WILEY BOOKS IN THE CERTMIKE SERIES

CompTIA ITF+ CertMike: *Prepare. Practice. Pass the Test! Get Certified! Exam FC0-U61* by Mike Chapple (ISBN 9781119897811)

CompTIA A+ CertMike: *Prepare. Practice. Pass the Test! Get Certified! Core 1 Exam 220-1101* by Mike Chapple and Mark Soper (ISBN 9781119898092)

CompTIA A+ CertMike: *Prepare. Practice. Pass the Test! Get Certified! Core 2 Exam 220-1102* by Mike Chapple and Mark Soper (ISBN 9781119898122)

CompTIA Network+ CertMike: *Prepare. Practice. Pass the Test! Get Certified! Exam N10-008* by Mike Chapple and Craig Zacker (ISBN 9781119898153)

CompTIA® A+® CertMike

Prepare. Practice. Pass the Test! Get Certified!

CompTIA® A+® CertMike

Prepare. Practice. Pass the Test! Get Certified!
Core 2 Exam 220-1102

Mike Chapple
Mark Soper

SYBEX®
A Wiley Brand

To my Aunt Jane, who has given so generously to me my entire life. I owe you more than I can ever express. Thank you.

—Mark

ACKNOWLEDGMENTS

From Mike Chapple:

This book marks the start of a new series of CertMike Test Prep books and I'd first like to thank the people who helped shape the vision for this series. The original idea was hatched over breakfast with two very supportive editors from the Wiley team: Ken Brown and Jim Minatel. I've worked with both Jim and Ken on many books over many years, and they're both insightful industry experts who know what it takes to produce a great book.

Mark Soper did the heavy lifting of putting this book together, and I am grateful to him for lending this series his expertise on end-user support and the A+ exams.

I'd also like to extend a special thank you to my agent, Carole Jelen of Waterside Productions. Carole is also an experienced industry pro who can deftly navigate the murky waters of publishing. Carole is the one who pushed me to create my own series.

Of course, the creation of any book involves a tremendous amount of effort from many people other than the authors. I truly appreciate the work of Adaobi Obi Tulton, the project editor. Adaobi and I have now worked together on many books, and she keeps the train on the tracks! I'd also like to thank Chris Crayton, the technical editor, who provided insightful advice and gave wonderful feedback throughout the book; and Magesh Elangovan, production editor, who guided me through layouts, formatting, and final cleanup to produce a great book. I would also like to thank the many behind-the-scenes contributors, including the graphics, production, and technical teams who make the book and companion materials into a finished product.

Finally, I would like to thank my family, who supported me through the late evenings, busy weekends, and long hours that a book like this requires to write, edit, and get to press.

From Mark Soper

My name is on the cover, but this book would not be a reality without the efforts of so many people behind the scenes. First, I want to thank CertMike, Mike Chapple, for the opportunity to work on this brand-new certification series. I am also deeply grateful to the editorial and production team at Wiley for all their hard work.

Many thanks to Ken Brown, acquisitions editor; Christine O'Connor, managing editor; Adaobi Obi Tulton, project editor; Chris Crayton, technical editor; Magesh Elangovan, production editor; Elizabeth Welch, copyeditor; and everyone else at Wiley who helped to make this book a reality.

I also want to thank my family for their support and for the many technology problems they've provided me with! It's been enjoyable to fix computer problems and to teach the next generation how things work. Thanks especially to my wife, Cheryl, for smiling and nodding as we've discussed tech issues during Christmas dinner.

Finally, thanks so much to Almighty God, who created everything visible and invisible, including the forces that make computers work, and for His great salvation.

About the Authors

Mike Chapple, Ph.D., CySA+, is author of the best-selling *CISSP (ISC)² Certified Information Systems Security Professional Official Study Guide* (Sybex, 2021) and the *CISSP (ISC)² Official Practice Tests* (Sybex 2021). He is an information technology professional with two decades of experience in higher education, the private sector, and government.

Mike currently serves as Teaching Professor in the IT, Analytics, and Operations department at the University of Notre Dame's Mendoza College of Business, where he teaches undergraduate and graduate courses on cybersecurity, cloud computing, data management, and business analytics.

Before returning to Notre Dame, Mike served as executive vice president and chief information officer of the Brand Institute, a Miami-based marketing consultancy. Mike also spent four years in the information security research group at the National Security Agency (NSA) and served as an active duty intelligence officer in the U.S. Air Force.

Mike has written more than 25 books. He earned both his B.S. and Ph.D. degrees from Notre Dame in computer science and engineering. Mike also holds an M.S. in computer science from the University of Idaho and an MBA from Auburn University. Mike holds the IT Fundamentals (ITF+), Cybersecurity Analyst+ (CySA+), Data+, Security+, Certified Information Security Manager (CISM), Certified Cloud Security Professional (CCSP), and Certified Information Systems Security Professional (CISSP) certifications.

Learn more about Mike and his other security certification materials at his website, CertMike.com.

Mark Edward Soper, MCP, CompTIA A+, is an instructor for University of Southern Indiana's Outreach and Engagement division. He has created and taught Microsoft Windows, Excel, Word, PowerPoint, Access, Outlook, and OneNote to staff, students, community, and corporate clients for USI for over a decade.

Mark is also the co-founder and president of Select Systems & Associates, Inc, a technology research, training, and writing organization. Mark is a world-class technology writer and trainer with an international reach, with books available in English, Spanish, Polish, French, Italian, Swedish, Russian, Chinese, and other languages. A proven bridge between users and technology, helping users to grasp, master, and seek new and better technologies, Mark is a 39-year tech veteran and a human tech multitool, having written or co-authored over 40 books on CompTIA tech certifications, computer hardware and software troubleshooting, operating systems, networking, digital photography, and self-service help desk topics. Mark has also taught these and other topics across the United States.

Mark has CompTIA A+ and Microsoft MOS – Microsoft Excel 2013 certifications, and blogs at www.markesoper.com.

About the Technical Editor

Chris Crayton is a technical consultant, trainer, author, and industry-leading technical editor. He has worked as a computer technology and networking instructor, information security director, network administrator, network engineer, and PC specialist. Chris has authored several print and online books on PC repair, CompTIA A+, CompTIA Security+, and Microsoft Windows. He has also served as technical editor and content contributor on numerous technical titles for several of the leading publishing companies. He holds numerous industry certifications, has been recognized with many professional and teaching awards, and has served as a state-level SkillsUSA final competition judge.

Contents at a Glance

CONTENTS

INTRODUCTION

If you're preparing to take the A+ Core 2 exam, you might find yourself overwhelmed with information. This exam covers a very broad range of topics, and it's possible to spend weeks studying each one of them. Fortunately, that's not necessary!

As part of the CertMike Test Prep series, *CompTIA A+ CertMike: Prepare. Practice. Pass the Test! Get Certified! Core 2 Exam 220-1102* is designed to help you focus on the specific knowledge that you'll need to pass the exam. CompTIA publishes a detailed list of exam objectives, and this book is organized around those objectives. Each chapter clearly states the single objective that it covers and then, in a few pages, covers the material you need to know about that objective.

You'll find two important things at the end of each chapter: Exam Essentials and Practice Questions. The CertMike Exam Essentials distill the major points from the chapter into just a few bullet points. Reviewing the Exam Essentials is a great way to prepare yourself right before the exam. Mike also recorded a free audio version of the Exam Essentials that you'll find on the book's companion website at www.wiley.com/go/sybextestprep. They're great listening when you're in the car, at the gym, or mowing the lawn!

Each chapter concludes with two Practice Questions that are designed to give you a taste of what it's like to take the exam. You'll find that they're written in the same style as the A+ exam questions and have detailed explanations to help you understand the correct answer. Be sure to take your time and thoroughly read these questions.

Finally, the book's website includes a full-length practice exam that you can use to assess your knowledge when you're ready to take the test. Good luck on the A+ Core 2 exam!

> **NOTE**
>
> Don't just study the questions and answers! The questions on the actual exam will be different from the Practice Questions included in this book. The exam is designed to test your knowledge of a concept or objective, so use this book to learn the objectives behind the questions.

THE A+ PROGRAM

A+ is designed to be a vendor-neutral certification for those seeking to enter the information technology field. CompTIA recommends this certification for individuals who want to be problem solvers in the world of endpoint management and technical support. Common job roles held by A+ certified individuals include the following:

- ► Helpdesk technician
- ► Field service technician
- ► Associate network engineer

▶ Junior systems administrator
▶ Desktop support specialist
▶ System support technician

The A+ certification is unique in that earning it requires passing two separate exams:

▶ **A+ Core 1 (220-1101),** which covers mobile devices, networking technology, hardware, virtualization, and cloud computing
▶ **A+ Core 2 (220-1102),** which covers operating systems, security, software, and operational procedures

This book focuses on the Core 2 exam, which covers four major domains of knowledge:

1. Operating Systems
2. Security
3. Software Troubleshooting
4. Operational Procedures

These four areas include a range of topics, from configuring operating system settings to preventing malware attacks, while focusing heavily on the basic knowledge expected of IT technicians.

The A+ exam uses a combination of standard multiple-choice questions and performance-based questions that require you to manipulate objects on the screen. This exam is designed to be straightforward and not to trick you. If you know the material in this book, you will pass the exam.

Each exam costs $239 in the United States, with roughly equivalent prices in other locations around the globe. You can find more details about the A+ exams and how to take it at:

www.comptia.org/certifications/a#examdetails

You'll have 90 minutes to take the exam and will be asked to answer up to 90 questions during that time period. Your exam will be scored on a scale ranging from 100 to 900, with a passing score of 700.

> **NOTE**
>
> CompTIA frequently does what is called *item seeding*, which is the practice of including unscored questions on exams. It does so to gather psychometric data, which is then used when developing new versions of the exam. Before you take the exam, you will be told that your exam may include these unscored questions. So, if you come across a question that does not appear to map to any of the exam objectives—or for that matter, does not appear to belong in the exam—it is likely a seeded question. You never really know whether or not a question is seeded, however, so always make your best effort to answer every question.

Taking the Exam

Once you are fully prepared to take the exam, you can visit the CompTIA website to purchase your exam voucher:

```
https://store.comptia.org
```

Currently, CompTIA offers two options for taking the exam: an in-person exam at a testing center and an at-home exam that you take on your own computer.

> **TIP**
>
> This book includes a coupon that you may use to save 10 percent on your CompTIA exam registration.

In-Person Exams

CompTIA partners with Pearson VUE's testing centers, so your next step will be to locate a testing center near you. In the United States, you can do this based on your address or your zip code, while non-U.S. test takers may find it easier to enter their city and country. You can search for a test center near you at the Pearson Vue website, where you will need to navigate to "Find a test center."

```
www.pearsonvue.com/comptia
```

Now that you know where you'd like to take the exam, simply set up a Pearson VUE testing account and schedule an exam on their site.

On the day of the test, take two forms of identification, and be sure to show up with plenty of time before the exam starts. Remember that you will not be able to take your notes, electronic devices (including smartphones and watches), or other materials in with you.

At-Home Exams

CompTIA began offering online exam proctoring in 2020 in response to the coronavirus pandemic. As of this writing, the at-home testing option was still available and appears likely to continue. Candidates using this approach will take the exam at their home or office and be proctored over a webcam by a remote proctor.

Due to the rapidly changing nature of the at-home testing experience, candidates wishing to pursue this option should check the CompTIA website for the latest details.

After the Exam

Once you have taken the exam, you will be notified of your score immediately, so you'll know if you passed the test right away. You should keep track of your score report with your exam registration records and the email address you used to register for the exam.

After you earn the A+ certification, you're required to renew your certification every three years by either earning an advanced certification, completing a CertMaster continuing education program, or earning 20 continuing education units over a three-year period.

Many people who earn the A+ credential use it as a stepping stone to earning other certifications in their areas of interest. Those interested in networking work toward the Network+ credential, data analytics professionals might go on to earn the Data+ certification, and the Security+ program is a gateway to a career in cybersecurity.

WHAT DOES THIS BOOK COVER?

This book covers everything you need to know to pass the A+ Core 2 exam. It is organized into four parts, each corresponding to one of the four A+ Core 2 domains.

Part I: Domain 1.0: Operating Systems

Chapter 1: Microsoft Windows Editions

Chapter 2: Microsoft Command-Line Tools

Chapter 3: Windows 10 Operating System Tools

Chapter 4: Windows 10 Control Panel

Chapter 5: Windows Settings

Chapter 6: Windows Networking

Chapter 7: Application Installation and Configuration

Chapter 8: Operating System Types

Chapter 9: Operating System Installations and Upgrades

Chapter 10: macOS

Chapter 11: Linux

Part II: Domain 2.0: Security

Chapter 12: Physical Security

Chapter 13: Logical Security

Chapter 14: Wireless Security

Chapter 15: Malware

Chapter 16: Social Engineering and Security Threats

Chapter 17: Windows Security

Chapter 18: Workstation Security Configuration

Study Guide Elements

This study guide uses a number of common elements to help you prepare. These include the following:

Exam Tips   Throughout each chapter, we've sprinkled practical exam tips that help focus your reading on items that are particularly confusing or important for the exam.

CertMike Exam Essentials   The Exam Essentials focus on major exam topics and critical knowledge that you should take into the test. The Exam Essentials focus on the exam objectives provided by CompTIA.

Practice Questions   Two questions at the end of each chapter will help you assess your knowledge and if you are ready to take the exam based on your knowledge of that chapter's topics.

Additional Study Tools

This book comes with a number of additional study tools to help you prepare for the exam. They include the following.

> **NOTE**
>
> Go to www.wiley.com/go/sybextestprep to register and gain access to this interactive online learning environment and test bank with study tools.

Sybex Test Preparation Software

Sybex's test preparation software lets you prepare with electronic test versions of the Practice Questions from each chapter and the Practice Exam that is included in this book. You can build and take tests on specific domains or by chapter, or cover the entire set of A+ Core 2 exam objectives using randomized tests.

Audio Review

Mike recorded an audio review where he reads each of the sets of chapter Exam Essentials. This provides a helpful recap of the main material covered on the exam that you can use while you're commuting, working out, or relaxing.

CORE 1 EXAM 220-1102 EXAM OBJECTIVES

CompTIA goes to great lengths to ensure that its certification programs accurately reflect the IT industry's best practices. They do this by establishing committees for each of its exam programs. Each committee consists of a small group of IT professionals, training providers, and publishers who are responsible for establishing the exam's baseline competency level and who determine the appropriate target-audience level.

Once these factors are determined, CompTIA shares this information with a group of hand-selected subject matter experts (SMEs). These folks are the true brainpower behind the certification program. The SMEs review the committee's findings, refine them, and shape them into the objectives that follow this section. CompTIA calls this process a job-task analysis.

Finally, CompTIA conducts a survey to ensure that the objectives and weightings truly reflect job requirements. Only then can the SMEs go to work writing the hundreds of questions needed for the exam. Even so, they have to go back to the drawing board for further refinements in many cases before the exam is ready to go live in its final state. Rest assured that the content you're about to learn will serve you long after you take the exam.

CompTIA also publishes relative weightings for each of the exam's objectives. The following table lists the four A+ Core 2 objective domains and the extent to which they are represented on the exam.

NOTE

The A+ exam covers both Windows 10 and 11. You should be familiar with how the information in these objectives applies to both operating systems.

Domain	% of Exam
1.0 Operating Systems	31%
2.0 Security	25%
3.0 Software Troubleshooting	22%
4.0 Operational Procedures	22%

CORE 2 EXAM 220-1102 CERTIFICATION EXAM OBJECTIVE MAP

Objective	Chapter(s)
1.0 Operating Systems	
1.1 Identify basic features of Microsoft Windows Editions	1
1.2 Given a scenario, use the appropriate Microsoft command-line tool	2
1.3 Given a scenario, use features and tools of the Microsoft Windows 10 operating system (OS)	3
1.4 Given a scenario, use the appropriate Microsoft Windows 10 Control Panel utility	4
1.5 Given a scenario, use the appropriate Windows settings	5
1.6 Given a scenario, configure Microsoft Windows networking features on a client/desktop	6

(continued)

Objective	Chapter(s)
1.7 Given a scenario, apply application installation and configuration concepts	7
1.8 Explain common OS types and their purposes	8
1.9 Given a scenario, perform OS installations and upgrades in a diverse OS environment	9
1.10 Identify common features and tools of the macOS/desktop OS	10
1.11 Identify common features and tools of the Linux client/desktop OS	11
2.0 Security	
2.1 Summarize various security measures and their purposes	12 and 13
2.2 Compare and contrast wireless security protocols and authentication methods	14
2.3 Given a scenario, detect, remove, and prevent malware using the appropriate tools and methods	15
2.4 Explain common social-engineering attacks, threats, and vulnerabilities	16
2.5 Given a scenario, manage and configure basic security settings in the Microsoft Windows OS	17
2.6 Given a scenario, configure a workstation to meet best practices for security	18
2.7 Explain common methods for securing mobile and embedded devices	19
2.8 Given a scenario, use common data destruction and disposal methods	20
2.9 Given a scenario, configure appropriate security settings on small office/home office (SOHO) wireless and wired networks	21
2.10 Given a scenario, install and configure browsers and relevant security settings	22

NOTE

Exam objectives are subject to change at any time without prior notice and at CompTIA's discretion. Please visit CompTIA's website (www.comptia.org) for the most current listing of exam objectives.

HOW TO CONTACT THE PUBLISHER

If you believe you've found a mistake in this book, please bring it to our attention. At John Wiley & Sons, we understand how important it is to provide our customers with accurate content, but even with our best efforts an error may occur. In order to submit your possible errata, please email it to our Customer Service Team at wileysupport@wiley.com with the subject line "Possible Book Errata Submission."

PART I

Domain 1.0: Operating Systems

Chapter 1 Microsoft Windows Editions
Chapter 2 Microsoft Command-Line Tools
Chapter 3 Windows 10 Operating System Tools
Chapter 4 Windows 10 Control Panel
Chapter 5 Windows Settings
Chapter 6 Windows Networking
Chapter 7 Application Installation and Configuration
Chapter 8 Operating System Types
Chapter 9 Operating System Installations and Upgrades
Chapter 10 macOS
Chapter 11 Linux

Operating Systems is the first domain of CompTIA's A+ Core 2 exam. It provides the foundational knowledge that IT professionals need to work with common operating systems, including Microsoft Windows, macOS, and Linux. This domain has 11 objectives:

1.1 Identify basic features of Microsoft Windows Editions.

1.2 Given a scenario, use the appropriate Microsoft command-line tool.

1.3 Given a scenario, use features and tools of the Microsoft Windows 10 operating system (OS).

1.4 Given a scenario, use the appropriate Microsoft Windows 10 Control Panel utility.

1.5 Given a scenario, use the appropriate Windows settings.

1.6 Given a scenario, configure Microsoft Windows networking features on a client/desktop.

1.7 Given a scenario, apply application installation and configuration concepts.

1.8 Explain common OS types and their purposes.

1.9 Given a scenario, perform OS installations and upgrades in a diverse OS environment.

1.10 Identify common features and tools of the macOS/desktop OS.

1.11 Identify common features and tools of the Linux client/desktop OS.

Questions from this domain make up 31% of the questions on the A+ Core 2 exam, so you should expect to see approximately 28 questions on your test covering the material in this part.

CHAPTER 1

Microsoft Windows Editions

Core 2 Objective 1.1: Identify basic features of Microsoft Windows editions.

Windows 10 and its successor, Windows 11, are available in a variety of editions. Understanding the differences and how upgrade paths are affected by those differences is essential to succeed as a computer tech.

In this chapter, you will learn everything you need to know about A+ Certification Core 2 Objective 1.1, including the following topics:

► **Windows 10 Editions**
► **Windows 10 versus Windows 11**
► **Feature Differences Between Editions**
► **Upgrade Paths**

WINDOWS 10 EDITIONS

Windows 10 is available in four major editions:

► Home
► Pro
► Pro for Workstations
► Enterprise

EXAM TIP

Windows 11 is currently being shipped as the standard version of Windows on new hardware. Existing Windows 10 Home and Pro editions can be upgraded to the corresponding Windows 11 version. Windows 11 is also available in Pro for Workstations and Enterprise.

These versions differ in features and supported hardware. The following sections cover core features common to all and differences by edition.

Core Windows 10 Features

Whichever edition of Windows 10 you use, you're looking at the following core features:

▶ The 64-bit operating system fully supports 64-bit processors from AMD and Intel and supports classic Windows and modern apps. Windows 10 supports multiple desktops, so you can have different desktops with different icons and backgrounds for different tasks. Windows 10 includes search, including Cortana voice search. Integrated antimalware and security features help keep Windows 10 protected from threats.

▶ Windows 10's Action Center provides messages from Windows and applications and makes it easy to change configurations such as wireless networking, Airplane mode, Bluetooth, and more. Windows 10 features a Start button and a two-pane menu with Live Tiles in Standard mode. The Tablet mode, which features a full-screen menu, can be toggled on/off manually or automatically when a tablet or convertible PC is used.

To determine which version of Windows is in use, open Settings, select System, and click About (Figure 1.1).

Home

As the name implies, Windows 10 Home is designed for people using their computers for home, including gaming, recreation, and small-office/home office (SOHO) scenarios. Windows 10 Home has all of the Core Windows 10 features, and adds wired and wireless Ethernet workgroup networking. You can't join a domain with Windows Home, but you're ready for basic networking. Windows 10 Home supports data backup with File History, and to keep your system up-to-date, there's Windows Update. Windows 10 Home can use less RAM than other versions, but its limit of 128 GB should be plenty for home and SOHO users, and that's much more than typical desktop and laptop PCs can currently support.

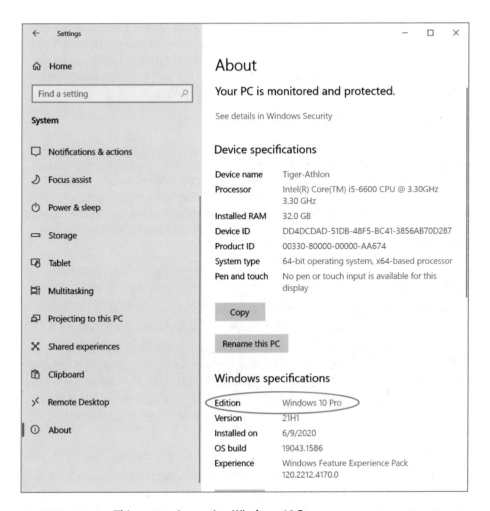

FIGURE 1.1 This system is running Windows 10 Pro.

Pro

Windows 10 Pro is designed to support modern business apps and high-end hardware requirements. It provides the same features as Windows 10 Home and adds a bunch of business-oriented features. The number one feature is domain networking, enabling centralized control of Pro workstations. Group Policy management works along with domain networking to enforce standardized settings across the domain. To protect data, Pro adds EFS (Encrypted File System) for individual files and folders, and BitLocker and BitLocker to Go to encrypt desktop and laptop drives.

Other Pro features include support for Remote Desktop, for remote access, and remote support; Windows Hello for Business, which includes no-password sign-in to Microsoft Windows and Azure; and integration with Microsoft Information Protection (previously known as Enterprise Data Protection). Pro also includes Microsoft's Hyper-V virtualization to create and manage virtual machines. Pro supports up to 2 TB of RAM.

Pro for Workstations

Windows 10 Pro for Workstations is designed to run apps such as those required for scientists, media productions, and graphics animators These users need high-performance hardware, so Windows 10 Pro for Workstations provides the same features as Windows 10 Professional but adds support for workstation-grade hardware, including up to four workstation-grade CPUs (AMD Opteron, Epyx, Intel Xeon); nonvolatile dual in-line memory modules (NVDIMM); remote direct memory access (RDMA); and ReFS (Resilient File System). Pro for Workstations supports up to 6 TB of RAM.

> **NOTE**
>
> NVDIMM combines flash memory and dynamic access memory (DRAM) for better performance and faster recovery from crashes. RDMA enables memory to be accessed remotely via a network adapter, bypassing the CPU and other components normally involved in memory transfers. ReFS is a filesystem designed to support enormous data sets up to terabytes, to access them at faster speeds, and to protect their contents from corruption. ReFS was originally designed for Windows Server editions.

Enterprise

Enterprise is built for Windows 10 systems in use on large networks, and as such, it takes the features of Windows 10 Pro and adds a lot of corporate management and enterprise networking features to the mix. Security features like Start Screen control with Group Policy, Credential Guard, Device Guard, and AppLocker are standard on Enterprise, as are networking features such as BranchCache and DirectAccess. Enterprise supports up to 6 TB of RAM.

> **NOTE**
>
> *DirectAccess* is an always-on remote management alternative to virtual private networks (VPNs) for clients. *AppLocker* provides improved software management, standardization, and protection against unwanted software. *BranchCache* optimizes wide area networking (WAN) bandwidth by using caching.

FEATURE DIFFERENCES BETWEEN EDITIONS

While the many flavors of Windows 10 have many features, the most important features in your day-to-day installation, support, and troubleshooting revolve are these:

▶ Support for domain access vs. workgroups
▶ Desktop styles and user interface
▶ Availability of Remote Desktop Protocol
▶ RAM limitations
▶ BitLocker
▶ Group Policy Editor (`gpedit.msc`)

The following sections provide the essential information you need to know about the differences in features between different editions of Windows.

Domain Access vs. Workgroup

Windows 10 Home offers only workgroup networking. In a workgroup, each computer can share printers or folders with others and maintains its own list of authorized users. There is no limit on the number of computers in a workgroup, but Windows is limited to 20 concurrent users for each shared resource.

Windows 10 Pro, Pro for Workstations, and Enterprise also support domain networking. A domain controller maintains a list of users, groups, and resources. Resources are connected directly to the network or to print and file servers, among others. The domain controller permits or denies access to resources per group or user.

To determine what type of network you are using:

1. Click Start.
2. Click System.
3. Click About.
4. Scroll down and click Rename This PC (Advanced).
5. The Computer Name tab of System Properties appears. It lists the domain name or the Workgroup name (Figure 1.2).

Desktop Styles/User Interface

Windows 10 can start in Standard mode or Tablet mode. It starts in Standard mode on desktop or laptop computers that have keyboards. Figure 1.3 illustrates a typical system's Start menu in Standard mode.

If you are using Windows 10 on a tablet or a convertible 2-in-1 PC that has its keyboard folded away or detached, it will start in Tablet mode (Figure 1.4). To switch between modes on a touchscreen computer, click Notifications, then Tablet Mode.

On a domain network,
the domain is listed here.

FIGURE 1.2 **This system is connected to a workgroup.**

FIGURE 1.3 **Typical Windows 10 Start menu in Standard mode**

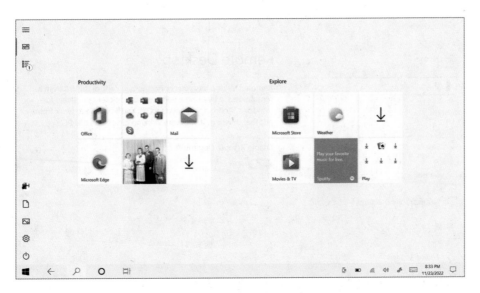

FIGURE 1.4 Typical Windows 10 Start menu in Tablet mode

To configure when Tablet mode starts, click Start ➤ System ➤ Tablet. To change how Tablet mode works, choose Change Additional Tablet Settings from the Tablet menu.

> **NOTE**
> Windows 11 also supports Standard and Tablet modes, but the difference is minimal and the switch is automatic.

Availability of Remote Desktop Protocol (RDP)

Remote Desktop Protocol (RDP) is a remote access/remote control protocol. You can configure a computer running Pro, Pro Workstations, and Enterprise editions to *receive* RDP connections, but not a computer using the Home edition.

After you enable RDP through the System Properties dialog box in Settings, click Select Users That Can Remotely Access This PC (Figure 1.5) to set up a list of authorized remote users.

The Remote Desktop Connection (RDC) apps used to connect to a system running RDP are available for Windows (including Home editions), iOS, and Android. Advanced settings allow you to configure additional security and remote network settings. Figure 1.6 illustrates using Remote Desktop Connection.

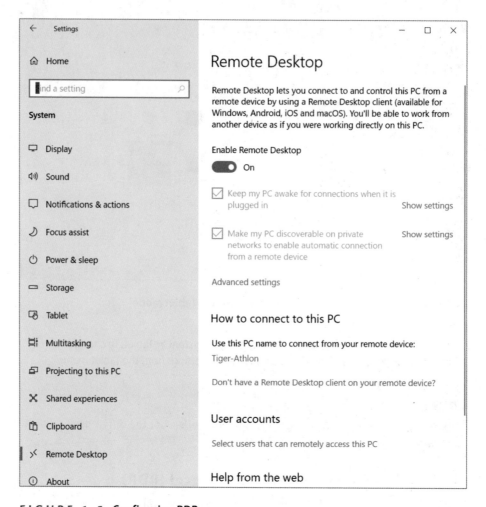

FIGURE 1.5 Configuring RDP

RAM Support Limitations

The amounts of memory (RAM) supported by Windows 10 editions vary but in most cases greatly exceed the amounts of RAM actually available in current hardware. See Table 1.1 for details.

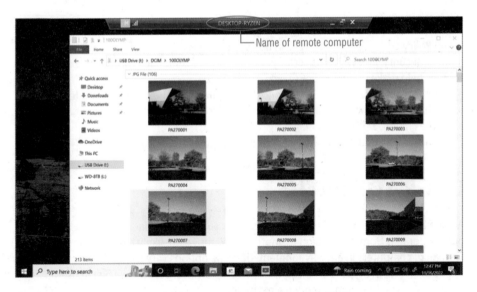

FIGURE 1.6 Viewing a folder on a remote system with RDC

TABLE 1.1 Windows 10 maximum memory sizes by edition

Version	x64 limit[*]
Windows 10 Home	128 GB
Windows 10 Pro	2 TB
Windows 10 Pro for Workstations	6 TB
Windows 10 Enterprise	6 TB

* 32-bit (x86) versions are all limited to 4 GB of RAM.

BitLocker

In an era in which stories of data compromised by lost laptops are common, using full disk encryption like BitLocker just makes sense. BitLocker (for internal drives) and BitLocker to Go (for external drives) can protect drives in most Windows 10 editions but is not available in Home.

To learn more about BitLocker and BitLocker to Go, see Chapter 17, "Windows Security."

Gpedit.msc (Group Policy Editor)

Group Policy Editor (`gpedit.msc`) can be used to configure computers, users, software, printers, security, and Windows settings. Administrative templates with a range of typical settings help make management easier.

When run on a workgroup, Group Policy Editor configures the current computer. When run on a domain network, it can configure settings for groups and users. It is not available on Home Edition.

To learn more about Group Policy Editor, see Chapter 13, "Logical Security."

UPGRADE PATHS

An operating system upgrade retains the existing software and data installed on a computer. Upgrades from one version to another of Windows are likely to occur through the lifespan of computers in any environment. Upgrade options vary with the version of Windows in use, the type (32-bit or 64-bit), and the licensing for the version in use. Upgrades can be free or may require a payment.

To learn more about upgrade methods, see Chapter 9, "Operating System Installations and Upgrades."

64-Bit Upgrade Paths

First, let's look at upgrade options for 64-bit versions of Windows Home and Windows Pro:

- ▶ You can upgrade Windows Home 7, 8/8.1 to Windows 10 Home and from Windows 10 Home to Windows 11 Home.
- ▶ You can upgrade Windows Pro 7, 8/8.1 to Windows 10 Pro and from Windows 10 Pro to Windows 11 Pro.
- ▶ You can upgrade Windows 10 Pro to Windows 10 Pro for Workstations or Enterprise.
- ▶ You can upgrade Windows 10 editions to the corresponding Windows 11 edition if hardware requirements are met.

32-Bit Upgrade Paths

If you have a 32-bit version of Windows 7 or 8/8.1, you can upgrade to Windows 10. However, Windows 11 is available only in 64-bit editions.

In-Place Upgrade

From the standpoint of time and effort, the preferred upgrade method is what Microsoft calls an *in-place upgrade*. This replaces your existing version of Windows while preserving your apps and data. The upgrade scenarios discussed earlier typically permit an in-place upgrade.

To learn more about in-place upgrades, see Chapter 9.

Here's a brief overview of how it works:

1. Use the Media Creation tool to create an ISO DVD or USB.
2. Start your system as you normally would.
3. Run the installer from File Explorer.
4. At the end of the process, you have a new version of Windows.

Moving from 32-Bit to 64-Bit Windows

Given the memory limitations of 32-bit Windows and the widespread application switch to 64-bit, the next logical question is. . . how about moving from 32-bit to 64-bit if you have a 64-bit processor?

Microsoft doesn't support an in-place upgrade. The official method is to back up the drive, erase it, install a clean copy of the new Windows edition, reinstall apps, and restore data files.

You can use third-party apps from many vendors (I like Laplink PCmover) as an alternative.

CERTMIKE EXAM ESSENTIALS

▶ Windows Home editions lack business networking, centralized management, and integrated disk encryption.

▶ Windows business-oriented editions (Pro, Pro Workstation, and Enterprise) support more RAM than the Home edition does and also supports domain networking, full-disk encryption, and centralized management.

▶ Moving from older to newer 64-bit editions is easy and supported by Microsoft, while moving from 32-bit to 64-bit editions is challenging if third-party tools are not used.

Practice Question 1

Your client has closed their offices and all office employees are now working from home. Client PCs are using a mixture of Windows 10 Home and Windows 10 Pro, and your client is concerned about supporting remote workers.

Which of the following upgrade strategies would best deal with this issue?

A. Upgrade all Windows 10 systems to Windows 11.
B. Upgrade all Windows 10 Home systems to Windows 10 Pro.
C. Install Remote Desktop Protocol on all Windows 10 systems.
D. Enable BitLocker on all systems.

Practice Question 2

You are helping a friend upgrade a computer that they picked up at a yard sale. It has a 64-bit processor and room for up to 16 GB of RAM. It has 4 GB of RAM. Your friend purchased additional RAM and has asked you to come over and install it. When you start the computer and go to System ➢ About, you notice that the Windows version installed is Windows 7 Home 32-bit edition. What should you do?

A. Install the additional RAM and assure your friend it will work.
B. Return the RAM since it can't work.
C. Do an in-place upgrade to a 64-bit edition of Windows before installing the RAM.
D. Perform a clean installation or use a third-party upgrade tool to install a 64-bit edition of Windows before installing the RAM.

Practice Question 1 Explanation

This question is designed to test your understanding of the differences between Windows editions and how to apply that knowledge in a real-world situation. You are likely to encounter this type of question on the exam.

Let's evaluate these choices one at a time.

1. The first suggested answer would make the support situation more of a challenge. Windows 11 has a different look and feel when compared to Windows 10. More significantly, this doesn't address any differences in remote support between Home and Pro editions. This is incorrect.

2. The next suggested answer, upgrade Windows 10 Home to Windows 10 Pro, reveals an understanding of one of the significant differences between Home and Pro: Pro has the ability to accept Remote Desktop Protocol (RDP) connections and Home doesn't. Systems running Pro can be connected to with RDP for use in remote support and access. This is the *best* answer.

3. The third suggestion, install RDP on all systems, shows an understanding of its importance in remote support. However, incoming RDP connections aren't supported on Windows 10 Home. Although RDP can be installed on Windows 10 Home, doing so requires an unofficial hack that violates Windows licensing. This is not a suitable solution.

4. The last option, enabling BitLocker, totally misunderstands the question. The issue is remote support, not data security. Using BitLocker is a good idea for computers being used remotely, but it doesn't address the support issue. Also, BitLocker is not available on Windows 10 Home. This is incorrect.

Correct Answer: B. Upgrade Windows 10 Home to Pro

Practice Question 2 Explanation

This question is designed to test your understanding of the differences between Windows editions in terms of hardware issues. You are likely to encounter this type of question on the exam.

Let's evaluate these choices one at a time.

1. The first suggestion, install the additional RAM and assure your friend it will work, is not a friendly thing to do. Memory above 4 GB can't be used by a 32-bit version of Windows. This is incorrect.

2. The next suggestion, return the RAM since it can't work, would be correct *if* nothing is done about the operating system. If a 64-bit operating system is installed, the additional RAM will be quite welcome. This is incorrect.

3. The third suggestion, do an in-place upgrade to a 64-bit version of Windows, can't work because you can't move from 32-bit to 64-bit Windows this way. This is incorrect.

4. The last option, perform a clean installation of a 64-bit version of Windows or use a third-party upgrade tool, is the *best* choice. A clean installation is the best option if there are no apps that the user has licenses for on the computer. To preserve existing apps, the third-party upgrade tool would preserve the apps, although some might require reinstallation afterwards.

Correct Answer: D. Clean installation of 64-bit version or use a third-party upgrade tool

CHAPTER 2

Microsoft Command-Line Tools

Core 2 Objective 1.2: Given a scenario, use the appropriate Microsoft command-line tool.

Although most users of Windows 10 and 11 use the GUI interface to move around the system or to run programs, there are times that the command-line interface is the way to go.

In this chapter, you will learn everything you need to know about A+ Certification Core 2 Objective 1.2, including the following topics:

▶ **Navigation**
▶ **Command-line Tools**

NAVIGATION

Opening up a command-prompt window provides access to a whole range of commands you can type in to move around local and network locations.

CMD, also known as the command prompt or Windows Command Processor, is the command-line interpreter built into Windows. To open the command prompt, click the Search box, type **CMD**, and press Enter. A window opens and the prompt shows the system drive and the path to the current user's home folder (refer to Figure 2.1 in the next section). You type commands at the >.

> **NOTE**
>
> Some commands, such as chkdsk, must be run from a command prompt in elevated mode. To open CMD in elevated mode, after searching for CMD, right-click the app and select Run As Administrator.

What Is a Folder?

A folder, also known as a subdirectory, is a type of file that holds other files and other folders. In Figure 2.1, the Users folder is one level beneath the root folder of C: and the Mark E. Soper folder is one level beneath the Users folder. Backslashes are used to separate each folder.

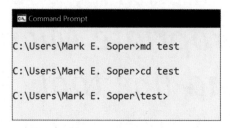

F I G U R E 2 . 1 Making and changing to a new folder. The prompt reflects the current location.

md

Use **md *foldername*** to make a new folder one level below the current folder (refer to Figure 2.1). In this and subsequent examples, replace the text in italics with the actual folder name, filename, website, URL, and so on.

> **EXAM TIP**
>
> Linux and macOS do not use the md command. They use the mkdir command for the same purpose.

Cd

Use **cd *foldername*** to change your current location to the specified folder (refer to Figure 2.1). When you change to a new folder, the prompt changes to show your new location.

Dir

With no options, dir lists files/folders in their current location. Add a drive letter or path to see files/folders in a specified location. To pause a listing, add **/p** to the command (Figure 2.2); to continue, press a key.

```
C:\Users\Mark E. Soper>dir /p
 Volume in drive C has no label.
 Volume Serial Number is 3CFC-BE75

 Directory of C:\Users\Mark E. Soper

04/18/2022  07:10 PM    <DIR>          .
04/18/2022  07:10 PM    <DIR>          ..
07/17/2018  05:14 PM               126 .gitconfig
08/15/2016  05:47 PM    <DIR>          .oracle_jre_usage
11/03/2016  01:35 PM    <DIR>          .Plays.tv
11/03/2016  01:35 PM    <DIR>          .QtWebEngineProcess
11/28/2018  02:31 PM    <DIR>          .SilverFast8
05/02/2017  01:41 PM    <DIR>          .swingsane
04/25/2017  10:12 PM    <DIR>          .swt
03/09/2021  09:23 PM    <DIR>          .thumb
03/24/2022  01:59 PM    <DIR>          .VirtualBox
04/13/2022  09:35 PM    <DIR>          .wdc
03/15/2022  06:40 PM    <DIR>          3D Objects
03/10/2021  01:10 PM     2,228,733,952 AliceChristmas_DVD2.iso
07/16/2018  01:04 PM    <DIR>          AppMods
02/20/2013  05:48 PM           232,503 APU+HD7800_WEI[Converted].xps
03/02/2010  03:06 PM            37,788 Blippo Light SF.ttf
07/15/2020  10:17 AM                50 BrazenConnect.txt
04/14/2022  01:51 PM    <DIR>          Creative Cloud Files
06/09/2020  11:16 AM    <DIR>          Desktop
09/18/2019  04:32 PM    <DIR>          Documents
04/11/2022  08:15 AM    <DIR>          Downloads
01/28/2022  11:14 AM    <DIR>          Dropbox
07/11/2016  03:58 PM    <DIR>          dwhelper
Press any key to continue . . .
```

FIGURE 2.2 Using dir /p to pause a long directory listing

EXAM TIP
Need help with the commands in this section? Use /? after the command to see its options.

rmdir

Use **rmdir** *foldername* to remove an empty folder (one that has no folders or files). Note that all folders contain two <DIR> entries: . (a single dot) is a shortcut to the drive's root folder, and .. (two dots) is a shortcut to one level up from the current folder.

To determine if a folder is empty, use this command: **dir *foldername***. As you can see at the top of Figure 2.3, there is nothing in the test folder. After using **rmdir *foldername***, use **dir *foldername*** again, and you will see File Not Found because the folder has been removed.

```
C:\Users\Mark E. Soper>dir test
 Volume in drive C has no label.
 Volume Serial Number is 3CFC-BE75

 Directory of C:\Users\Mark E. Soper\test

04/18/2022  07:10 PM    <DIR>          .
04/18/2022  07:10 PM    <DIR>          ..
               0 File(s)              0 bytes
               2 Dir(s)  93,981,720,576 bytes free

C:\Users\Mark E. Soper>rmdir test

C:\Users\Mark E. Soper>dir test
 Volume in drive C has no label.
 Volume Serial Number is 3CFC-BE75

 Directory of C:\Users\Mark E. Soper

File Not Found
```

FIGURE 2.3 Removing a folder with **rmdir**

Drive Navigation Inputs

With most commands, you can specify a particular drive for the command to work on:

Use **D:** to switch to the current location on drive D:.

Use **MD E:\Test** to create a folder called Test in the root folder of drive E:.

When you see command examples given, sometimes the lower-case x: is used as a place-holder for the actual drive letter. Keep in mind that sometimes there actually is a drive X: (usually a network folder mapped to a drive letter).

COMMAND-LINE TOOLS

In addition to navigational commands built into CMD, Windows includes a lot of command-line tools that can be used for network diagnostics, system maintenance, and disk storage management and use.

TIP

Use the command **CLS** to clear the screen between commands if you want to. Use the Up Arrow key to scroll through previous commands.

ipconfig

Use **ipconfig** to display TCP/IP configuration about all the network connections on a Windows system. Use **ipconfig /all** to see detailed information for each connection (Figure 2.4).

```
C:\Users\Mark E. Soper>ipconfig /all

Windows IP Configuration

    Host Name . . . . . . . . . . . . : Tiger-Athlon
    Primary Dns Suffix  . . . . . . . :
    Node Type . . . . . . . . . . . . : Hybrid
    IP Routing Enabled. . . . . . . . : No
    WINS Proxy Enabled. . . . . . . . : No

Wireless LAN adapter Wi-Fi:

    Connection-specific DNS Suffix  . :
    Description . . . . . . . . . . . : TP-Link Wireless MU-MIMO USB Adapter
    Physical Address. . . . . . . . . : 98-48-27-C5-23-79
    DHCP Enabled. . . . . . . . . . . : Yes
    Autoconfiguration Enabled . . . . : Yes
    Link-local IPv6 Address . . . . . : fe80::4cb:6d01:7cd1:d326%2(Preferred)
    IPv4 Address. . . . . . . . . . . : 192.168.1.109(Preferred)
    Subnet Mask . . . . . . . . . . . : 255.255.255.0
    Lease Obtained. . . . . . . . . . : Wednesday, April 13, 2022 9:58:24 PM
    Lease Expires . . . . . . . . . . : Wednesday, April 20, 2022 9:13:29 AM
    Default Gateway . . . . . . . . . : 192.168.1.1
    DHCP Server . . . . . . . . . . . : 192.168.1.1
    DHCPv6 IAID . . . . . . . . . . . : 43534375
    DHCPv6 Client DUID. . . . . . . . : 00-01-00-01-26-71-6C-6F-40-8D-5C-1C-B3-19
    DNS Servers . . . . . . . . . . . : 192.168.1.1
    NetBIOS over Tcpip. . . . . . . . : Enabled
```

FIGURE 2.4 Portions of an **ipconfig /all** report showing the Wi-Fi connection

ping

Use **ping** *URL* or **ping** *website* to test TCP/IP and Internet connectivity to the URL or website entered (Figure 2.5). Enter **ping** by itself to see options. Some websites block ping for security.

```
Command Prompt

C:\Users\Mark E. Soper>ping www.evansville.net

Pinging www2.windstream.net [162.39.145.20] with 32 bytes of data:
Reply from 162.39.145.20: bytes=32 time=50ms TTL=51
Reply from 162.39.145.20: bytes=32 time=40ms TTL=51
Reply from 162.39.145.20: bytes=32 time=42ms TTL=51
Reply from 162.39.145.20: bytes=32 time=42ms TTL=51

Ping statistics for 162.39.145.20:
    Packets: Sent = 4, Received = 4, Lost = 0 (0% loss),
Approximate round trip times in milli-seconds:
    Minimum = 40ms, Maximum = 50ms, Average = 43ms
```

FIGURE 2.5 Using **ping** to check connectivity

hostname

This command displays the name of the local device (host).

netstat

Use **netstat** with no options to display active connections. To display the interface list and IPv4 routing table, use **netstat -r** (Figure 2.6) To display open TCP and UDP ports,

```
C:\Users\Mark E. Soper>netstat -r
===========================================================================
Interface List
 29...40 8d 5c 1c b3 19 ......Intel(R) Ethernet Connection (2) I219-V
 17...0a 00 27 00 00 11 ......VirtualBox Host-Only Ethernet Adapter #2
 48...9a 48 27 c5 23 79 ......Microsoft Wi-Fi Direct Virtual Adapter #7
 79...98 48 27 c5 23 79 ......Microsoft Wi-Fi Direct Virtual Adapter #8
 11...00 50 56 c0 00 01 ......VMware Virtual Ethernet Adapter for VMnet1
 12...00 50 56 c0 00 08 ......VMware Virtual Ethernet Adapter for VMnet8
 30...98 48 27 c5 23 79 ......TP-Link Wireless MU-MIMO USB Adapter
  1...........................Software Loopback Interface 1
 24...00 15 5d c8 ba 3c ......Hyper-V Virtual Ethernet Adapter
 59...00 15 5d 72 a4 72 ......Hyper-V Virtual Ethernet Adapter #2
 64...00 15 5d fd c7 2c ......Hyper-V Virtual Ethernet Adapter #3
 69...00 15 5d ab 05 3a ......Hyper-V Virtual Ethernet Adapter #4
 74...00 15 5d 03 79 c1 ......Hyper-V Virtual Ethernet Adapter #5
===========================================================================

IPv4 Route Table
===========================================================================
Active Routes:
Network Destination        Netmask          Gateway       Interface  Metric
          0.0.0.0          0.0.0.0      192.168.1.1   192.168.1.109     45
        127.0.0.0        255.0.0.0         On-link         127.0.0.1    331
        127.0.0.1  255.255.255.255         On-link         127.0.0.1    331
  127.255.255.255  255.255.255.255         On-link         127.0.0.1    331
      169.254.0.0      255.255.0.0         On-link    169.254.80.105    281
```

FIGURE 2.6 Using **netstat -r** to display the interface list and IPv4 routing table use **netstat -a** to list all ports regardless of their protocol or state; use **netstat -at** to list all TCP ports; use **netstat -au** to list all UDP ports; and use **netstat -l** to list all listening ports. For other options, use **netstat /?**. netstat is also available in Linux.

nslookup

Use **nslookup** with no options to display current DNS server and its IP address. At the NSLookup prompt >, enter a URL to see its default server, IP address, and aliases (Figure 2.7). Type **exit** to return to the command prompt.

```
Command Prompt - nslookup

C:\Users\Mark E. Soper>nslookup
Default Server:  router.asus.com
Address:  192.168.1.1

> wiley.com
Server:  router.asus.com
Address:  192.168.1.1

Non-authoritative answer:
Name:    wiley.com
Address:  63.97.118.67

> www.bing.com
Server:  router.asus.com
Address:  192.168.1.1

Non-authoritative answer:
Name:    dual-a-0001.dc-msedge.net
Addresses:  2a01:111:202c::200
          131.253.33.200
          13.107.22.200
Aliases:  www.bing.com
          a-0001.a-afdentry.net.trafficmanager.net
          www-bing-com.dual-a-0001.a-msedge.net

>
```

FIGURE 2.7 Using **nslookup** to view this computer's current server and IP addresses for two websites

chkdsk

Use **chkdsk** to perform a variety of disk checks on the specified drive. The command must be run in elevated mode. If not, the error message shown in Figure 2.8 appears.

Use **chkdsk** without options to scan a drive for errors (Figure 2.9). Use **chkdsk /f** to scan and fix a drive that may have errors. Specify a drive to check for errors with **chkdsk x:** (substitute your actual drive letter for *x:* and add options as needed).

```
Command Prompt

C:\Users\Mark E. Soper>chkdsk
Access Denied as you do not have sufficient privileges or
the disk may be locked by another process.
You have to invoke this utility running in elevated mode
and make sure the disk is unlocked.
```

FIGURE 2.8 An error triggered when **chkdsk** is run from the command prompt in normal mode

```
Stage 3: Examining security descriptors ...
Security descriptor verification completed.
 Phase duration (Security descriptor verification): 25.66 milliseconds.
  235287 data files processed.
 Phase duration (Data attribute verification): 0.26 milliseconds.
CHKDSK is verifying Usn Journal...
  37803208 USN bytes processed.
Usn Journal verification completed.
 Phase duration (USN journal verification): 93.27 milliseconds.

Windows has scanned the file system and found no problems.
No further action is required.

 975436319 KB total disk space.
 895994044 KB in 1724813 files.
   1000104 KB in 235288 indexes.
         0 KB in bad sectors.
   2259535 KB in use by the system.
     65536 KB occupied by the log file.
  76182636 KB available on disk.

      4096 bytes in each allocation unit.
 243859079 total allocation units on disk.
  19045659 allocation units available on disk.
Total duration: 1.21 minutes (72917 ms).
```

FIGURE 2.9 The end of a **chkdsk** run with no errors detected

net user

With no options, net user displays network accounts on the current system (Figure 2.10). Options include changing passwords and adding/removing users.

net use

When run with no options, **net use** displays existing mappings of a shared resource on the network to a drive letter (Figure 2.11). Use **net use /help** for complete syntax and options.

```
Administrator: Command Prompt

C:\WINDOWS\system32>net user

User accounts for \\TIGER-ATHLON

-------------------------------------------------------------------------
Administrator           ASPNET                    Bill
DefaultAccount          geekc                     Guest
HelpAssistant           marcu                     Marcus
Marcus-VP81             Mark E. Soper             pi
SUPPORT_388945a0        WDAGUtilityAccount
The command completed successfully.


C:\WINDOWS\system32>net user /?
The syntax of this command is:

NET USER
[username [password | *] [options]] [/DOMAIN]
        username {password | *} /ADD [options] [/DOMAIN]
        username [/DELETE] [/DOMAIN]
        username [/TIMES:{times | ALL}]
        username [/ACTIVE: {YES | NO}]
```

F I G U R E 2 . 1 0 Displaying network accounts with **net user**

tracert

Use **tracert *website*** or **tracert *IP address*** to trace the route between your PC and a specified website or IP address (Figure 2.12). The equivalent command in macOS and Linux is traceroute.

```
Administrator: Command Prompt

C:\WINDOWS\system32>net use
New connections will be remembered.


Status       Local      Remote                    Network

-------------------------------------------------------------------------------
Disconnected P:          \\CHERYLHP\Users          Microsoft Windows Network
Unavailable  Z:          \\EPSON-XP800\MEMORYCARD  Microsoft Windows Network
The command completed successfully.


C:\WINDOWS\system32>net use /?
The syntax of this command is:

NET USE
[devicename | *] [\\computername\sharename[\volume] [password | *]]
        [/USER:[domainname\]username]
        [/USER:[dotted domain name\]username]
        [/USER:[username@dotted domain name]
        [/SMARTCARD]
        [/SAVECRED]
        [/REQUIREINTEGRITY]
        [/REQUIREPRIVACY]
        [/WRITETHROUGH]
        [[/DELETE] | [/PERSISTENT:{YES | NO}]]

NET USE {devicename | *} [password | *] /HOME

NET USE [/PERSISTENT:{YES | NO}]
```

F I G U R E   2 . 1 1 **Viewing drive mappings with net use and getting condensed help with net use /?**

format

Use **format** (Figure 2.13), specifying a drive letter and options as needed, to create or re-create the specified filesystem on recordable or rewritable storage (magnetic, flash, or optical). In the process, the contents of the drive are overwritten. Use **format x:** to format the specified drive with its default settings. Use **format /?** for other options.

copy

Use **copy** to make a copy of one or more files to another folder or drive. The copy command, unlike xcopy or robocopy, cannot copy folders.

Use **dir *destination*** to verify that the copied files are in the destination you specified. Figure 2.14 illustrates the use of a wildcard character (*) to substitute for the filename in a command.

```
Administrator: Command Prompt

C:\WINDOWS\system32>tracert www.evansville.net

Tracing route to www2.windstream.net [162.39.145.20]
over a maximum of 30 hops:

  1     1 ms     1 ms     1 ms  router.asus.com [192.168.1.1]
  2    17 ms    10 ms    18 ms  142-254-146-121.inf.spectrum.com [142.254.146.121]
  3    17 ms     9 ms    10 ms  lag-62.evvninas01h.netops.charter.com [74.128.4.121]
  4    21 ms    15 ms    15 ms  lag-27.lsvqkydb01r.netops.charter.com [65.29.30.36]
  5    25 ms    33 ms    26 ms  lag-24.rcr01clevohek.netops.charter.com [65.189.140.166]
  6    32 ms    33 ms    32 ms  lag-27.vinnva0510w-bcr00.netops.charter.com [66.109.6.66]
  7    35 ms    32 ms    33 ms  lag-11.asbnva1611w-bcr00.netops.charter.com [66.109.6.30]
  8    38 ms    33 ms    33 ms  lag-310.pr2.dca10.netops.charter.com [209.18.43.59]
  9     *        *       33 ms  eqix-dc5.intellifiber.com [206.126.237.16]
 10     *        *       38 ms  ae1.cr01.asbn07-va.us.windstream.net [169.130.193.68]
 11    41 ms    40 ms    42 ms  ae3-0.agr03.ephr01-pa.us.windstream.net [40.129.34.17]
 12    49 ms    39 ms    39 ms  162.39.143.14
 13    42 ms    43 ms    45 ms  www2.windstream.net [162.39.145.20]

Trace complete.
```

FIGURE 2.12 Tracing the route to a website. Each * indicates no response from the listed URL/website on the route.

```
C:\Users\Mark E. Soper>format m:
Insert new disk for drive M:
and press ENTER when ready...
The type of the file system is RAW.
The new file system is FAT.
Verifying 1.9 GB
Initializing the File Allocation Table (FAT)...
Volume label (11 characters, ENTER for none)?
Format complete.
        1.9 GB total disk space.
        1.9 GB are available.

        32,768 bytes in each allocation unit.
        62,835 allocation units available on disk.

           16 bits in each FAT entry.

Volume Serial Number is BA13-90E8
```

FIGURE 2.13 Formatting a 2 GB SD card using its default setting

```
CL Command Prompt

C:\Users\Mark E. Soper>copy *.log logs
Patcher.log
rpro.log
Sti_Trace.log
        3 file(s) copied.

C:\Users\Mark E. Soper>dir logs
 Volume in drive C has no label.
 Volume Serial Number is 3CFC-BE75

 Directory of C:\Users\Mark E. Soper\logs

04/20/2022  02:23 PM    <DIR>          .
04/20/2022  02:23 PM    <DIR>          ..
02/27/2014  04:17 PM             1,123 Patcher.log
01/12/2022  04:11 PM         3,304,882 rpro.log
08/25/2013  02:07 PM            10,761 Sti_Trace.log
               3 File(s)      3,316,766 bytes
               2 Dir(s)  79,429,902,336 bytes free

C:\Users\Mark E. Soper>
```

FIGURE 2.14 Using **copy *.log _foldername_** and **dir _foldername_** to verify the files copied

---

EXAM TIP

Wildcards are used to substitute for one or more characters in commands. * matches any number of characters and can be used anywhere in a character string. ? matches a single alphanumeric character in a specific position. [ ] matches characters inside the brackets. [!] excludes characters after the ! between brackets from searches.

---

xcopy

Use **xcopy** to copy files and folders. Use **xcopy _folder1_ _folder2_** to copy the contents of one folder to another. Use **xcopy _files_ _folder_** to copy one or more files and folders to another folder. Use **xcopy _files_ _x:_** to copy to the current folder on another drive. The xcopy command, unlike copy, can create a new folder as the destination and can copy folders (Figure 2.15).

```
C:\Users\Mark E. Soper>xcopy logs logs2
Does logs2 specify a file name
or directory name on the target
(F = file, D = directory)? d
logs\Patcher.log
logs\rpro.log
logs\Sti_Trace.log
3 File(s) copied
```

FIGURE 2.15 Using xcopy to create a folder and copy the contents of another folder into it

robocopy

Robocopy is a highly configurable file/folder copy and move app. Use **robocopy** when you need to mirror, purge, synchronize, exclude, create log files of operations, create and run jobs, and much more. Of the file copying command-line utilities in Windows, copy is the simplest and least powerful, xcopy is next, and robocopy is the most flexible and powerful. In Figure 2.16, robocopy is used to create a folder and move files into it.

```
C:\Users\Mark E. Soper>robocopy logs logs3 /move

-------------------------------------------------------------------------------
   ROBOCOPY     ::     Robust File Copy for Windows
-------------------------------------------------------------------------------

  Started : Tuesday, April 19, 2022 12:52:18 PM
   Source : C:\Users\Mark E. Soper\logs\
     Dest : C:\Users\Mark E. Soper\logs3\

    Files : *.*

  Options : *.* /DCOPY:DA /COPY:DAT /MOVE /R:1000000 /W:30

-------------------------------------------------------------------------------

            New Dir       3    C:\Users\Mark E. Soper\logs\
100%        New File          1123        Patcher.log
100%        New File          3.1 m       rpro.log
100%        New File          10761       Sti_Trace.log

-------------------------------------------------------------------------------

               Total    Copied   Skipped  Mismatch    FAILED    Extras
    Dirs :         1         1         0         0         0         0
   Files :         3         3         0         0         0         0
   Bytes :    3.16 m    3.16 m         0         0         0         0
   Times :   0:00:00   0:00:00                       0:00:00   0:00:00


   Speed :             221117733 Bytes/sec.
   Speed :             12652.458 MegaBytes/min.
   Ended : Tuesday, April 19, 2022 12:52:18 PM
```

FIGURE 2.16 Using robocopy to create a folder and copy the contents of another folder into it

gpupdate

Use **gpupdate** to refresh Group Policy on local or Microsoft Active Directory (AD) managed systems (Figure 2.17).

```
Command Prompt

C:\Users\Mark E. Soper>gpupdate
Updating policy...

Computer Policy update has completed successfully.
User Policy update has completed successfully.


C:\Users\Mark E. Soper>gpresult /r

Microsoft (R) Windows (R) Operating System Group Policy Result tool v2.0
© Microsoft Corporation. All rights reserved.

Created on ⌈ 4/⌈ 19/⌈ 2022 at 1:12:11 PM


RSOP data for TIGER-ATHLON\Mark E. Soper on TIGER-ATHLON : Logging Mode
---------------------------------------------------------------------------

OS Configuration:          Standalone Workstation
OS Version:                10.0.19043
Site Name:                 N/A
Roaming Profile:           N/A
Local Profile:             C:\Users\Mark E. Soper
Connected over a slow link?: No


USER SETTINGS
-------------

    Last time Group Policy was applied: 4/19/2022 at 1:01:36 PM
    Group Policy was applied from:       N/A
    Group Policy slow link threshold:    500 kbps
    Domain Name:                         TIGER-ATHLON
    Domain Type:                         <Local Computer>

    Applied Group Policy Objects
    -----------------------------
        Local Group Policy

    The user is a part of the following security groups
    ---------------------------------------------------
        High Mandatory Level
        Everyone
        Local account and member of Administrators group
        Authors
        Debugger Users
        HomeUsers
        BUILTIN\Administrators
        BUILTIN\Users
        NT AUTHORITY\INTERACTIVE
        CONSOLE LOGON
        NT AUTHORITY\Authenticated Users
        This Organization
        markesoper@hotmail.com
        Local account
        LOCAL
        Cloud Account Authentication
```

FIGURE 2.17 Using **gpupdate** and **gpresult /r**

gpresult

Use **gpresult** to display the Resultant Set of Policy (RSoP) for the specified computer and user based on applied Group Policy settings. Use **gpresult /r** to display RSoP for the local system (refer to Figure 2.17).

sfc

Use **sfc /scannow** to scan system files and replace damaged or missing files immediately (Figure 2.18); the command must be run in elevated mode.

```
Administrator: Command Prompt

C:\WINDOWS\system32>sfc /scannow

Beginning system scan.  This process will take some time.

Beginning verification phase of system scan.
Verification 100% complete.

Windows Resource Protection found corrupt files and successfully repaired them.
For online repairs, details are included in the CBS log file located at
windir\Logs\CBS\CBS.log. For example C:\Windows\Logs\CBS\CBS.log. For offline
repairs, details are included in the log file provided by the /OFFLOGFILE flag.
```

F I G U R E   2 . 1 8   Scanning and repairing Windows system files with sfc

[command name] /?

[command name] /? displays help for the specified command. See Figure 2.11 for an example where net use /? is entered.

diskpart

Use **diskpart** to list and change disks and partitions. Use this command to perform tasks (such as cleaning the entire contents of a drive) that cannot be performed with the Windows Disk Management utility. Diskpart must be run in elevated mode, but if you run it in standard mode, you are prompted to permit it to run. Figure 2.19 illustrates disk cleaning. Type **exit** to close diskpart and return to the command prompt.

pathping

Use **pathping** to provide information about network latency and network loss at the intermediate hops between a source and destination (Figure 2.20); pathping can be used in place of tracert. Use **pathping IP address** or **pathping URL**.

```
■⁚ C:\WINDOWS\system32\diskpart.exe

Microsoft DiskPart version 10.0.19041.964

Copyright (C) Microsoft Corporation.
On computer: TIGER-ATHLON

DISKPART> list disk

  Disk ###  Status         Size     Free     Dyn  Gpt
  --------  -------------  -------  -------   ---  ---
  Disk 0    Online          931 GB  1024 KB         *
  Disk 1    Online         3726 GB     0 B          *
  Disk 2    Online         7452 GB  1024 KB         *
  Disk 3    No Media          0 B      0 B
  Disk 4    Online         1964 MB     0 B
  Disk 5    No Media          0 B      0 B
  Disk 6    No Media          0 B      0 B
  Disk 7    Online           12 TB     0 B          *
  Disk 8    Online         2794 GB     0 B          *

DISKPART> select disk 4

Disk 4 is now the selected disk.

DISKPART> clean all

DiskPart succeeded in cleaning the disk.
```

FIGURE 2.19 Cleaning all contents of a disk with **diskpart**

```
C:\ Command Prompt

C:\Users\Mark E. Soper>pathping www.evansville.net

Tracing route to www2.windstream.net [162.39.145.20]
over a maximum of 30 hops:
  0  Tiger-Athlon [192.168.1.109]
  1  router.asus.com [192.168.1.1]
  2  142-254-146-121.inf.spectrum.com [142.254.146.121]
  3  lag-62.evvninas01h.netops.charter.com [74.128.4.121]

Computing statistics for 325 seconds...
              Source to Here   This Node/Link
Hop  RTT     Lost/Sent = Pct  Lost/Sent = Pct  Address
  0                                             Tiger-Athlon [192.168.1.109]
                                0/ 100 =  0%    |
  1   3ms     2/ 100 =  2%     2/ 100 =  2%     router.asus.com [192.168.1.1]
                                0/ 100 =  0%    |
  2  13ms     1/ 100 =  1%     1/ 100 =  1%     142-254-146-121.inf.spectrum.com [142.254.146.121]
                                0/ 100 =  0%    |
  3  13ms     2/ 100 =  2%     2/ 100 =  2%     lag-62.evvninas01h.netops.charter.com [74.128.4.121]
                                0/ 100 =  0%    |
```

FIGURE 2.20 Portions of the output from a typical **pathping** run

winver

Use **winver** to display the Windows edition, build number, and Microsoft license terms. winver displays this information in a GUI window.

CERTMIKE EXAM ESSENTIALS

▶ Command-line commands and tools provide a wide range of information that goes beyond what is available from the standard Windows graphical user interface (GUI).

▶ Unlike Windows GUI commands that provide immediate visual feedback, using the dir command with the appropriate options is very useful in determining the results of a command.

▶ Some commands require the user to open the command prompt in elevated mode, also known as Run As Administrator.

Practice Question 1

Your client is trying to run chkdsk on an external drive to determine if it has a problem. After getting a message that says "Access Denied . . . the disk may be locked by another process. You have to evoke this command in elevated mode . . ." the client wants to know how to unlock the disk. Which of the following responses is the *best* answer?

A. Run **UNLOCK.EXE** and specify the disk to be unlocked.

B. Close the command prompt and open it with the Run As Administrator option.

C. Try the chkdsk command again with the /UNLOCK switch.

D. Run the command ELEVATE.EXE first.

Practice Question 2

Your client is seeing a wide variety of Windows problems, including periodic loss of network connection and slow program performance. Which of the following Windows tools is most likely to solve these problems?

A. chkdsk

B. pathping

C. winver

D. sfc

Practice Question 1 Explanation

This question is designed to test your understanding of command-line commands and their requirements. Let's evaluate these choices one at a time.

1. The first suggested answer, run UNLOCK.EXE and specify the disk to be unlocked, is not possible. There is no UNLOCK.EXE in Windows.

2. The next suggestion, close the command prompt and open it with the Run As Administrator option, is the right one. The disk isn't actually locked. Run As Administrator is the same as elevated mode and will enable chkdsk to run properly.

3. The third suggestion, run chkdsk with the /UNLOCK switch, is not possible. There is no /UNLOCK switch.

4. The fourth suggestion, run ELEVATE.EXE first, is not possible. There is no ELEVATE.EXE command in Windows.

Correct Answer: B. Run CMD as administrator

Practice Question 2 Explanation

This question is designed to test your ability to understand the capabilities of the Windows tools in this chapter.

Let's evaluate these choices one at a time.

1. The first suggestion, chkdsk, can help improve slow program performance caused by disk structure problems. However, chkdsk does nothing about network connections.

2. Next suggestion, pathping, is designed to provide detailed information about Internet/network connections to a specified IP address or URL. However, it cannot repair a network problem, nor can it help with program performance.

3. The third suggestion, winver, reports the installed Windows version. It has no diagnostics capabilities.

4. The last option, sfc, is designed to solve problems caused by corrupted or missing Windows system files. Windows system files affect all parts of a Windows installation, including network connections, applications, and much more. sfc is the *best* choice.

Correct Answer: D. Run SFC

CHAPTER 3

Windows 10 Operating System Tools

Core 2 Objective 1.3: Given a scenario, use features and tools of the Microsoft Windows 10 operating system (OS).

Windows 10 and 11 include a wide variety of tools to view, manage, and help improve performance and security.

In this chapter, you will learn everything you need to know about A+ Certification Core 2 Objective 1.3, including the following topics:

▶ **Task Manager**
▶ **Microsoft Management Console (MMC) Snap-ins**
▶ **Additional Tools**

TASK MANAGER

Task Manager provides five ways to view the tasks that Microsoft Windows is performing at a given time. Start Task Manager in any of these ways:

▶ Click Search, type **Task Manager**, and click the matching app.
▶ Click Search, type **taskmgr**, and click the matching app.
▶ Press the Ctrl+Alt+Del keys at the same time and choose Task Manager from the list of tasks.
▶ Press the Ctrl+Shift+Esc keys at the same time.

Depending on how Task Manager was last used, the Fewer Details dialog box that lists active apps might show up first (Figure 3.1). To get to the More Details view, click the More Details button.

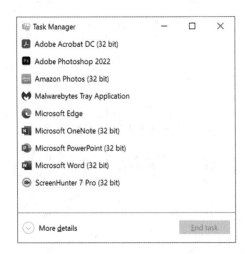

F I G U R E 3 . 1 **The Fewer Details view of Task Manager shows only active apps.**

Processes

The Processes tab is the tab you see first when you open Task Manager in More Details view (Figure 3.2). Scroll down to see Apps, Background Processes, and Windows Processes and the amount of CPU, memory, disk, and network resources used by a process.

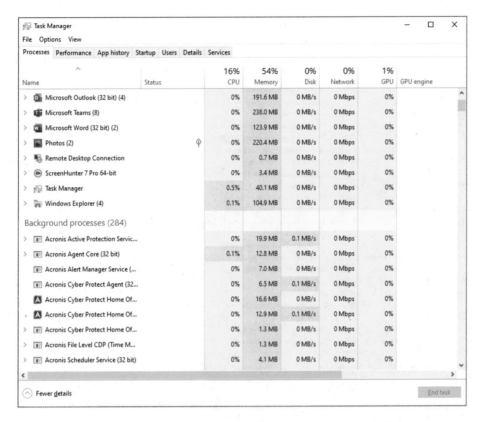

FIGURE 3.2 Viewing background processes with the Processes tab

Scroll to the right to see GPU and power usage information. The green leaf icon in the Status column indicates Windows processes that are suspended temporarily to improve performance. To end a task, highlight it and click End Task.

Services

The Services tab in Task Manager (Figure 3.3) provides a shortcut to view Windows and third-party services. At a glance, you can see the name of the process, its process ID (PID), what it does, its status, and its group.

If you need to make any changes to a service, right-click the service and choose an option from the menu. To work with multiple services, click the Open Services link at the bottom of the dialog box.

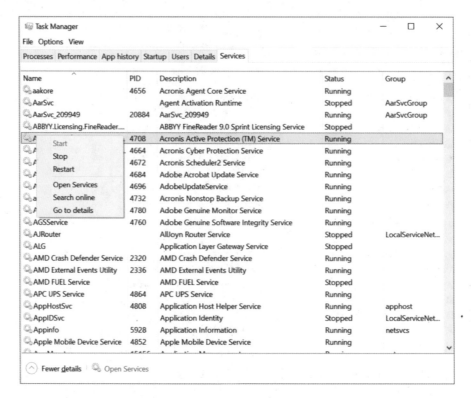

FIGURE 3.3 The Services tab lists all services, with options to manage a selected service.

EXAM TIP

The Windows taskkill command-line app can be used to shut down a malfunctioning app or service with `taskkill PID` (specify the actual PID value).

Startup

If you need to find out exactly what's loading at startup and how much effect it has on loading time, click the Startup tab (Figure 3.4). To learn more about a Startup item, right-click it and choose Properties. To disable a Startup item, select it and then click Disable.

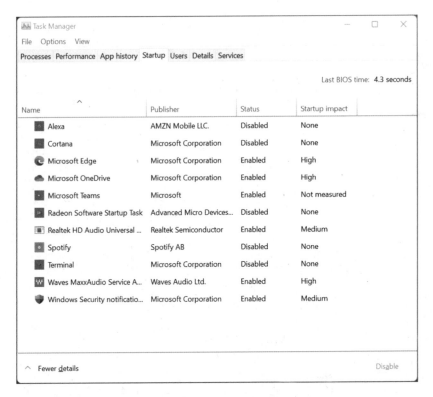

FIGURE 3.4 The Startup tab on a system with a few Startup events

Performance

Use the Performance tab (Figure 3.5) to check real-time performance of CPU, memory, drives, network, and GPU components. For even more details, click the Open Resource Monitor link (we cover Resource Monitor later in this chapter).

Users

Whether the current system has one user or more signed in, the Users tab (Figure 3.6) provides a quick look at who is signed in and how much resource usage is involved. It also provides easy Sign Out and Switch User options.

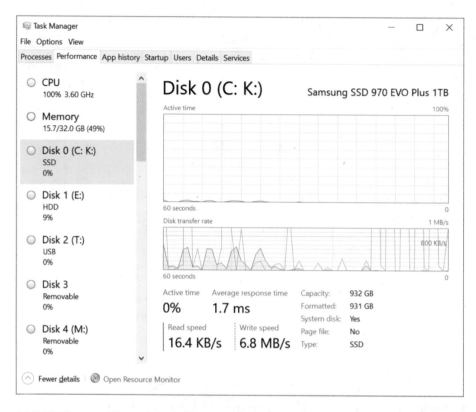

F I G U R E   3 . 5   The real-time drive transfer rate, read, and write speeds, and disk details for the system drive as shown on the Performance tab

MICROSOFT MANAGEMENT CONSOLE (MMC) SNAP-IN

Instead of creating a wide variety of separate apps for managing Windows, Microsoft has a single extensible app called the Microsoft Management Console (*MMC*). The Microsoft Management Console (*MMC*) is a framework for Microsoft and third-party tools called *snap-ins*.

To open a blank MMC session, press the Windows+R keys to open the Run menu, type MMC, and press the Enter key. You can then add a snap-in from the MMC snap-in library as shown in Figure 3.7.

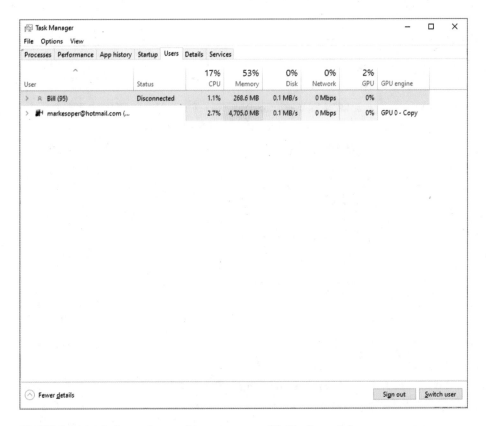

FIGURE 3.6 Preparing to sign out a user with the Users tab

In this section, you will learn about MMC snap-ins already installed in Windows 10/11. To start any of these snap-ins, open the Search window and type in the name or the command; then click the matching app.

> **TIP**
> Right-click the Start button to gain access to important Windows management features, including the Disk Management, Computer Management, Device Manager, and Event Viewer MMC snap-ins.

> **EXAM TIP**
> Make sure you know what each of the following snap-ins do and how to start them by searching for their name or executable file.

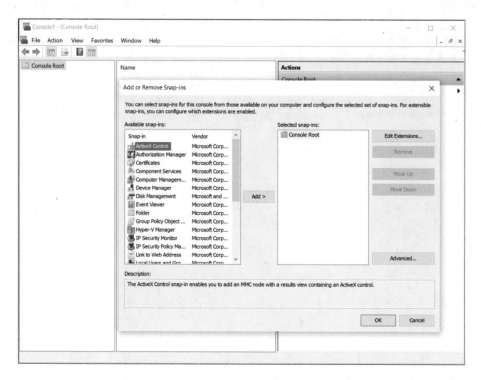

FIGURE 3.7 Preparing to install a snap-in for MMC; start the process by selecting File ➢ Add/Remove Snap-in.

Event Viewer (*eventvwr.msc*)

You can use Event Viewer to see listings of critical, error, warning, information, and audit success events by clicking the appropriate log type or view in the left-hand pane.

> **EXAM TIP**
>
> For the Core 2 1102 exam, focus on Windows Application, Security, and System Event logs and their associated error messages.

Use the Actions menu to create customized filters and views. In Figure 3.8, a custom Windows event log has been created to display Critical events. The window at lower center provides details of the selected event.

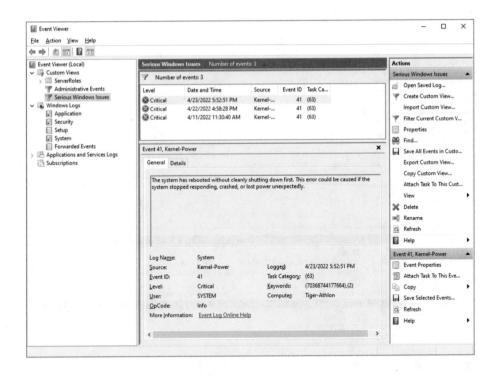

FIGURE 3.8 Viewing details of a critical event recorded in a custom log in Event Viewer

Disk Management (*diskmgmt.msc*)

Disk Management displays the status of all connected internal and external hard drives, including disk partitions (volumes), drive letters, and Windows RAID configurations (Figure 3.9). Disk Management can turn an unallocated drive into one or more drive letters with its New Simple Volume Wizard and can extend or shrink volumes, assign a different drive letter, and create spanned, striped (RAID 0), mirrored (RAID 1), and, with three or more drives, RAID 5 arrays. As with hardware RAID arrays, use identical drives or at least drives with the same capacity.

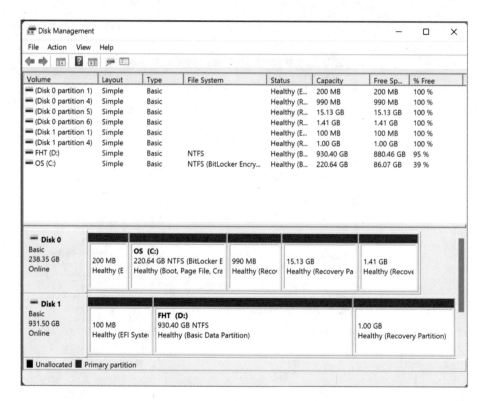

F I G U R E 3 . 9 Disk Management displaying the configurations of a system drive and an external drive

---

EXAM TIP

A drive that cannot be used with Disk Management may be managed with the command-line diskpart tool.

Task Scheduler (*taskschd.msc*)

Both Windows and third-party apps use Task Scheduler to schedule updates and other tasks that need to run at a particular time or when a particular event takes place. Task Scheduler stores existing tasks in the Task Scheduler Library (Figure 3.10).

To create a new task, click Create Task in the right-hand window. As the wizard runs, you are prompted to describe the task and specify triggers (conditions or events that will start the task), what actions to perform, what conditions change how the task runs, the task's settings, and task history (enable this from the Actions menu).

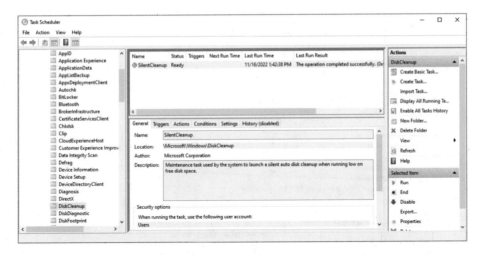

FIGURE 3.10 **Reviewing conditions for an existing task in Task Scheduler**

Device Manager (*devmgmt.msc*)

Device Manager lists the devices built into or connected to a computer by category and provides status, driver information, Registry information, and more. Click a category to see the items in that category.

When Device Manager is opened, any devices with issues are listed (Figure 3.11). Click the item to see what the issue is. Use the solution button on the General tab of the Properties dialog box to solve the problem. In Figure 3.11, the solution button says "Enable Device." Select the Driver tab to update or roll back the driver or to disable/enable the device. Select the Details tab to view technical details, and select the Power Management tab on USB hubs to determine whether the computer can turn off or wake a device. The Events tab lists time-stamped events such as device installation, device configuration, and so on.

Certificate Manager (*certmgr.msc*)

Security certificates are used to confirm the identity of secured websites or software developers. A website's security certificate is downloaded to a device when a connection is made. Similarly, when a digitally signed app is installed, its security certificate is installed during the process.

Certificate Manager provides a list of security certificates installed on the system (Figure 3.12). Certificates can also be removed, imported, or exported. Trusted root certificate authorities are entities that are responsible for providing security certificates to application and website providers.

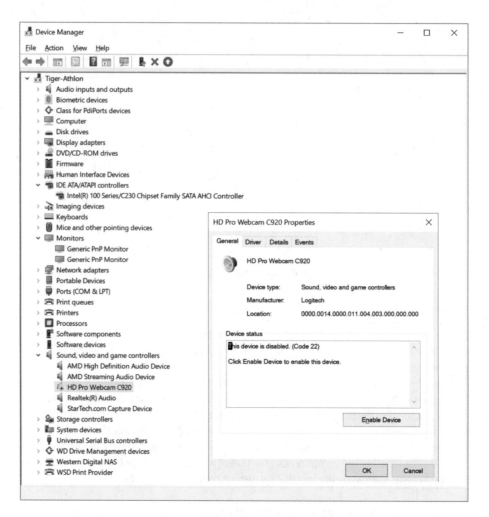

F I G U R E   3 . 1 1   Device Manager listing for a disabled device

Local Users and Groups (*lusrmgr.msc*)

Local Users and Groups (Figure 3.13) is used to display and manage users and groups on the current system (domains use Microsoft Active Directory Users and Groups to perform similar tasks for domain members).

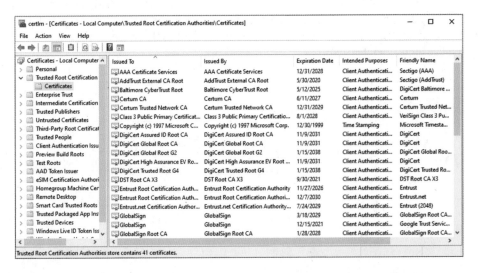

FIGURE 3.12 Certificate Manager list of trusted root certificate authorities

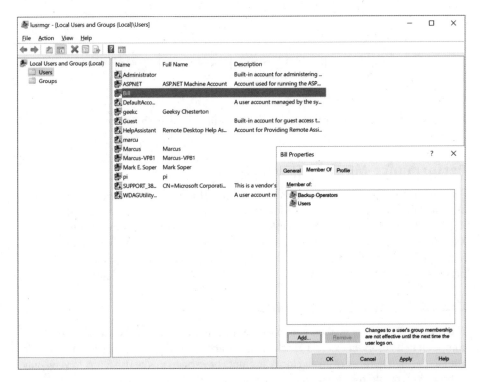

FIGURE 3.13 Adding a user to the Backup Operators group with Local Users and Groups

If you add a specific user to the group, the user will inherit the group's access rights and be able to run commands associated with that group. Double-click a user to view, add, or remove group memberships.

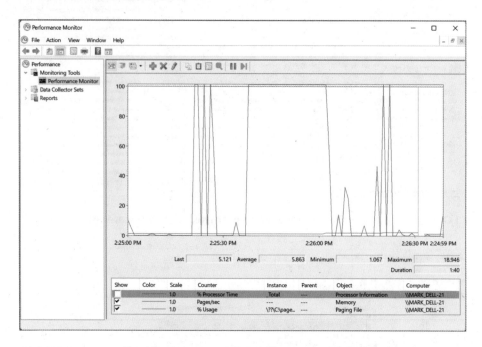

FIGURE 3.14 Checking memory and pagefile usage with Performance Monitor

Performance Monitor (*perfmon.msc*)

Performance Monitor provides a real-time system performance summary, options to create Data Collector Sets to capture performance of selected subsystems, and access to the Resource Monitor (discussed later in this chapter). In the example shown in Figure 3.14, Memory Pages/Sec and Pagefile Usage counters have been selected to help determine if the system needs more RAM. Open the Reports section to start, create, or view performance or diagnostic reports.

Group Policy Editor (*gpedit.msc*)

The Group Policy Editor enables you to view and configure a wide variety of settings for a computer or its users. In Figure 3.15, changes are about to be made to lock out an account after a specified number of invalid login attempts have been made. Use filters to view only policies that match specific criteria.

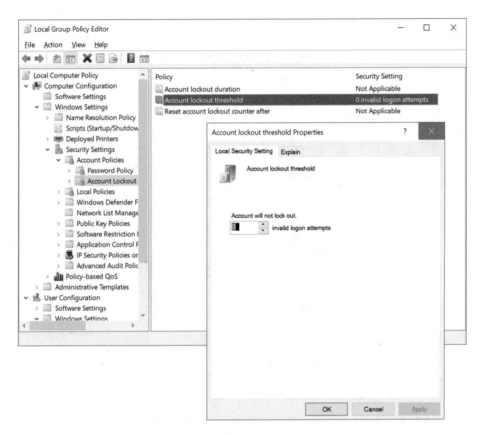

FIGURE 3.15 Using Group Policy Editor to change the Account Lockout Threshold policy

ADDITIONAL TOOLS

Windows includes additional tools to help you manage your system. They are covered in the following sections.

System Information (*msinfo32.exe*)

System Information provides basic information about a computer's hardware, Windows configuration, and software. MSInfo32's opening dialog box provides a summary of the computer's hardware, including motherboard, processor, memory size, and Windows version (Figure 3.16). Expand the categories in the left pane and click an item for more details.

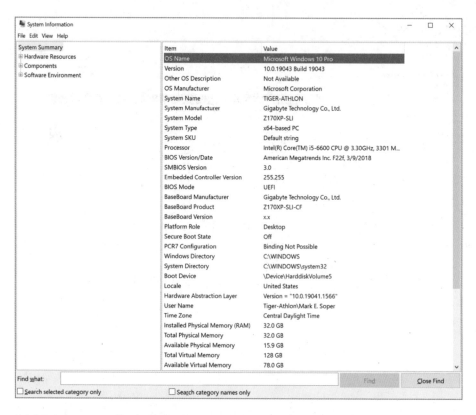

FIGURE 3.16 Reviewing a system summary with System Information

Resource Monitor (*resmon.exe*)

Resource Monitor can be opened directly as well as through Performance Monitor. Resource Monitor provides an overview (Figure 3.17) of system performance for CPU, Disk, Network, and Memory components as well as real-time graphs and specific PIDs using the selected resource. Use the Monitor menu to start and stop monitoring as desired.

System Configuration (*msconfig.exe*)

Use System Configuration (`msconfig.exe`) to control the drivers and apps used at startup (General tab), how the system boots (Boot tab), to enable/disable Microsoft and third-party services (Services tab), and get access to various tools (Tools tab). Figure 3.18 shows the General and Boot tabs (the Startup tab's former functions are now controlled in Task Manager).

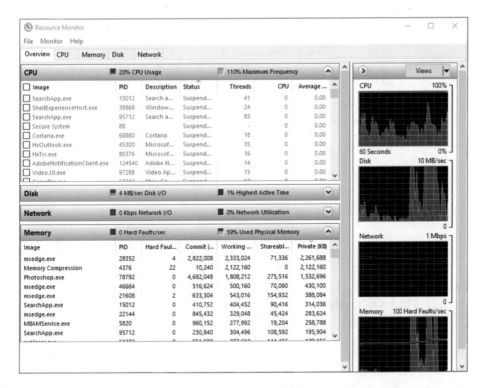

FIGURE 3.17 Reviewing system performance with Resource Monitor

Disk Cleanup (*cleanmgr.exe*)

The longer that a Windows PC is in service, the more likely it is that leftover files of various types will accumulate. Use Disk Cleanup (Figure 3.19) to remove unneeded files of various kinds. When you run Disk Cleanup from the EXE file, as opposed to running it from the Tools tab of the Disk Properties menu, you must specify the drive. You must provide administrator credentials to clean up system files. Click the View Files button to see what will be removed.

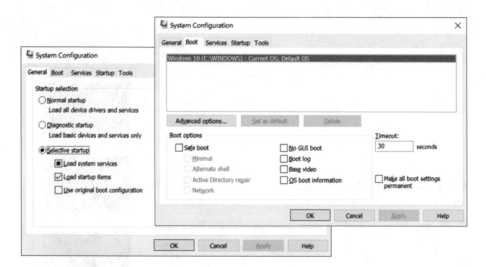

FIGURE 3.18 General and Boot tabs for a Windows 10 system, with some changes to its default system services

FIGURE 3.19 Reviewing suggested cleanup items with Disk Cleanup

Disk Defragment (*dfrgui.exe*)

Disk defragmentation (Optimize Drives), which reassembles files stored in noncontiguous sectors into contiguous sectors for faster operation, is run automatically in Windows for mechanical drives (solid-state drives do not need defragmentation). Thus, it is seldom run manually. However, if a drive with data is connected to a new computer, the user can analyze it manually and start the defragmentation process if necessary.

After starting Disk Defragment, review the list of drives. If a drive is listed as Never Run, click Analyze. If the drive has fragmentation, click Optimize to start the process. The default is weekly. Click Change Settings to change the frequency.

Registry Editor (*regedit.exe*)

Although Windows includes a large number of management tools and many menu adjustments, it is sometimes necessary to make changes to the Windows Registry, which is the central repository for all Windows settings. Registry Editor (Figure 3.20) is the tool used to view and change the Registry.

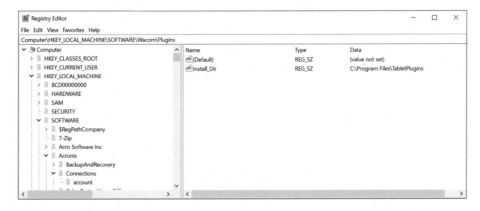

FIGURE 3.20 Viewing Registry branches and a specific Registry entry

EXAM TIP

Before using Registry Editor, back up the Registry. To back up the entire Registry, right-click Computer, select Export, and assign a name to the backup (it is stored with a .reg extension).

Most Registry changes are made by importing a Registry file (with the extension .reg), but you can make other changes by opening an entry and changing existing values or by inserting a new entry and adding the appropriate value. Be sure to verify that suggested changes come from a reliable source and make the recommended Registry backups before making changes.

CERTMIKE EXAM ESSENTIALS

▶ Windows includes a number of apps, snap-ins, and tools that display real-time operations. Many can also be used to log performance over time.

▶ The Microsoft Management Console (MMC) provides a common interface for a variety of important features. More snap-ins can be added as needed.

▶ Before making configuration changes with any app or tool, be sure to note the current configuration so it can be reversed.

Practice Question 1

Your client is looking for performance bottlenecks that happen on some systems when running a photo editor to make changes to large images. The client wants to log performance under normal and heavy system loads. Which of the following tools would you recommend?

A. Task Manager
B. Event Viewer
C. Performance Monitor
D. System Configuration

Practice Question 2

Your client needs to enable some security functions they have learned about in Windows. Which of the following should you recommend?

A. Teach them how to safely use Registry Editor.
B. Configure their company's workstations to boot in Safe Mode with System Configuration.
C. Remove Disk Management from the standard Windows image.
D. Help them use Group Policy Editor.

Practice Question 1 Explanation

This question is designed to test your understanding of both real-time and logging features for the tools discussed in this chapter.

Let's evaluate these choices one at a time.

1. The first suggested answer, Task Manager, shows real-time program and process loads on CPU, memory, disk, network, and GPU components. However, Task Manager has no capabilities for logging performance.

2. The next suggestion, Event Viewer, is designed primarily to capture events such as critical failures, warnings, and information messages generated by software and hardware. It logs this information, but it is not logging performance events.

3. The third suggestion, Performance Monitor, provides both real-time and logged information about hardware performance. Set up Data Collector Sets to log performance and click the link to Resource Monitor to see real-time performance. This is the *best* choice.

4. The last option, running System Configuration (`msinfo32.exe`), doesn't provide the level of detail needed. It reports CPU type and speed, and memory size, but it doesn't provide module-level information.

Correct Answer: C. Performance Monitor

Practice Question 2 Explanation

This question is designed to test your understanding of Windows tools and their applicability.

Let's evaluate these choices one at a time.

1. The first suggestion, Registry Editor, is potentially very dangerous as well as not necessary. Although security settings can be changed with Registry Editor, there are far easier and safer ways to do it.

2. The next suggestion, booting in Safe Mode, would cripple computer operation. Safe Mode itself doesn't support networking and limits a system's capabilities. This is not the safety your client is looking for.

3. The third suggestion, remove Disk Management from the standard Windows image, would only guard against disk-based mischief and would hamper technicians who need to use it.

4. The last option, Group Policy Editor (GPE), is a winner. There are many security settings that can be enabled with GPE. GPE is well documented, far easier to use than Regedit, and far less likely to crash a system. This is the *best* option.

Correct Answer: D. Group Policy Editor

CHAPTER 4

Windows 10 Control Panel

Core 2 Objective 1.4: Given a scenario, use the appropriate Microsoft Windows 10 Control Panel utility.

Windows Control Panel has been the backbone of Windows configuration for many years. Although more Windows configuration functions are being moved to Settings in each subsequent release of Windows 10 and Windows 11, Control Panel is still an important feature to understand and use.

In this chapter, you will learn everything you need to know about A+ Certification Core 2 Objective 1.4, including the following topics:

▶ **Internet Options**
▶ **Devices and Printers**
▶ **Programs and Features**
▶ **Network and Sharing Center**
▶ **System**
▶ **Windows Defender Firewall**

▶ **Mail**

▶ **Sound**

▶ **User Accounts**

▶ **Device Manager**

▶ **Indexing Options**

▶ **Administrative Tools**

▶ **File Explorer Options**

▶ **Power Options**

▶ **Ease of Access**

CONTROL PANEL OVERVIEW

Control Panel contains dozens of applets (small applications) that are used to configure various parts of Windows functions, including network, security, hardware, file management, power, and more. Techs use Control Panel to discover details about the hardware and the Windows installation and to troubleshoot and solve problems with both.

Keep in mind that because of the continued movement of traditional Control Panel functions that some Control Panel applets actually open the corresponding feature in Settings (discussed in Chapter 5, "Windows Settings"). We'll point these out throughout this chapter.

OPENING CONTROL PANEL

To open Control Panel, click Search, type **Control Panel**, and click the app shortcut (Figure 4.1). You can also get to Control Panel by using the Search tool in Settings.

The default arrangement of Control Panel is the Category view. To switch to the individual settings we discuss in this chapter, open the View By menu and choose either Large Icons (Figure 4.2) or Small Icons.

> **TIP**
> One of the advantages of using the Large or Small icons view is that the default Category view doesn't include all of the Control Panel applets.

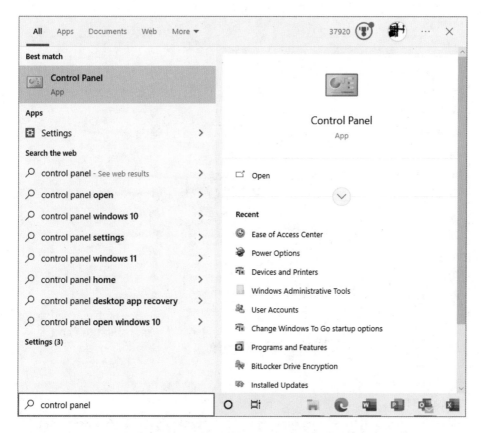

FIGURE 4.1   Using Windows 10 Search to open Control Panel

INTERNET OPTIONS

Internet Options is used to configure the default behavior of Internet Explorer (IE). When you open Internet Options, the dialog is called Internet Properties.

Use the General tab to set home page tabs, startup behavior, tabs, control over browsing history, and appearance. Use the Security tab to configure security settings for web browsing. Use the Privacy tab to enable the pop-up blocker and InPrivate browsing controls. Use the Content tab to view certificates used by IE, settings for AutoComplete, and news feeds. Use Connections to configure VPN, dialup, and LAN settings, including proxy servers. Use Programs to set IE as the default for browsing or other actions. Use Advanced to configure a variety of settings, including encryption, appearance, and more.

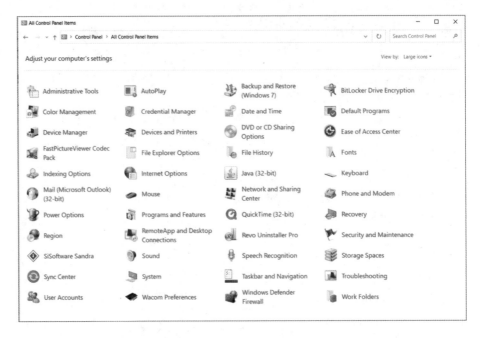

FIGURE 4.2 Control Panel's Large Icons view

> **EXAM TIP**
>
> Most Internet Options settings apply to Internet Explorer, not to Microsoft Edge or third-party browsers. You should know what the different tabs do, but most of them you won't use in the field since IE is now obsolete.

DEVICES AND PRINTERS

Devices and Printers (Figure 4.3) is one of the most versatile Control Panel applets. It provides you with one-stop access to major hardware devices, right-click access to properties sheets and configuration options, file browsing for computers and storage devices, and easy installation.

> **TIP**
>
> Consider making Devices and Printers the first Control Panel item you check when you want to get the "big picture" of what's connected to a system because you can also get to the details you need.

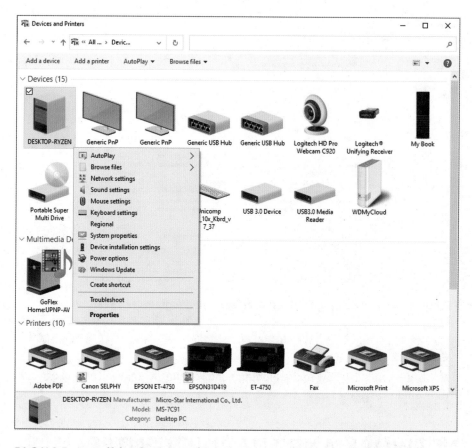

FIGURE 4.3 Using Devices and Printers to see information about hardware attached to the user's computer

PROGRAMS AND FEATURES

Programs and Features (Figure 4.4) lists all the programs installed in Windows 10, including version numbers and installation dates. Use it to uninstall or change (repair or add/remove features) programs, and use the options in the left pane to view installed updates or turn Windows features on or off.

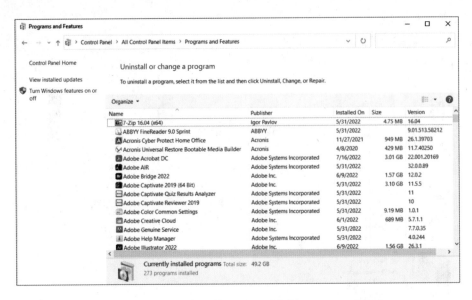

FIGURE 4.4 Preparing to uninstall an app with Programs and Features

EXAM TIP

Make sure you know how to use Programs and Features to uninstall an app or turn Windows features on or off.

NETWORK AND SHARING CENTER

The Network and Sharing Center (Figure 4.5) displays your active networks, sets up a new connection or network, and troubleshoots network problems. Use the options in the left pane to change network adapter settings, advanced sharing settings, and media streaming options.

SYSTEM

Clicking System (Figure 4.6) opens the About page in Settings, listing your hardware (device) specifications first, followed by Windows specifications. Use the Copy buttons to copy the information to the Windows Clipboard so that you can paste it into another application. Use the Rename This PC button to change the name of the PC.

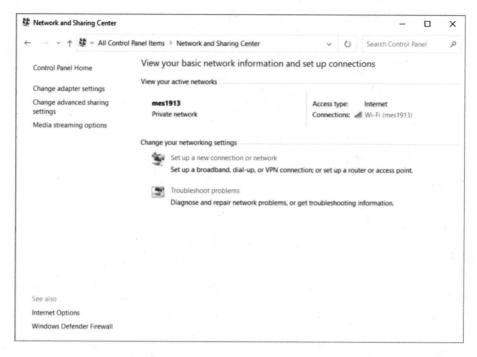

FIGURE 4.5 The Network and Sharing Center

WINDOWS DEFENDER FIREWALL

Windows Defender Firewall (Figure 4.7) blocks unwanted apps from accessing your device. It shows the current network connection type and status. To change how it works, click the appropriate option on the left.

If a third-party application with a firewall has been installed, Defender Firewall will display a banner indicating that the other app is protecting your system (Figure 4.8).

MAIL

Mail (Figure 4.9) is used to configure Outlook's email accounts, data file locations, and profiles. If this applet is missing from Control Panel, you can also access these dialog boxes from within Outlook.

FIGURE 4.6 The About page in Settings opens when you click System in Control Panel.

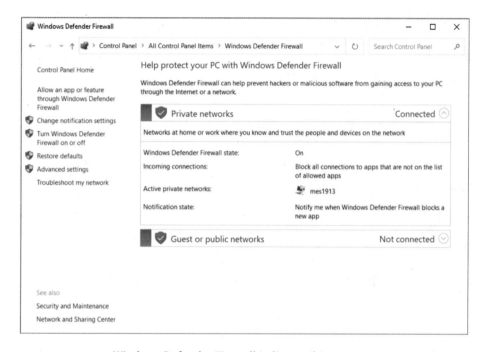

FIGURE 4.7 Windows Defender Firewall indicates this system is connected to a private network and is protected from unwanted incoming connections.

FIGURE 4.8 Windows Defender Firewall indicates this system is being protected by a Norton application.

SOUND

Use the Sound applet (Figure 4.10) to configure playback and recording settings for audio hardware. Select the Sounds tab to select or modify a sound scheme (a sound scheme is the collection of sounds played during various events). Select the Communications tab to specify how Windows adjusts the volume of sounds when telephone calls are being made on your PC.

F I G U R E   4 . 9   **The Mail applet in Control Panel is used with the 32-bit version of Outlook.**

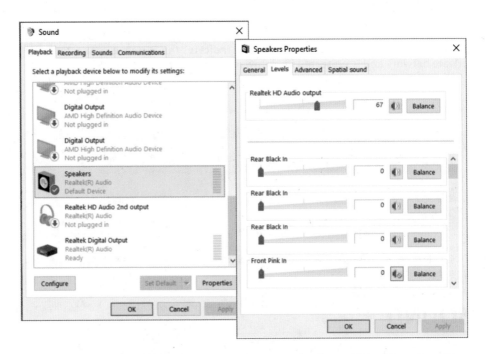

F I G U R E   4 . 1 0   **Adjusting Speakers properties in the Control Panel Sound applet**

USER ACCOUNTS

User Accounts (Figure 4.11) is no longer used for all account settings. You can use it to change your account type (Standard or Administrator), manage another account, and change User Account Control (UAC) settings. To add user accounts or make other changes to your account, use Accounts in Settings.

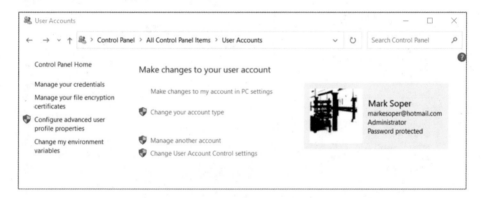

FIGURE 4.11 The User Accounts applet in Control Panel is used for account management, not creation.

DEVICE MANAGER

Device Manager lists all devices connected to your computer by category. Any problem device in a category is displayed (Figure 4.12) so that you can take action by installing the driver, enabling the device, or other actions as needed. Common symbols used to indicate problems in Device Manager include a down arrow in a circle (which indicates the device needs to download a driver) or a yellow exclamation point (which indicates the device is not recognized).

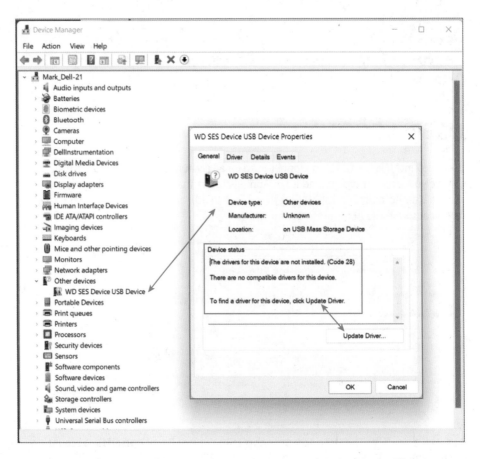

FIGURE 4.12 A WD drive shown in Device Manager has problems. Click the device listing to show its properties sheet (see inset).

Click the device to see the error code. In this example, the error code indicates that no device drivers are available. Depending on the device, drivers may be available directly from the manufacturer or via Windows Update. After we went to Windows Update, checked for optional updates, and downloaded the drivers found there, the problem device shown in Figure 4.12 is now working properly (Figure 4.13).

EXAM TIP

Know how to update drivers, roll back drivers, disable devices, and uninstall devices in Device Manager. Refer to Figures 4-12 and 4-13.

FIGURE 4.13 Installing drivers supplied by Windows Update resolved the problem. Click the Driver tab for details (see inset).

INDEXING OPTIONS

File searches in Microsoft Windows are much faster because Windows indexes the contents of documents and other library folders and other locations. To see what is being indexed and make changes, open Indexing Options (Figure 4.14). In this example, Modify has been selected so the user can also index the contents of the F: drive. After the user selects the additional location(s) to index and clicks OK, the indexing feature indexes the new location.

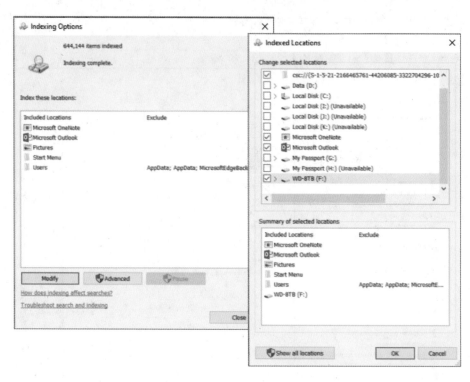

FIGURE 4.14 Preparing to add a location to the index with Indexing Options

ADMINISTRATIVE TOOLS

Administrative Tools (Figure 4.15) is a collection of advanced tools for managing Windows. Many of these apps were covered in detail in Chapter 3, "Windows 10 Operating System Tools." Others you might use from time to time include Recovery Drive (used to create bootable recovery media for Windows), Print Management (manages print servers), and ODBC Data Sources (32-bit and 64-bit; used for managing connections to external data sources for use with the Microsoft programs Access and Excel).

> **EXAM TIP**
>
> Make sure you can identify and understand the use of the following Administrative Tools for the Core 2 exam: Event Viewer, Local Security Policy, ODBC Data Sources, Print Management, Registry Editor, Services, System Information, Computer Management, Disk Cleanup, Performance Monitor, Resource Monitor, System Configuration, Task Scheduler, and Windows Memory Diagnostic. Be certain you know how to use these tools as part of a process.

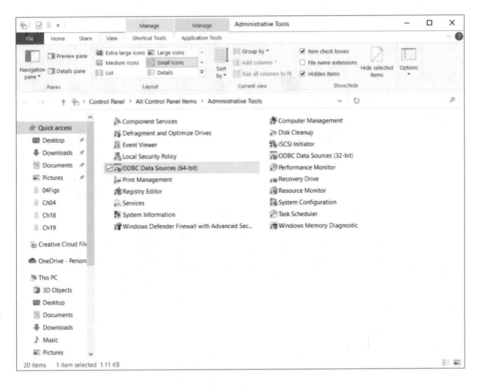

FIGURE 4.15 Administrative Tools in Windows 10

In Windows 11, these tools as well as others are available in Control Panel as Windows Tools. Windows Tools (Figure 4.16) also includes apps that were previously found in the Windows Accessories folder, including Character Map, Windows Media Player, and others. In both Windows 10 and 11, right-clicking the Start button brings up a menu where you can access several of these tools.

FILE EXPLORER OPTIONS

Use File Explorer Options to configure how File Explorer works. The default settings for File Explorer are designed to make File Explorer easy to use for most users. However, technicians and others who need to see more information about files will want to use File Explorer Options to make additional information about files visible. The Search tab is used to configure how searches are performed.

FIGURE 4.16 Windows Tools in Windows 11

General Options

The General tab is used to configure Browse folders, whether to use single-click or a double-click to open an item, and Privacy settings (Figure 4.17).

FIGURE 4.17 The General tab in File Explorer Options

View Options

The View tab is used to configure many different options for viewing files, folders, and drives. The following sections discuss some of the most common uses for Advanced settings on the View tab.

Show Hidden Files

By default, some folders such as AppData are hidden. Typical users don't need to see these files, but if you are trying to fix problems with Windows or Windows apps, you do. To make hidden files and folders visible with File Explorer Options, click the View tab, scroll down to Hidden Files And Folders in the Advanced Settings menu, click Show Hidden Files, Folders, And Drives, and click Apply (Figure 4.18).

FIGURE 4.18 Showing hidden files and preparing to unhide protected operating system files with File Explorer Options

To make protected operating system files visible, scroll down a little further in the View menu and deselect Hide Protected Operating System Files (Recommended). A Warning dialog box appears asking if you want to do this. Answer Yes to make the change.

Figure 4.19 compares the appearance of the C:\ (root) folder before and after showing hidden files.

Figure 4.20 compares the default appearance of a different part of the C:\ folder before and after unhiding protected operating system files.

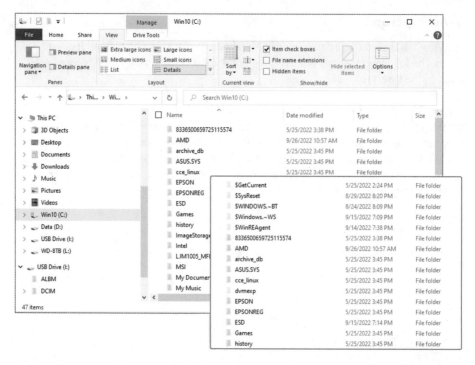

F I G U R E   4 . 1 9   The C:\ folder before (left) and after (right) showing hidden files and folders

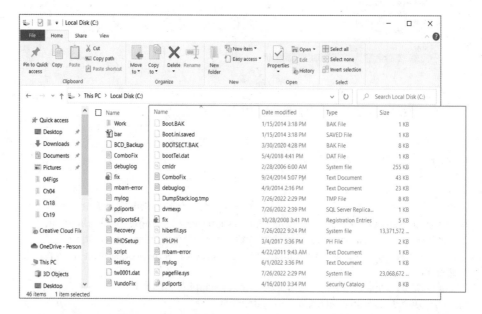

F I G U R E   4 . 2 0   The C:\ folder before (left) and after (right) unhiding protected operating system files

Hide Extensions

By default, file extensions for known file types are hidden. A known file type is a file type that is recognized as belonging to an installed application, such as .docx for Microsoft Word, .xlsx for Microsoft Excel, .jpg for photo editors, and so on. If there are multiple files with the same name but different extensions, it can be useful to show the file extensions in File Explorer: open the View menu, deselect Hide Extensions For Known File Types, and click Apply.

Figure 4.21 compares a portion of a pictures folder before and after unhiding file extensions.

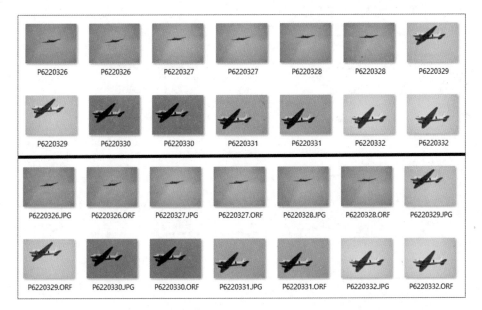

FIGURE 4.21   **A view of a pictures folder with file extensions hidden (top) and visible (bottom)**

EXAM TIP

Make sure you know the major uses of File Explorer Options and Power Options. Know how to use these tools as part of a process—for example, unhiding extensions and making hidden files visible as part of removing unneeded files.

POWER OPTIONS

Power Options are used to configure how long your computer stays awake when not in use, whether it saves power when in operation, and ways to have it sleep or shut down while retaining current open apps. Figure 4.22 shows the main Power Options menu from a desktop computer (top) and a laptop computer (bottom).

FIGURE 4.22 Choose power plans and select power settings to change from the main Power Options menu.

Power Plans

A power plan includes settings for how long the display stays on and when the computer goes to sleep. On a laptop computer, it also includes separate settings for AC power and battery power. To get to these settings, click Change Plan Settings in the main menu for the plan you want to edit.

You can change how long the display and computer will stay on before going to sleep, and you can change additional settings by clicking the Change Advanced Power Settings link.

Some systems offer two or more plans. To see additional plans, click the down arrow next to Show Additional Plans.

Hibernate

The Hibernate option records open apps and files in a hidden file called `hiberfil.sys` before the system shuts down. This enables a system to be ready to use in just moments after you turn it on. Hibernate is most often used by laptops and 2-in-1 convertible laptops, but it can also be used on desktop computers. To enable Hibernate, click Choose What The Power Buttons Do in the left pane of Figure 4.22 and select the Hibernate option in Shutdown Settings (Figure 4.23).

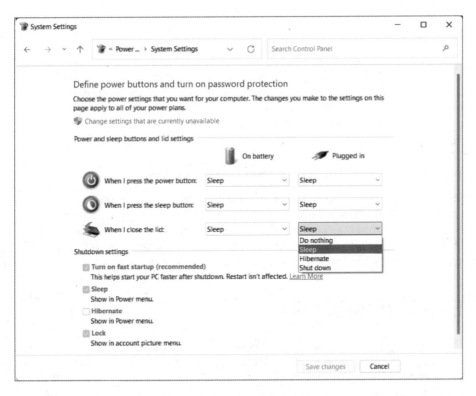

FIGURE 4.23 Turn On Fast Startup (Recommended), Sleep, And Lock are enabled on this system; Hibernate can be enabled.

Turn On Fast Startup

Turn On Fast Startup is the default setting in Windows 10 and 11. If a system is started after being turned off, this setting loads the operating system faster. In some cases, fast startup causes problems. To disable it, click Choose What The Power Buttons Do and deselect the Turn On Fast Startup (Recommended) check box, also shown in Figure 4.23.

Sleep/Suspend

The Sleep mode in Windows 10 and 11 saves a lot of power, but programs can still run. Systems can go into Sleep mode automatically after being idle for a specified period of time. Systems can come out of Sleep mode in just a few seconds. You can also enable Sleep as a shutdown option using the Shutdown Settings options shown in Figure 4.23.

Standby

Standby was an older power-saving feature that systems offered before Sleep mode. Today, Standby is synonymous with Sleep.

Choose What Closing the Lid Does

On a laptop or 2-in-1 convertible laptop, closing the lid can perform one of four functions, and you can set different actions if the computer is on AC power or battery power. To change the setting, click Choose What Closing The Lid Does from the main Power Options menu (refer to Figure 4.22) and open the When I Close The Lid menu for AC or battery power. Choose the option desired: Do Nothing, Sleep, Hibernate, or Shut Down (refer to Figure 4.23).

Universal Serial Bus (USB) Selective Suspend

USB Selective Suspend turns off power to USB ports when the system is idle. This option is enabled by default in Power Options, but it can be disabled if USB devices malfunction. To access it, click Change Plan Settings for the Power Plan setting you want to change, select Change Advanced Power Plan Settings, and expand the USB Settings section. You can disable this option for battery or plugged in (AC power). Click Apply, then click OK.

EASE OF ACCESS

Ease of Access makes Windows 10 and 11 easier to use for people with vision, hearing, or mobility issues. Click Ease Of Access Center to get started. From the main menu, choose the options you want to use. Settings include Magnifier, On-screen Keyboard, Narrator,

High Contrast, Screen Reader, Visual Alerts, and more. Figure 4.24 illustrates the main menu of the Ease of Access Center after enabling High Contrast. You can switch between Ease of Access Center optimizations and normal settings by using the menu or by pressing assigned keystrokes, depending on the setting.

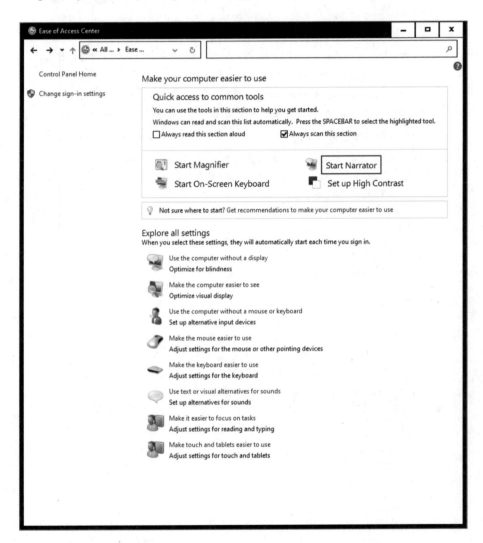

FIGURE 4.24 The Ease of Access Center main menu in High Contrast mode

CERTMIKE EXAM ESSENTIALS

▶ Use Control Panel to manage a wide variety of Windows features, such as hardware, networking, user configuration, indexing, file viewing, ease of access, and more.

▶ Control Panel settings are best run from the View By menu's Large Icons or Small Icons view as they provide access to every option, unlike the default Category menu.

▶ Some of the settings in Control Panel are available from the right-click Start Menu, from individual properties sheets, or from the Windows 10/11 Settings menu. However, Control Panel provides a one-stop shop for most advanced system settings.

▶ Use Programs and Features to uninstall an app or turn Windows features on or off.

▶ Use Device Manager to update drivers, roll back drivers, disable devices, and uninstall devices. The down arrow next to a device in Device Manager means that the device is disabled.

Practice Question 1

Your client wants to hibernate their new laptop by closing the lid. Which of the following Control Panel applets will enable them to make these settings?

A. Power Options
B. Device Manager
C. Ease of Access
D. Administrative Tools/Windows Tools

Practice Question 2

Your client needs to make changes to the contents of the `AppData` folder but is unable to find it. Which of the following Control Panel settings can be used to make it visible?

A. AutoPlay
B. Programs and Features
C. System
D. File Explorer Options

Practice Question 1 Explanation

This question is designed to test your real-world understanding of Control Panel features. Let's evaluate these answers one at a time.

1. The first answer, Power Options, is the right one. Select this option to open The Define Power Buttons And Turn On Password Protection menu. This menu includes options for setting up what happens on a laptop when the lid is closed.

2. The next answer, Device Manager, won't help because it has no options for working with power settings. This is incorrect.

3. The next answer, Ease of Access, also has nothing to do with power settings and is not correct.

4. The last answer, Administrative Tools, is also incorrect. Although there are many settings in Administrative Tools/Windows Tools, none of them pertain to power settings.

Correct Answer: A. Power Options

Practice Question 2 Explanation

This question is designed to test your knowledge of file management troubleshooting.

Let's evaluate these answers one at a time.

1. The first answer, AutoPlay, has nothing to do with folder visibility. AutoPlay is used to determine how removable-media drives are handled by Windows.

2. The second answer, Programs and Features, is used to uninstall, change, or repair applications and is incorrect.

3. The third answer, System, is used to display information about the device's hardware and software. Incorrect again.

4. The last answer, File Explorer Options, is used to change how files, folders, and drives are viewed and used in Windows. This is the correct answer.

Correct Answer: D. File Explorer Options

CHAPTER 5

Windows Settings

Core 2 Objective 1.5: Given a scenario, use the appropriate Windows settings.

Originally, almost all Windows configuration was done through Control Panel. However, with Windows 10 and Windows 11, many functions formerly performed in Control Panel are now performed in Settings.

In this chapter, you will learn everything you need to know about A+ Certification Core 2 Objective 1.5, including the following topics:

▶ **Time & Language**
▶ **Update & Security**
▶ **Personalization**
▶ **Apps**
▶ **Privacy**
▶ **System**
▶ **Devices**
▶ **Network & Internet**
▶ **Gaming**
▶ **Accounts**

ACCESSING SETTINGS

To access the Settings menu in Windows 10 or 11, click the Start button. In Windows 10, click the gearbox icon alongside the alphabetical Apps menu. In Windows 11, click the gearbox icon that appears in the Apps menu. Both are shown in Figure 5.1.

FIGURE 5.1 Settings icon for Windows 10 (left) and Windows 11 (right)

TIP

Other ways to access Settings include: press Windows key+I; in the Windows Search box type **Settings**; or open the command prompt or Microsoft Power-Shell and enter `start ms-settings`.

The Settings menu for Windows 10 is shown in Figure 5.2.

Compared to the Windows 10 version, the Settings menu for Windows 11 has some differences, as shown in Figure 5.3.

EXAM TIP

The differences in Windows 11's version of Settings are provided for your reference. The important things to know for the Core 2 1102 exam include the categories in Settings (Time & Language, Update & Security, Personalization, Apps, Privacy, System, Devices, Network & Internet, Gaming, and Accounts) and what each is used for. This is a "Given a scenario" objective. You need to know where each setting is located and what each one does. So, practice, and practice performing a scenario, rather than just studying commands in isolation.

FIGURE 5.2 Settings menu for Windows 10

TIME & LANGUAGE

The Time & Language menu has four sections in Windows 10: Date & Time, Region, Language, and Speech. The Date & Time menu (Figure 5.4) helps you keep your clock in sync and helps you manually select a time zone.

Use Region to configure region-specific formats for date and time. Use Language to confirm or change your display language and to switch input methods. Use Speech to set up the language used for reading the screen aloud and to set up your microphone.

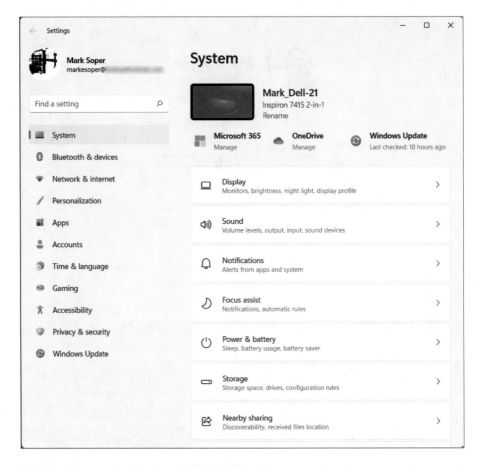

FIGURE 5.3 Settings menu for Windows 11

NOTE

In Windows 11, the sections are Date & Time, Language & Region, Typing, and Speech. Use the Typing menu to configure touch keyboards, to enable or disable autocorrection, and to switch input methods.

UPDATE & SECURITY

Update & Security in Windows 10 includes options to update, back up, reset, and trouble-shoot Windows, and an option to locate your device, among others.

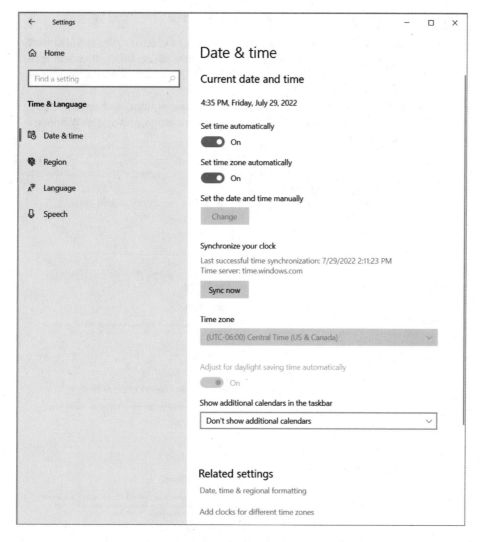

F I G U R E 5 . 4 Date & Time menu for Windows 10

Windows Backup (Figure 5.5, left) is used to set up and run File History, which backs up libraries and other folders you specify and stores different versions of the same backed-up file so that you can retrieve either the latest or older files. It also allows you to create and restore whole-computer backups using the Windows 7 Backup and Restore tool.

The Recovery menu (Figure 5.5, right) includes these options:

▶ Reset This PC, which reinstalls Windows and can keep user files and Microsoft Store apps (other apps are removed) or remove all user information and apps.

▶ Go Back To The Previous Version Of Windows 10 can be used for up to 10 days after an update.

▶ Advanced Startup lets you access UEFI firmware settings, start up from a USB or optical disc, restore Windows from a system image, and change Windows startup settings,

---

EXAM TIP

Make sure you know what each of the options in the Recovery menu can do.

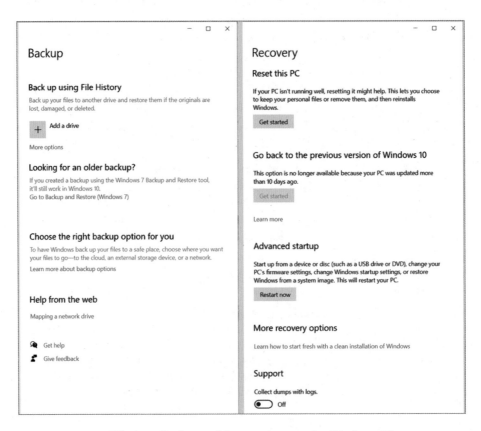

F I G U R E 5 . 5 Windows Backup and Recovery menus for Windows 10

Other Update & Security options include the following:

- ▶ Delivery Optimization lets you use multiple local and Internet PCs to down-load files.
- ▶ Windows Security allows you to configure security for devices and family members. Learn more about Windows Security features in Chapter 17, "Win-dows Security."
- ▶ Select Troubleshoot when you need to fix Windows problems. Learn more in Chapter 23, "Troubleshooting Windows."
- ▶ Activation allows you to check on Windows activation or to change license keys.
- ▶ Enable Find My Device makes it easy to track down a missing Windows device.
- ▶ You can use For Developers as a one-stop shop for adjusting file extensions, installing software, configuring Remote Access, and other useful settings for software developers. Some development apps require this setting be enabled before they'll work properly.
- ▶ Use Windows Insider Program to join, leave, or change Insider settings (which permit you to install pre-release Windows builds and try new features).

NOTE

In Windows 11, some of these options are found in the Windows Update menu. Also, you must configure and run File History and Backup and Restore (Windows 7) from Control Panel.

PERSONALIZATION

The Personalization menu is used to configure the appearance of Windows. Figure 5.6 illustrates the Background and Colors menus. Other settings include Lock Screen, Themes (preset or custom combinations of colors, backgrounds, sounds, and the mouse cursor), Fonts (font installation), Start, and taskbar settings.

NOTE

In Windows 11, the Personalization menu is also used to configure the touch key-board and to configure device usage.

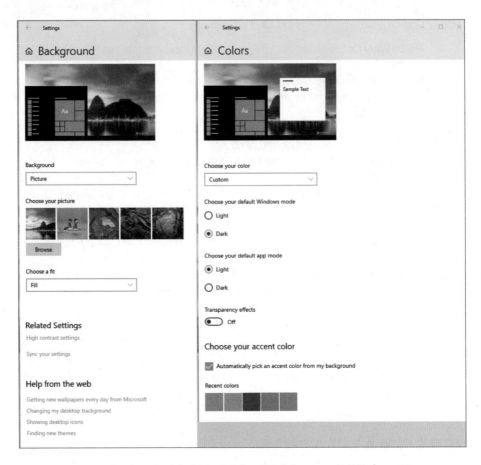

FIGURE 5.6 Background (left) and Colors (right) menus in Windows 10

APPS

The Apps menu in Windows 10 and 11 is used for listing and uninstalling or changing Apps & Features and for controlling app sources. Default Apps lets you specify the apps you want to use for music, photo viewing, and other functions. You can use Apps For Websites to specify whether to use a web browser or an app for some functions. You can download maps with the Offline Maps feature, and adjust video quality with Video Playback. Specify which apps you want to run at startup with the Startup option. Figure 5.7 illustrates the Apps & Features and Startup menus.

> **NOTE**
> In Windows 11, you can also add optional Windows features from the Apps menu.

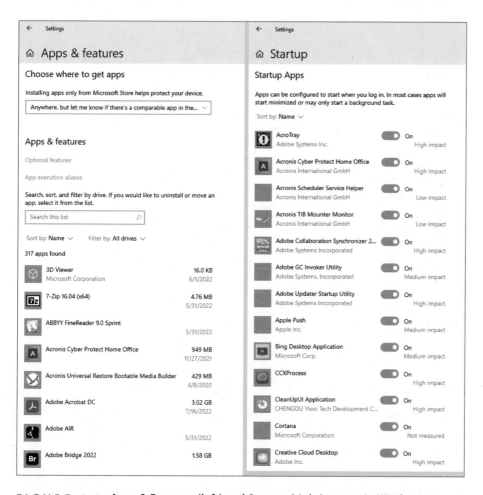

FIGURE 5.7 Apps & Features (left) and Startup (right) menus in Windows 10

PRIVACY

Use the Privacy menus to set up General privacy options, permissions for Speech, Inking & Typing personalization, Diagnostics and Feedback, and Activity History. Use App permissions to control how apps can interact with your system. Figure 5.8 shows the General and Camera menus. The Camera options are typical of the app permissions privacy options. For each one, you specify whether the feature can be used by apps and which specific apps can use the feature.

> **NOTE**
> In Windows 11, this menu is known as Privacy & Security, and it also includes Security settings.

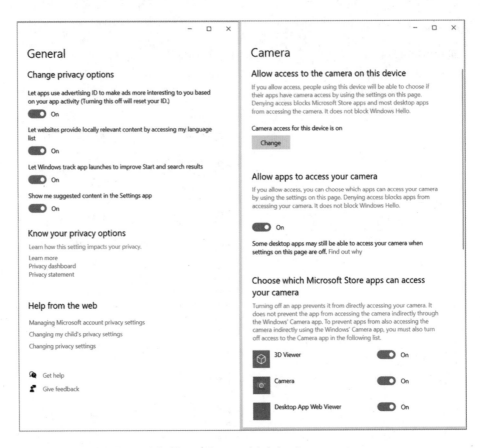

FIGURE 5.8 General (left) and Camera (right) privacy menus

SYSTEM

You can use the System settings in both Windows 10 and 11 for a quick look "under the hood" of your system with the About menu; get details about your Windows edition, version, and build number and hardware configuration; copy Windows and hardware information to other apps; and rename your PC (Figure 5.9).

Other options in System include the following:

▶ Adjust speaker and microphone settings with Sound.
▶ Configure notifications with the Notifications & Actions menu.
▶ Turn on Focus Assist to limit distractions from notifications.
▶ Use the Power & Sleep menu to adjust screen and system sleep settings and power mode.

- ▶ Use Storage to view the space on your system drive, and turn on Storage Sense to get rid of temporary files and Recycle Bin contents automatically.
- ▶ Configure how Windows 10 works with a tablet with Tablet Mode.
- ▶ Configure multiple windows, Timeline, and Alt-Tab settings with Multitasking.
- ▶ Configure your PC to display screens from another PC or phone with Projecting To This PC.
- ▶ Enable Shared Experiences to share accounts and data across devices.
- ▶ Enable Clipboard History and configure your Clipboard with the Clipboard option. Enable and configure Remote Desktop with Remote Desktop.
- ▶ Use the right sidebar to configure BitLocker, access Device Manager, use Remote Desktop, enable System Protection, and Rename This PC (Advanced).
- ▶ Use the Advanced System Settings link to configure Performance, User Profiles, and Startup and Recovery.

FIGURE 5.9   **About dialog from the System menu**

With the Display menu (Figure 5.10), you can perform a variety of tasks, including:

▶ Configure all connected displays.

▶ Set up additional displays as extended desktop or mirrored.

▶ Configure Windows HD color on supported displays.

▶ Modify the display scale (changing the size of text, apps, and other items), display resolution, and display orientation (landscape or portrait).

▶ Access display information such as refresh rate and graphics settings.

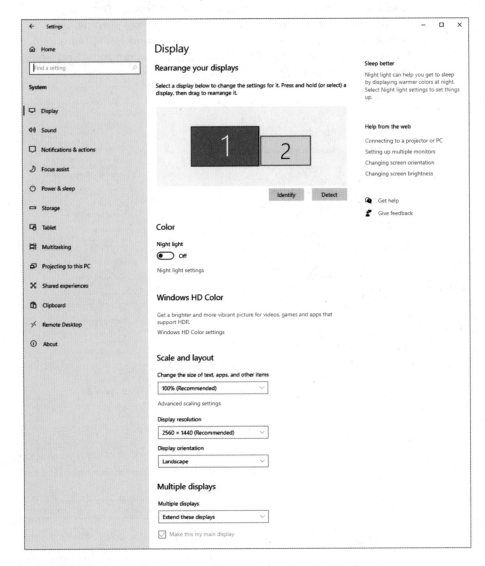

FIGURE 5.10   Setting up extended desktop using the Display menu

DEVICES

You can view and configure devices with the Devices menu. Use Bluetooth & Other Devices to add Bluetooth and remove many categories of devices. Configure what happens when you connect removable media with AutoPlay, including taking no action or running a particular app. Both of these menus are shown in Figure 5.11.

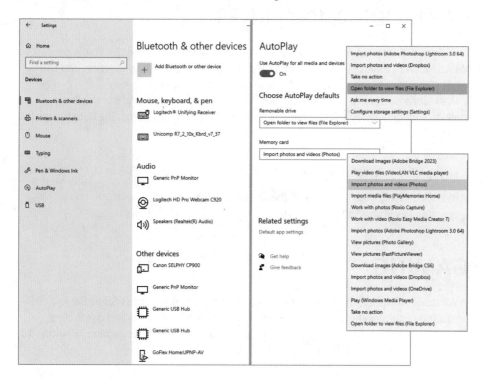

FIGURE 5.11 Bluetooth & Other Devices and AutoPlay menus in Windows 10

Using the Devices menu, you can:

▶ Install printers and view installed printers and scanners with Printers & Scanners.
▶ Configure basic mouse settings with Mouse.
▶ Configure both software and hardware keyboards with Typing.
▶ Configure Windows Ink and pens with Pen & Windows Ink.
▶ Access USB settings with USB.

NOTE

In Windows 11, this menu is known as Bluetooth & Devices and also includes support for accessing Android phones' contents with Your Phone and configuration for connected cameras with Cameras.

NETWORK & INTERNET

The Network & Internet menu shows the status of your connection on the Status page. Menus for Wi-Fi, Ethernet, Dial-up, and VPN provide details of each connection. You can select Airplane mode to temporarily disable connections when necessary.

Use Mobile Hotspot to share a Wi-Fi connection with other users, and use the Proxy menu to configure proxy settings/servers to filter or monitor web traffic. See both menus in Figure 5.12.

NOTE

In Windows 11, this menu uses Advanced network settings to perform the same functions as Status in Windows 10.

GAMING

In Windows 10 and 11, the Gaming options are used to configure Xbox Game Bar keyboard and controller shortcuts, set up Captures to record screenshots and game clips (Figure 5.13), and enable/disable Game Mode to optimize your PC for gaming. Windows 10 also displays the status of Xbox Networking.

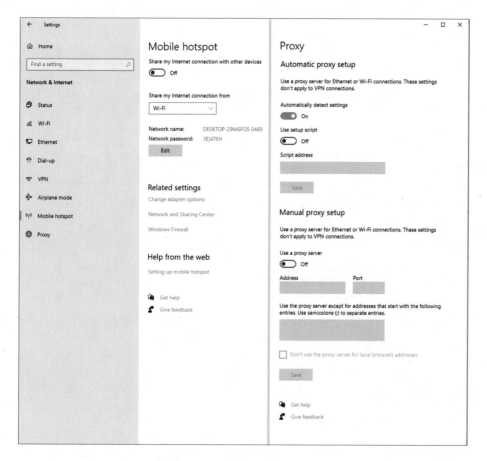

FIGURE 5.12 Mobile Hotspot and Proxy menus in Windows 10

ACCOUNTS

In Windows 10, Accounts is used to:

- ▶ Configure your personal account (Your Info).
- ▶ Set up email accounts used by Mail, Calendar, and Contacts with Email & Accounts.
- ▶ Configure Windows Hello, password, and other sign-in options (Figure 5.14).
- ▶ Connect to work or school networks with Access Work Or School.
- ▶ Add family and other users to your device and set it up for use as a kiosk with assigned access with Family & Other Users.
- ▶ Sync your settings to use the same settings across devices with your Microsoft account.

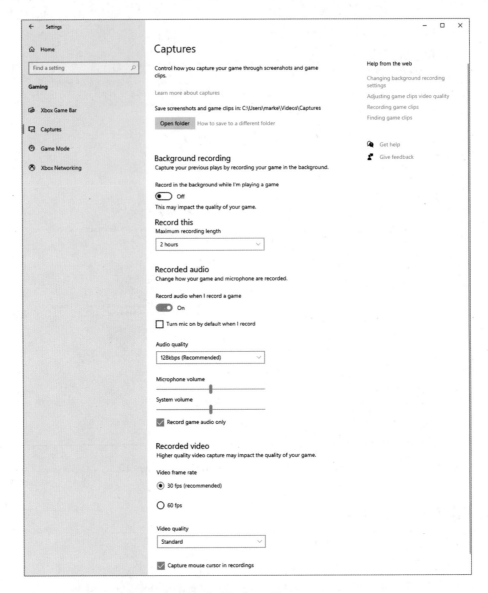

FIGURE 5.13 Captures menu in Windows 10

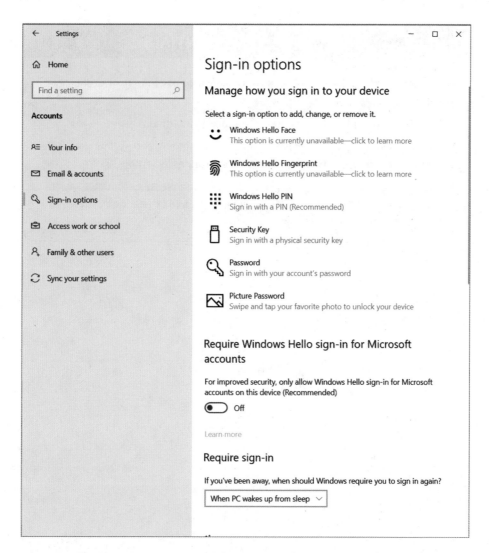

FIGURE 5.14 Sign-in options available in Accounts on Windows 10

NOTE

In Windows 11, Accounts also includes Windows backup settings for OneDrive Sync and preferences.

CERTMIKE EXAM ESSENTIALS

▶ Use Settings to manage a wide variety of Windows features, from Time & Language to Network & Internet and much more.

▶ Many Settings menus offer a slider for configuring a setting.

▶ Many Settings menus overlap with Control Panel options, and as time goes on, Microsoft will continue to move Control Panel features to Settings.

▶ There are several ways to access Settings, including pressing Windows key+I, entering **Settings** in the Search box, or entering `start ms-settings` at a command prompt or in PowerShell.

Practice Question 1

You have been working on a client's Windows installation after someone in the firm decided to "help" configure it. As a result, the installation is hopelessly fouled up. The best solution is to reset it back to its original condition and start over. Which of the following Settings categories has the Reset This PC feature?

A. Apps
B. System
C. Network & Internet
D. Update & Security

Practice Question 2

Your client uses a lot of removable USB and optical media in their work and is tired of constantly having to ignore the prompts to open the media when they connect it. Which of the following options are they looking for?

A. AutoPlay
B. Mobile Hotspot
C. Storage
D. Windows Security

Practice Question 1 Explanation

This question is designed to test your real-world understanding of Settings features. Let's evaluate these answers one at a time.

1. The first answer, Apps, is incorrect. The Apps menu is used to view and configure apps, set up startup apps, and other app-related functions.

2. The next answer, System, won't help because it displays hardware and software information but has no repair functions.

3. The next answer, Network & Internet, also has nothing to do with system reset options.

4. The last answer, Update & Security, is correct. The Recovery menu contains the Reset This PC feature.

Correct Answer: D. Update & Security

Practice Question 2 Explanation

This question is designed to test your knowledge of specific Settings options. Let's evaluate these answers one at a time.

1. The first answer, AutoPlay, is the right choice. AutoPlay can turn off prompts when media is connected as well as perform a variety of actions based on installed apps.

2. The second answer, Mobile Hotspot, is used to share an Internet connection with others and thus is incorrect.

3. The third answer, Storage, is used to display information about space on the system drive and to configure Storage Sense. Incorrect again.

4. The last answer, Windows Security, is used to view and configure various security features in Windows.

Correct Answer: A. AutoPlay

CHAPTER 6

Windows Networking

Core 2 Objective 1.6: Given a scenario, configure Microsoft Windows networking features on a client/desktop.

The Windows operating system was created to be a true network operating system. Both the Windows client and server operating systems allow for accessing and serving files, printers, and any other applications that can be networked. In this chapter, you will learn what you need to know about the A+ Certification Core 2 Objective 1.6, including the following topics:

► **Workgroup vs. domain setups**
► **Local OS firewall settings**
► **Client network configuration**
► **Establish network connections**
► **Proxy settings**
► **Public network vs. private network**
► **File Explorer navigation – network paths**
► **Metered connections and limitations**

WORKGROUP VS. DOMAIN SETUP

A workgroup-based network is generally used for a small office/home office (SOHO) setup. Authentication in workgroup-based networks is local and decentralized. Workgroups require a minimal amount of supporting resources to support authentication and security. Both the Windows client and server operating systems are capable of serving files, printers, and even specialized applications, such as fax services. If you share files or printers on a workgroup-based computer, you can only secure the resource with the local user or groups from the local Security Account Manager (SAM) database on the resource-sharing computer. Therefore, if remote users connect to the resource-sharing computer, they must either supply local account credentials or their username and password must be configured as an account on the resource-sharing computer.

Domain-based networks are extremely scalable and are found in small to enterprise-sized networks. A domain-based network requires dedicated resources, such as a server that is installed as a domain controller for Active Directory (AD). Authentication in domain-based networks is centralized with the AD domain controller, and user accounts can be centrally managed by the organization's administrator.

When computers are joined to a domain-based network, users will log in with their Active Directory account in lieu of the local credentials in the local SAM. To join a domain in Windows 10/11, perform the following steps:

1. Click Start ➤ Settings ➤ Accounts ➤ Access Work Or School ➤ Connect ➤ Join This Device To A Local Active Directory Domain. You will be prompted to enter a domain name.
2. Enter your credentials on the domain when prompted, which allows the joining of the operating system.
3. Reboot the operating system for the changes to take effect.

NOTE

You can read more about Active Directory domains and their functional parts in Chapter 13, "Logical Security."

EXAM TIP

Workgroups provide decentralized administration and are typical in SOHO settings. Domains provide centralized administration and are typically found in organizations, both small and large.

Shared Resources

Various resources can be shared from the Windows operating system. Files and printers are probably the two dominant resources shared on a network. There are plenty of other resources that can be shared on the network, such as email, specialized applications, and fax services. Any service that can be shared and that has a finite amount of utility can be considered a shared resource.

> **EXAM TIP**
>
> File shares and printer shares are the two dominant shared resources on the Windows operating system. Any service with a finite amount of utility should be considered a resource, and if it is shareable over the network, it can be considered a shared resource.

Printers

Printers are probably one of the most common resources shared on a network. If you are sharing a printer on a small office home office (SOHO) network, the Windows operating system will directly connect to the printer. However, in larger networks the volume can be higher, so networked printers are often shared from a server or a workstation in the network. Sharing a printer from Windows also allows for the centralized control of the resource by using permissions to restrict printing. You can also centrally control default settings, such as toner saving settings.

You can share your printer on Windows with the following procedure:

1. Click Start, then select Settings ➤ Devices ➤ Printers & Scanners.
2. Choose the printer you want to share, then select Manage.
3. Select Printer Properties, then select the Sharing tab.
4. On the Sharing tab, select Share This Printer.
5. Edit the Share Name of the printer; you'll use this name to connect to the printer from a secondary computer.

When you need to access a shared printer, you just need to map the printer. Mapping a printer can be accomplished in one of two ways: via the command line or via the GUI. To map a printer via the command line, use syntax like this: net use lpt1: *server*\ *printername*. This command will map the LPT1 device to the Universal Naming Convention (UNC) path of *server**printername*. You can also use the GUI method of connecting a printer by right-clicking the printer after browsing to the server, and then selecting Connect, as shown in Figure 6.1.

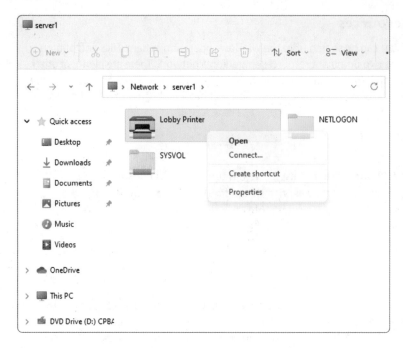

FIGURE 6.1 Connecting to printers

File Servers

Next to print resources, file sharing is probably the most important function for any network. In small networks of 20 clients or fewer, workstations can serve files to others in the network. We also have the limitation on a workstation operating system of 20 simultaneous connections. This is where the function of a dedicated file server is advantageous for small or large networks.

On the file server you will often have a volume separate from the operating system with the data to be shared. The folders on the volume are then shared, and permissions are applied on the various network shares to prevent unauthorized access. The client will then browse to the server with File Explorer and select the share where their files are located. The client can also directly visit the shared files on the file server with a shortcut or mapped drive.

Mapped Drives

A mapped drive is a function of the operating system that allows for a drive letter to be mapped to a network location that contains files. This makes the file resource appear to be part of the operating system and local to the computer even though it is located on the network.

The net use command can be used to establish a mapped drive at a command prompt, for example. If you want to connect to a shared network drive and make it your R: drive, the syntax is net use R: \\server\share. The \\server\share portion of the command is the UNC path and describes the server and share for the mapping. The UNC path is a standard way to describe the server and file share to the Windows operating system, as well as shared printers.

In addition to using the command line, you can use the GUI to map a network share. After browsing to the server by typing **\\server** in the File Explorer address bar, right-click the file share and select Map Network Drive. If you are using Windows 11, you will need to click Show More Options first. You will then be prompted with some options for mapping the network share, as shown in Figure 6.2.

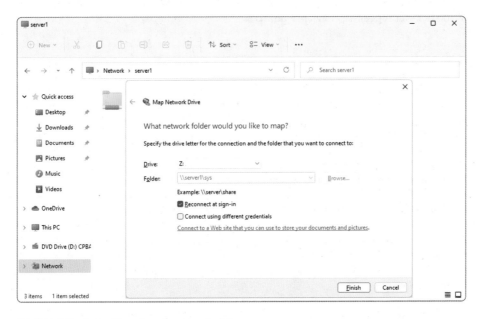

F I G U R E   6 . 2   Mapping a network drive

> **NOTE**
>
> By default, the Reconnect At Sign-in option is selected. In order to ensure that the mapped drive is reconnected when the user signs in, this option must be selected. The net use command is explored in Chapter 2, "Microsoft Command-Line Tools," and you'll learn more about scripting and mapping in Chapter 35, "Scripting."

LOCAL OS FIREWALL SETTINGS

Windows 10/11 ships with a built-in host-based firewall called Windows Defender Firewall. It allows for bidirectional firewall capabilities of both inbound and outbound connections. By default the firewall blocks all inbound connections, and as features are configured, firewall rules to permit traffic are enabled. You can also configure the firewall to block outbound connections, but this defeats the intended purpose of the Windows operating system and the firewall is really intended to protect unused services.

There are several ways to launch the Windows Defender Firewall settings dialog box. You can access the basic firewall controls by clicking Start ➢ Windows System ➢ Control Panel ➢ Windows Defender Firewall. Alternately, you can click Start and type **firewall** until it appears in the search results. In either case the basic Windows Defender Firewall settings dialog box will appear, as shown in Figure 6.3.

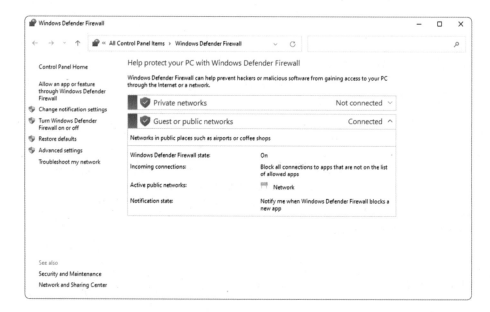

FIGURE 6.3 **Windows Defender Firewall**

> **NOTE**
>
> Microsoft is slowly replacing configuration dialog boxes in Windows and encouraging users to use the Settings app. If you are on Windows 11, you can navigate to the new configuration page by clicking Start ➢ Settings ➢ Network & Internet ➢ Advanced Network Settings ➢ Windows Firewall.

Application Restrictions and Exceptions

Windows Defender Firewall has a friendly interface for the average user. The mechanism exists to allow the firewall to easily configure itself while providing information to the end user. When a program is launched that listens to an incoming port, an Allow Access or Cancel notification is sent to the user, as shown in Figure 6.4. The end user can click Allow

Access for the application and a rule will automatically be generated allowing connections, or the user can click Cancel and the port will remain blocked.

FIGURE 6.4 Windows Security Alert

There are a number of applications and services that are preconfigured in the firewall. As an example, when you share a folder, the ports associated with file sharing are automatically enabled. To access the individual preconfigured rules, the Windows Defender Firewall with Advanced Security Microsoft Management Console (MMC) can be launched by clicking the Start menu and typing the word **firewall** until the result of Windows Defender Firewall with Advanced Security appears. The Windows Defender Firewall with Advanced Security MMC is shown in Figure 6.5. The rules can be examined and configured within this MMC.

> **EXAM TIP**
>
> Applications can be exempted through the Windows Defender Firewall. When the program opens with a listening port, the user is prompted on the screen to allow the firewall exemption, or deny the firewall exemption. Applications can also be exempted manually with the Windows Defender Firewall with Advanced Security MMC.

Configuration

Along with both the automated mechanism in which firewall rules can be added and the manual mechanism of allowing or configuring a rule, you can specify which network profile the rules are active in. A network profile is a collection of rules that are active or inactive in certain network circumstances, such as public versus private (your home). As an example, you might want to allow Network Discovery at home but not in a public setting.

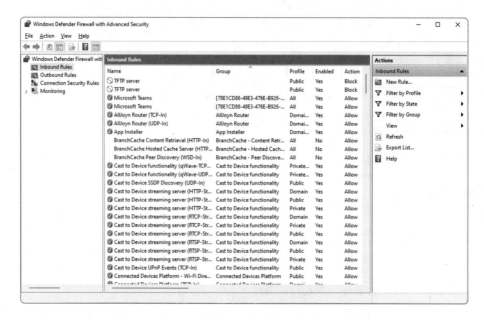

F I G U R E 6 . 5 Windows Defender Firewall with Advanced Security

There are three different network profiles that firewall rules can be active for: public, private, and domain. You can control if your laptop is public or private, but if a domain controller exists and the laptop is joined to a domain, then the domain profile becomes active. In both the basic Windows Defender Firewall Control Panel applet and the Windows Defender Firewall with Advanced Security MMC, you can enable or disable the firewall for any of the network profiles. However, the Windows Defender Firewall with Advanced Security MMC does allow for the maximum amount of control over the Windows firewall. Certain settings, such as logging, can only be found in the MMC.

Rules can also be manually created to allow for maximum granularity. You can add a rule based on a program, port, predefined rule, or something totally custom. For example, if you wanted to allow an incoming port of 8080 via TCP only to a specific application awaiting its request for a specific network profile, the MMC interface will allow you to do so. The New Inbound Rule Wizard can be seen in Figure 6.6.

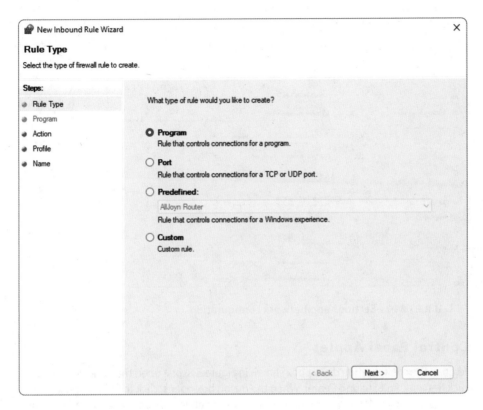

FIGURE 6.6   New Inbound Rule Wizard

CLIENT NETWORK CONFIGURATION

Most of the time we take network configuration for granted. This is mainly because routers support the Dynamic Host Configuration Protocol (DHCP) and the client will automatically configure itself with an IP address, subnet mask, default gateway, and the appropriate Domain Name System (DNS) servers. However, you should be familiar with all of these elements so that you can troubleshoot problems. There are also times where you might need to configure a computer with a static address, such as a server. You can configure the clients network configuration with both the Settings app and the Control Panel applet, as described in this section.

Settings App

You can open the network Settings app by clicking Start, then clicking the Settings gear, selecting Network & Internet and clicking Properties, and then clicking Edit under IP Settings. You can then configure the network interface, as shown in Figure 6.7.

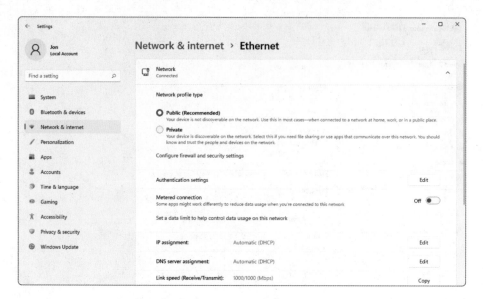

FIGURE 6.7 Settings app network configuration

Control Panel Applet

To open the configuration dialog box shown in Figure 6.8, first open the Control Panel, then click Network And Sharing Center. When the dialog box opens, click the Change Adapter Settings link on the left side and then right-click the network adapter and select Properties.

> **NOTE**
>
> Throughout this section, we will refer to the Control Panel applet settings. Although the Settings app can be used for configuration, it has changed slightly from Windows version to version.

Internet Protocol (IP) Addressing Scheme

The IP addressing can be modified from the Control Panel applet by selecting Internet Protocol version 4 (TCP/IPv4) or Internet Protocol version 6 (TCP/IPv6). The IPv4 address is a 32-bit number represented as a dotted-decimal notation, such as 192.168.1.1. An IP address is a logical address that is structured in a way to create networks and nodes, similar to numbering the chairs in a room.

You can open the IP address dialog box in Windows 11 with the following procedure:

1. Select Start, then type **settings**. Select Settings ➢ Network & Internet.
2. Select a Wi-Fi network or Ethernet network.

3. Next to IP assignment, select Edit.
4. Under Edit Network IP Settings or Edit IP Settings, select Automatic (DHCP) or Manual.

FIGURE 6.8 Control Panel network configuration

Subnet Mask

The subnet mask is the second most important piece of information for the purpose of network addressing systems. The subnet mask defines the network that a computer belongs to. Subnet masks can be written as doted-decimal notations such as 255.255.255.0, or the total number of bits occupying the subnet mask, such as /24.

EXAM TIP

A valid IP address requires both an IP address and subnet mask. The IP address specifies the network and node number, and the subnet mask defines the delimitation in the IP address between the network and the node number.

Gateway

When the destination computer is not in the same network, the packet must be sent to the default gateway. Once sent to the default gateway, also known as a router, the packet is routed accordingly to the destination network. The default gateway must always be in the same network as the computer, because it routes packets from your immediate network to other remote networks.

Domain Name System (DNS) Settings

DNS servers translate www.certmike.com to 162.255.119.133, because numbers are too hard to remember for humans. The dialog box will often require two DNS servers: a primary and a secondary address. If you only have one DNS server address, that is fine, but having a secondary address gives you redundancy in the event of failure on the first DNS server.

Static vs. Dynamic

Now that you understand the basic elements for network configuration, let's examine the various ways that configuration can happen. A computer can be configured one of three ways, as described next, and there are advantages and disadvantages for each method.

Static

Static addressing is typically only used for servers or in a situation where you always want the IP address to always be the same. The advantage to static addressing computers is that infrastructure such as a DHCP server is not needed. However, the disadvantage is that the manual entry of IP addressing information is error prone.

Dynamic

Dynamic addressing is the most common and preferred method to configure network addressing on computers. The DHCP server serves IP addresses along with a lease time; when the time is 50 percent of the lease duration, the client will renew its lease. In addition to IP addressing, DHCP servers can provide network options, such as DNS servers and the gateway address. The advantage to dynamic addressing is it takes the guesswork out of assigning IP addresses and their associated options. The disadvantage is a computer might not always have the same IP address.

APIPA

Automatic Private IP Addressing (APIPA) might be considered dynamic IP addressing, but it is not. The APIPA address is automatically configured if a static IP address is not defined, and a DHCP server is not available. The APIPA address always begins with 169.254.x.x. The advantage is it allows two or more computers to communicate without any infrastructure.

ESTABLISH NETWORK CONNECTIONS

Establishing a proper network connection between a computer and the network is a key element to any successful network. This section covers a number of ways to connect to a network. Regardless of the connection method, a computer will function identically. For example, if you are playing a video, as long as the bandwidth is the same for your connection the experience is identical whether you connect wirelessly or wired.

Virtual Private Network (VPN)

A VPN is typically used over a public network to provide a secure and tamperproof connection between a computer and a remote network. When a VPN is used to connect a computer to a remote network, it is considered a host-to-network connection; this is often used for remote workers. Network-to-network connections also exist to connect two networks together over a public Internet connection. In both of these instances, end-to-end encryption is used to prevent eavesdropping from threat actors. Signing of packets also prevents replay attacks or the modifying of payloads in transit.

Establishing a VPN connection will require information from the organization's VPN appliance or server. You will need the VPN protocol, server address, and the sign-in information. You can create a VPN connection by selecting Start ➢ Settings ➢ Network & Internet ➢ VPN; from here you can add a VPN connection, as shown in Figure 6.9.

Wireless

Connecting to a wireless network, also known as a wireless local area network (WLAN), is a little different than a wired connection, also known as a local area network (LAN). Wired connections have a light that indicates whether you have a connection; wireless equipment rarely has a visual identifier. Windows 10/11 will display a radio wave wireless icon in the notification area. If the radio wave is grayed out with an asterisk at the upper left, then there are wireless connections detected and you are not connected to any of them. If you click the wireless icon, all of the wireless networks available will be displayed, along with their security status, as shown in Figure 6.10.

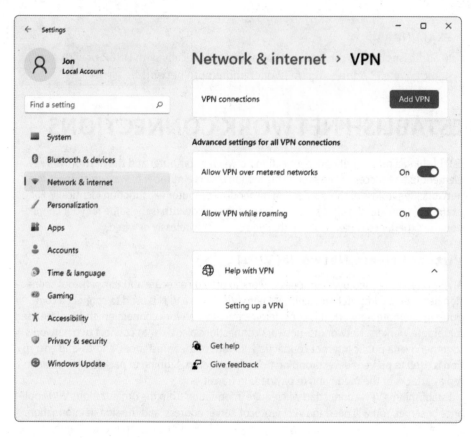

FIGURE 6.9 VPN connectivity

The other nuance to wireless is the security. After you choose a wireless network and select Connect, you will be prompted to enter additional security, such as a preshared key (PSK). By default, wireless networks that you connect to will automatically reconnect when you are in range.

NOTE

You can learn more about wireless security in Chapter 14, "Wireless Security."

FIGURE 6.10 Wireless connectivity

Wired

A wired connection does have a huge benefit: constant speed. A wired connection does not suffer from poor signal strength, as does wireless. A wired connection is also the easiest to diagnose when there are problems. The network link light gives you a visual indicator that you have a network connection. Windows 10/11 will also place a visual notification of a computer with a cable in the notification area when a wired connection is detected.

Wireless Wide Area Network (WWAN)

A wireless wide area network (WWAN) network connection is a connection that is created with the use of a WWAN adapter and a cellular data provider, such as T-Mobile, Verizon, or AT&T, just to name a few. The WWAN adapter might be USB, built-in, or even a hotspot.

You connect to a cellular network by selecting Start ➢ Settings ➢ Network & Internet ➢ Cellular, as shown in Figure 6.11. If your laptop does not have a WWAN adapter installed, then the Cellular section will not appear on the Network & Internet screen. After selecting Cellular, you can then configure roaming options, as well as the preference of cellular over Wi-Fi, and you can configure Windows to treat the connection as a metered connection.

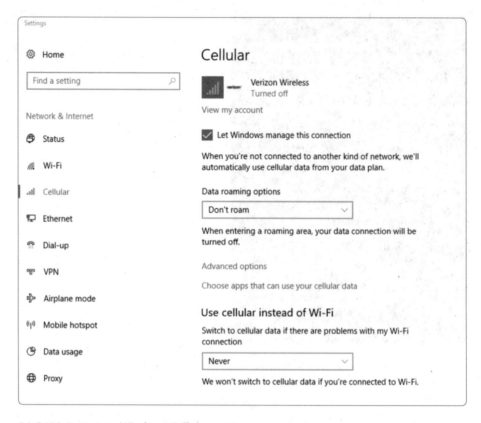

FIGURE 6.11 Windows Cellular settings

EXAM TIP

VPN connections provide security over an untrusted network. Wireless connections provide portability and convenience. Wired connections provide dedicated connections, and wireless wide area network (WWAN) connections provide coverage outside of your organization or SOHO.

PROXY SETTINGS

After you have established a connection, your organization might require the use of a proxy server to access the Internet. A proxy server will accept requests for websites from the user's browser, and it will retrieve the web page on behalf of the user. The use of a proxy server is generally found in an organization and not in a SOHO setup.

To configure the proxy settings for Microsoft Edge and Internet Explorer, select Start ➤ Settings ➤ Network & Internet ➤ Proxy. From the proxy screen you can configure the operating system to automatically use a setup script by clicking Use Setup Script and specifying the script address, as shown in Figure 6.12.

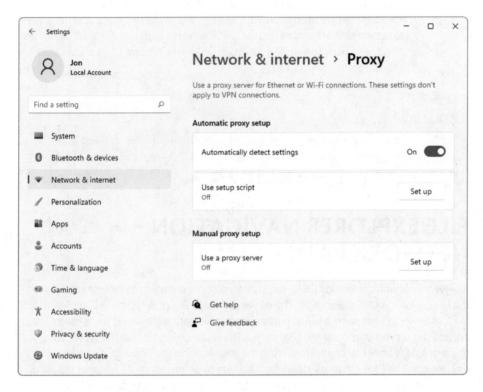

FIGURE 6.12 Windows Proxy settings

PUBLIC NETWORK VS. PRIVATE NETWORK

When configuring and troubleshooting a network there are three different types of IP addresses you will encounter: public, private, or link-local.

- ▶ **Public:** A public address is publicly routable on the Internet. A public address is usually not found within a network or configured directly on a computer; it is often found on a router.
- ▶ **Private:** A private address is not publicly routable on the Internet. The addresses are intended to be used in the private network of the organization.

Private addresses are defined by the RFC 1918 standard. The standard reserves addresses between 192.168.0.0 to 192.168.255.255 (192.168.0.0/16) for small-sized networks, 172.16.0.0 to 172.31.255.255 (172.16.0.0/12) for medium-sized networks, and 10.0.0.0 to 10.255.255.255 (10.0.0.0/8) for large networks.

▶ **Link-local:** A link-local address is not routable in public or private networks. The addresses are used to create a fast connection to another computer where no network infrastructure such as DHCP servers exists. Link-local addresses are called Automatic Private IP Addressing (APIPA) in Windows and always start with the prefix 169.254.x.x.

EXAM TIP

Public addresses are routable on the Internet, private addresses defined in the RFC 1918 and are not routable on the Internet, and link-local connections (also known as APIPA) always start with 169.254.x.x.

FILE EXPLORER NAVIGATION – NETWORK PATHS

A universal naming convention (UNC) path is the most common way to browse servers with the File Explorer. A UNC path defines the server and the resource. A typical UNC path will look like \\server\fileshare; the first portion of the UNC path is the server the resource is on, and the second portion of the UNC path is the resource location on the server. In this example, server is the server serving the resource and the resource is named fileshare. The UNC can also extend the file share to define a specific folder or file. Also, the File Explorer is not the only thing that uses the UNC; you can also find UNCs at the command line.

METERED CONNECTIONS AND LIMITATIONS

A metered connection is a connection in which you pay for a specific amount of data to be downloaded. When the data limit is reached, you can be responsible for an overage fee, typically by the gigabytes of data. Many features in Windows, such as Windows Updates, can work differently depending on whether the connection is a metered connection or a standard connection.

You can specify that this connection is a metered connection by selecting Start ➢ Settings ➢ Network & Internet ➢ Ethernet, and then sliding the Metered Connection slider to On, as shown in Figure 6.13.

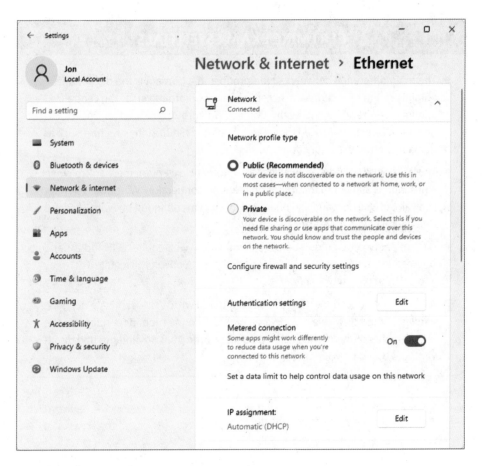

FIGURE 6.13 Ethernet connection options

CERTMIKE EXAM ESSENTIALS

▶ The main difference between a workgroup and a domain is the decentralized administration of security and accounts for a workgroup versus the centralized administration and security with a domain. Workgroups are used for small SOHO networks. Domains are used for organizations and require infrastructure, such as domain controllers, to function.

▶ The Windows Defender Firewall has an automatic exception mechanism when a program is started that requires an inbound connection. Windows Defender Firewall can also be manually configured for custom configurations with Windows Defender Firewall for Advanced Security.

▶ A client's network configuration at bare minimum will require an IP address and subnet mask. If the computer is talking to other networks, it will require a gateway and a DNS server to be configured.

▶ A client's network connection can be configured with a virtual private network, wireless, wired or wireless wide area network connection, depending on the requirements of the client. Each type of connection has advantages and disadvantages based on your needs.

Practice Question 1

You are setting up a small office network that requires centralized administration of user accounts. Which setup will best fit the situation?

A. Workgroup
B. Domain
C. Static IP addressing
D. Dynamic IP addressing

Practice Question 2

You receive a call that a computer is not communicating with the network and discover an IP address of 169.254.23.22 configured on the computer. What type of IP address is this?

A. Public
B. Private
C. APIPA
D. DHCP

Practice Question 1 Explanation

This question is designed to test your knowledge of workgroups versus domains.

1. The first answer (A, Workgroup) is incorrect. A workgroup is best used for decentralized administration.

2. The next answer (B, Domain) is correct. A domain model is best used when centralized administration of user accounts and security is desired.

3. The next answer (C, Static IP addressing) is incorrect. Static IP addressing will have no direct effect on centralized administration.

4. The last answer (D, Dynamic IP addressing) is incorrect. Although DHCP allows for the centralized administration of IP addresses, it does not affect user accounts.

Correct Answer: B. Domain

Practice Question 2 Explanation

This question is designed to test your knowledge of the various IP addresses presented in this chapter.

Let's evaluate these answers one at a time.

1. The first answer (A, Public) is incorrect. Although a public IP address can be anything, this particular IP address is an APIPA and is nonroutable.

2. The second answer (B, Private) is incorrect. A private IP address follows the RFC 1918 standard of 10.0.0.0/8, 172.16.0.0/12, or 192.168.0.0/16.

3. The third answer (C, APIPA) is correct. Any IP address that starts with 169.254.x.x is an APIPA address and is automatically configured because of the lack of DHCP on the network.

4. The last answer (D, DHCP) is incorrect. Although a DHCP address can be anything, the fact that an APIPA address is automatically configured shows that DHCP is not working on the network.

Correct Answer: C. APIPA

CHAPTER 7

Application Installation and Configuration

Core 2 Objective 1.7: Given a scenario, apply application installation and configuration concepts.

There's more to installing applications than preparing an ISO file for transfer to USB or DVD media or downloading and clicking on an EXE file. For a successful application installation, you need to ensure hardware and operating system compatibility and consider the impacts (good or bad) on your organization.

In this chapter, you will learn what you need to know about A+ Certification Core 2 Objective 1.7, including the following topics:

▶ **System Requirements for Applications**
▶ **OS Requirements for Applications**
▶ **Distribution Methods**
▶ **Other Considerations for New Applications**

SYSTEM REQUIREMENTS FOR APPLICATIONS

Before you install an application on a particular system, you need to make sure that the application and the device are compatible with each other. The following sections discuss in detail how to make sure they'll work properly with each other.

32-Bit vs. 64-Bit Dependent Application Requirements

Although almost all new systems running Windows, macOS, or Linux use 64-bit processors, 32-bit applications are still widespread. 32-bit applications were written for 32-bit processors such as early Pentiums, 486, and 386 processors. 32-bit applications can't use more than 4 GB of RAM and have other limitations compared to 64-bit applications. However, they still work on today's 64-bit processors because 64-bit processors are designed to work with both 64-bit and 32-bit applications.

Running Windows 32-Bit Apps on 64-Bit Windows

64-bit Windows versions are designed to run 32-bit apps by separating 32-bit and 64-bit applications and their support files. On a 64-bit version of Windows, the system drive (normally C:\) has two Program Files folders: C:\Program Files is used for 64-bit apps, and C:\Program Files (x86) is used for 32-bit apps.

Although 64-bit Windows is designed to run 32-bit apps, some apps might need help in running properly. The Compatibility tab on the app's properties sheet (Figure 7.1) and the Program Compatibility Troubleshooter (Figure 7.2) enable apps made for older versions of Windows to run properly by tweaking Windows version requirements, resolution and color settings, and other adjustments. These compatibility features can be used with both 32-bit and 64-bit apps that might not work properly on the installed version of Windows; 32-bit apps tend to be older and need help more often.

> **EXAM TIP**
>
> Use the Compatibility tab or Compatibility Troubleshooter to run an older 32-bit app on 64-bit Windows versions when necessary. Be prepared to answer questions that involve these tools in a scenario. Practice using them with older apps!

Running Linux 32-Bit Apps on 64-Bit Linux

64-bit Linux requires the installation of additional software to enable it to run 32-bit apps. Older Debian-based distros such as Ubuntu 18 and earlier can install shared libraries, a process known as Multiarch, with commands such as the following (on some distros, the i386 package may have a different name):

```
sudo dpkg --add-architecture i386
sudo apt update
```

```
sudo apt install -y ia32-libs
sudo apt install package-name:i386
```

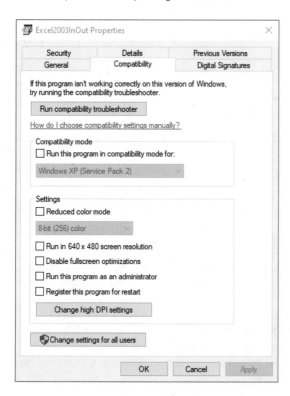

FIGURE 7.1 If an older app won't run on a current 64-bit version of Windows, use the Compatibility tab to change how it works.

Other methods include creating a 32-bit VM for a 32-bit version of Linux and 32-bit apps or creating a container (a more powerful version of a VM) containing a 32-bit version of Linux and 32-bit apps. These methods work with current 64-bit Linux distros such as Ubuntu 22.04 and above.

NOTE

Learn more about running 32-bit apps on 64-bit Linux at `https://faun .pub/32-64-de608b0896e`. Check your Linux distro's website for specific information about 32-bit support.

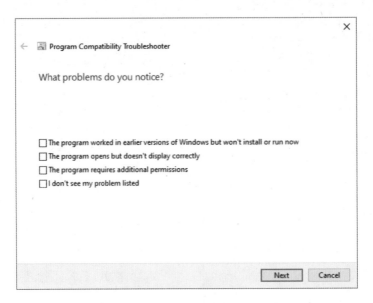

FIGURE 7.2 The Program Compatibility Troubleshooter can be run from the Compatibility tab to provide interactive help to tweak an older program's operation.

Running macOS 32-Bit Apps on 64-Bit macOS

The Mojave version of macOS (10.14), introduced in 2018, is the last version of macOS to support 32-bit apps. Third-party apps such as CleanMyMac X can be used to update 32-bit apps to their 64-bit versions (if available), or you can install macOS Mojave or older versions into a VM and install your 32-bit apps there.

> **NOTE**
>
> Learn more about running 32-bit apps on 64-bit macOS at `https://macpaw`
> `.com/how-to/32-bit-apps-not-working-catalina`.

Dedicated Graphics Card vs. Integrated

Office apps and casual games can be run with either integrated graphics or a dedicated graphics card because they don't require high graphics performance. When it comes to 3D gaming, photo editing, CAD, or video editing, look for DirectX 12 support and at least 2 GB of video RAM (more is better).

A dedicated graphics card typically supports more advanced 3D features, offers more dedicated video RAM, and provides more advanced monitor ports (such as multiple DisplayPort connections) than integrated video.

NOTE

Be sure to check the recommended (not minimum) hardware requirements for your favorite games, your CPU, and your computer's PCIe slots and version before you purchase a new graphics card.

Video RAM (VRAM) Requirements

If you are planning to work (or play) at 4 K or higher display resolutions, the amount of video RAM (VRAM) on your graphics card is an important consideration. *VRAM* (video RAM) is the RAM used by the graphics processing unit (GPU) to load and store video data. On systems with dedicated graphics cards, VRAM is on the card. On systems with integrated graphics, VRAM is a designated portion of system memory. The more pixels in a display, the more video RAM necessary to support the display.

For example, Windows versions of Adobe Photoshop CC 2023 edition require at least 1.5 GB of video memory for up to 1080p displays (1920×1080). However, if you want to work with 4 K or higher-resolution displays, you need at least 4 GB of video memory. Windows versions of Adobe Premiere Pro 2023 edition require at least 2 GB of video RAM for HD workflows, but if you're planning to work in 4 K or higher resolutions, you need at least 6 GB of video RAM.

3D gamers need at least 4 GB of VRAM for many current game titles. Going up to 8 GB improves performance.

EXAM TIP

Make sure you know the apps you can use to check the DirectX version, installed video RAM, system RAM, CPU, and available disk space. You can use DXDiag (DirectX Diagnostic) and MSInfo32 (System Information) to find this information in Windows.

Figure 7.3 and Figure 7.4 illustrate using DXDiag's System and Display tabs to display essential system information. On systems with more than one display connected to the same video card (Figure 7.4), click any display tab for the information needed.

Figure 7.5 illustrates using MSInfo32 to check available disk space.

RAM Requirements

One of the reasons that 32-bit apps are fading away is because the limitations of 32-bit addressing cap available memory size at 4 GB. However, with 64-bit apps, the limitations of the motherboard's memory capacity are the only practical limitation.

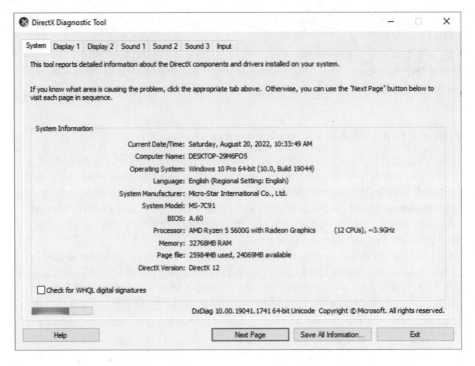

F I G U R E   7 . 3 DXDiag's System tab provides a quick view of the Windows version, processor, installed memory, and DirectX version.

8 GB is the smallest amount of RAM you should have in a 64-bit Windows system, and if you plan on doing a lot of multitasking, running demanding 3D games, photo editing, or video editing, you need more. Table 7.1 provides a sample of RAM recommendations for popular 64-bit Windows apps.

T A B L E   7 . 1 RAM recommendations for popular Windows 64-bit apps

Application	Application type	Recommended RAM
Adobe Photoshop Elements 22	Photo editing	16 GB
Adobe Premiere Elements 22	Video editing	16 GB dual-channel (HD video)
		32 GB dual-channel (4 K and above video)

Application	Application type	Recommended RAM
AutoCAD 2022	CAD	16 GB
Resident Evil 3 (2020)	3D gaming	8 GB or more
F1 2022	3D gaming	16 GB
Spider-Man Remastered	3D gaming	16 GB

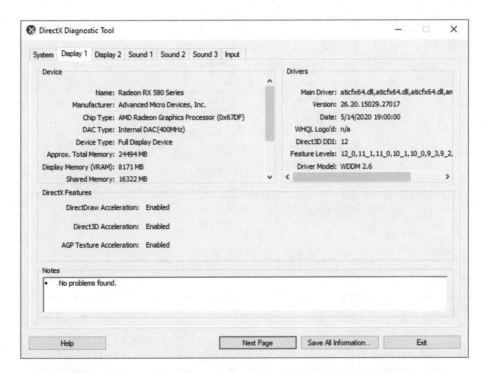

F I G U R E 7 . 4 DXDiag's Display 1 tab lists the display memory (VRAM) installed.

CPU Requirements

A few years ago, most apps simply listed CPU requirements as 64-bit processors running at a speed of 1 GHz or faster. However, with the increasing numbers of both productivity and gaming apps supporting multicore and multithreaded processors, processor requirements have become more complex.

FIGURE 7.5 After starting MSInfo32 (System Information), click Components ➢ Storage ➢ Drives to see installed drives and free space for each drive.

Many 3D games recommend a minimum of multicore recent model Intel i3 or i5 or similar AMD Ryzen processors because they need multicore and multithreading support for best performance. Although productivity apps typically don't require multicore or multithreading features, if you want to run multiple apps or multiple processes at the same time, you're better off with CPUs with these features, along with at least 16 GB of RAM installed in a system.

External Hardware Tokens

External hardware tokens is how CompTIA refers to smart cards, USB dongles, or other security features needed for some software or some computing environments. If you are running software that requires some type of external hardware token, make sure your computer has support built in.

NOTE

The most common use for external hardware tokens based on USB (USB dongles) is to prevent expensive software from being pirated. Smart cards are typically used to secure computers in business, government, or military environments.

Storage Requirements

Storage requirements for applications can range up to 50 GB of available disk space. Typically, 3D games are among the biggest disk hogs. For better performance, some apps are also recommending the use of SSDs instead of hard disks.

Before installing apps that require multiple gigabytes of disk space, you should check free disk space using MSInfo32 or the properties sheets for your drives to determine free space on your system drive (almost always C: drive), as shown in Figure 7.6.

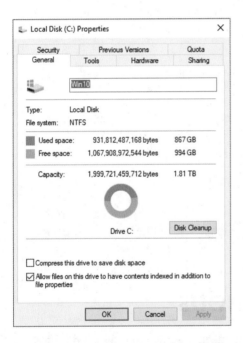

FIGURE 7.6 The system drive (C:) has plenty of room remaining for apps.

OS REQUIREMENTS FOR APPLICATIONS

Before you purchase or download an app, make sure it will work with your operating system.

Application to OS Compatibility

A few years ago, Windows apps required Windows 7 or later to run. Now, with Windows 7 at end of life (EOL) and out of support and Windows 8/8.1 not far behind, Windows 10 is the minimum version most new apps are looking for. Windows 10 will reach EOL in 2025, and don't be surprised if down the road Windows 11 becomes a minimum operating system requirement for apps. Learn more about vendor life-cycle limitations such as EOL in Chapter 8, "Operating System Types."

Although 64-bit Windows can run 32-bit Windows apps, some older apps need help from the Windows Compatibility Wizard or the Compatibility tab to work properly, typically due to screen handling. Compatibility fixes are not designed to help antivirus or disk utilities made for older versions of Windows to run on current versions, however. If you have apps that have problems running in Windows 10 or 11 and compatibility fixes don't work, you have two choices:

▶ Upgrade the app to a version that works with your version of Windows.
▶ Create a VM with an older version of Windows and install your app in the VM.

32-Bit vs. 64-Bit OS

As discussed earlier in this chapter, 64-bit Windows is designed to run both 64-bit and 32-bit applications using its side-by-side technology, which includes the use of separate folders for 32-bit and 64-bit applications and their support files.

The most recent macOS and Linux versions require the use of VMs or similar container technologies to create environments where 32-bit apps can run. See "32-Bit vs. 64-Bit Dependent Application Requirements" earlier in this chapter for details.

> **EXAM TIP**
>
> Be sure you understand the OS requirements for installing new apps: app to OS compatibility and 32-bit vs. 64-bit OS. Be prepared to apply this information in scenarios.

DISTRIBUTION METHODS

Software distribution methods include physical media, downloadable files, and ISO files. The following sections look at how these vary and what you are likely to encounter when installing apps.

> **EXAM TIP**
>
> Understand the implications of various distribution methods, including physical, downloadable, and ISO mountable, and be prepared for questions using them in a scenario.

PHYSICAL MEDIA VS. DOWNLOADABLE

In the last decade, the switch from physical media (CDs and DVDs, which had replaced floppy disks) to downloadable media has become almost complete. Although stores still have a lot of software boxes on the shelf, most of them contain key cards with serial numbers and instructions for downloading and installing the software instead of CDs or DVDs.

Downloadable software is easier to maintain, as the vendor can update software provided online so that you can download the latest version. If updates are needed, they are also provided online. Downloadable software is also less expensive to produce, as vendors no longer need to press optical media, buy media cases, or print multipage instruction booklets to be inserted into the media cases.

What may be physical media's last stand is the continued use of driver discs with printers, scanners, and multifunction devices. Although it's recommended that you download updated drivers for devices that include a driver disc, don't discard the disc since it may contain software that is not licensed for download, such as photo editors and page recognition apps.

Downloadable software comes in various forms. Operating systems and office suites are typically downloaded as ISO files (see the next section). However, drivers for Windows are typically downloaded as self-extracting EXE files or as ZIP archive files, which are extracted with operating system tools. While self-extracting EXE files automate the installation process, ZIP archive files must be manually extracted and the contents might need to be moved into a specific location to run.

ISO MOUNTABLE

As discussed in the previous section, operating systems and office suites for Windows are often downloaded as ISO files. An ISO file is an image of a CD or DVD that can be burned to the appropriate type of optical disc for installation. However, recent versions of Windows support direct mounting of ISO files for installing applications and for upgrading to newer versions of Windows (Figure 7.7).

FIGURE 7.7 Preparing to mount an ISO file with Windows 10's File Explorer

ISO files can also be mounted by means of virtual optical drives for installation into virtual machines.

OTHER CONSIDERATIONS FOR NEW APPLICATIONS

Beyond issues of software compatibility, it's also important to consider the impact that new software can have on devices, networks, operations, and businesses before purchasing and installing apps.

> **EXAM TIP**
>
> Be prepared to answer questions about impacts to device, network, operation, and business.

Impact to Device

Earlier in this chapter, we emphasized the need to research the device's hardware and operating system version before choosing a new app. Part of the reason is that software can require you to provide additional disk space, upgrade RAM, and upgrade the operating system so that it will work. In addition, some software might have compatibility issues with existing software. Careful examination of existing hardware, software, and operating systems on a computer or device can help you avoid these kinds of traps.

Impact to Network

Impact to network can happen if a new application increases the load on the network. If the software generates more network traffic than the current network can handle, it could lead to an expensive upgrade. The impact on network resources is one of the reasons that many companies and universities banned the use of peer-to-peer file downloading tools some time back.

Network impact is an even bigger issue today with the rise of cloud-based apps from Gmail to Microsoft 365. Redundant Internet and LAN connections are strongly encouraged for businesses that are running cloud-based apps.

Impact to Operation

Ideally, new software should enhance an organization's operation. However, software that requires extensive user training for even basic operations means that, in the short term, at least, it can have a moderate to severe impact on operations.

The change from Microsoft's traditional menu system in its Office app from the 2003 and earlier versions to 2007 caused some temporary productivity loss. However, the switch from Windows 7 to Windows 8 was much more significant. Even experienced Windows users struggled to figure out how to use the operating system, and some users resorted to software add-ons that made Windows 8 resemble Windows 7. Eventually, Microsoft went back to a more traditional menu system in Windows 10.

Other effects on operation go deeper than the user interface, however. Changes to default file formats, proprietary programs that don't work on the new operating system, changes in application programming (such as VBA coding and macros), and changes to disk structures are just a few of the issues that can have substantial impacts on operation.

> **NOTE**
>
> One of the biggest changes happening in office apps is the changeover to Microsoft 365 from Microsoft Office. This can have significant effects on VBA macros and add-ins. Microsoft's Readiness Toolkit for Office can help find these issues so that the affected macros and add-ins can be updated. Search for **Readiness Toolkit for Office** at `https://docs.microsoft.com` to learn more.

Impact to Business

The final area of concern in choosing software is its impact on business. An upgrade to an application that runs a business needs to be tested more thoroughly than one that is used in a small department. Software bugs or system outages can cripple an organization that depends on a particular app.

Ideally, new business-critical apps should be run in parallel with the old system for some time before the changeover takes place.

Be sure to review Chapter 29, "Change Management," for details on how to plan upgrades and the importance of rollback plans if upgrades don't work as expected.

CERTMIKE EXAM ESSENTIALS

▶ To avoid purchasing an app that's unsuitable for your requirements, take advantage of trial offers, but make sure to track the amount of time you can use the app before you must start paying for it, especially if you are asked to provide a credit card to start the trial.

▶ Most applications, whether sold online or in retail stores, use downloads instead of physical media. If your Internet connection has download limits, plan your download of large apps or operating systems to occur at off-peak hours.

▶ Check reviews from reliable sources and comparison charts to help narrow down candidates for major application or operating system purchases.

Practice Question 1

Your client has just upgraded from 32-bit Windows 7 to 64-bit Windows 10 and is concerned about using existing 32-bit software with Windows 10. Which of the following will occur during the installation of the 32-bit software on 64-bit Windows 10?

A. The software will be installed to \Program Files\32-bit.
B. The software can't be installed and must be replaced with 64-bit versions.
C. The software must go through a conversion process during installation.
D. The software will be installed in \Program Files (x86).

Practice Question 2

You are considering installing a new application that uses much more RAM than its predecessor. Upgrades will be necessary for some of the computers that will use the new app. If you decide to purchase this app, which of the following impacts can you expect to see *first*?

A. Impact to business
B. Impact to device
C. Impact to operation
D. Impact to network

Practice Question 1 Explanation

This question is designed to test your knowledge of Windows upgrade limitations.

Let's evaluate these answers one at a time.

1. The first answer (A, The software will be installed to \Program Files\32-bit) is incorrect. This folder name isn't created during installation and would exist only if the user creates it.

2. The second answer (B, The software can't be installed and must be replaced with 64-bit versions) is incorrect. 64-bit Windows can accept and run 32-bit applications.

3. The third answer (C, The software must go through a conversion process during installation) is incorrect. No special conversion process is needed to enable 32-bit applications to run on 64-bit Windows.

4. The last answer (D, The software will be installed in \Program Files [x86]) is correct. Windows uses separate folders for 64-bit applications (\Program Files) and 32-bit applications (\Program Files (x86)).

Correct Answer: D. The software will be installed in \Program Files (x86)

Practice Question 2 Explanation

This question is designed to test your real-world understanding of the impact of new software. Let's consider each of these answers.

1. The first answer (A, Impact to business) is incorrect. Impact to business, if any, is likely to take place only after the app is installed and in use for a while.

2. Next answer (B, Impact to device) is correct. Computers that are not ready to use the application will need to be upgraded with more RAM before the app can be installed.

3. Next answer (C, Impact to operation) is incorrect. The upgrades can be done in off-hours and won't require any changes to currently installed software.

4. The last answer (D, Impact to network) is incorrect. Upgrading the RAM will have no impact on the network.

Correct Answer: B. Impact to device

CHAPTER 8

Operating System Types

Core 2 Objective 1.8: Explain common OS types and their purposes.

Computers and mobile devices use different operating systems (OSs). What makes them different? What makes one more suitable for some jobs than others? You need to understand their differences when you are supporting computers and mobile devices. In this chapter, you will learn what you need to know about A+ Certification Core 2 Objective 1.8, including the following topics:

▶ **Workstation OSs**
▶ **Cell Phone/Tablet OSs**
▶ **Various Filesystem Types**
▶ **Vendor Life-Cycle Limitations**
▶ **Compatibility Concerns Between OSs**

WORKSTATION OSs

The choice of a particular workstation operating system (OS) should take into account the features of the OS, the software available, its compatibility with the intended hardware, and compatibility with other OSs already in use in the organization. Workstation OSs run office apps, web browsers, and email clients, and may also be used for graphics, photo editing, and video editing. There are four major OS families to consider: Windows, macOS, Linux, and Chrome OS.

Although these operating systems vary in many ways, one common feature shared by Windows, macOS, and Linux are their use of a hardware abstraction layer. A hardware abstraction layer (*HAL*) enables an operating system to run on many different types of hardware by using device drivers.

> **NOTE**
>
> For a more detailed explanation of what a HAL does, visit `www.techopedia .com/definition/4288/hardware-abstraction-layer-hal`.

Windows

Microsoft Windows is the dominant OS in business and home use. Windows is a commercial product that can run on computers from many manufacturers. It features a graphical user interface (*GUI*) as its primary user interface for use by mouse or touchpad or pen, but it also has a command-line interpreter used primarily by technicians for diagnostics and advanced tasks. Figure 8.1 illustrates Windows 10's desktop GUI and command-line (Command Prompt) interfaces.

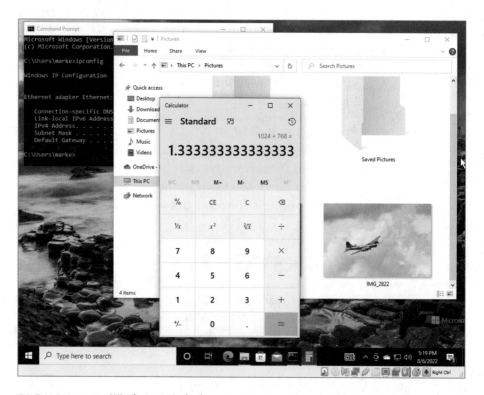

FIGURE 8.1 Windows 10's desktop GUI and command-line interfaces

Windows supports Intel and AMD processors as well as some Advanced RISC Machine (ARM) processors, so it supports the dominant computing architectures. Windows is available in versions for home (Home), professional (Pro), workstation (Pro for Workstations), education (Education), enterprise networks (Enterprise), servers (Server), and Internet of Things (IoT) devices.

Windows has an enormous software library of 32-bit apps and 64-bit apps of all types. Programs designed to run on both 64-bit and 32-bit AMD and Intel processors are collectively known as Windows Desktop apps or Classic apps. Programs designed specifically for Windows 8 and later, including versions for ARM and IoT processors, are collectively known as Windows or Modern apps.

Windows also dominates in terms of device support, with Windows support the top priority for device vendors of all types, from display and storage to printer, scanner, and networking.

Windows is also very flexible, able to run on everything from low-powered thin clients where most of the processing is done by a server to high-performance workstations optimized for graphics, CAD, and video editing.

Windows 10 and its major features were discussed in Chapter 3, "Windows 10 Operating System Tools."

Linux

Linux is a family of Unix-like operating systems that run on Intel or ARM hardware. Many different Linux distros (distributions) exist, most of which are free and open source for easy modification and improvement. Linux distros range from those made to appeal to Windows users (Debian, Ubuntu, and others) to those made especially to support servers and back-end computing (SUSE Linux Enterprise Server, Red Hat Enterprise Linux, and others). As a primarily free and open source OS, Linux also enjoys enormous support from developers of open source (mostly free) software.

Linux was originally a command-line OS, and the command-line interface is the core of serious Linux use to this day. To master Linux, users need to be familiar with many commands and the most common variations. The built-in man (manual) is a very important learning and reference tool for all levels of Linux users.

> **EXAM TIP**
>
> All Linux distros include man pages for each command. To access the man page for `apt-get`, for example, open a Terminal session and type **man apt-get**.

Although many Linux distros are bundled with GUIs (Figure 8.2), Linux GUIs are separate from the core OS. This enables users to switch between various versions of GUIs such as GNOME, KDE Plasma, XFCE, and many others.

Linux can run on simple computers like the Raspberry Pi all the way up to the servers powering data centers, providing extreme scalability.

Learn more about Linux and its major features in Chapter 11, "Linux."

FIGURE 8.2 Ubuntu Linux 22.04's desktop GUI and command-line interfaces

macOS

macOS differs a great deal from both Windows and Linux. While Windows and Linux run on hardware from many different manufacturers, macOS, created by Apple, runs strictly on Apple hardware. Apple is the only manufacturer of computers authorized to run macOS. Although macOS is also descended from a Unix-like operating system, BSD, it is primarily GUI-driven, with a Terminal command-line mode used for technical issues (Figure 8.3).

macOS currently runs on two families of processors. Until recently, it ran on the same Intel CPUs used by most Windows and Linux desktops. However, Apple is now producing its own M1 and M2 ARM processors and current Mac models use them. These processors are not compatible with Intel macOS operating systems or apps. The macOS software library is heavily weighted toward creative apps (graphics, video, sound) as well as office suites.

Learn more about macOS and its major features in Chapter 10, "macOS."

FIGURE 8.3   macOS Monterey's desktop GUI and command-line interfaces

Chrome OS

Chrome OS was developed by Google as a web-based operating system. Essentially, a Chromebook (a computer that runs Chrome OS) is a thin client that uses Google Chrome and its related apps (Google Drive, Google Docs) with an active web connection (Figure 8.4). Chromebooks are very popular in elementary and secondary schools because it's difficult to hack the hardware or the software.

Originally, Chromebooks were very low-powered devices that ran either ARM processors or low-end Intel ATOM processors and lacked touchscreens. However, many Chromebooks now feature touchscreens and some are equipped with mid-range AMD (Ryzen 3) and Intel (Core i5) or even faster processors.

> **EXAM TIP**
>
> Know the common OS types, including Windows, Linux, macOS, and Chrome OS, and be able to explain their purposes.

FIGURE 8.4 Chrome OS uses Google web apps.

CELL PHONE/TABLET OSs

Apple and Android are the only two players of any importance in cell phone and tablet OSs. The following sections cover their major features and differences. Keep in mind that all of these OSs are designed primarily for information viewing and gaming rather than for information creation.

iOS

Apple's iOS operating system supports its iPhone smartphones. It offers an easy-to-use touchscreen GUI and a large library of apps via the App Store. The iOS operating system is app-oriented, but recent versions have added the Files app for easier access to recent files and support for browsing folders on iCloud. The latest versions of iOS are 15 (Figure 8.5) and 16.

iPadOS

Until recently, Apple, the creator of iPad, iPhone, and iPod devices, used the same operating system (iOS) on all of their devices. Now iPads have their own OS, known as iPadOS.

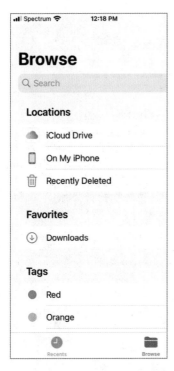

FIGURE 8.5 Browsing files with iOS 15.5's Files app

Compared to iOS, iPadOS has several improvements, including support for multiple windows with multitasking (Figure 8.6), Sidecar (enabling some iPad models to work as second monitors for macOS computers), support for Apple Pencil, and an improved Files app for file management. The latest versions of iPadOS are 15 and 16.

Android

Although Google is the creator of Android, a touchscreen smartphone and tablet OS derived from Linux, Google is not the only source for Android devices. Google licenses Android to many other smartphone and tablet vendors and supports modifications to the basic user interface and bundled apps.

Android is also available in different versions that support older and newer devices. So, don't be surprised to discover differences in Android on devices from Samsung, Google, Lenovo, and other Android smartphone and tablet vendors. Android and its apps are typically distributed using the Android Package (*APK*) file format.

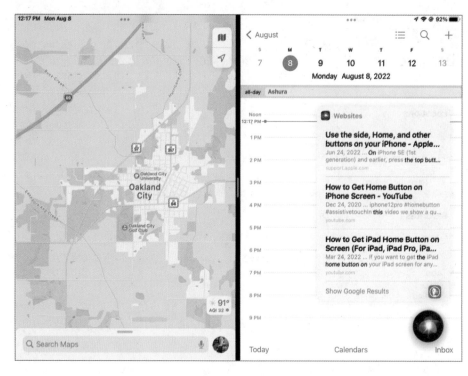

FIGURE 8.6 Using the split-screen multitasking feature of iPadOS

Figure 8.7 shows the home screen for a typical Android smartphone, a Samsung A20, running Android 11 and the Galaxy Showcase, Android apps chosen for (and possibly modified) for Samsung Galaxy smartphones.

EXAM TIP

Know the purposes and features of the various cell phone/tablet OSs.

VARIOUS FILESYSTEM TYPES

A filesystem (also referred to as file system) is how files are stored, named, and retrieved from a storage device. Choosing the best filesystem for a specific device is based on compatibility with the operating system, the size of the storage device, and its intended use. In the following sections, we take a close look at the filesystems most commonly used by Windows, Linux, and macOS, including cross-platform options.

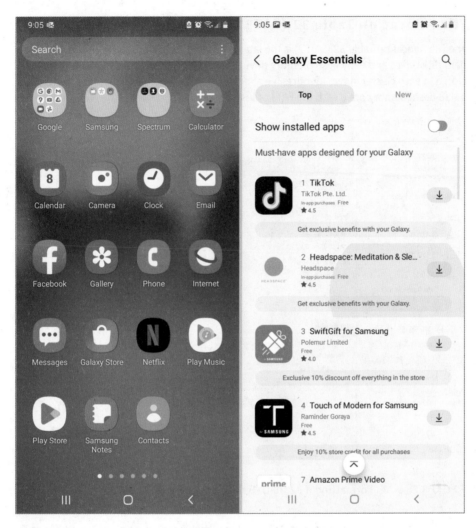

FIGURE 8.7 Two screens from the Samsung A20 smartphone, running a modified version of Android

EXAM TIP

Know the purposes and features of the various filesystems and be prepared to answer questions about which one to use in a specific scenario.

File Allocation Table 32 (FAT32)

The File Allocation Table 32 (FAT32) is the latest version of the FAT filesystems used by small hard disk drives and early flash memory devices. A *FAT* filesystem keeps track of the data stored in each cluster in two identical file allocation tables. Figure 8.8 illustrates formatting a USB flash memory drive with the FAT32 filesystem.

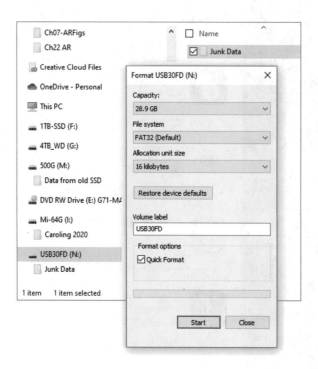

FIGURE 8.8 Formatting a 32 GB USB flash drive with FAT32

FAT32 uses 32-bit numbering for cluster sizes, and most implementations support up to 2 TB size drives using 512-byte sectors and file sizes up to 4 GB. FAT32 is primarily used today for small (up to 32 GB) flash memory drives and cards. FAT filesystems, including FAT32, lack the security features of NTFS.

New Technology File System (NTFS)

The New Technology File System (NTFS) isn't exactly new anymore: it was introduced with Windows NT 3.1. However, it is a big advance over the original file allocation tab (FAT) filesystems. Major features of *NTFS* include its structure, which features a master file table with backup, journaling, access control lists (ACLs), and support for file-level encryption with the Encrypting File System (EFS) on all versions except Home editions of Windows. NTFS is the preferred filesystem for Windows backup programs, and most do not support non-NTFS drives.

Journaling keeps track of changes that haven't yet been stored. Journaling makes file systems like NTFS more robust and faster and easier to recover from crashes. ACLs are used to permit varying levels of access to files and folders based on user or group membership. EFS is the encrypted file system. In NTFS, files can be compressed by the file system or be encrypted, but not both (Figure 8.9).

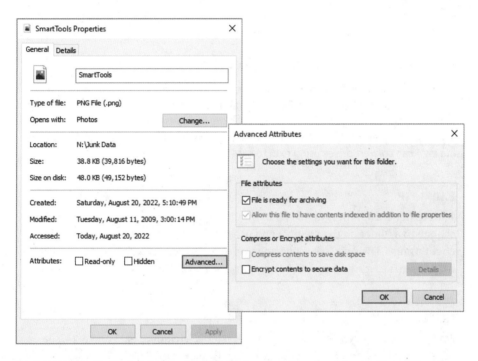

FIGURE 8.9 Click Advanced on the file's properties sheet to see the options for compression or encryption with EFS.

EXAM TIP
To determine what file system a Windows drive is using, open its properties sheet and view the General tab.

Third Extended File System (ext3)

The first filesystem created for use with Linux, *ext*, sets up virtual directories on physical drives and creates an inode table on each drive to track the filename, size, owner, group, access permissions, and pointers to the data block storing the drive.

> **EXAM TIP**
>
> Much of what ext filesystems store about files is displayed when you use the `ls -l` command to view the contents of a folder.

The Third Extended filesystem (ext3) improves on ext by adding ordered mode journaling to store inode data, and ext3 also continues the improved file storage method introduced in ext2 to reduce file fragmentation. ext3 is widely supported by current Linux distros, but it has been replaced by ext4 as the default Linux filesystem.

Fourth Extended Filesystem (ext4)

The Fourth Extended filesystem (ext4) has several improvements over ext3, including more efficient file storage by using Extents (a range of contiguous physical blocks) for data storage and inodes, delayed allocation disk caching, no limits to the number of subdirectories in a directory, and volume sizes up to 1 exabyte (EB) and file sizes up to 16 TB. Systems using ext4 can convert drives using ext3 to ext4.

> **EXAM TIP**
>
> To determine what filesystem a Linux volume is using, open a Terminal session, change to a folder on the volume, and use the command `findmnt`. To learn more about using `findmnt`, see `www.howtogeek.com/774913/ how-to-use-the-findmnt-command-on-linux`.

> **NOTE**
>
> For much more information about ext filesystems, including ext3 and ext4, see `www.partitionwizard.com/partitionmanager/ ext2-vs-ext3-vs-ext4.html`.

In addition to ext3 and ext4 file systems, UNIX, Linux, and macOS also use the network file system (*NFS*) for networking. The current version of NFS, NFSv4, uses TCP or UDP port 2049. Although NFS can be used across multiple platforms, other network filesystems are more popular.

Apple File System (APFS)

The Apple File System (APFS) supports Apple-compatible devices such as hard drives, flash memory, and other devices with built-in storage. APFS supports iOS, macOS, tvOS, and watchOS devices. *APFS* supports 64-bit file signatures, improves use of disk capacity, copies files more quickly than its predecessors HFS and HFS+, and supports Space Sharing to extend a partition across multiple devices.

NOTE

For much more information about the features of APFS, see `https://developer.apple.com/documentation/foundation/file_ssystem/about_apple_file_system`.

Extensible File Allocation Table (exFAT)

The Extensible File Allocation Table (exFAT) was developed by Microsoft and later made available to other vendors. The *exFAT* filesystem is designed to support large drives, including flash drives over 32 GB in size and USB hard drives, supporting files up to 16 EB and drives up to 128 petabytes (PB), and over 2.7 million files per folder. However, it lacks journaling and other security features of NTFS.

Linux, macOS, and many smart TVs support exFAT devices, so exFAT is a good filesystem to use for cross-platform file transfers. Figure 8.10 illustrates formatting a 64 GB flash drive with exFAT.

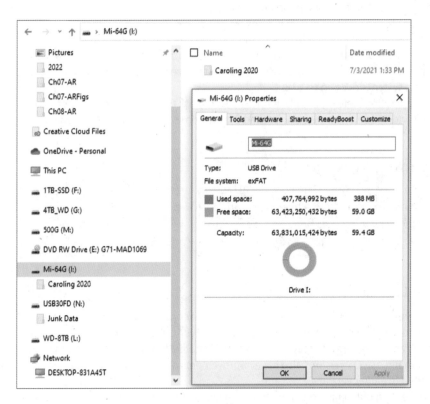

FIGURE 8.10 Formatting a 64 GB flash drive with the exFAT filesystem

VENDOR LIFE-CYCLE LIMITATIONS

No operating system lasts forever. Windows 98, Windows XP, and Windows 7 are just three of the long-lasting operating systems that have become outdated. There are two reasons why operating systems become obsolete: end of life and update limitations.

End-of-Life (EOL)

End-of-life (*EOL*) is defined as the point at which computing hardware or software is no longer being produced, supported, or repaired. For organizations that must keep using EOL hardware, the supplies of old motherboards, video cards, and hard drives shrink over time while the prices for this type of equipment can go up.

With software, the problem with EOL software isn't a physical one, but rather the continuing need for security and hardware support updates. For example, when Windows XP was first released, it was designed to support system hard drives up to 137 GB—a size almost impossible to find today. Later releases raised the size limit, but Windows XP SP3 can only support system drives up to 2 TB.

Any EOL operating system or application is a security risk that will be targeted by hackers. Windows 7 and Windows 8 have now reached EOL. Windows 10 will reach EOL in 2025.

Update Limitations

The second reason for EOL is the inability to update older operating systems to handle modern hardware and modern security threats. Windows 10 and 11, for example, support Secure Boot and other security features unheard of in earlier Windows versions. Similarly, newer Linux and macOS versions also have improvements at the kernel level that cannot be retrofitted to earlier versions.

To take the sting out of moving up to newer versions, Linux free and open source distros and macOS offer free upgrades to the latest OSs, even if you haven't upgraded every time an upgrade was previously offered. Windows 7 and 8/8.1 can be upgraded to Windows 10, and Windows 10 can be upgraded to Windows 11. However, in all cases, you must check your system's hardware to verify that it can handle an upgraded operating system.

COMPATIBILITY CONCERNS BETWEEN OSs

If an organization uses the same version and release of an operating system, there would never be any worries about compatibility. But in the real world, there are likely to be some older systems that can't be upgraded, some macOS systems in the creative departments tucked away in a sea of Windows PCs, and some Linux servers and even a few desktops.

When transferring files between devices via networks, network operating systems take care of the differences between local filesystems. However, if external drives are shared between different OSs, choosing a cross-platform filesystem, such as exFAT, is important. When this is not possible, drivers are available to help filesystems such as NTFS, ext3, ext4, and APFS to be read by computers that normally use a different filesystem. Some drivers are read-only, whereas others are read-write.

CERTMIKE EXAM ESSENTIALS

▶ Workstation operating systems such as Windows, macOS, and Linux are used for office apps and for business and creative tasks, whereas cell phone and tablet operating systems such as Android, iOS, and iPadOS are designed to view information.

▶ Windows uses the New Technology File System (NTFS) and File Allocation Table 32 (FAT32) filesystems, Linux uses Extended File System 3 and Extended File System 4 filesystems, and macOS uses the Apple File System. The exFAT filesystem is supported by Windows, macOS, and Linux, so it is cross-platform. These filesystems vary in the operating systems they support, the drive sizes they support, and their support for security features such as journaling and user/group-based access controls.

▶ Operating systems that reach end-of-life (EOL) do so because they can no longer be updated for the latest hardware, software support, or security issues. When it is necessary to continue to support EOL operating systems, installing them in virtual machines provides an extra measure of safety against security threats for the operating system and its apps.

Practice Question 1

You are preparing a group of external 4TB portable drives that will be used for file copying by Linux, macOS, and Windows users. Currently, these drives are formatting with the NTFS filesystem. Which of the following would be the *best* way to use these drives with all three types of computers?

A. Install NTFS drivers for Linux and macOS.
B. Reformat the drives using ext4.
C. Reformat the drives using FAT32.
D. Reformat the drives using exFAT.

Practice Question 2

Your client has a computer that is running Windows 7. Due to the desired software only running on newer versions of Windows, your client wants to upgrade to Windows 11. Which of the following needs to happen *first*?

A. Check system compatibility with Windows 10 and Windows 11.
B. Check system compatibility with Windows 11.
C. Create installation media for Windows 11.
D. You need to inform your client it's not possible.

Practice Question 1 Explanation

This question is designed to test your real-world understanding of filesystems' cross-platform compatibility. Let's evaluate these answers one at a time.

1. The first answer (A, Install NTFS drivers for Linux and macOS) is incorrect. Using drivers for accessing not-normally supported filesystems is risky.

2. The next answer (B, Reformat the drives using ext4) is incorrect. The ext4 filesystem is supported by Linux, but macOS and Windows would need to install special drivers.

3. The next answer (C, Reformat the drives using FAT32) is incorrect. FAT32 supports drives up to only 2 TB.

4. The last answer (D, Reformat the drives using exFAT) is correct. exFAT is supported by macOS, Linux, and Windows.

Correct Answer: D. Reformat the drives using exFAT

Practice Question 2 Explanation

This question is designed to test your knowledge of Windows upgrade limitations.

Let's evaluate these answers one at a time.

1. The first answer (A, Check system compatibility with Windows 10 and Windows 11) is correct. The upgrade path is Windows 7 to 10, then Windows 10 to 11. It's important to make sure that both Windows 10 and 11 can run on the computer before starting.

2. The second answer (B, Check system compatibility with Windows 11), is incorrect. The system must be upgraded to Windows 10 first.

3. The third answer (C, Create installation media for Windows 11) is incorrect. Until you check compatibility with both versions of Windows, there's no need to create installation media.

4. The last answer (D, You need to inform your client it's not possible) is incorrect. The upgrade can be done, but in two stages (Windows 7 to 10, then Windows 10 to 11) if the computer is compatible.

Correct Answer: A. Check system compatibility with Windows 10 and Windows 11

CHAPTER 9

Operating System Installations and Upgrades

Core 2 Objective 1.9: Given a scenario, perform OS installations and upgrades in a diverse OS environment.

During the lifespan of a typical Windows, macOS, or Linux computer, operating system upgrades and installations are common occurrences and take on many forms. In this chapter, you will learn what you need to know about A+ Certification Core 2 Objective 1.9, including the following topics:

► **Boot methods**
► **Types of installations**
► **Partitioning**
► **Drive format**
► **Upgrade considerations**
► **Feature updates**

BOOT METHODS

There are more methods available today than ever before for booting a system to start an operating system upgrade, including various types of media, network, and internal storage. The following sections discuss these in detail.

USB

USB (Universal Serial Bus) is an external interface built into just about every desktop or portable PC. It supports storage, input/output data transfers, and video output. USB 3.0/3.1/3.2 and USB-C storage devices (which run at speeds from 5 Gbps up) are suitable for operating system installation sources. Learn more about USB at www.usb.org.

The most common type of boot media for starting an operating system upgrade is USB. A USB drive with a capacity of 8 GB or higher can store a bootable Windows or Linux image (ISO file).

Windows

You can purchase Windows 10 or Windows 11 on a USB drive ready for installation. To create a USB bootable drive for installing Windows 10, you can use the Windows 10 Media Creation tool available from www.microsoft.com/en-us/software-download/windows10. When you run it, select the option to create installation media for another PC and select USB Flash Drive. To create a USB bootable drive for installing Windows 11, you can use the Windows 11 Media Creation tool available from www.microsoft.com/en-us/software-download/windows11. When you run it, select USB Flash Drive.

You can also download an ISO file using the media creation tools and use it to create a USB bootable drive. The free Rufus tool (available at https://rufus.ie/en) is a popular choice for creating Windows 10, Windows 11, and Linux bootable USB media because of its speed and its ability to create a customized Windows 11 installation drive that bypasses default settings such as compatibility checks (Figure 9.1).

> **NOTE**
>
> See www.supereasy.com/how-to-create-your-windows-10-bootable-usb-drive-using-rufus for more about Rufus and Windows. To boot from a USB drive to install Windows or Linux, insert the drive into the appropriate USB port. Restart the computer and access UEFI/BIOS settings and change the boot order to make the USB drive the first boot device. Save changes, reboot, and start the installation process.

Linux

To install most Linux distros from USB, download the ISO file for the distro and use a tool such as Rufus (Figure 9.2) to create a bootable USB installation drive. For Fedora, use Fedora Media Writer. The Persistent Partition Size setting shown in Figure 9.2 enables the user to save changes back to the Linux USB media.

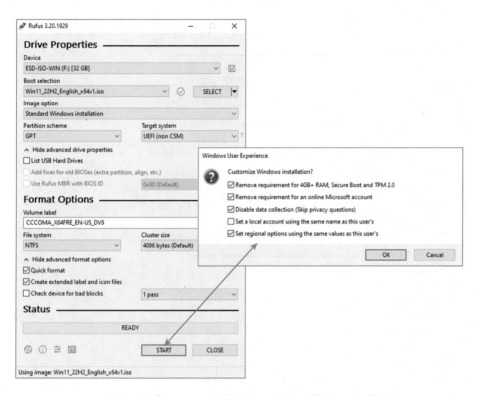

F I G U R E   9 . 1   **Using Rufus to create Windows 11 installation media that bypasses default settings**

NOTE

To learn more about persistent storage in Linux, visit www.pendrivelinux
.com/what-is-persistent-linux. For a tutorial on creating a bootable
USB drive for installing Ubuntu Linux, see https://ubuntu.com/
tutorials/create-a-usb-stick-on-windows#1-overview.

Optical Media

Until recently, the most common way to install Windows or Linux was via optical media. Windows 11 is the first Windows version that is not available in a packaged DVD version for sale. Many computers no longer include DVD drives, so you would need to purchase a USB or SATA internal optical drive if you want to install an operating system or software from optical disc. You will also need to change the UEFI/BIOS settings to permit booting from the drive.

If you prefer to use optical media rather than USB, you can use the Windows media creation tools to download an ISO file. An ISO file is an image file that stores the files and layout necessary to create a bootable DVD. Linux distros are also supplied as ISO files.

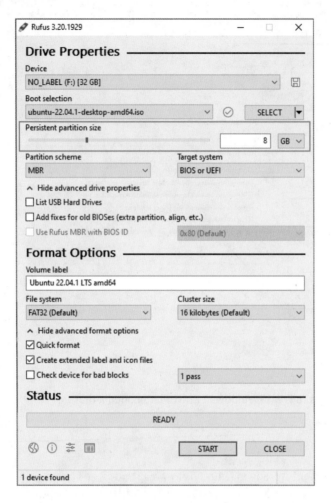

FIGURE 9.2 Using Rufus to create Ubuntu Linux installation media with the optional Persistent Partition Size setting enabled

The Windows File Explorer can be used to burn any ISO file to a CD or DVD (Figure 9.3), depending on the size of the ISO file, or you can use a third-party app like ImgBurn (www .imgburn.com). In macOS, you can use the File menu in the Finder to burn a disk image from an ISO file.

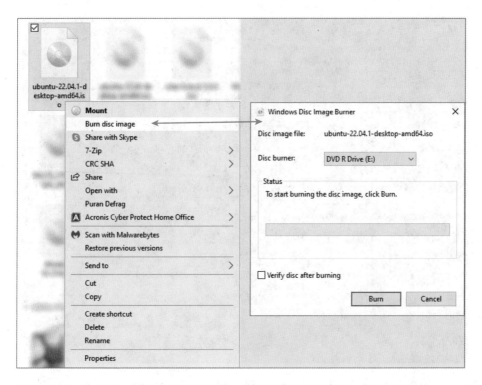

FIGURE 9.3 Burning an Ubuntu Linux ISO to an optical disc with Windows File Explorer

Network

To install an operating system by booting from a network location, you must set up a network location to provide the boot and installation images and a DHCP server to provide an IP address during the network boot process. You can use Windows Deployment Services (WDS) or third-party tools such as Serva and AIOCreator to set up the network location.

After you set up a network location, you access it by configuring your computer to use network booting. The setting is usually called PXE (Preboot Execution Environment) on a system with Legacy BIOS or UEFI Network on a system with UEFI firmware. In Figure 9.4, the system is configured with the network port as UEFI Boot Option #1.

> **NOTE**
>
> To learn more about installing Windows over the network using WDS, see www
> .itechguides.com/install-windows-10-from-network. To learn
> more about using AIO Boot, see www.aioboot.com/en/network-boot.
> To learn more about using Serva, see www.vercot.com/~serva/default
> .html and www.digitalcitizen.life/
> how-install-any-version-windows-other-network-computers.

F I G U R E 9 . 4 Configuring a system to boot from the network

Solid-State/Flash Drives

To boot from a solid-state or flash drive for an operating system installation, make sure the drive has bootable media. To prepare a USB flash memory card, use the same media preparation tools discussed earlier. To prepare an external SSD, install the operating system to it and set it up as a bootable device using the system's Boot dialog box in BIOS/UEFI firmware.

Internet-Based

An Internet-based installation can refer to either a cloud-based installation of an operating system or a web-based operating system (such as ChromeOS). The most common reasons to perform an Internet-based installation is to perform a recovery installation with Windows or Chrome OS.

To reset a Windows installation using the Internet:

1. Click Start ➢ Settings ➢ Update & Recovery (Windows 10) or Start ➢ Settings ➢ System (Windows 11).
2. Click Recovery ➢ Get Started (Windows 10) or Recovery ➢ Reset PC (Windows 11).

3. Choose either Keep My Files or Remove Everything.
4. Click Cloud Download to reinstall Windows from the Internet. If you're on a limited data plan, keep in mind that this will require over 4 GB of data.

To recover a ChromeOS installation on a Chromebook from the Internet:

1. Enter recovery mode (specific instructions differ by model).
2. Select Recover Using Internet Connection and follow the prompts to complete the reinstallation.

External/Hot-Swappable Drive

You can install an operating system from external USB, optical, or other types of hot-swappable drives, including eSATA. Make sure the drive is recognized as a hot-swappable and bootable drive in the BIOS/UEFI settings and that it has the operating system you want to install.

Internal Hard Drive (Partition)

By configuring the boot sequence to boot from an internal hard drive that is configured as a bootable drive and has a bootable operating system, you can boot from that drive's operating system and then use it to prepare a different internal or external drive as a bootable drive. For example, you can boot from an internal Windows hard drive and format a different internal hard drive as a bootable Windows drive. You can then use the newly formatted drive to start your system.

If you are replacing a lower-capacity hard drive with a higher-capacity hard drive, the easiest way to achieve this is with disk-cloning software, a feature built into many backup programs. This transfers the entire contents of your original drive to a new drive (internal or external) and resizes the existing partitions to fit the new drive's capacity.

EXAM TIP

Make sure you know the different types of boot methods used for operating system installation.

TYPES OF INSTALLATIONS

There are many types of operating system installations you need to be familiar with for the A+ Core 2 1102 certification exam. The following sections discuss these.

NOTE

Keep in mind that the Windows 10/11 Reset (this) PC can also be used to perform a reinstallation of Windows. Refer to "Internet-Based" earlier in this chapter for details.

Upgrade

An upgrade installation works this way: Boot the system as you would normally. Connect a drive that has an installable copy of the upgraded operating system: for example, an ISO of the latest Windows 11 release if you have Windows 10 or an earlier version of Windows 11 installed. Start the installation by opening the ISO or drive and selecting the install program.

> **NOTE**
>
> Before starting an upgrade installation, back up your important data and settings files and make sure you have access to your apps' install files in case you might need to reinstall some of them after the upgrade installation.

Recovery Partition

A recovery partition is a hidden partition on some brands and models of desktop or laptop computers that is used to store installation media. Depending on the system, you may need to create media from the recovery partition, or you can start the installation process directly from the recovery partition. In either case, running this type of installation wipes out the contents of the boot drive and restores a system to its as-shipped condition, so be sure to have a complete backup of your system, including data, before you use this installation method.

Clean Installation

Use a clean installation to configure a blank drive as a bootable drive. Start the computer with its installation media. During the process, you will determine how much of the drive to use for the operating system, format the specified capacity, and set up users and configuration settings.

Image Deployment

Use an image deployment installation to set up a blank drive with specific apps and settings. To start, create an image with backup software that creates an image file, such as Acronis, AOMEI Backupper, Arcserve ShadowProtect, Paragon Hard Disk Manager, or others.

Create bootable media with the backup software. Boot the system with the bootable media and restore the image to a drive of the same size or larger as the original drive.

> **NOTE**
>
> A free version of Acronis that supports full and image backups is available for Western Digital drive users. See Acronis True Image for Western Digital at https://support.wdc.com/downloads.aspx. A free version of Acronis

that supports full and image backups is available for Seagate drive users as part of its DiscWizard utility. See `www.seagate.com/support/downloads/discwizard`.

Repair Installation

A repair installation replaces your existing operating system with a fresh copy. It is known as an in-place upgrade in Microsoft Windows. See Chapter 1, "Microsoft Windows Editions," for more about upgrade paths.

After downloading an ISO file of the same version of Windows as the one installed, open File Explorer, right-click the ISO, and select Mount. The ISO will open in its own File Explorer folder. Double-click Setup. During the preparation process, you're asked if you want to keep your personal files and apps or keep personal files only. Unless you suspect that your apps need reinstallation, I recommend you choose the keep personal files and apps option. Click Install and wait for the process to complete.

To perform a repair installation in macOS, restart the system, press Command+R to start Recovery mode, and select Reinstall macOS. With Linux, check the documentation for the specific distro for the steps needed.

Remote Network Installation

A remote network installation uses servers to store an image of the operating system and provide DHCP services to remote computers. Remote computers boot from the network using PXE, and scripts guide the remainder of the installation process. As mentioned earlier, Windows includes Windows Deployment Services (WDS). WDS can also be used to install Linux distros.

> **NOTE**
>
> For the complete process including prerequisites, see `https://learn.microsoft.com/en-us/windows/deployment`. To learn more about using WDS to deploy Windows and Linux VMs remotely, see `www.veeam.com/blog/windows-deployment-service-guide.html`.

Remote network installation and other types of scripted installations use a special version of Windows called Windows PE or WinPE. *WinPE* is a command-line version of Windows used for installation, repair, recovering data from unbootable devices, and more. In addition to being built into Windows, WinPE can also be downloaded as an add-on to the Windows Assessment and Deployment Kit.

> **NOTE**
>
> To learn more about using WinPE, visit `https://learn.microsoft.com/en-us/windows-hardware/manufacture/desktop/winpe-intro`.

Other Considerations

With any type of installation, you need to make sure that software drivers are provided for network, mass storage, and display hardware.

Third-Party Drivers

Third-party drivers are drivers that are not bundled with the operating system. Windows includes standard video, SATA, network, and USB drivers but might not include drivers for 3D chipsets, third-party storage RAID, wireless or wired network, or USB chipsets.

During a manual installation process, you are prompted to install third-party storage drivers during installation. To avoid this prompt, incorporate the drivers into your Windows installation source. You can also install video and other types of drivers after the installation process is complete, using drivers provided by the motherboard or system vendor on optical media or by download.

> **NOTE**
>
> For the step-by-step process for incorporating drivers into Window 10 and 11 installation media, see `https://learn.microsoft.com/en-us/ windows-hardware/manufacture/desktop/add-device- drivers-to-windows-during-windows-setup?view=windows-11`.

> **EXAM TIP**
>
> Make sure you understand the different types of installations and their purposes. Use virtual machines (VMs) to practice if you don't have spare computers to work with.

PARTITIONING

During a clean installation or when adding an additional hard drive to a system, the drive must be partitioned. Partitioning creates one or more areas on the drive that can be assigned drive letters. This section discusses the two partition types used: MBR and GPT.

Master Boot Record (MBR)

The Master Boot Record (*MBR*) partition type is the only partition type supported by legacy ROM BIOS systems, but it is also supported by BIOS/UEFI. MBR drives have a maximum size of 2.2 TB and have two types of partitions: primary and extended.

A primary partition can be bootable, and there can be up to four primary partitions on a drive, only one of which can be active. An extended partition acts as a container for nonbootable logical drives. For example, if you wanted to set up a drive with C: (bootable) and D: and E: drives (nonbootable, logical), you would create a primary partition occupying part of the drive capacity for the C: drive, an extended partition for the remainder of the disk's capacity, and then create logical D: and E: drives in the extended partition. Only one extended partition can be created on an MBR drive.

GUID (Globally Unique Identifier) Partition Table (GPT)

The GUID (Globally Unique Identifier) Partition Table (*GPT*) is a partitioning scheme introduced with BIOS/UEFI firmware, supporting up to 128 primary partitions and drives up to 9.4 ZB (1 ZB = 1 billion TB). Compared to its predecessor, MBR, GPT improves reliability by having backup partition entries and a protective MBR that protects the drive's contents from being damaged by disk utilities that don't understand GPT partitions. GPT drives are bootable with 64-bit operating systems. However, 32-bit operating systems can use GPT drives as data drives.

A Globally Unique Identifier (*GUID*) is a unique ID used by Windows and Windows applications to refer to many Windows components and features.

> **EXAM TIP**
>
> Make sure you understand the differences between GPT and MBR partition schemes, including the MBR size limits and the improvements that GPT makes over MBR.

DRIVE FORMAT

During a clean installation, the drive used for the installation must be formatted, wiping out any existing data on the drive. In Windows, the format type is NTFS, whether the drive is set up as GPT or MBR. Formatting can be performed using Windows Disk Management (see Chapter 3, "Windows 10 Operating System Tools" to learn more) or at the command line using diskpart (see Chapter 2, "Microsoft Command-Line Tools" to learn more).

To format an entire blank drive during a Windows installation, click Custom for the installation type, then Format. To specify how much of the drive to use, click New, then specify the size you want to format (Figure 9.5). This method is recommended if you want to use part of the drive as a different drive letter or for a different operating system.

> **EXAM TIP**
>
> Make sure you understand that clean installations require drive formatting.

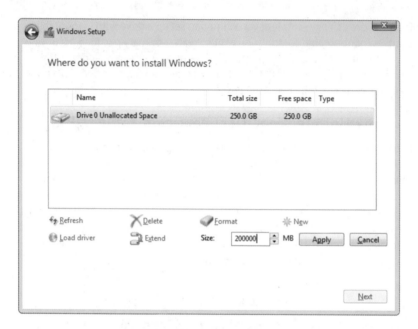

FIGURE 9.5 Preparing to format a portion of a blank drive for use with Windows

UPGRADE CONSIDERATIONS

Planning to upgrade to a new version of Windows? Make sure you follow these guidelines as you prepare for it.

Backup Files and User Preferences

Backing up should include more than just your data files. Make sure you back up user preferences, such as customized templates and spelling dictionaries in Microsoft Office, Adobe actions, and other user preferences. You can do this by running a file-by-file backup, using tools such as Windows 10 and 11 OneDrive, File History, and Backup and Restore (Windows 7) (see Chapter 30, "Workstation Backup and Recovery" to learn more about backup). Make sure your backup app is set to back up hidden files and folders, as the Windows AppData folder used for some user preferences is a hidden folder.

> **TIP**
> An image backup is designed to be restored completely; image backups do not support file-by-file restoration. Be sure to perform a file-by-file backup, which does allow individual files to be restored.

Application and Driver Support/Backward Compatibility

To discover which installed apps might not work or might need compatibility tweaks on a Windows 10 system being upgraded to Windows 11, download the Microsoft Assessment and Deployment Kit for Windows 11 (ADK). Get it from `https://learn.microsoft .com/en-us/windows-hardware/get-started/adk-install` and install the Application Compatibility Tools. Run the Compatibility Administrator (64-bit) from the Windows 10 Start menu and have it search the default path for your applications. When it is finished, it lists installed applications that have fixes in its Search For Fixes window. Click the app to view the fixes that will be applied by Windows 11 after it's installed. You can also use the Compatibility Administrator to look up apps that are not installed and see if they will work.

Hardware Compatibility

One way to discover any hardware compatibility issues with an upgrade to Windows 11 from Windows 10 is to run the Windows 11 Installation Assistant, available from the Microsoft download page for Windows 11 (`www.microsoft.com/en-us/ software-download/windows11`). Click Download Now in the Windows 11 Installation Assistant section of the page. To start the upgrade, click Accept And Install. To quit, click Decline.

To research hardware compatibility for hardware that is not installed or that you are considering purchasing, open the Microsoft Hardware Compatibility List (HCL). The HCL (`https://partner.microsoft.com/en-us/dashboard/hardware/ search/cpl`) can be searched by vendor, model, or Windows version to determine compatible products.

> **EXAM TIP**
> Make sure you know that upgrade preparations include backing up data and settings, checking application and driver compatibility, and verifying hardware compatibility. Practice these steps with physical or virtual machines.

FEATURE UPDATES

With current versions of Windows (Windows 10 and Windows 11), Microsoft is providing major updates about twice a year, using the last two digits of the year and suffixes 1H and 2H to name the update, such as Windows 11 22H2. These updates typically include new and improved features as well as updates to improve reliability and security.

Apple's macOS major updates (such as from macOS 12, Monterey to macOS 13, Ventura) occur about once a year, with minor updates between. Linux distro updates vary greatly in frequency, but updates for one of the most popular distros, Ubuntu, occur about every six months.

Product Life Cycle

With updates to Windows occurring much more frequently than in the past, the product life cycle for any Windows release is much shorter now than in the days of Windows 7. For example, releases of Windows 10 prior to 21H1 all reached their end of servicing dates in 2021 or before. However, because Microsoft provides free Windows 10 updates, Windows 10 will be supported through October 25, 2025. Windows 11 releases 22H2 and earlier will not be serviced after October 8, 2024, but Windows 11 has no announced end-of-support date.

For specific information about all types of operating systems for desktop and mobile devices as well as applications, see the End of Life website at `https://endoflife.date`.

To keep an operating system or application supported until the end of support, be sure to install all updates as they become available. When planning operating system or application upgrades to a new version, keep the end-of-support dates in mind.

> **NOTE**
>
> To determine the life cycle of any Microsoft operating system or application, go to `https://learn.microsoft.com/en-us/lifecycle`. You can search by product or by year.

> **EXAM TIP**
>
> Make sure you understand product life cycles and how to keep operating systems and applications up-to-date.

CERTMIKE EXAM ESSENTIALS

► If you are maintaining existing systems, repair or upgrade installations are the most common. However, new system builds or drive replacements often involve clean installations.

► Checking hardware and software compatibility before starting installations helps you avoid the frustration of abandoning an installation because the hardware or software won't work with the new or upgraded operating system.

► Be prepared to download application and driver updates before or immediately after an operating system upgrade to keep the system working.

Practice Question 1

You are preparing to install Windows and Linux on a variety of systems in your office. You want to use the same software tool for both installations. Which of the following is the best choice to prepare your installation media?

A. DHCP
B. Rufus
C. GPT
D. Recovery Partition

Practice Question 2

Your client has discovered some problems with missing data files and user preferences after completing an operating system upgrade. Which of the following provides the best solution?

A. Restore from an image backup.
B. Restore from a file-by-file backup.
C. Run a repair installation.
D. Check the compatibility administrator report.

Practice Question 1 Explanation

This question is designed to test your real-world understanding of software installation tools. Let's consider each of these answers.

1. The first answer (A, DHCP) is incorrect. DHCP is used to assign IP addresses to computers on a network. While network installations use DHCP, it is not an installation tool.

2. The next answer (B, Rufus) is the best choice. Rufus can prepare installation media for both Windows and Linux operating systems.

3. The next answer (C, GPT) is incorrect. GPT is an advanced disk partitioning method used with drives larger than 2.2 TB, but it is used during installation, not as an installation tool.

4. The last answer (D, Recovery Partition) is incorrect. Recovery Partition is used to restore a system to its as-shipped configuration, not for a new installation.

Correct Answer: B. Rufus

Practice Question 2 Explanation

This question is designed to test your knowledge of solving upgrade problems.

Let's evaluate these answers one at a time.

1. The first answer (A, Restore from an image backup) is incorrect. An image backup doesn't store individual files but rather a complete image of the system in its current condition. Restoring an image backup wipes out the upgrade and the upgrade would need to be restarted.

2. The second answer (B, Restore from a file-by-file backup) is the best option. Individual data files and user preferences can be restored. In a worst-case scenario, the image backup could be restored if the file-by-file restore process doesn't work.

3. The third answer (C, Run a repair installation) is incorrect. A repair installation will not restore missing files lost during the upgrade process.

4. The last answer (D, Check the compatibility administrator report) is incorrect. The report identifies applications that will need fixes after an operating system upgrade or those that are incompatible. It doesn't identify lost files.

Correct Answer: B. Restore from a file-by-file backup

macOS

Core 2 Objective 1.10: Identify common features and tools of the macOS/ desktop OS.

Computers running macOS are popular in schools, at home, and for creative work in corporations. Thus, it's likely you will probably be working on them at some point in your career.

In this chapter, you will learn everything you need to know about A+ Certification Core 2 Objective 1.10, including the following topics:

▶ **Installation and Uninstallation of Applications**
▶ **Apple ID and Corporate Restrictions**
▶ **Best Practices**
▶ **System Preferences**
▶ **Features**
▶ **Disk Utility**
▶ **FileVault**
▶ **Terminal**
▶ **Force Quit**

INSTALLATION AND UNINSTALLATION OF APPLICATIONS

Most installations of macOS apps are performed through the App Store, but unless macOS is configured to block other sources, you can also install apps from direct downloads or from media (USB, network, optical disc). In the following sections, we'll look at the file types used for installation, how to install apps from the App Store, and how to uninstall apps.

File Types

There are three file types that can be installed in macOS:

▶ DMG
▶ PKG
▶ APP

Here's how they differ and how they are installed.

DMG

A DMG file (with the extension `.dmg`) is a disk image file used by Apple for distributing macOS operating systems and updates, and it is also used by many third-party app vendors as well. To install an app stored as a DMG file, you can double-click or Control-click it and select Open With ➢ DiskImageMounter (Default), as shown in Figure 10.1. Follow the prompts to install the app.

FIGURE 10.1 Installing a DMG file from the Downloads folder

PKG

A PKG file (with the extension `.pkg`) is an installer file for macOS software (see the `XZ.pkg` file shown in Figure 10.1). It is a self-extracting compressed archive file that can contain multiple files and folders. To install a PKG file, double-click it to open it with Installer, or Control-click the file and select Open With ➢ Installer.

APP

An APP file (with the extension `.app`) is what Apple calls a "package bundle," a folder (or directory) that contains the files needed for the app to run. The preinstalled apps in macOS as well as apps from the App Store are stored as APP files. To see the contents of an APP file, open the Finder and go to the `Applications` folder. Control-click the application and select Show Package Contents. Click the `Contents` folder, and you will then see the `MacOS` and other folders (Figure 10.2). The `MacOS` folder contains the executable file.

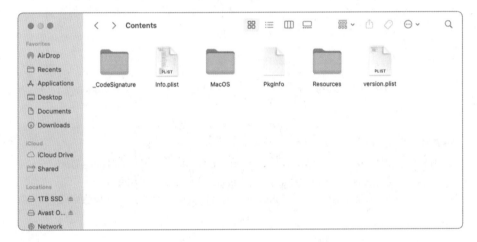

FIGURE 10.2 Examining the contents of an APP folder

App Store

When you install an app from the App Store, the app is copied directly from the store listing into your computer's `Applications` folder. It is installed as an APP file in the `Applications` folder.

Uninstallation Process

To uninstall any macOS application, regardless of how it is installed, follow these steps:

1. Open the Finder and click the app icon, then either drag the app icon to the trashcan icon (Trash) or Control-click the icon and select File ➢ Move To Trash.
2. Provide the administrator name and password to continue.
3. Open the Trash.

4. Click the app icon.
5. Click Empty Trash (Figure 10.3).

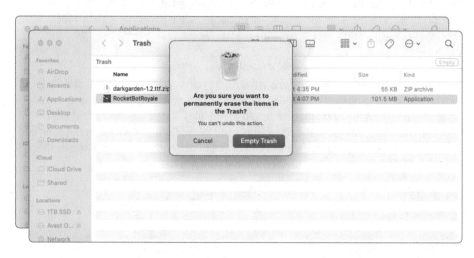

FIGURE 10.3 **Emptying the Trash to finish uninstalling a macOS app**

EXAM TIP

For the Core 2 1102 exam, be sure you can identify the macOS file types DMG, PKG, and APP. Know that App Store apps are installed as APP files in the Applications folder. And be familiar with the app uninstallation process.

APPLE ID AND CORPORATE RESTRICTIONS

An Apple ID enables a macOS user to add or remove software, use iCloud for music and for backups, and perform other tasks that are not necessarily okay with IT management. Apple enables a company to create Managed Apple IDs to improve the security of the macOS devices used in their business.

Managed Apple IDs are created using Apple Business Manager from standard Apple IDs. Managed Apple IDs support Google Workspace or Microsoft Active Directory (Azure AD) domains.

Managed Apple IDs don't support personal-oriented features such as Apple Pay, some iCloud services, for-pay or free downloads from the App Store/iTunes Store/Apple Books, media services, Find My (Device), some continuity features, adding of HomeKit devices to the Home app, or channel management with News Publisher.

> **NOTE**
>
> To learn more about Managed Apple IDs and Apple Business Manager, visit `https://support.apple.com/guide/apple-business-manager/welcome/web`.

BEST PRACTICES

As with other operating systems, it's important for you to know how to apply best practices for backup, antivirus, and updates/patches to macOS. The following sections cover these important issues.

Backups

The macOS Time Machine provides easy-to-use backup for the contents of your system, excluding log files, cache files, and some app settings. It creates backup versions so you can get back either the most recent version of a file or an earlier version. See "Time Machine" later in this chapter for details.

Antivirus

Although macOS is not targeted as often by malware and viruses as Windows, protecting macOS systems from malware and viruses is important. Although the App Store has some antivirus and antimalware apps available, most of the major vendors' products, both free and for-pay, for macOS are available from their own websites. These include TotalAV, Avast, Bitdefender, Norton, AVG, Malwarebytes, and Kaspersky, among others.

> **EXAM TIP**
>
> If you want to install an antivirus/antimalware app not available from the App Store, you must use Security & Privacy's General tab to permit downloads from other locations. See Figure 10.9 in the section "Security & Privacy" later in this chapter.

Updates/Patches

System Preferences has a software update feature that informs you of updates for macOS and for apps installed from the App Store. An indicator on the Software Update icon in System Preferences lets you know the number of updates available. Click it, then click Update Now to start the update. If you prefer automatic updates, select Automatically Keep My Mac Up-To-Date. Click Advanced to choose whether to automatically install as well as download updates (see Figure 10.4).

FIGURE 10.4 Using Software Update to install a macOS update

If you use apps other than those from the App Store, check individual apps for their update and patch procedures.

SYSTEM PREFERENCES

System Preferences (Figure 10.5) is the macOS equivalent of Windows' Control Panel and Settings menus. Use it to configure macOS hardware, backup, and security settings. Let's look at some of these preferences.

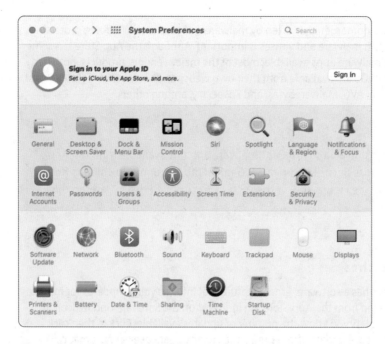

FIGURE 10.5 System Preferences reminds you to sign in with your Apple ID to finish setting up your system.

Displays

Use Displays (Figure 10.6) to set up one or more displays, including resolution, brightness, color profile, and with two or more displays, their arrangement. Each display has separate settings. Click the Night Shift button to set up a schedule for adjusting the screen colors after dark.

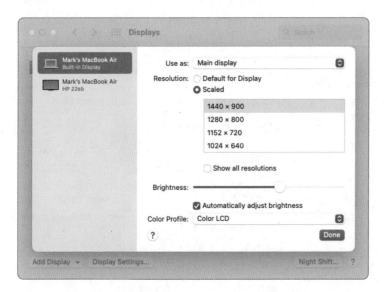

FIGURE 10.6 Displays lets you configure the resolution and other settings for each display separately.

Network

Use Network to display and configure network connections. For details, select a network connection and click Advanced. The Advanced dialog box has tabs for the connection type (Wi-Fi in this example), TCP/IP settings, DNS servers, WINS settings used on Windows networks, 802.1X security, Proxies, and Hardware (network adapters). Figure 10.7 shows the Network dialog box and the Hardware tab of the Advanced dialog box for a Wi-Fi connection.

Printers & Scanners

Use Printers & Scanners to add and manage printers, scanners, and multifunction devices (Figure 10.8). Note that CompTIA lists Printers and Scanners as separate objectives.

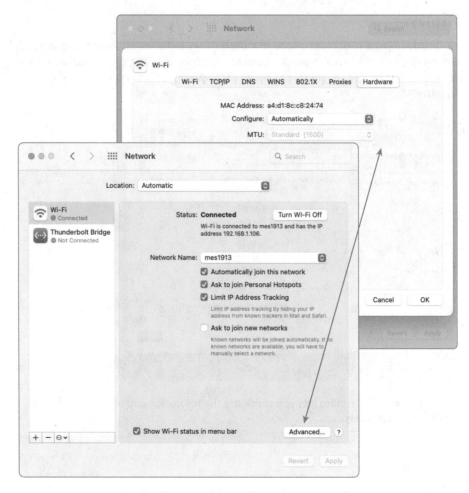

FIGURE 10.7 Network dialog boxes

Security & Privacy

Use Security & Privacy to adjust a variety of ways to protect your system and your privacy. The General tab (Figure 10.9) is used to configure when the Lock Screen function starts after a period of idleness and to choose whether to permit non–App Store software installations.

FIGURE 10.8 Scanning an old photo with Printers & Scanners

The Privacy tab (Figure 10.9) is used to determine which apps can use a particular service or feature. FileVault is covered later in this chapter, and Firewall is used to enable or disable the macOS firewall. Note that CompTIA only lists Privacy as an objective, but Privacy is part of Security & Privacy in the macOS.

> **EXAM TIP**
> Security & Privacy and some other preferences in System Preferences require you to click the closed padlock icon shown in Figure 10.9 and provide administrator login information before you can make changes.

Accessibility

Accessibility (Figure 10.10) provides a wide variety of settings to make macOS use easier for users with physical limitations. It's comparable to the Ease of Access feature in Windows.

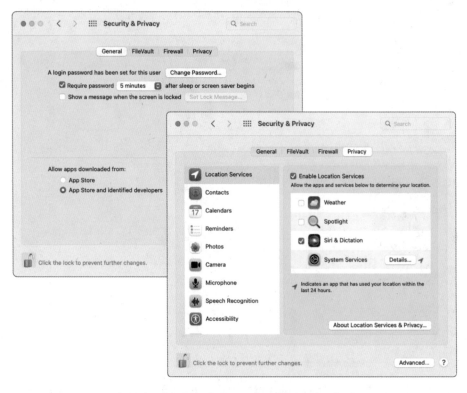

FIGURE 10.9 Security & Privacy's General and Privacy tabs

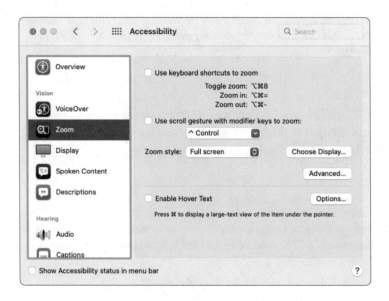

FIGURE 10.10 Accessibility's Zoom options

> **NOTE**
>
> The keystrokes (keyboard shortcuts) shown in Figure 10.10 for Zoom are Option+Command+8 (toggle zoom), Option+Command+= (zoom in), and Option+Command+- (zoom out).

Time Machine

Use Time Machine (Figure 10.11) to configure the macOS backup utility. Time Machine can back up to local drives connected by USB or Thunderbolt ports, AirPort Time Capsules, or network-attached storage (using the SMB protocol).

FIGURE 10.11 Running Time Machine

When setting up Time Machine, you must enter a password and provide a hint. Lose the password, and your backups can't be accessed. Apple recommends using the Apple File System (APFS) or APFS Encrypted filesystems for a Time Machine drive, but it also supports backing up to MacOS Extended filesystems as well as Xsan drives. Time Machine creates scheduled backups and will make local backup snapshots if the backup drive is not available.

To learn more about APFS, see Chapter 8, "Operating System Types."

To restore a file to its original location (Figure 10.12), navigate to the location with the Finder, search for **Time Machine On This PC**, start it, select the backup with the version you want, select the file(s) you want to restore, and click Restore.

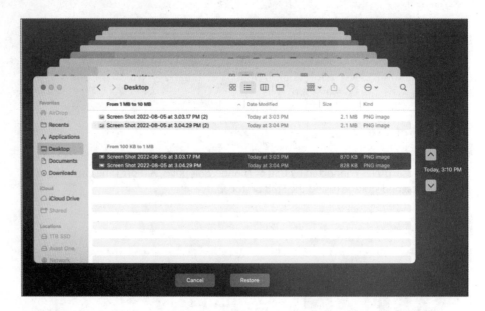

FIGURE 10.12 Restoring selected files to the desktop with Time Machine

---

EXAM TIP

To be prepared, practice with macOS System Preferences. For the exam, you need to be familiar with Displays, Networks, Printers & Scanners, Security & Privacy, Accessibility, and Time Machine.

FEATURES

The macOS operating system also has a variety of features to make your work easier, including multiple desktops with Mission Control, iCloud, Keychain for secure password and network setup storage, Spotlight search, iCloud media storage and Find My Device location, gestures for mice and touchpads, the Finder file manager, Remote Disc optical drive access, and Dock app listing.

Multiple Desktops and Mission Control

The macOS operating system supports multiple desktops. Use the Mission Control app to copy or move apps between different desktops. You can use keyboard or mouse shortcuts to make Mission Control even more convenient (Figure 10.13).

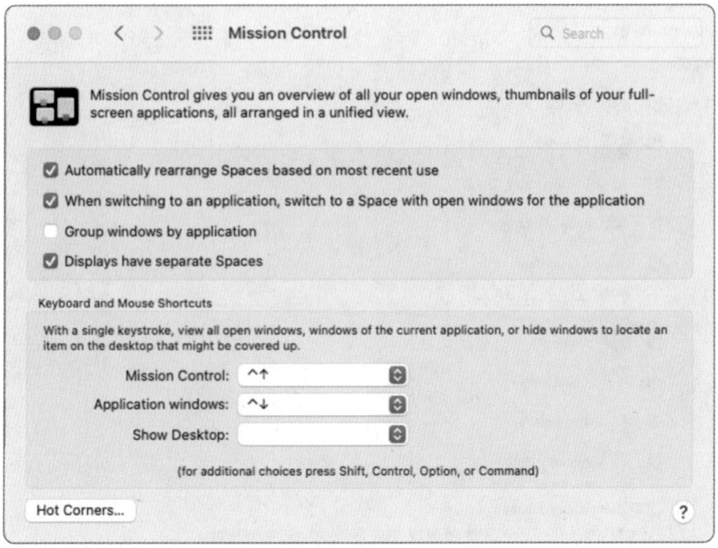

FIGURE 10.13   Mission Control's options

iCloud

The iCloud app can store passwords, photos, and documents, and can be used to help find your Apple devices. Apple ID is used to enable iCloud, Keychain, and other services. Note that all Apple devices for this account are listed in the Apple ID dialog box (Figure 10.14).

> **NOTE**
>
> For more details about iCloud, see www.apple.com/icloud.

Keychain

When you browse to a new website that requires a login and Keychain is enabled, Keychain offers to store your username and password securely. It can also store credit cards, Internet accounts, and Wi-Fi passwords for you. To view your saved passwords, open Passwords in System Preferences.

Spotlight

Spotlight is the macOS search tool. You can open it by pressing Command+spacebar, or by clicking the magnifying glass icon in the top-level menu. Spotlight searches your system for matching or related apps and content as well as the web. In Figure 10.15, the search for **Screen Shot** has found the keyboard (used to create screen shots), a number of Screen Shot files, and matching web content. Click a match to open it.

FIGURE 10.14 Enabling iCloud and other services with Apple ID

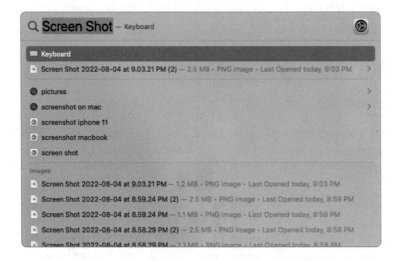

FIGURE 10.15 Searching for Screen Shot with Spotlight

Gestures

Macs don't have touchscreens, but the support for gestures using the trackpad (Apple-speak for touchpad) and the Magic Mouse help to make up for it. Some useful gestures for trackpad are:

- ▶ Launchpad—Pinch to close using four or five fingers.
- ▶ Switching apps in full-screen—Use three or four fingers to left-swipe or right-swipe.
- ▶ Mission Control—Swipe up using two fingers.

Want more? Go to Trackpad in System Preferences (Figure 10.16) where you can select gestures you want to add. Don't want a gesture? Deselect its check box.

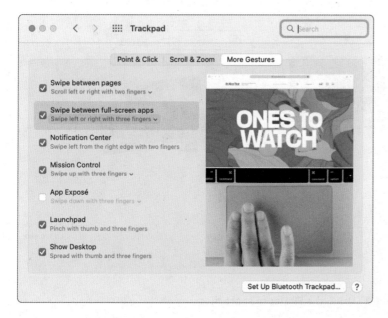

FIGURE 10.16 Enabling more trackpad gestures

Some useful gestures for Magic Mouse (which has a touch-sensitive cover) are:

- ▶ Zoom up—Control key plus one-finger scroll.
- ▶ Switching apps in full screen—Use two fingers to left-swipe or right-swipe.

Want more? Open Mouse in System Preferences.

Finder

The macOS equivalent of Windows File Manager is the Finder. To go quickly to particular types of content, use the shortcuts in the left pane. Use the top-level menu to change how files are viewed, share them, and tag them in categories. In Figure 10.17, the Finder is used to select recent files, determine their total size and creation date(s), and share them.

> **NOTE**
>
> For more details about the Finder, visit `https://support.apple.com/en-us/HT201732`.

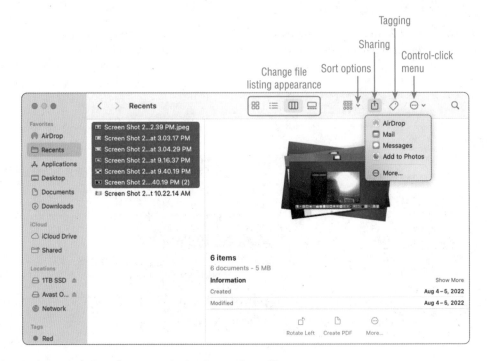

FIGURE 10.17 Using the Finder to share files

Remote Disc

The Remote Disc feature is designed to share a built-in optical drive on a Mac with another Mac that lacks an optical drive. This feature is used only for reading media, not for burning media. This is performed through the System Preferences menu on the Mac with an optical drive with Sharing. For more details, see `https://support.apple.com/en-us/HT203973`.

If you want to share a Windows PC's optical drive with a Mac, the official answer is to install DVD or CD Sharing Update 1.0 for Windows and enable sharing in the Control Panel.

TIP

The DVD or CD Sharing software hasn't been updated in years and doesn't work with Windows 10 or 11. With these versions of Windows, set up the optical drive as a shared drive in Windows, make sure there's a user account on the Windows PC that the Mac can log into, make sure the Mac and the PC are on the same network, and use the Finder on the Mac to find the computer, log into it, and open the drive.

Dock

Dock provides shortcuts to commonly used apps, and its default location shows running apps (marked with a dot under the icon) along the bottom edge of the screen. Click Dock & Menu Bar in System Preferences to change the size of the Dock & Menu bar, to enable magnification as you point to an icon, the position (left, right, or bottom edges), and other behaviors. Click a category in the left pane (not all are shown) for more settings. Learn more about the Dock & Menu Bar at `https://support.apple.com/en-us/HT201730`. Figure 10.18 shows Dock & Menu Bar and its System Preferences after turning on Magnification.

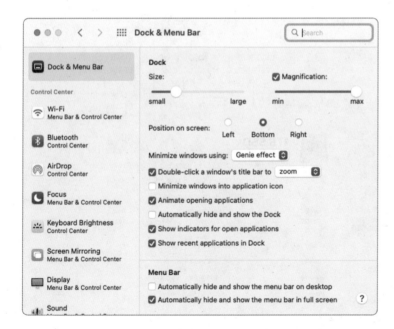

FIGURE 10.18 Using the Dock & Menu Bar in System Preferences to enable Magnification

DISK UTILITY

Use Disk Utility (Figure 10.19) to prepare drives for use with macOS, including for additional storage, for use with Time Machine, or for image backups. Disk Utility can be run at startup by pressing and holding the Command and R keys until it starts. You can then run the First Aid disk repair program from Disk Utility. You can also start Disk Utility by using Spotlight Search to locate it, or from the Finder or Launchpad. You can prepare a drive with any of the filesystems supported by Time Machine, or if you want to use the drive with both macOS and Windows, you can use exFAT or MS-DOS (exFAT is recommended unless you are working with a very old version of Windows). Linux can also use exFAT, so it's the best filesystem to use when all three operating systems need to share an external drive.

To learn more about filesystems supported by Windows, macOS, and Linux, see Chapter 8.

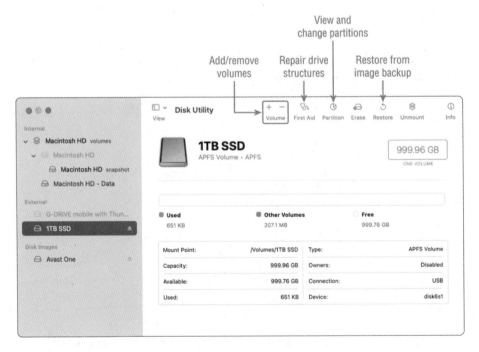

FIGURE 10.19 Using Disk Utility to view an SSD's details

In Apple-speak, the term "Restore" is used when you copy from a source to a destination, even if you are making an image file.

To create an image of a macOS system:

1. Erase the drive you want to use for the image.
2. Select the volume you created during erasure; it will be the destination drive.
3. Choose Edit ➤ Restore from the Disk Utility top-level menu.
4. Confirm the source drive (Macintosh HD).
5. Click Restore to copy the source to the destination (Figure 10.20).
6. To restore the image, boot the computer to Disk Utility and choose Edit ➤ Restore.

> **TIP**
>
> See https://support.apple.com/guide/disk-utility/ restore-a-disk-image-to-a-disk-dskutl14078/mac for more information about the macOS image creation process.

External drive icon

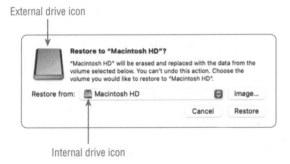

Internal drive icon

FIGURE 10.20 Using Disk Utility to restore the onboard macOS drive to an external drive as an image file

FILEVAULT

Any system with valuable personal or business information should be encrypted. FileVault is macOS's whole-disk encryption program (similar to Microsoft's BitLocker). It makes the system drive unreadable if the encryption key is not provided. Even if the drive is removed from the Mac, no key = no access.

To turn on FileVault, open System Preferences, click Security & Privacy, select the FileVault tab, and click the lock to make changes. Click Turn On FileVault.

You have the option to use your iCloud account to unlock your drive and reset your password or make a recovery key. The iCloud or recovery key is necessary only if a user cannot log into the system.

After you make a recovery key (recommended), be sure to keep it safe by printing or making a screen shot of it and keep it stored away from your Mac for safekeeping. The encryption process can take several hours, so do it as the last thing you do before going home from work or going to sleep.

TERMINAL

The macOS Terminal functions similarly to the Linux Terminal, and supports many of the same commands, including top, ps, ping, and sudo (for superuser/root, similar to Windows Administrator privileges for some commands). Some other commands you will want to know are shutdown, du (subdirectory space usage), whois (domain), ifconfig, and kill PID. Figure 10.21 illustrates using top, kill, and pmset -g batt (displays battery charge/AC power status) in macOS Terminal.

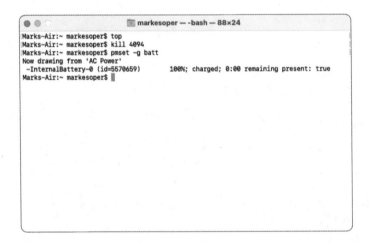

FIGURE 10.21 Running ps, kill, and pmset -g batt in macOS Terminal

TIP

Visit www.igeeksblog.com/macos-terminal-commands for a list of useful macOS Terminal commands.

FORCE QUIT

If you have a balky app in Windows, you can open Task Manager to kill it. In macOS, you open Force Quit Applications to choose the app you want to shut down. You can open Force Quit Applications by pressing Command+Option+Esc, by choosing it from the Apple menu, or by clicking the app's icon in the Dock. From the Force Quit menu (Figure 10.22), select the app you want to close and click Force Quit.

FIGURE 10.22   Preparing to force quit Photos

EXAM TIP

Prepare for the Core 2 1102 exam by making sure you understand the purpose of each of the three file types used for installation (DMG, PKG, and APP); how Managed Apple IDs are used for corporate restrictions; how System Preferences (Displays, Networks, Printers & Scanners, Privacy, Accessibility, and Time Machine) are used; how multiple desktops and Mission Control, Keychain, Spotlight, iCloud, Gestures, Finder, Remote Disc, and Dock are used; and how Disk Utility, File Vault, Terminal, and Force Quit are used.

CERTMIKE EXAM ESSENTIALS

▶ Backups and updates/patches use macOS features that are built into the OS, but for antivirus and antimalware protection you must use third-party apps.

▶ The macOS application interface uses a relatively small window because their file and other menus are always located at the top of the screen. As you click each app, its menu shows up at the top of the screen.

▶ Some features such as iCloud and Keychain are not available until you create an Apple ID and use it to sign in when prompted.

Practice Question 1

You are preparing a portable hard disk to use as a cross-platform data shuttle between macOS and Windows computers with Disk Utility. Which of the following filesystems should you use?

A. APFS

B. exFAT

C. HFS+

D. Any of the above

Practice Question 2

Your client wants to encrypt a macOS drive using BitLocker but is chagrined to discover that macOS doesn't have BitLocker. When you remind the client that there is full-disk encryption in macOS called FileVault, the next question is, where is it? Which of the following menus or features is used to set up and use FileVault?

A. Disk Utility

B. Dock

C. Security & Privacy

D. Time Machine

Practice Question 1 Explanation

This question is designed to test your real-world understanding of macOS and Windows filesystems. Let's evaluate these answers one at a time.

1. The first answer (A, APFS) is incorrect. APFS is an Apple-specific filesystem. Windows would require using special drivers to use the drive.

2. The next answer (B, exFAT) is correct. The exFAT filesystem was designed for large drives in a cross-platform environment.

3. The next answer (C, HFS+) is incorrect. Although this is no longer the default filesystem for macOS, it is still supported, but like APFS, Windows does not support it without special drivers.

4. The last answer (D, Any of the above) is incorrect because only exFAT is supported by both macOS and Windows.

Correct Answer: B. exFAT

Practice Question 2 Explanation

This question is designed to test your knowledge of specific macOS preferences and features. Let's evaluate these answers one at a time.

1. The first answer (A, Disk Utility) is incorrect. FileVault sets up the drive encryption itself.

2. The second answer (B, Dock), is incorrect. Dock is used to display running programs and shortcuts to other popular programs.

3. The third answer (C, Security & Privacy) is correct. Security & Privacy has a FileVault tab where you can configure and run full-disk encryption.

4. The last answer (D, Time Machine) is incorrect. Time Machine is used to make periodic backups of the macOS system drive.

Correct Answer: C. Security & Privacy

CHAPTER 11

Linux

Core 2 Objective 1.11: Identify common features and tools of the Linux client/desktop OS.

Linux is the unsung operating system, working quietly in the background on everything from tiny Raspberry Pi single-board computers to web servers—and sometimes showing up on desktops as well. In this chapter, you will learn everything you need to know about A+ Certification Core 2 Objective 1.11, including the following topics:

▶ **Common Commands**
▶ **Best Practices**
▶ **Tools**

COMMON COMMANDS

It's not necessary for an A+ Certified technician to become an expert on Linux, but knowing what the commands in this section do and how to use them for typical tasks is definitely necessary to your success on the exam and in an increasingly diverse computing environment afterward.

The commands in the following sections are run from Terminal. Terminal is the equivalent of the Windows command prompt. If you are running Linux in command mode, you are using Terminal. If you are running Linux with a GUI, open the program listing (Activities in Ubuntu, a popular Debian-based Linux distro used in this chapter), and click Terminal to get started (Figure 11.1). To exit Terminal, type **exit**. macOS also has Terminal, and many of the commands are the same as in Linux.

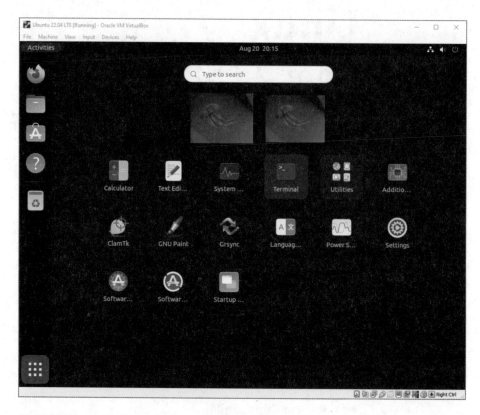

FIGURE 11.1 Preparing to open Terminal from Ubuntu's Activities (programs) menu

TIP

If you do not have access to a computer or a VM running Linux, you can practice Linux commands online free. Visit the Linux Survival website at `https://linuxsurvival.com` to get started.

EXAM TIP

For the Core 2 1102 exam you need to be able to identify the purpose of common Linux commands. For example, the `ls` command is used to list directory contents. The `man` command is used to learn what a command does and its available options. Practice with each command and remember what it does!

ls

The `ls` command is used to display the contents of a directory (folder). Using `ls -l` shows permissions for each file. Use `ls -l directoryname` to show the contents of a folder with permissions. Figure 11.2 shows the results of using `ls -l Pictures` with Ubuntu.

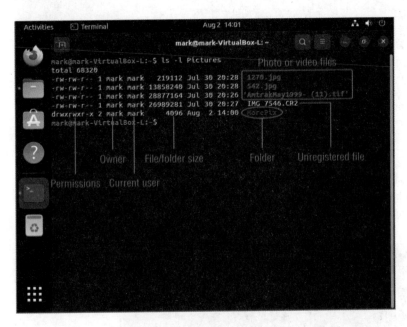

FIGURE 11.2 Using `ls -l` to view the contents of the `Pictures` folder in Ubuntu

The permissions for the files are in three groups. The first group is the permissions granted to the owner (creator) of the file; the second group is the permissions granted to the group (a collection of users defined by the contents of the /etc/group file); and the third group is the permissions granted to everyone else (public).

Note that the `ls -l` listing also shows the owner and the current user of the file. In Figure 11.1, the owner is the current user, but later in this chapter (in the section "chown"), you will see a listing in which the owner is not the current user. For more information about `ls`, type **man ls**.

man

The `man` command displays the manual (command options) for a specified command. For example, `man ls` displays the manual for the `ls` command.

> **TIP**
>
> Use the man *command* (replace *command* with the actual command) to discover additional options and uses for the commands covered in this chapter.

pwd

The `pwd` (print working directory) command shows the name of the current (working) directory (see Figure 11.2). For more information about pwd, use **man pwd**.

df

The `df` ("disk-free") command checks disk space use in Linux. Use `df` to display free space in bytes. Use `df -h` to see free space in MB and GB (see Figure 11.3). For more information about `df`, type **man df**.

```
mark@mark-VirtualBox-L:~$ pwd
/home/mark
mark@mark-VirtualBox-L:~$ df
Filesystem     1K-blocks     Used Available Use% Mounted on
tmpfs              99456     1584     97872   2% /run
/dev/sda3       19946096  8698164  10209392  47% /
tmpfs             497268        0    497268   0% /dev/shm
tmpfs               5120        4      5116   1% /run/lock
/dev/sda2         524252     5364    518888   2% /boot/efi
tmpfs              99452     2412     97040   3% /run/user/1000
mark@mark-VirtualBox-L:~$ df -h
Filesystem     Size  Used Avail Use% Mounted on
tmpfs           98M  1.6M   96M   2% /run
/dev/sda3       20G  8.3G  9.8G  47% /
tmpfs          486M     0  486M   0% /dev/shm
tmpfs          5.0M  4.0K  5.0M   1% /run/lock
/dev/sda2      512M  5.3M  507M   2% /boot/efi
tmpfs           98M  2.4M   95M   3% /run/user/1000
mark@mark-VirtualBox-L:~$
```

FIGURE 11.3 Using pwd, df, **and** df -h **in Ubuntu**

mv

The mv (move) command moves specified files to a specific location. To move a file to a location one level below the current level, type **mv *filename(s) foldername*** as shown in Figure 11.4. For more information about mv, type **man mv**.

```
mark@mark-VirtualBox-L:~/Pictures$ mv 1270.jpg MorePix
mark@mark-VirtualBox-L:~/Pictures$ ls MorePix
1270.jpg
mark@mark-VirtualBox-L:~/Pictures$
```

FIGURE 1 1 . 4   Using mv **and** ls **(to confirm the move) in Ubuntu**

cp

The cp (copy) command copies specified files to a specific location. If no location is provided, the copy is created in the current folder. The syntax of the command shown in Figure 11.5 is cp *filename newfilename*. For more information about cp, type **man cp**.

```
mark@mark-VirtualBox-L:~/Pictures$ ls
542.jpg  'AmtrakMay1999- (11).tif'   IMG_7546.CR2   MorePix
mark@mark-VirtualBox-L:~/Pictures$ cp 542.jpg 542copy.jpg
mark@mark-VirtualBox-L:~/Pictures$ ls
542copy.jpg   542.jpg  'AmtrakMay1999- (11).tif'   IMG_7546.CR2   MorePix
mark@mark-VirtualBox-L:~/Pictures$
```

FIGURE 1 1 . 5   Using cp **and** ls **(to confirm the copy) in Ubuntu**

rm

Use rm to remove (erase) a file. Use the command rm *filename* to erase a file in the current folder (to remove a directory, use rmdir). For more information about rm, type **man rm**.

chmod

Use chmod to change permissions for a specified file or directory. The syntax for chmod is chmod *permissions filename*. The permissions are identified by numbers, as shown in Table 11.1.

TABLE 1 1 . 1   chmod permissions key

Execute	Write	Read	No Permission
7	6	4	0

The first number in the *permissions* part of the command is the permissions for the owner. The second number is the permissions for the group. The third number is the permissions for the public (all other users). For example, 640 would grant write (and read) permissions (6) to the owner; read permissions (4) to the group, and no permissions (0) to the public. Figure 11.6 illustrates viewing the permissions for the file 542.jpg with ls -l and changing them from write, write, read to 640 (write, read, none) using chmod. For more information about chmod, type **man chmod**.

FIGURE 11.6 Using chmod **in Ubuntu**

TIP

Learn more about using chmod and how to convert between letters (as displayed with ls -l) and numbers in permissions by using the Chmod Calculator at www
.chmod-calculator.com.

---

su/sudo

Some Linux commands can be run by any user. However, some commands require you to run a command as another user, typically the root user (equivalent to the Administrator on a Windows system). Use sudo *command* to run the command as the root user (also known as the superuser). The user is prompted to provide the root user's password before the command is completed. For more information about sudo, type **man sudo**.

The su command is used to switch between accounts. If su is run by itself, the user is switched to root after providing the root user's password. For more information about su, type **man su**.

EXAM TIP

Remember the differences between su and sudo! The su command switches the Terminal session to another user in order to run one or more commands. The sudo command allows a user to run a single command as another user such as root.

chown

Use chown to change the ownership of a specified file or directory. chown must be run as the superuser; regular users must add sudo at the beginning of the command. The syntax for regular users is sudo chown *newowner filename*, as shown in Figure 11.7. Using ls -l before and after using chown shows the ownership change. For more information about chown, type **man chown**.

FIGURE 11.7 **Using** chown **in Ubuntu**

apt-get

Use apt-get in Debian-based distributions such as Ubuntu to work with new programs; it requires sudo or a superuser to run. The syntax for regular users is sudo apt-get *function appname*. Two common tasks to perform with apt-get are apt-get *update* to get a new list of packages (programs) and apt-get install *package* to install a specified package (Figure 11.8). Note that you must agree to continue (Y) to perform the installation. For additional information, type **man apt-get**.

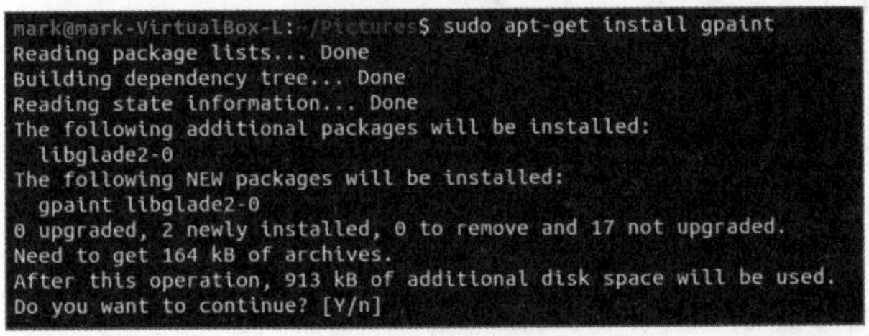

FIGURE 11.8 **Installing gpaint using** apt-get **in Ubuntu**

> **TIP**
>
> If you work with Linux distros that use dnf, learn more about the differences between dnf and apt at https://opensource.com/article/21/7/dnf-vs-apt.

yum

The yum command is the original package manager for Red Hat and similar distros (such as Fedora). It is used for installing, upgrading, and updating packages. Many Red Hat–based distros now use dnf instead. You must be a superuser or use sudo to use yum. To install a package if you are a regular user, use this syntax: sudo yum install *package*. To get a list of all installed and available packages, use sudo yum list. For additional information, type **man yum**.

ip

The ip command is used to display and manage IP connections in Linux. Some useful options are:

▶ ip address displays the IP address of each network connection (see Figure 11.9).

▶ ip route list displays network routes in use (see Figure 11.9).

▶ ip link displays the status (UP or DOWN) of each network connection.

For additional information, type **man ip**.

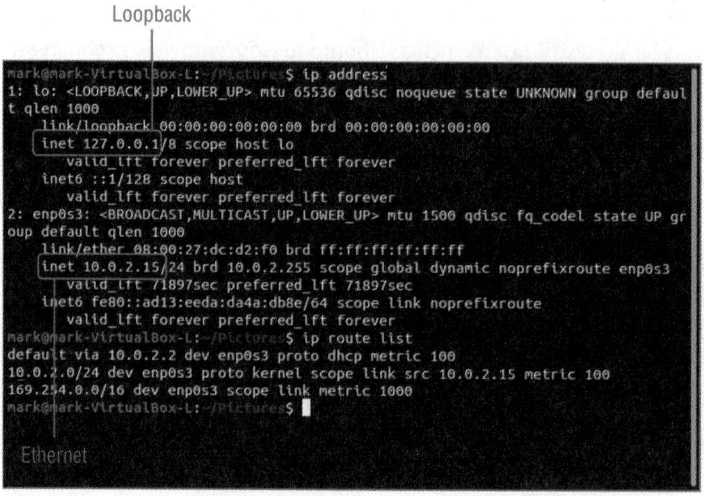

FIGURE 11.9 **Viewing IP addresses and routes with** ip **in Ubuntu 22.04**

grep

The grep command is used to perform text searches. It defaults to exact matches, but it can also perform searches that ignore case, and it can perform searches of all directories beneath the current directory (recursive searching). In Figure 11.10, grep is used to look for a particular CPU manufacturer in the /proc/cpuinfo file (which identifies the CPU in use) with the syntax grep -i *searchterm* /*folder*/*file*. There were two matches in the file. For more information about grep, type **man grep**.

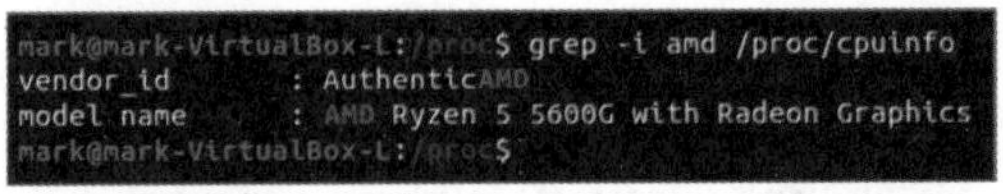

FIGURE 11.10 Finding a word in a file using grep in Ubuntu

ps and *kill*

The ps command displays process IDs (PIDs) for the current user in the current environment. For example, if you are running Terminal from within a GUI version of Linux, you will see only processes happening inside Terminal (refer to Figure 11.11). The kill command is used to terminate running processes using the PIDs displayed by ps. For example, kill 999 kills a process with a PID of 999. For more information about ps, type **man ps**. For more information about kill, type **man kill**.

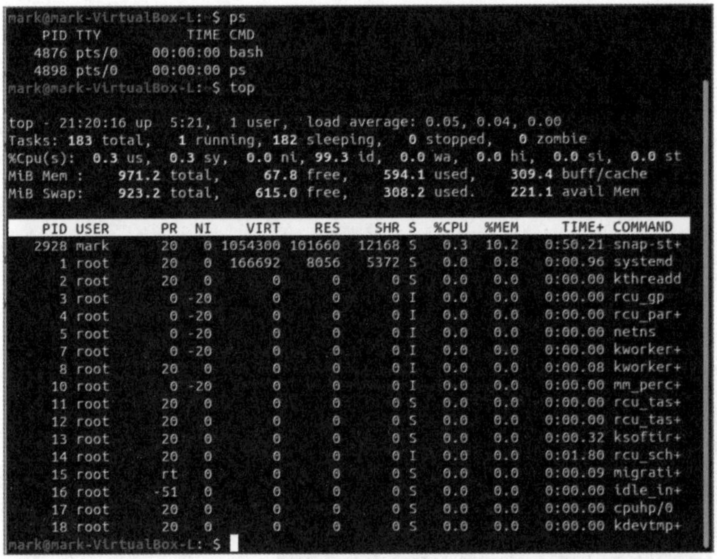

FIGURE 11.11 Comparison of ps and top in Ubuntu

top

The top command displays system resources usage and running processes for all current users (Figure 11.11). For more information about top, type **man top**.

find

The find command can be used to find all kinds of information, including file and folder names, file types by extension, files by owner, find and run scripts by name, and much more. In Figure 11.12, find is used to locate JPEG files and to find files owned by user charlie. For more information about find, type **man find**.

```
mark@mark-VirtualBox-L:~$ find . -name "*.jpg"
./Pictures/MorePix/542.jpg
./Pictures/MorePix/542copy.jpg
./Pictures/542.jpg
./Pictures/542copy.jpg
./snap/firefox/common/.cache/mozilla/firefox/ozf3b5i2.default/settings/main/quick
suggest/icon-160380814674521.jpg
mark@mark-VirtualBox-L:~$ find . -user charlie
./Pictures/542.jpg
```

FIGURE 11.12 Using find **to locate JPEG files and to view files owned by charlie in Ubuntu**

dig

The dig (Domain Information Groper) command is used to display information about DNS. If dig is not installed on Ubuntu or other Debian-based distros, use this command to install it: sudo apt-get install dnsutils. On Red Hat–based distros, use sudo yum install bind-utils.

Use dig with no options to display the DNS server. Use dig *URL* to display the IP address of the URL and the DNS server IP address (Figure 11.13). For more information about dig, type **man dig**.

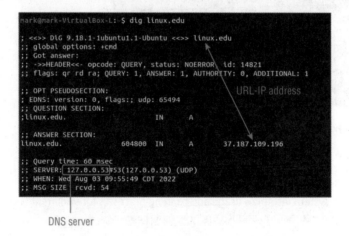

FIGURE 11.13 Using dig **to display the IP address of a website and the DNS server in Ubuntu**

cat

The `cat` command can be used to display the contents of one or more files, create a file, append text to a file, and more. In Figure 11.14, `cat> filename` is used to create a new file, `cat >> filename` is used to append text to a file, and `cat filename` is used to display the contents of the file. For more information about `cat`, type **man cat**.

> **TIP**
>
> After entering **cat>*filename*** or **cat>>*filename***, type the text you want in the file. Press Ctrl+D to save the file. To learn more about using > and >> for redirection with `cat` and other Linux commands, see www.`linuxfordevices`
> .`com/tutorials/linux/`
> `append-text-to-the-end-of-a-file-in-linux`.

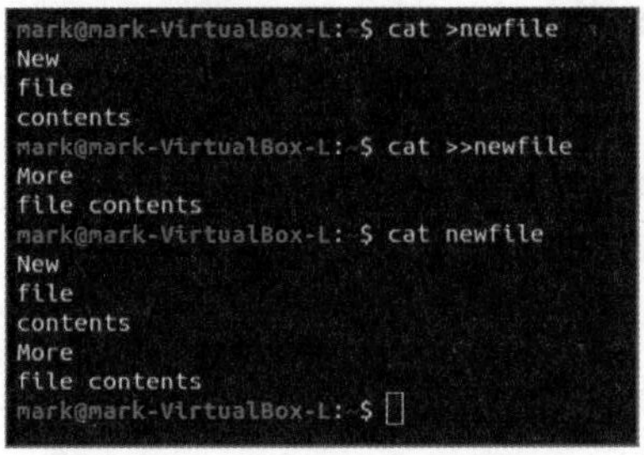

```
mark@mark-VirtualBox-L:-$ cat >newfile
New
file
contents
mark@mark-VirtualBox-L:-$ cat >>newfile
More
file contents
mark@mark-VirtualBox-L: $ cat newfile
New
file
contents
More
file contents
mark@mark-VirtualBox-L: $ []
```

FIGURE 11.14 Using `cat` to create, append text to, and view a file

nano

The nano command starts the popular text editor (replacement for vim and vi), which features easy Control-key menus displayed at the bottom of the screen. In Figure 11.15, nano is being used to view the complete information about the system's CPU by opening / `proc/cpuinfo`. For more information about nano, type **man nano**.

> **EXAM TIP**
>
> For the Core 2 1102 exam, make sure you know the names and major uses of these Linux commands: `ls`, man, pwd, `df`, mv, cp, rm, chmod, su, sudo, chown, apt-get, yum, ip, grep, ps, top, `find`, dig, `cat`, and nano.

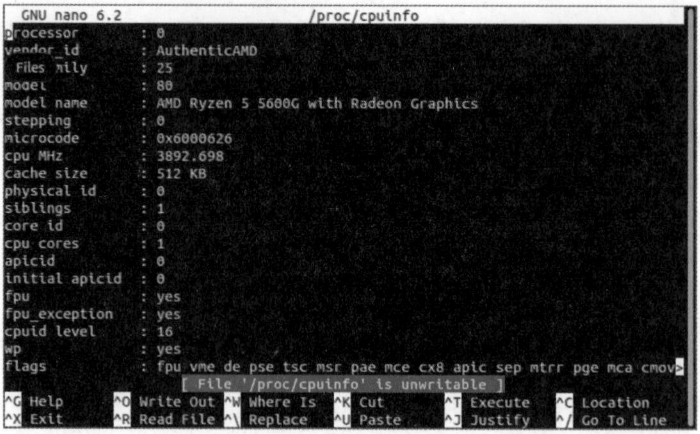

FIGURE 11.15 Using nano **to view the contents of** cpuinfo

BEST PRACTICES

Best practices for Linux include creating backups, installing antivirus and antimalware apps, and regularly checking for and installing updates and patches. The following sections discuss these in more detail.

Backups

Backup software is designed to make copies of your important information so that you can restore it in case of data loss or a system crash. Linux offers a wide variety of backup apps.

A popular choice for Linux GUIs is Deja Dup, which is preinstalled in some distros and can be installed in others using sudo apt-get install deja-dup (Debian-based, including Ubuntu) or other package manager commands used by other Linux distros. Popular command-line backups include rsync, BackupNinja, and Clonezilla.

Look for the ability to make different types of backups, such as periodic full backups with backups of only changed files between full backups, and scheduled backups, and decide if you want local or cloud storage. Some backup apps, such as rsync, have GUI front-ends (Grsync, as shown in Figure 11.16) or can be used to easily create a backup script.

Antivirus

Although Linux is not as widely targeted by viruses and malware, you should still guard against these threats. A wide variety of free and commercial antivirus/antimalware apps are available. ClamAV can be installed and run from the command line. Its GUI front-end, ClamTK, is also run from the command line (Figure 11.17).

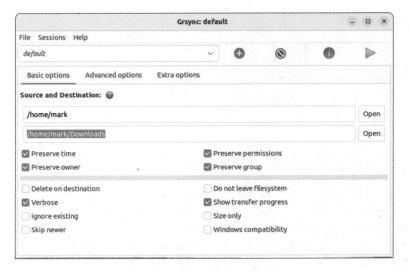

FIGURE 11.16 Setting up a backup with Grsync

FIGURE 11.17 Preparing to scan a system with ClamTK Virus Scanner

TIP

If you are running Linux in a VM, be sure to install antivirus on the VM as well as on the host computer.

Updates/Patches

Whether you manage just one Linux system or dozens, you need to check for updates and patches on a schedule. If you only manage one or a few systems, checking for updates with your package manager (`apt-get` or an equivalent) will do. You can automate the process by creating a script or by opening the GUI's software collection app and clicking Updates.

> **TIP**
>
> The Addictive Tips website has an excellent guide for creating an update script for Ubuntu Linux. It can be adapted to other distros by changing the references to the package manager. See `www.addictivetips.com/ ubuntu-linux-tips/make-updating-ubuntu-simpler`. For distros using yum, see `www.thegeeksearch.com/how-to-install-and- update-software-packages-using-the-yum-command`. For distros using dnf, see `https://linux-audit.com/ automatic-security-updates-with-dnf`.

For larger fleets of Linux systems, consider commercial patch management utilities from companies such as JetPatch (`www.jetpatch.com`), `ManageEngine.com`, and others. Commercial patch management utilities can provide support for multiple Linux distros and avoid the need to create custom scripts for different setups.

TOOLS

Linux has a variety of tools that support other apps and functions of the operating system. In this section we discuss the Shell/terminal and Samba tools.

Shell/Terminal

Unlike Windows, which offers only two command shells, `cmd.exe` and PowerShell (which runs as "Terminal" in Windows 10/11), Linux has a wide variety of shells, which are command interpreters and can also perform additional tasks. The most common one is bash, which is used in Ubuntu and many other distros.

You can use bash and other shells to run a wide variety of scripts, which are like batch files in the Windows command line but are much more powerful. You can create scripts by using a text editor such as `nano` or by using `cat`.

> **TIP**
>
> For many script examples for bash, see `www.howtogeek.com/ 808593/bash-script-examples`. To learn more about other shells, see `www.ubuntupit.com/ linux-shell-roundup-15-most-popular-open-source-linux- shells`.

Samba

Samba enables file and printer sharing between Linux/Unix and Windows systems. Install samba using the default package manager for your distro. Samba runs as a server on Linux. The default is to configure it with the smb.conf configuration file, which is created when samba is installed. Files stored in the shared folder you create during configuration can be accessed by Linux, macOS, or Windows users who have SMB support installed.

> **TIP**
>
> For a great step-by-step tutorial on installing and using Samba on Ubuntu (the steps are similar for other Debian-based distros), see `https://ubuntu.com/tutorials/install-and-configure-samba#1-overview`. For other distros, see `www.linuxfordevices.com/tutorials/linux/linux-samba`.

CERTMIKE EXAM ESSENTIALS

▶ The Linux commands discussed in this chapter work with almost all Linux distros. Although you can use graphical user interface (GUI) equivalents for many of these, we recommend that you learn how to use Terminal and the command-line versions so that you can work confidently with any installation.

▶ It's essential to remember that Linux is case-sensitive. Some command switches are capitalized, and others are lowercase. Also, Linux commands make extensive use of dashes and other punctuation characters. Read examples carefully before you type them in.

▶ Linux best practices are similar to those for Windows and macOS: make backups, use antivirus, and perform updates and install patches.

Practice Question 1

You are using the command `cat` to create a file called `config`. After you create it, your supervisor informs you it needs additional text. Which of the following commands will add text to `config`?

A. `cat>config`

B. `cat<config`

C. `cat -u config`

D. `cat>>config`

Practice Question 2

You need to determine who is the owner of a file. Which of the following commands would you use?

A. `cat`

B. `find`

C. `grep`

D. `chown`

Practice Question 1 Explanation

This question is designed to test your real-world understanding of cat. Let's evaluate these answers one at a time.

1. The first answer (A, cat>config) is incorrect. This command is used to create a file called config.

2. The next answer (B, cat<config) displays the contents of the config file. The < (less than) redirect symbol is not used in config and is ignored. It is not the right answer.

3. The next answer (C, cat -u config) is used to display the contents of the config file (the -u option is ignored). It is not the right answer.

4. The last answer (D, cat>>config) is the right answer. The additional text you type will be added to the end of config when you press Ctrl+D on a blank line.

Correct Answer: D. cat >>config

Practice Question 2 Explanation

This question is designed to test your knowledge of different Linux commands. Let's evaluate these answers one at a time.

1. The first answer (A, cat) is incorrect. cat is used to create, append to, and display the contents of text files.

2. The second answer (B, find) is correct. find locates files by owner, file types by extension, and many other file-related tasks.

3. The third answer (C, grep) is incorrect. grep is used to perform text searches.

4. The last answer (D, chown) is incorrect. chown is used to change the ownership of a file.

Correct Answer: B. find

Domain 2.0: Security

Security is the second domain of CompTIA's A+ Core 2 exam. It covers the core knowledge that IT technicians must understand to be able to secure workstations, mobile devices, operating systems, networks, browsers, and facilities. This domain has 10 objectives:

2.1 **Summarize various security measures and their purposes.**

2.2 **Compare and contrast wireless security protocols and authentication methods.**

2.3 **Given a scenario, detect, remove, and prevent malware using the appropriate tools and methods.**

2.4 **Explain common social-engineering attacks, threats, and vulnerabilities.**

2.5 **Given a scenario, manage and configure basic security settings in the Microsoft Windows OS.**

2.6 **Given a scenario, configure a workstation to meet best practices for security.**

2.7 **Explain common methods for securing mobile and embedded devices.**

    2.8 **Given a scenario, use common data destruction and disposal methods.**

    2.9 **Given a scenario, configure appropriate security settings on small office/home office (SOHO) wireless and wired networks.**

    2.10 **Given a scenario, install and configure browsers and relevant security settings.**

Questions from this domain make up 25% of the questions on the A+ Core 2 exam, so you should expect to see approximately 22 questions on your test covering the material in this part.

CHAPTER 12

Physical Security

Core 2 Objective 2.1: Summarize various security measures and their purposes.

Keeping technology safe involves both physical and electronic security measures. In this chapter, you will learn about physical security measures covered in Core 2 Objective 2.1. The remainder of Objective 2.1 is covered in Chapter 13, Logical Security. This chapter covers what you need to know about:

▶ **Physical security**
▶ **Physical security for staff**

PHYSICAL SECURITY

Physical security uses structures and physical objects to protect offices, laboratories, and warehouses, as well as the information they contain. The different types of physical security are covered in this section.

Access Control Vestibule

One of the most obvious ways to control access into a secure area is an access control vestibule, otherwise known as a *mantrap*. It has two locking doors: one is used for initial entry and the other for entry into the secured area. Before a person entering the first door can access the second door, the person must present some type of credentials to pass through. Credential checking might be in the form of a security guard, an access code, or a badge reader. In any event, without proper authorization, the individual will not be able to continue. An access control vestibule might allow individuals to exit the first door or strand the unauthorized person inside until security can arrive.

Badge Reader

Badge readers can permit users to pass through an access control vestibule or other type of secure access doorway. Badge readers use radio frequency identification (RFID) technology or barcodes to identify the carrier. If the badge information doesn't match a list of authorized users, the carrier cannot enter.

Video Surveillance

Video surveillance can be used to record activity at entrances and exits to a location, as part of an access control vestibule, or to view multiple locations at the same time. Although analog recording systems that use tape are still in use, their low image quality and poor low-light performance has led to greater popularity of digital systems, including systems that use IP wired or wireless networks, cloud storage, and hard drive storage.

Motion Sensors

Motion sensors can be used to turn lights and heating, ventilation, and air conditioning (HVAC) services on and off depending on room occupancy. After normal work hours, they can alert security to abnormal movements in a surveilled space.

Alarm Systems

Alarm systems that use glass-break sensors, motion sensors, video surveillance, heat and smoke detectors, or other means to protect a facility are used in offices, factories, warehouses, and home offices. Although some systems use proprietary wiring, others use UTP or STP network wiring, and many smaller systems use Wi-Fi wireless networking. Alarm systems are typically monitored by in-house or remote monitoring services that can alert fire or law enforcement in the event of an emergency.

Door Locks

Door locks are the most fundamental kind of protection of secure areas. Main entrances, server rooms, wiring closets, computer labs, and technical rooms should be locked and access to each locked room should be on a "need to access" basis.

What type of lock is best? It depends on the situation. Physical locks that use traditional keys can't be hacked remotely. Locks that use access codes or smart cards avoid the need to rekey locks in the event of personnel changes or lost keys.

Equipment Locks

If you want to keep equipment from "walking away," you can go beyond locking the location to locking the equipment in place. Many computers and peripherals include support for the Kensington security lock shown in Figure 12.1.

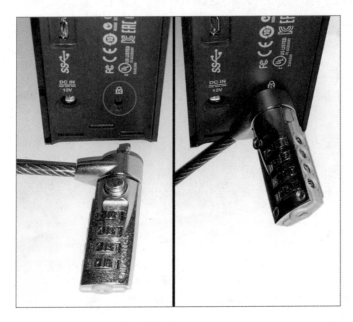

FIGURE 12.1 **A Kensington security lock before attachment (left) and after attachment (right) to a desktop USB hard drive**

USB port locks prevent USB ports from hosting connections, including storage devices. USB port locks are available from companies such as Smart Keeper, Lindy, LogiLink, and others.

Guards

Security guards are the vital human component in physical security. Guards help make access control vestibules more effective, provide an extra layer of security along with other methods discussed here, and can provide on-premises monitoring of security cameras and alarm systems.

Bollards

Bollards are posts, balls, and pillars that permit pedestrian entrance but block motor vehicles. Bollards can be fixed or made removable when occasional vehicle access is needed.

NOTE

To learn more about bollard types and installation best practices, see `www.bollardshop.com.au/blog/` `bollard-installation-best-practices`.

Fences

Fences are useful for providing a barrier to casual entry and to indicate the outer limit of a secured space. The most common type of security fence is chain link. To make this type of fence more effective, it can be combined with alarms, motion detectors, electrification, and barbed wire.

NOTE

To learn more about chain link fences for security, see `https://` `chainlinkinfo.org/security-fencing-guidelines`.

EXAM TIP

Make sure you understand the essential features and benefits of using access control vestibules, badge readers, video surveillance, alarm systems, motion sensors, door locks, equipment locks, guards, bollards, and fences.

PHYSICAL SECURITY FOR STAFF

Physical security isn't just for buildings and structures—it's also for staff. Some physical security measures for staff are designed to make sure that only authorized users can access specific locations and resources, whereas others are designed to protect staff from intruders or each other. Both varieties of physical security are discussed next.

Key Fobs

Key fobs provide access to secured areas by using Bluetooth, RFID, or near-field communication (NFC) to open or close electronic locks.

NOTE

To learn more about how key fob access control works, see `http://blog` `.nortechcontrol.com/key-fob-access-control`.

Smart Cards

A smart card is a credit card–sized card that contains stored information. Smart cards are often used on secure laptops to make certain only the cardholder can start and use the laptops. Other uses for smart cards include stored-value debit cards, hotel guest room access, and other functions.

A smart card used for laptop access or secure facility access might contain identification information, and in that case, it usually has an on-board microprocessor, such as the Europay, Mastercard, & Visa (EMV) chip used on credit and debit cards to create more secure transactions. Contactless smart cards also have an antenna inlay. Smart cards often use a PIN along with the card for access.

> **NOTE**
>
> To learn more about how smart cards work, see `https://electricalfundablog.com/smart-card-works-specifications-types`.

Keys

Mechanical keys continue to be used for securing doors, lockers, toolboxes, and access panels in schools and businesses. Some lock companies offer multiple security levels of locks and keys, enabling keys for a higher-level lock to open lower-level locks. This allows locks of different security levels to be placed as needed while enabling a master key to unlock all locks if desired.

> **NOTE**
>
> To learn more about keys and locks, see `www.sargentlock.com/en` and `www.masterlock.com`.

Biometrics

Biometrics, the use of biological information such as fingerprints, face recognition, voice measurements, and retina scanning, have become increasingly common in both commercial and home technology. Many laptops and mobile devices now include fingerprint readers, and Windows 10/11 computers that support Windows Hello can use built-in or USB-connected fingerprint readers or infrared cameras to identify users.

> **NOTE**
>
> For an introduction to biometric authentication, visit `www.spiceworks.com/it-security/identity-access-management/articles/what-is-biometric-authentication-definition-benefits-tools`.

(continued)

> To learn more about Windows Hello and its setup process, see `https://support.microsoft.com/en-us/windows/learn-about-windows-hello-and-set-it-up-dae28983-8242-bb2a-d3d1-87c9d265a5f0` or search `https://support.microsoft.com` for **Windows Hello set up**.

Retina Scanner

Retina scanners use infrared light to map the blood vessel patterns in the retina, the light-sensitive portion of the rear of the eye. The data created by a retinal scan is stored into an 80-byte computer code and, compared to fingerprint scans, can't be compromised by dirt or incorrect finger placement.

> **NOTE**
>
> Learn more about retina scanning at `www.securityx.ca/blog/retina-scan-security` and `https://getsmarteye.com/how-accurate-are-retinal-security-scans`.

Fingerprint Scanner

Fingerprint scanners work by using a charge coupled device to emit light to illuminate your fingerprint. The fingerprint is converted into an encrypted number that is stored and used for comparison to subsequent scans. The encrypted number, rather than the actual fingerprint, is stored to minimize the risk of privacy violations.

> **NOTE**
>
> Learn more about fingerprint scanning at `https://microkeeper.com.au/blog_item.php?id=Biometric-Fingerprint-Scanner-FAQs` and `https://getsmarteye.com/how-accurate-are-retinal-security-scans`. For help in trouble-shooting fingerprint scanners in Windows 10 and 11, visit `www.asus.com/us/support/FAQ/1047028`.

Palmprint Scanner

Palmprint scanners, more accurately referred to as palm vein scanners, use near-infrared light to read blood vessel patterns in the human hand. Compared to fingerprint scanners, palmprint scanners store up to over a million data points for greater accuracy.

> **NOTE**
>
> Learn more about palmprint scanning at `www.matrixaccesscontrol`
> `.com/blog/facts-about-palm-vein-recognition-system-all-`
> `you-need-to-know` and `https://recfaces.com/articles/`
> `palm-vein-scan`.

Lighting

Security lighting helps detect or deter illegal activity in a specified location, such as a parking lot, building exterior, or building interior. Security lighting that is arranged to help improve video quality for security cameras helps provide higher-quality recording of activity for better identification of vehicles, license plates, and intruders.

For maximum security, security lighting should be arranged to avoid glare, installed in protective light fixtures, and powered by auxiliary generators or high-performance battery backups to keep the lights on in the event of accidental or deliberate loss of power.

> **NOTE**
>
> Learn more about security lighting at `https://commercialledlights`
> `.com/outdoor-lighting` and `www.lightningbugelectric.com/`
> `blog/2016/february/the-importance-of-security-lighting`.

Magnetometers

A magnetometer is similar to a metal detector but is designed to detect ferrous metals (iron and steel) only. A magnetometer can detect ferrous metals at a greater distance than conventional metal detectors. For example, a magnetometer can detect a large object, such as a car at a range of over 30 feet, while a metal detector's typical range is less than 7 feet.

Some security experts believe that by disregarding nonferrous metals, a magnetometer is more useful for detecting weapons than conventional metal detectors and enables faster clearing by allowing people to be scanned to simply walk through.

> **NOTE**
>
> Learn more about the advantages of magnetometers at `https://blog`
> `.uspatriottactical.com/`
> `magnetometers-the-most-practical-personnel-screening-device`.

> **EXAM TIP**
>
> Make sure you understand the essential features and benefits of using key fobs; smart cards; keys; biometrics such as retina scanners, fingerprint readers, and palmprint scanners; lighting; and magnetometers.

CERTMIKE EXAM ESSENTIALS

▶ Physical security measures should be used in combination for maximum protection. For example, use fences, bollards, security lighting, motion sensors, magnetometers, alarm systems, and video surveillance to control the exterior of a facility.

▶ To control access to specific locations inside a facility, use security measures such as access control vestibules and guards. Use door locks and equipment locks to help prevent theft and unauthorized access to equipment. Security lighting and video surveillance are also useful for interior security.

▶ Similarly, use security measures such as access control vestibules, door locks, equipment locks, and guards to control access inside the facility.

▶ Key fobs, smart cards, keys, and biometrics are types of security that control access based on workers' roles and responsibilities.

▶ Security devices such as key fobs, smart cards, keys, and biometrics are some of the ways to control access based on employees' or contractors' roles and responsibilities. For example, office staff with non-line-of-business roles could be restricted from accessing production facilities without an escort, or second-shift or third-shift employees could be restricted from accessing offices after normal business hours.

Practice Question 1

You are responsible for improving internal security for an organization that has leased space in a large warehouse. The leasing company is responsible for external security. Which of the following security measures can you have installed to control access inside the building? (Choose two.)

A. Install magnetometers.
B. Install fences.
C. Use bollards.
D. Install biometric identification systems.

Practice Question 2

Your client is considering purchasing laptop computers that support Windows Hello. Which of the following biometric security features are supported by Windows Hello? (Choose two.)

A. Retina scanner
B. Face recognition
C. Palmprint scanner
D. Fingerprint scanner

Practice Question 1 Explanation

This question is designed to test your understanding of external versus internal physical security. Let's evaluate these answers one at a time.

1. The first answer (A, Install magnetometers) is correct. Magnetometers can easily be installed within leased space for security.

2. The next answer (B, Install fences) is incorrect. Fences are located outside the building and are the responsibility of the leasing company.

3. The next answer (C, Use bollards) is incorrect. As with fences, bollards are external security and are the responsibility of the leasing company.

4. The last answer (D, Install biometric identification systems) is also correct. Biometric identification systems can be used to control access into the leased space and into specified locations.

Correct Answer: A. Install magnetometers and D. Install biometric identification systems

Practice Question 2 Explanation

This question is designed to test your knowledge of the features of Windows Hello. Let's evaluate these answers one at a time.

1. The first answer (A, Retina scanner) is incorrect. Laptops with Windows Hello do not include retina scanners.

2. The second answer (B, Face recognition), is correct. Laptops with Windows Hello include support for face recognition or fingerprint scanners.

3. The third answer (C, Palmprint scanner) is incorrect. Laptops with Windows Hello do not include support for palmprint scanners

4. The last answer (D, Fingerprint scanner) is also correct. Laptops with Windows Hello include support for face recognition or fingerprint scanners.

Correct Answer: B. Face recognition and D. Fingerprint scanner

CHAPTER 13

Logical Security

Core 2 Objective 2.1: Summarize various security measures and their purposes.

Logical security is a security method or measure that can be established with software or a logical process. These logical security measures typically do not fit into the category of physical security or something physically restricting you, as you learned in Chapter 12, "Physical Security." However, the theory of logical security can be applied to physical security to complement it. In this chapter, you will learn what you need to know about the A+ Certification Core 2 Objective 2.1, including the following topics:

► **Logical security**
► **Mobile device management (MDM)**
► **Active Directory**

LOGICAL SECURITY

Physical security is focused on preventing unauthorized individuals and threat actors from physically entering your organization. Logical security is focused on preventing unauthorized individuals and threat actors from accessing your organizations data or systems. In addition, logical security protects you from malware, ransomware, and data leakage, which is an added benefit of preventing unauthorized access. Logical security employs a wide area of devices and methods, such as firewalls, antimalware software, directory permissions, multifactor authentication, and best practices, just to name a few. Each of these topics is addressed in this section.

Principle of Least Privilege

The principle of least privilege is a security concept that states a user should be restricted to the least amount of privileges that they need to do their job. If the end user has administrative privilege on their computer, they have the ability to circumvent security. If the end user circumvents security, then they are an insider threat. If a threat actor exploits the administrative access the end user has, then it is an external threat. This scenario could play out as a malicious email that the user clicks on. In either case, if the end user doesn't need the permission to perform their duties, they should simply not have the permissions. Therefore, providing the user with the least privilege to perform their task is a best practice. As an added benefit, limiting workers' ability to modify the operating system can prevent unintentional misconfigurations.

> **EXAM TIP**
>
> The principle of least privilege is a concept of applying the least amount of permissions to the user for them to do their job.

Access Control Lists (ACLs)

Access control lists (ACLs) are used to restrict the access to applications or data. ACLs can be implemented on network devices to control the flow of network traffic to prevent access to applications. If you had a web server and needed to restrict traffic to the server, as shown in Figure 13.1, you would construct an ACL. It will contain access control entries (ACEs) to allow traffic to the application for the networks you determine should have access and deny access to the application for everyone else. In this example, pseudocode was used; the HR network would be allowed to the web server and all other networks would be denied access to the web server. The last statement in the pseudocode is a permit statement for all other traffic. Network ACLs usually have a default deny statement at the end of their ACLs that is implied.

> **NOTE**
>
> Pseudocode is general code that is not specific to any vendor. It allows a person to convey general concept through code. You can then go back and write the specific code that matches the concept.

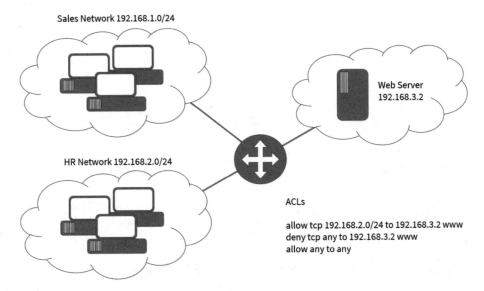

Sales Network 192.168.1.0/24

HR Network 192.168.2.0/24

Web Server
192.168.3.2

ACLs

allow tcp 192.168.2.0/24 to 192.168.3.2 www
deny tcp any to 192.168.3.2 www
allow any to any

F I G U R E   1 3 . 1   Network ACL example

Each vendor will have their own unique syntax for an ACE, but they all follow an action
and condition statement and usually read from left to right, the source of the traffic to the
destination of the traffic. As an example, in the first line of the previous ACL example, the
`allow` is the action.

An ACL can also be used to prevent unauthorized file access on the operating system.
Although it is a similar concept, it is implemented a totally different way and has nothing
to do with restricting network traffic. NTFS is the default filesystem for Windows 10/11,
because it has this inherent security built-in and supports discretionary access control lists
(DACLs), which are nothing more than a list of ACEs. If you want to restrict the access to data
for a Windows group of users, the NTFS filesystem will allow you to create multiple ACEs to
do so. The result is, even if the user is locally logged on and not given explicit permissions,
they will not be able to access the data. The NTFS filesystem will allow for very granular permissions. In Figure 13.2, the Administration Team has read and execute access to the data in
the ACL editor for the data folder.

> **NOTE**
>
> In Chapter 17, "Windows Security," you will learn more about NTFS and share per-
> missions.

> **EXAM TIP**
>
> The key takeaway from this section is that ACLs can be applied to network traf-
> fic or files.

FIGURE 13.2 NTFS ACL example

Multifactor Authentication (MFA)

Authentication is the act of verifying a person's credentials and ultimately proving who they claim to be. Typical security on operating systems and applications has been a combination of a person's username and their password. Username and password combinations are a single factor of identification, and anyone who guesses or steals the username and password can steal the person's credentials.

There are three common authentication factors:

Something You Know   A piece of knowledge that you have in your mind. This authentication factor has historically been based on a username and password combination.

Something You Have   This is based on something you physically have. Typically you will have a key fob or smartcard, but there are several other physical token types.

Something You Are   This authentication factor is based on biometrics: physical characteristics of your body, such as your fingerprint, your voice, or your iris or retinal patterns.

When more than one unique factor is used to authenticate a user, this is known as multifactor authentication (MFA). A best practice is to use two or more unique factors of authentication to authenticate a user. For examples, using a password and fingerprint is a valid MFA method. Using a password and a PIN is not, because they are both something that you know. However, most MFA will consist of two factors of authentication, also known as 2FA.

NOTE

The use of the terms MFA and 2FA are practically interchangeable. 2FA requires that at least two factors of authentication be present for the user to be authenticated. MFA requires the use of authentication techniques from at least two different factors, if not more, for the user to be authenticated. It is rare for any consumer application to require more than two factors of authentication.

EXAM TIP

The use of multifactor authentication (MFA) is a best practice to combat credential theft.

Email

The use of email as an alternate authentication technique is popular with low-security websites, gaming services, and social media, just to name a few, and the list is ever increasing. This is mainly due to the fact almost everyone has an email address and your email address is typically the first piece of information the providers request during sign-up.

When you initially log into a site protected with email as a second factor of authentication, you will initially use the username and password combination you established with the provider during the sign-up process. If this factor of authentication is successful and the username and password are correct, then the second factor will be checked via email. An email containing a 4- to 8-character code will be sent to the email address that you originally established with the provider. The site will then ask you to enter the code emailed to you before you can proceed to log into the site.

WARNING

While you should be familiar with the use of email-based authentication as you prepare for the A+ exam, it's important to know that this is a very weak authentication approach and depends on the security of the user's email account. For example, if a user uses the same password for both their account on your site and their email account, sending an email to that account does not provide any significantly better security benefit than the password alone. If an attacker has the user's password, they will also be able to access the confirmation email.

Hard Token

A hard token is a physical device, which often looks like a key fob or USB thumb drive if you are using a Fast Identity Online (FIDO) key: both serve as a "something you have" authentication factor. A key fob is shown in Figure 13.3. The device works by providing a number that is unique and synchronized with the login server on a time basis, also known as a one-time password (OTP). The number shown on the key fob will typically change every 1 to 5 minutes and will usually be 6 digits in length. A FIDO key will send a series of letters to your keyboard when the device is physically touched, and this is a unique time-based passcode. The devices themselves don't have any communication or ongoing connection with the login server (or site).

FIGURE 13.3 **Hard token example**

The user experience is very simple, but it requires the user to actually have the hard device on their person. After the user enters their initial username and password, the login server or site will require the user to enter their unique number from the hardware token or physically touching the FIDO key depending on the method you are using. If this number matches the number on the server side, then the user is logged on.

Soft Token

A soft token operates identically to a physical (hard) token, except it is software based, hence the name. In an effort to make security more convenient for everyone, hardware token vendors have adopted soft token cellphone apps. These soft token apps are considered a "something you have" authentication factor, as people tend to have their cellphone on them at all times.

An authenticator application is a form of a soft token app, and an example can be seen in Figure 13.4. The cellphone app contains a rotating code to secure sites with 2FA. Using an authenticator app such as Google Authenticator will require a self-enrollment. Typically, you will turn on 2FA on the website and you'll be presented with an initial code to enter or a QR code to scan. Once you have verified the initial code, your login is set up with 2FA and you are typically presented with recovery codes in case you lose your phone. Keep these in a safe place in the event you need to override the authenticator application. Because time can be much more precise on a cell phone, these apps will rotate the code every minute.

FIGURE 13.4 Soft token example

Short Message Service (SMS) and Voice Calls

Short Message Service (SMS), also known as texting, is one of the original forms of "something you have" authentication. In this approach, the user will first log into a website with their username and password, satisfying the first factor of authentication. They will then receive a code on their cellphone and be prompted on the site for the code, satisfying the second factor of authentication.

Alternatively, voice calls may be used to read a code to the user when they answer the telephone. This code is then used in the same way as one sent via SMS.

> **WARNING**
>
> SMS and voice call authentication are no longer considered secure and should be used with extreme caution. The reason for this is that phone numbers may be hijacked by attackers and redirected to a device belonging to the attacker, rendering them insufficient as a "something you have" factor.

MOBILE DEVICE MANAGEMENT (MDM)

Some organizations allow employees to use their personal devices for work purposes. This puts the organization at risk if the device is compromised, stolen, or just misplaced. To help control both corporate-owned and bring-your-own-device (BYOD) personal devices and protect the organization's information on those devices, many organizations use mobile device management (MDM) software. MDM software ensures that a device is of a certain specification; has the proper updates; has antimalware software and encryption; and meets other organizational requirements. Workers will either opt in and comply or the device cannot access company data. MDM software can also allow an organization to partition a device so that any work-related content is put into a special partition on the device. If the device is lost or stolen, or the person leaves the company, the MDM software can delete the organization's data without affecting the personal storage.

ACTIVE DIRECTORY

Active Directory is an incredibly scalable directory service that uses the Lightweight Directory Access Protocol (LDAP) to provide lightning-fast object lookup across an enterprise. Active Directory's main purpose is to organize, file, and look up objects, and although it assists in the authentication process, it doesn't really authenticate the users. Kerberos is used in conjunction with Active Directory to provide authentication of users and computers.

Active Directory consists of several different partitions that serve various functions for the domain, intra-domain functionality, replication, DNS, and most important, the schema of objects. The schema partition describes the attributes of each class of objects in the directory. For example, there are up to 375 attributes that are defined for a user class in Active Directory. However, an average user account will typically have only a few attributes configured, such as first name, last name, middle initial, description, display name and account, just to name a few. Most of your account management is performed in the GUI Microsoft Management Console (MMC) called Active Directory Users and Computers. From this tool you can configure a number of other attributes for the user. You can also manage accounts using PowerShell and other domain tools such as the `net` command.

Domain

A domain is a hierarchical grouping of users, computers, policies, and other objects. This hierarchical grouping allows for centralized administration of user accounts and centralized login. Active Directory domains are named with a Domain Name System (DNS) name, such as `certmike.com`, called the root domain. If you needed to create subdomains, you would add the namespace to the left of the root domain, such as `comptia .certmike.com`. This is why Active Directory is considered scalable and hierarchical. Organizations create subdomains for various reasons; some might be logical separations of objects, regulatory reasons, or regional reasons. However, most organizations never need more than one domain for all their user and computer objects.

A user authenticating to Active Directory is very similar to a person reporting to work and picking up a set of keys to do their job. When the user authenticated to Active Directory, the domain access token is issued, as shown in Figure 13.5. These keys will open various ACLs on resources, as you previously learned in this chapter. When a user is a member of a security group, that key gets attached to the user's domain access token. Then when an ACL is encountered in the operating system, if the key fits the ACL the user is allowed access or denied, depending on the permissions set.

username: mike@certmike.com
password: *************

FIGURE 13.5 **Active Directory security tokens**

> **EXAM TIP**
>
> An Active Directory domain is a hierarchical grouping of users, computers, policies, and other objects for centralized administration of users and computer accounts.

Security Groups

Organizations adopt Active Directory domains for the centralized administration model of user accounts. Organizations also gain the ability to secure resources with these centralized accounts. It is always a best practice to secure resources with groups rather than individual user accounts. By using groups, you maintain the ability to scale Active Directory, because as time goes on it will get increasingly harder to control individual permissions on resources.

All security should be configured with security groups, even if there are only a few users assigned to the resource. There are many reasons for this best practice. The first is that it is simpler to assign a permission once to a group, versus multiple times for each user who needs the same permission.

A second benefit to using security groups is the centralized auditing of permissions. If you need to know who had access to a resource, you just have to open the security group in the Active Directory User and Computers MMC and look at the membership of the security group associated with the resource. Alternately, if you want to know which resources a user has permissions to, open the user in the MMC and view their membership of security groups.

Another best practice related to security groups is the naming of the group upon creation. The name should signify the permission and resource that it will be used to secure, and the group should not be reused for additional permission. As an example, the group `perm_print_colorprinter` allows you to determine the permission level and the resource just by reading the group name. If you have more than one color printer, then add location into the naming of the security group.

> **EXAM TIP**
>
> Security groups are used to assign permissions on resources for ease and scalability of assigning permissions, as well as providing a way to centralize auditing of resource access.

Organizational Units

As you've learned, domains are hierarchal groupings of users and computers. The method of grouping users and computers in Active Directory is the organizational unit (OU). The organization unit allows you to group objects together based on their class, geographic location, function, or cross-function of two or more. You can then apply policies to the OU, so they can apply to the grouping of computers or users. You can even delegate administration of an OU to a junior administrator without having to assign them full permission to Active Directory. OUs should be designed to group objects by the following criteria:

Object Class   Objects can be organized based on their class or type of object. For example, computers and users can be organized into their respective OUs.

Suborganization   Objects can be organized based on their suborganization in the overall organization, such as Sales, Marketing, and HR.

Function   Objects can be organized based on their function in the network, such as servers, workstations, and users.

Geographic Location   Objects can be organized based on their location. Typically, it is best practice to use the airport codes as the OU names to describe the location of the branch.

Hybrid   The OU groupings can be combined so that you can form your own unique hierarchy for your organization. For example, you can use airport codes to represent the various branches, with functions under each airport code, as shown in Figure 13.6.

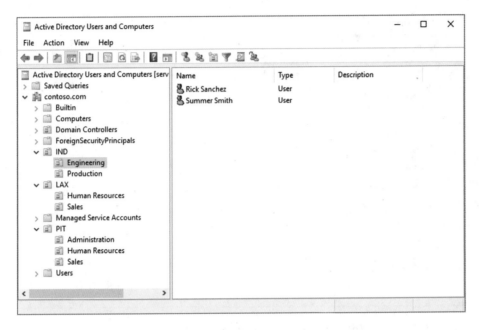

FIGURE 13.6 A hybrid OU structure

Group Policy/Updates

Group Policy is one of the many features of Active Directory, and it enables you to apply policies to control groups of users or computers. An administrator can configure Group Policy and apply it to an organizational unit containing users or computers. You cannot link policies to individual users or computers; instead, you link the Group Policy Object to an organizational unit containing a group of users or computers. Group Policy Objects are created, linked, and edited in the Group Policy Management Console (GPMC), as shown in Figure 13.7.

You can control thousands of settings for both the user and computer objects, as shown in Figure 13.8. These settings are policed by reapplying during the background refresh cycle every 90 minutes to ensure that any user changes are not persistent. However, most of the time if a setting is policed by a GPO it will be grayed out for the user, and they will not be able to change the setting. Group Policy also allows configuration of preferences, which allow for files, Registry, environment variables, and Control Panel items to be modified. Preferences are initially applied on startup of the operating system for computer preferences and at logon for user preferences. The user can then change them after the initial application.

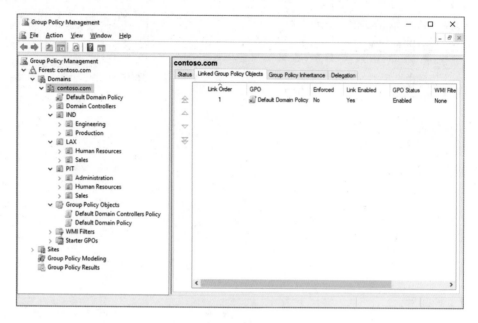

FIGURE 13.7 The Group Policy Management Console

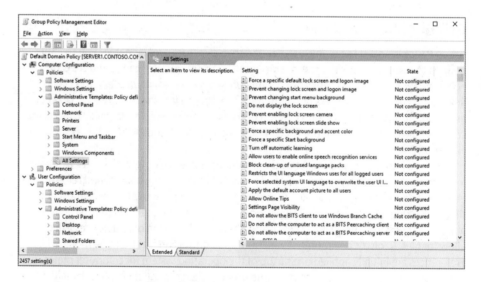

FIGURE 13.8 Group Policy Object settings

Folder Redirection

When a user logs into a computer joined to the network and the user has a roaming profile configured, the profile is completely downloaded to the computer from the network server. When the user logs out of the computer, the profile is completely written back to the network server. During both the logon and logoff, the user should sit and wait until the process is done or risk loss of data. During logon, end users are anxious to get to work, and during logoff they are anxious to leave. Profiles contain user registry, roaming AppData, desktop files, the documents folder, and several other folders. Over time the profile can really swell in file size, sometimes gigabytes in size, which can equate to longer logon and logoff times.

Folder redirection is an operating system feature that is controlled via Group Policy settings. It allows the redirection of portions of users' profile folders to a network location in lieu of a complete download. When the folder redirection feature is configured for a user, their roaming profile is still downloaded. The redirected folders are not downloaded; they are redirected to the network location specified in the Group Policy folder redirection setting. By implementing folder redirection, you can speed up logon and logoffs for your end users.

Home Folder

Home folders are private network locations that a user can store their personal documents in. The folder can be automatically mapped to a drive letter so that the storage looks like it is local to the user. Home folders can be configured by first making a share on a file server that is writable by everyone. Then each user must be configured in the Active Directory Users and Computers MMC for their own unique Home Folder on the setting in the Profile tab, as shown in Figure 13.9. The location can be a local path if the user will use the same computer and the files should be stored locally for the user. Or it can be a local drive letter, which is more useful if the user roams between computers. The driver letter will be automatically mapped to the remote file server. Implementing a home folder located on a network server allows for centralized file storage, and you can perform backups on the centralized data.

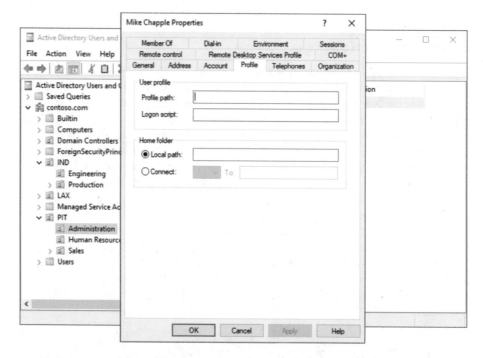

FIGURE 13.9 The Profile tab in Active Directory Users and Computers MMC

EXAM TIP

With home folders, network locations appear to the user as local drive letters.

Login Script

Login scripts allow tasks to be automated and repeatable every time the user logs in. You can create login scripts to map network drives, map printers, and automate administrative tasks, such as logging users or copying files.

There are a number of languages to choose from, such as Windows batch scripting, PowerShell, and VBScript. After you write the login script, you will copy it to the \\domain\NETLOGON folder. You can then configure the user account that needs to call the script. You can do this on the Profile tab in the Active Directory Users and Computers MMC.

NOTE

You can learn more about scripting in Chapter 35, "Scripting."

CERTMIKE EXAM ESSENTIALS

▶ The principle of least privilege defines the least permission that a user needs to do their job. By limiting a user's permission, you can prevent misuse of privileges and/or prevent unintentional misconfigurations.

▶ Access control lists (ACLs) are security rules that can govern network traffic flow or file access. ACLs are typically configured on routers/firewalls to restrict network access. ACLs can also be configured on files and folders to restrict filesystem access to documents.

▶ Multifactor authentication (MFA) is two or more factors of authentication used to authenticate a user. By using two or more authentication factors, you can limit credential theft. Authentication factors include username and passwords, biometrics, tokens, GPS position, signature, and others outlined in this chapter.

▶ Mobile device management (MDM) software allows an organization to police and control bring-your-own-device (BYOD) and corporate-owned devices. MDM assures the organization's data is safe in the event a device is lost or stolen. Organizational data can be remotely deleted and policed with MDM policies.

▶ Domains are a grouping of users, computers, groups, policies, and other objects to centralize administration and logon credentials. Security groups are used to assign access to groupings of users for resources. Organizational units (OUs) allow users and computers to be organized by object class, suborganization, function, geographic location, or a combination of these. Group Policy can be applied to an OU to in turn apply policies to users and computer objects. Folder redirection, home folders, and login scripts provide faster login times, convenience, and support for centralized backups.

Practice Question 1

A banking website requires you to install an application that creates a rotating code for authenticating to the site. What is this logical security method being used?

A. Access control list
B. Hard token
C. Short Message Service
D. Soft token

Practice Question 2

You need to create a Group Policy Object to restrict settings. Which type of objects will allow you to apply the Group Policy Object so that it takes effect?

A. Groups
B. Organizational units
C. Computers
D. Users

Practice Question 1 Explanation

This question is designed to test your knowledge of the various factors of authentication.

1. The first answer (A, Access control list) is incorrect. An access control list is a way to govern the access of network traffic or files.

2. The next answer (B, Hard token) is incorrect. A hard token is a hardware device with a rotating number that represents a factor of something that you have.

3. The next answer (C, Short Message Service) is incorrect. SMS is a factor of authentication in which a code is texted to you.

4. The last answer (D, Soft token) is correct. A soft token is similar to a hardware token but implements a software program to display the rotating code.

Correct Answer: D. Soft token

Practice Question 2 Explanation

This question is designed to test your knowledge of the various components of Active Directory, specifically GPO. Let's evaluate these answers one at a time.

1. The first answer (A, Groups) is incorrect. You cannot link a Group Policy Object to a group.

2. The second answer (B, Organizational units) is correct. The Group Policy Object is to be linked to an organizational unit containing the users or computers you want to police.

3. The third answer (C, Computers) is incorrect. Although you will ultimately police a computer, you cannot link a Group Policy Object to computers.

4. The last answer (D, Users) is incorrect. Just like the previous answer, you cannot link a Group Policy Object to users directly.

Correct Answer: B. Organizational units

CHAPTER 14

Wireless Security

Core 2 Objective 2.2: Compare and contrast wireless security protocols and authentication methods.

From tiny home networks with just a couple of PCs and a few smartphones to gigantic enterprises, devices connected to wireless networks are everywhere—and they need to be secure. In this chapter, you will learn everything you need to know about A+ Certification Core 2 Objective 2.2, including the following topics:

▶ Protocols and Encryption
▶ Authentication

PROTOCOLS AND ENCRYPTION

Since the first Wi-Fi networks were introduced about 20 years ago, there have been encryption standards and protocols designed to protect those networks. With an encrypted wireless network, a device must have the appropriate encryption key (password) stored in it to be able to join the wireless network.

The earliest encryption standard, WEP, was, sadly, almost completely useless except for slowing down systems. Today, we have much improved encryption standards and protocols to protect our wireless networks. In the following sections, you will learn about them.

> **EXAM TIP**
>
> Keep in mind that many wireless networks do not have encryption enabled by default. Therefore, it's necessary to enable encryption on wireless routers and access points (APs) and to set up devices to store the encryption key so that they can make the connection. Be sure you know which encryption standards use particular types of encryption and how authentication processes work. In the field, you will often need to make correct choices in setting up secure wireless networks. Don't be surprised if you are asked to simulate the process of creating a secure wireless network on your A+ exams.

Wi-Fi Protected Access 2 (WPA2)

Until recently, the best encryption standard used for Wi-Fi networks was Wi-Fi Protected Access 2 (WPA2), the second generation of WPA. *WPA* (Wi-Fi Protected Access) uses a pre-shared encryption key of up to 63 ASCII characters and the TKIP protocol to encrypt connections. *WPA2* (Wi-Fi Protected Access 2) uses variable-length encryption keys along with the more powerful AES-based CCMP protocol for encryption(see later in this chapter for details of both TKIP and AES).

Depending upon your router, you might find WPA identified as WPA-TKIP and WPA2 identified as WPA-AES. Some routers allow WPA to use both types of encryption to improve its security (Figure 14.1).

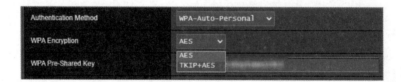

FIGURE 14.1 A router that offers both TKIP and AES encryption with WPA

> **EXAM TIP**
>
> When configuring WPA/WPA2 encryption, most routers offer the option of WPA or WPA2-Personal or WPA or WPA2-Enterprise. Choose WPA2-Personal (preferred) or WPA-Personal to use an encryption key if you are setting up a home or small-business network. If you are setting up a network that has a RADIUS server for user authentication, choose WPA2-Enterprise (preferred) or WPA-Enterprise.

WPA3

WPA3, introduced in 2018, has several improvements over WPA2, including replacement of PSK with Simultaneous Authentication of Equals (SAE)/Dragonfly Key Exchange and forward security (preventing third-party eavesdropping on connections). WPA3 continues to use AES encryption.

WPA3 is supported in many Wi-Fi 6 and 6E routers as well as some Wi-Fi 5 routers. These routers also support earlier WPA2 standards so that existing wireless adapters will still work: choose WPA2/WPA3 during router setup for networks with existing WPA2 wireless adapters (Figure 14.2). Check the specifications for new built-in or add-on wireless adapters to find models that support WPA3.

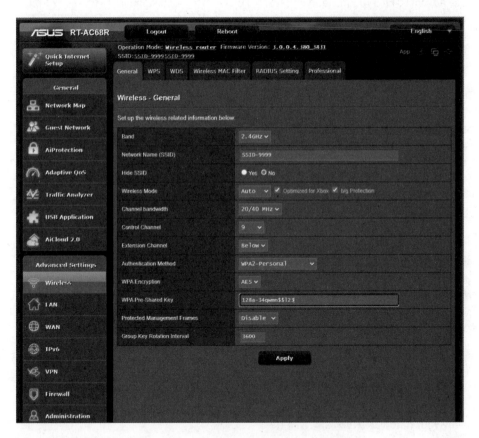

FIGURE 14.2 A router that supports WPA2/WPA3 encryption

NOTE

To learn more about the differences between WPA2 and WPA3, see www
.diffen.com/difference/WPA2_vs_WPA3.

Temporal Key Integrity Protocol (TKIP)

WPA is designed to use Temporal Key Integrity Protocol (*TKIP*) encryption. TKIP uses a longer key than the RC4 encryption used by the first Wi-Fi security standard, WEP. TKIP uses 128-bit encryption along with longer keys to make it harder to crack without requiring users with WEP-compliant routers and wireless adapters to have to replace their hardware. TKIP, although harder to crack than WEP's RC4, has been recognized as insecure for over a decade, and it should not be used unless it is the strongest encryption method available.

Advanced Encryption Standard (AES)

The Advanced Encryption Standard (*AES*) is a block encryption standard that uses 128-bit blocks with keys of 128, 192, or 256 bits. Simply put, AES is far more secure than TKIP. AES isn't simply a wireless standard; it is widely used by full-disk encryption programs such as BitLocker (Windows), FileVault (macOS) and others; most popular ZIP compression programs; and NTFS Encrypting File System (EFS) and other file-level encryption programs, among others.

AES is used by both WPA2 and WPA3 Wi-Fi security standards. For maximum security on a home network, use WPA2-AES or WPA3-AES (when supported by router and adapter hardware). When authentication (see the next section) is used, select WPA2 or WPA3-Enterprise (preferred) or WPA-Enterprise (Figure 14.3) and also set up the authentication method.

AUTHENTICATION

In a home or small-business wireless network that uses file and printer sharing on individual workstations, authentication is simply creating user accounts and setting up each wireless workstation with the appropriate encryption key (password) for the wireless router(s) or APs it will connect to. However, in enterprise wireless networking, centralized authentication is used. The following sections discuss the major authentication standards you might encounter, including RADIUS, TACACS+, Kerberos, and multifactor.

> **EXAM TIP**
>
> When configuring a wireless router or AP that uses RADIUS or TACACS+ authentication, choose the Enterprise version of the strongest WPA standard supported by your hardware (typically WPA2).

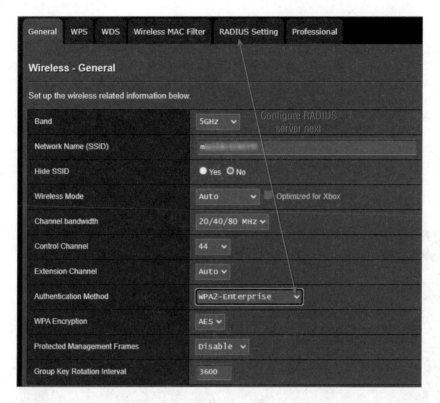

FIGURE 14.3 A router with WPA2-Enterprise enabled must also be configured to use RADIUS authentication.

Remote Authentication Dial-In User Service (RADIUS)

A *RADIUS* (Remote Authentication Dial-In User Service) server is used to:

▶ Authenticate users by matching the user's credentials to its list of users.

▶ Authorize authenticated users to have access to specific resources.

▶ Account for the resources each user consumes while using the network, such as time, data sent, or data received.

TIP

Because RADIUS servers perform Authentication, Authorization, and Accounting, they are sometimes referred to as AAA servers.

Despite its name, RADIUS servers are used by many types of networks. In addition to ISPs using all types of connections, RADIUS is used by cellular network providers and business and education enterprise-level networks for a wide variety of secure networks, including VPNs as well as wireless and wired Ethernet networks.

The RADIUS service is nonproprietary, so implementations are available from many vendors. In a typical network configuration, the RADIUS server is connected to the network access server and user databases. The RADIUS server receives requests for authentication from the network and matches the users to those stored in the user database. If there's a match, the RADIUS server permits access to the network. RADIUS uses UDP port 1812 for its authentication and authorization activities and UDP port 1813 for accounting. Figure 14.4 illustrates the RADIUS configuration options in a typical wireless router.

The other major access system is the TACACS+ system discussed in the following section.

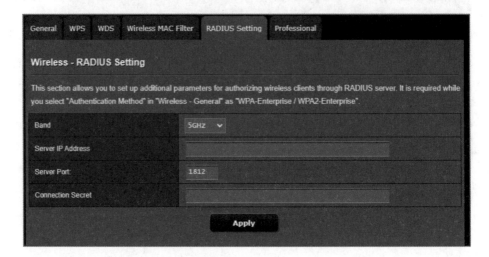

FIGURE 14.4 To enable RADIUS authentication on this wireless router, enter the IP address for the server and its connection secret (password).

Terminal Access Controller Access-Control System (TACACS+)

The Terminal Access Controller Access-Control System (*TACACS+*) is a proprietary Cisco access control system that is used to authenticate users. Use it when you have only Cisco network hardware; if you use other vendors, you must use RADIUS instead.

TACACS+ does not include authorization but connects to third-party authorization services such as Kerberos (see the next section). TACACS+ can also be configured to provide accounting of user activity. TACACS+ uses TCP port 49.

TIP

For a useful comparison of RADIUS and TACACS+, see `www.geeksforgeeks`
`.org/difference-between-tacacs-and-radius`.

Kerberos

Kerberos is described as a network authentication protocol by its creators at MIT
(`https://web.mit.edu/Kerberos`), but it is actually used as an authorization protocol by networks. Kerberos is widely used in single sign-on (SSO) networks this way; the
user is authenticated by RADIUS or TACACS+, but still needs to be authorized to use network resources. The Kerberos server provides a "ticket" that can be used to receive access to
the services (files, folders, printers, etc.) the user is authorized for. Instead of needing to log
in using the original login credentials, the Kerberos "ticket" is assigned to the user and provides access to services for the remainder of the computing session.

Kerberos is included in a wide variety of freeware and commercial authorization packages.

NOTE

For a good discussion of how RADIUS and Kerberos are complementary
technologies, visit `https://security.stackexchange.com/`
`questions/124092/`
`whats-the-difference-between-radius-and-kerberos`.

Multifactor

From social media sites like Facebook to large organizations, using multifactor security
has become very popular. Instead of using a single means of authentication (such as
username/password or an access code), organizations are adding a second authentication
method you must respond to before you can access a secure network.

Here are typical methods of authentication:

▶ Something you have (token or ID card)
▶ Something you know (PIN or password)
▶ Something you are (biometric characteristic)

When multifactor authentication is enabled, you need to provide at least two different
methods of authentication to prove your identity and gain access to a location or computing
resource. For example, a PIN and a password count as a single method of authentication.
However, a PIN or a password plus biometrics would count as two factors.

Multifactor authentication is often referred to as layered security, and if you use an
ATM, you have encountered it; the ATM card is something you have, and your PIN is
something you know.

EXAM TIP

To prepare for the 1102 Core 2 exam, be sure you can apply WPA/WPA2/WPA3 protocols; TKIP/AES encryption; and RADIUS, TACACS+, Kerberos, and multifactor authentication to security scenarios.

A common method for using multifactor authentication for remote work is to have users provide a means of accepting notifications of login requests via text or email. When a login attempt is made with the user's credentials, the user receives a notification and must approve or reject it. This helps prevent a purported user in one location from successfully impersonating the actual user who is somewhere else. We have seen this method stop a number of attempted logins to college and social media resources.

NOTE

To learn more about multifactor authentication, visit `https://support .microsoft.com` and search for **What is: Multifactor Authentication**.

CERTMIKE EXAM ESSENTIALS

▶ To protect your system, use the strongest encryption standard supported by all of your devices, typically WPA2. WPA3 is supported by the most recent hardware and operating systems. Having a mixture of older hardware that does not support WPA3 and devices supporting WPA3 forces your network to use the lower-protection standards for all devices.

▶ AES is virtually unbreakable, and when combined with long encryption keys makes a home or small-business wireless network very secure.

▶ Authentication, authorization, and accounting are three essential parts of secure centralized networking. RADIUS can perform all three, whereas TACACS+ uses third-party authorization from sources such as Kerberos.

▶ Multifactor authentication requires you to provide two or more authentication factors to prove your identity and gain access. The possible factors are something you know, such as a password; something you have, such as a smartphone; and something you are, such as a fingerprint.

Practice Question 1

You are configuring a small-business wireless network with a new router and you select WPA3 as the security protocol in the router configuration. Some workstations cannot connect to the router. Which of the following is the most likely reason?

A. You forgot to configure the RADIUS server.
B. The workstations support WPA2, not WPA3.
C. The workstations are using Cisco network adapters.
D. You forgot to configure the TACACS+ server.

Practice Question 2

Your client has an urgent question about the authentication server used on his network. Unfortunately, the client, who has called you at 11 p.m. because he can't sleep, can only remember that the server uses UDP ports 1812 and 1813. Which of the following is the client worrying about?

A. TACACS+
B. WPA3-Personal
C. RADIUS
D. WPA3-Enterprise

Practice Question 1 Explanation

This question is designed to test your real-world understanding of wireless security. Let's evaluate these answers one at a time.

1. The first answer (A, You forgot to configure the RADIUS server) is incorrect. A RADIUS server is not used in small-business networks. Workstations are configured to use the encryption key set up in the router for the network.

2. The next answer (B, The workstations support WPA2, not WPA3) is the most likely answer. Because older wireless adapters support WPA2, routers should be configured to support WPA2/WPA3 to avoid this problem.

3. The next answer (C, The workstations are using Cisco network adapters) is incorrect. Because this network does not use TACACS+ authentication, there is no problem in mixing Cisco and other brands of Wi-Fi hardware.

4. The last answer (D, You forgot to configure the TACACS+ server) is incorrect. A TACACS+ server is used on large networks that use Enterprise settings, not on a small-business network.

Correct Answer: B. The workstations support WPA2, not WPA3

Practice Question 2 Explanation

This question is designed to test your knowledge of the network ports used by authentication servers. Let's evaluate these answers one at a time.

1. The first answer (A, TACACS+) is incorrect. TACACS+ uses TCP port 49, and does not use UDP ports.

2. The second answer (B, WPA3-Personal), is incorrect. WPA3-Personal uses Dragonfly Key Exchange for encryption keys. It is not an authentication server.

3. The third answer (C, RADIUS) is correct. The RADIUS AAA server uses UDP ports 1812 and 1813.

4. The last answer (D, WPA3-Enterprise) is incorrect. While it requires a RADIUS server (non-Cisco hardware) or a TACACS+ server (Cisco hardware) in router configuration, WPA3-Enterprise is not an authentication server.

Correct Answer: C. RADIUS

CHAPTER 15

Malware

Core 2 Objective 2.3: Given a scenario, detect, remove, and prevent malware using the appropriate tools and methods.

Malicious software, or malware, poses a significant threat to the security and stability of computers and other devices. Created for a variety of purposes, malware infects systems and then undermines their security controls. Malware infections may prevent users from accessing resources on their system, steal personal information, or encrypt data until the victim pays a ransom. Computer technicians must understand how to detect, remove, and prevent malware infections.

In this chapter, you'll learn everything you need to know about A+ Core 2 objective 2.3, including the following topics:

▶ **Malware**
▶ **Tools and Methods**

MALWARE

As you prepare for the A+ Core 2 exam, you should understand the many different types of *malware*, or malicious software, that exist. Understanding these threats will help you implement controls that protect against them.

Viruses

Viruses are malicious code objects that spread from system to system after some human action. They might be transported on removable media or spread via email attachments, for example. They carry a malicious payload that carries out the virus author's intent, such as stealing data or disrupting system activity.

Boot Sector Viruses

The *boot sector virus* is one of the earliest known forms of virus infection. These viruses attack the boot sector—the portion of bootable media (such as a hard disk or flash drive) that the computer uses to load the operating system during the boot process. Because the boot sector is extremely small, it can't contain all the code required to implement the virus's propagation and destructive functions. To bypass this space limitation, boot sector viruses store the majority of their code on another portion of the storage media. When the system reads the infected boot sector, the virus instructs it to read and execute the code stored in this alternate location, thereby loading the entire virus into memory and potentially triggering the delivery of the virus's payload.

Trojan Horses

Trojan horses pretend to be legitimate pieces of software that a user might want to download and install. When the user runs the program, it does perform as expected; however, the Trojan horse also carries a malicious, hidden payload that performs some unwanted action behind the scenes.

Rootkits

The root account is a special superuser account on a system that provides unrestricted access to system resources. It's normally reserved for system administrators, but it's also the ultimate goal of many hackers.

　　Rootkits are a type of malware that originally were designed for privilege escalation. A hacker would gain access to a normal user account on a system, and then use the rootkit to "gain root," or escalate the normal user access to unrestricted superuser access. Use of the term *rootkit* has changed over the years, however. It is now used to describe software techniques designed to hide other software on a system.

> **NOTE**
> The Secure Boot technology included with newer UEFI-based motherboards helps protect against rootkit attacks. For more information, see `https://docs.microsoft.com/en-us/windows-hardware/design/device-experiences/oem-secure-boot`.

Spyware

Spyware is malware that gathers information without the user's knowledge or consent. It then reports that information back to the malware author, who can use it for any type of purpose, which might be identity theft or access to financial accounts—or even in some cases, espionage. Spyware uses many different techniques.

Keyloggers

Keyloggers, or keystroke loggers, are a type of spyware that captures every key a user presses so that they can report everything back to the malware author. Or they might monitor for visits to certain websites and capture the usernames and passwords used to access banks or other sensitive sites.

Ransomware

Ransomware blocks a user's legitimate use of a computer or data until a ransom is paid. The most common way of doing this is encrypting files with a secret key and then selling that key for ransom.

A recent example of that is the WannaCry ransomware, which struck many Internet-connected systems in 2017. WannaCry spread from system to system by exploiting a vulnerability called EternalBlue that affected Windows systems. Once it infected a system, WannaCry encrypted several files on the hard drive. These included office documents, images, or CAD drawings—some of the files that are most important to end users. The decryption key for those files was kept on a server under the control of the malware author, and the user was given a deadline to pay a ransom of several hundred dollars.

The big question when a ransomware infection occurs is whether you should pay. Your first response might be to say, no, you don't want to pay the malware author. But it's a very difficult question when they're your files that have been encrypted and are no longer accessible. A 2021 survey showed that over 40 percent of those infected with ransomware actually did pay the ransom (`https://thycotic.com/resources/ransomware-survey-and-report-2021`), and an analysis of Bitcoin payments for an earlier piece of ransomware called CryptoLocker shows that malware authors have received over $27 million to date.

Cryptominers

Cryptominers are a form of malware that takes over the computing capacity of a user's system and uses that capacity to mine cryptocurrencies, such as Bitcoin, generating revenue for the malware author.

EXAM TIP

It's easy to confuse ransomware and cryptominers because both employ cryptography. Ransomware uses cryptography to encrypt files and demand a ransom from a user. Cryptominers steal compute capacity from a user's system and use it to mine cryptocurrency. If you get confused, remember that the beginning of the name is what the attacker hopes to get. In ransomware, the attacker hopes to get a ransom whereas cryptominers hope to mine cryptocurrency.

MALWARE PREVENTION AND REMOVAL TOOLS AND METHODS

Computer technicians should understand how to implement security controls that both prevent malware infections from occurring in the first place and assist with the removal of malware from infected systems. You'll find more information on this topic in Chapter 25, "Troubleshooting Malware."

Preventive Controls

Preventive security controls are designed to stop a security threat from successfully violating the security of a system in the first place. Common preventive controls against malware include antivirus/antimalware packages, firewalls, and user education.

Antivirus/Antimalware

You can use the same tools to protect against many different types of malware threats. Modern *antivirus/antimalware* software protects against viruses, worms, Trojan horses, and spyware. Figure 15.1 shows an example of the Windows Security antimalware package provided by Microsoft as part of the Windows operating system.

To find Windows Security, in Windows 10 go to Windows Settings ➤ Update & Security ➤ Windows Security. Then click the Open Windows Security button. In Windows 11, go to Windows Settings ➤ Privacy & Security ➤ Windows Security. Then click the Open Windows Security button.

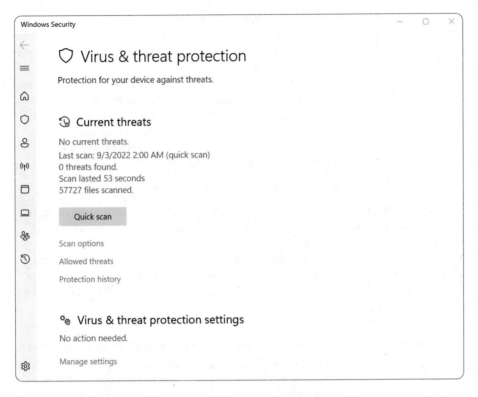

FIGURE 15.1 Windows Defender antimalware package

Antivirus software uses two mechanisms to protect systems against malicious software:

▶ *Signature detection* uses databases of known malware patterns and scans the files and memory of a system for any data matching the pattern of known malicious software. If it finds suspect contents, it can then remove the content from the system or quarantine it for further analysis. When you're using signature detection, it is critical that you frequently update the virus definition file to ensure that you have current signatures for newly discovered malware.

▶ *Behavior detection* takes a different approach. Instead of using patterns of known malicious activity, these systems attempt to model normal activity and then report when they discover anomalies—activity that deviates from that normal pattern.

Behavioral detection techniques are found in advanced malware protection tools known as *endpoint detection and response (EDR)* solutions. These advanced tools go beyond basic signature detection and perform deep instrumentation of endpoints. They analyze memory and processor usage, Registry entries, network communications, and other system behavior characteristics. They offer advanced real-time protection against malware and other security threats by using agents installed on endpoint devices to watch for signs of malicious activity and trigger automated responses to defend systems from attack.

In addition, EDR tools often have the capability of performing *sandboxing*. When a system receives a suspicious executable, the advanced malware protection system sends that executable off to a malware sandbox before allowing it to run on the protected system. In that sandbox, the malware protection solution runs the executable and watches its behavior, checking for suspicious activities. If the malware behaves in a manner that resembles an attack, it is not allowed to execute on the protected endpoint.

Software Firewalls

Firewalls are an important security control. They act as the security guards of the network, monitoring attempts to start communications and only allowing those connections that match the enterprise security policy.

Firewalls follow the "default deny" principle that says that any network connection that is not explicitly allowed should be blocked. Connections to a computer should only be made when the administrator determines that the connection is necessary to meet business requirements.

Firewalls come in two forms:

▶ *Network firewalls* are hardware devices that sit in between two networks and control the connections between those networks. For example, organizations place network firewalls at the border of their networks, in between the organization's network and the Internet. This network firewall forms an important part of the organization's perimeter defense. The network firewall only restricts those connections that pass through the firewall. Connections between systems on the same network are not restricted by the network firewall because they don't pass through it.

▶ *Host-based firewalls,* or software firewalls, work in a similar manner but are not hardware devices. They are software, normally a part of the operating system, that sits on an individual workstation or server. The host firewall restricts any attempt to connect to that individual computer from any other system on the network. They are an important part of a defense-in-depth approach to information security.

Figure 15.2 shows an example of the host firewall capabilities built into Windows.

The Windows Defender Firewall is discussed in more detail in Chapter 4, "Windows 10 Control Panel."

User Education

Security depends on the behavior of individuals. An intentional or accidental misstep by a single user can completely undermine many security controls, exposing an organization to unacceptable levels of risk. Security training programs that include user education regarding common threats help protect organizations against these risks. In particular, they help educate users about how they can avoid falling victim to malware and phishing attacks.

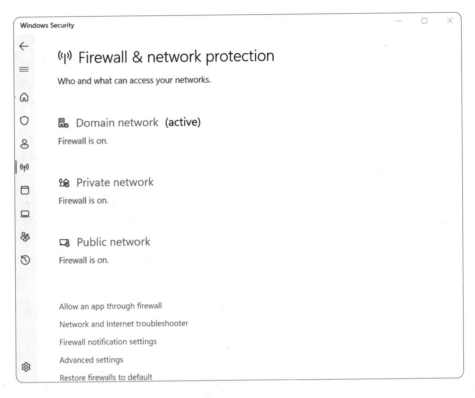

FIGURE 15.2 Windows Firewall

Security education programs include two important components:

▶ *Security training* provides users with the detailed information they need to protect the organization's security. These may use a variety of delivery techniques, but the bottom-line goal is to impart knowledge. Security training demands time and attention from students.

▶ *Security awareness* is meant to remind employees about the security lessons they've already learned. Unlike security training, it doesn't require a commitment of time to sit down and learn new material. Instead, it uses posters, videos, email messages, and similar techniques to keep security top-of-mind for those who've already learned the core lessons.

Organizations may use a variety of methods to deliver security training. This may include traditional classroom instruction, providing dedicated information security course material, or it might insert security content into existing programs, such as a new employee orientation program delivered by Human Resources. Students might also use online computer-based training providers to learn about information security or attend classes offered by vendors. Whatever methods an organization uses, the goal is to impart security knowledge that employees can put into practice on the job.

EXAM TIP

User education regarding common threats is the best defense in preventing malware.

Anti-Phishing Training

Anti-phishing training programs add an interesting twist. Instead of simply providing security awareness training, the company PhishMe allows you to measure the success of your training efforts by actually conducting simulated phishing attacks. Users receive fake phishing campaigns in their inboxes and, if they respond, they're directed to training materials that warn them of the dangers of phishing and help prevent them from falling victim to a real attack. Back-end reporting helps security professionals gauge the effectiveness of their security education efforts by measuring the percentage of users who fall victim to the simulated attack.

Recovery Controls

Recovery controls are designed to restore a system to normal operation after a security incident occurs. Common recovery controls used after malware infections include recovery mode and operating system reinstallation.

Recovery Mode

In many cases, antimalware software will be able to remove malware from a system and restore it to normal working order. In cases where that is not successful, you may be able to use the operating system's recovery mode to restore the system to working order. The Advanced options of Windows recovery mode, shown in Figure 15.3, offer administrators several choices:

▶ Restore the system from a previous known good state.
▶ Restore the system using a specific system image file.
▶ Repair the startup sequence.
▶ Access a command prompt.
▶ Change Windows startup behavior.

WARNING

If you choose to restore a system to a prior configuration, you'll want to be certain that you're choosing a point when the malware was not already on the system or you will soon find yourself repeating this process! Also, be sure to correct any vulnerability that allowed the malware to infect the system in the first place. You'll learn more about this in Chapter 25.

Operating System Reinstallation

If other methods are not successful, your last-ditch approach for recovering a system from a malware infection is to wipe the hard drive and reinstall the operating system. This is a drastic, time-consuming measure, but it may be the only viable option in some cases.

After reinstalling the operating system, you may then install applications required by the end user and restore data from backups.

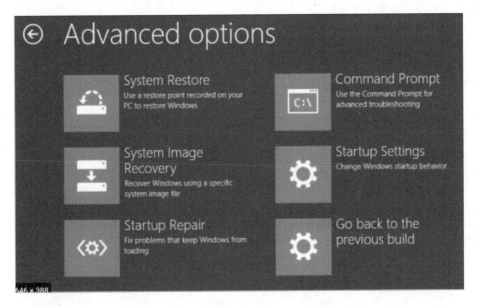

FIGURE 15.3 Windows recovery mode Advanced options

CERTMIKE EXAM ESSENTIALS

▶ Viruses are malicious code objects that spread from system to system after some human action. Trojan horses pretend to be legitimate pieces of software that a user might want to download and install. Rootkits use software techniques designed to hide other software on a system.

▶ Spyware is malware that gathers information without the user's knowledge or consent. Keyloggers, or keystroke loggers, capture every key a user presses.

▶ Ransomware uses cryptography to encrypt files and demand ransom from a user. Cryptominers steal compute capacity from a user's system and use it to mine cryptocurrency.

▶ Preventive controls used against malware threats include antivirus/antimalware software, software firewalls, and user education about common threats and anti-phishing training.

▶ Recovery controls used against malware threats include recovery mode and operating system reinstallation.

▶ If you suspect a malware infection, first run an antimalware scan. If that scan is unable to remove the infection, you may try restoring the system to a previous configuration or reinstalling the operating system.

Practice Question 1

You are inspecting a system that you believe has been infected by malware. What should be your first step?

A. Run an antimalware scan.
B. Reinstall the operating system.
C. Restore the system to the last known good configuration.
D. Wipe the hard drive.

Practice Question 2

You are examining a system that has been infected by malware. Discussing the situation with the end user, you learn that they recently downloaded a new game and that the malware symptoms appeared immediately afterward. What type of malware should you expect?

A. Virus
B. Trojan horse
C. Rootkit
D. Ransomware

Practice Question 1 Explanation

This question is designed to test your real-world understanding of malware processes. All of these steps may take place during the troubleshooting process, but you are being asked to identify which step should occur first.

1. Option A (run an antimalware scan) is correct because you should begin by running this scan to determine whether the system actually is infected by malware.

2. Option B (reinstall the operating system) is incorrect because that is not the first step you should follow. You should begin by running an antimalware scan to determine whether the system is infected by malware. If that scan does turn up malware, the antimalware package may be able to remove the infection. If that is not successful, you may then turn to more drastic steps, such as restoring the system to a previous configuration, wiping the hard drive, or reinstalling the operating system.

3. Option C (restore the system to the last known good configuration) is incorrect because it is not the first step you should follow. You should begin by running an antimalware scan to determine whether the system is infected by malware.

4. Option D (wipe the hard drive) is incorrect because it is not the first step you should follow. You should begin by running an antimalware scan to determine whether the system is infected by malware.

Correct Answer: A. Run an antimalware scan

Practice Question 2 Explanation

This question is testing your knowledge of different malware types.

1. Option A (virus) is incorrect because a virus is a piece of malicious software that spreads after the user takes some action. The situation in this scenario could also be described as a virus, but that is a more general term and Trojan horse is a better answer.

2. Option B (Trojan horse) is correct because a Trojan horse is a type of malware that appears to be legitimate software but that carries out malicious actions in the background. The symptoms here make it likely that the game was a Trojan horse.

3. Option C (rootkit) is incorrect because there is no indication that the malware used rootkit techniques to hide itself from detection.

4. Option D (ransomware) is incorrect because there is no indication that any data access was restricted or that any ransom demand took place. Therefore, it is not likely that this malware is ransomware.

Correct Answer: B. Trojan horse

CHAPTER 16

Social Engineering and Security Threats

Core 2 Objective 2.4: Explain common social-engineering attacks, threats, and vulnerabilities.

Although computers and technology are found in almost all parts of any business or organization, they don't operate themselves. People do, and people are the attack vector used by hackers running social-engineering attacks and threats.

In this chapter, you will learn everything you need to know about the A+ Certification Core 2 Objective 2.4, including the following topics:

▶ **Social Engineering**
▶ **Threats**
▶ **Vulnerabilities**

SOCIAL ENGINEERING

Social engineering is a blanket term for a variety of methods used by hackers to convince computer users to permit access to restricted systems. Today, most social engineering involves using devices rather than face-to-face interaction, but the goal is the same: using deceit to get information the hacker has no right to.

Phishing and Vishing

Phishing uses fake websites or emails to persuade respondents to provide banking, financial, or personal information. Figure 16.1 illustrates a typical recent phishing email attempt that contains some of the hallmarks of phishing emails: a link pointing to a website different from the purported source and foreign-language characters substituted for normal letters.

Foreign-language characters

Customer No. #9112663702 You are our September Winner!

CR   CVS Rewards
To markesoper@hotmail.com; markesoper@hotmail.com
Cc markesoper@hotmail.com

↩ Reply   ↩ Reply All   → Forward   ...
Thu 9/8/2022 12:31 PM

Original URL:
http://liked.busterhot.com/lo=ivs9zy3vifj.
yf29fi73s/jyz9b37z7-ys2/
x3scjnyzxzdegivhjl3vzxckhkmkhkmkcuek
zfmva/3iojohyb3deqryir73byx7l%22
Click or tap to follow link.

fer Valid Till - (08-09-2022)

Float mouse over link
to see actual URL

♥ CVS
pharmacy®

Congratulations!

You Are Our **September Winner**

Your Consumer Number Code

FDR-145A89F

FIGURE 16.1 A phishing email purportedly from a major drugstore chain

TIP

Other signs of phishing emails include asking you to open a compressed (zip) file to view a document, addressing you as "customer" instead of your name or account number, and containing poor spelling and grammar. See more phishing examples at www.phishing.org/phishing-examples.

A variation on phishing is known as "vishing", voice phishing, or phone phishing. In this version, an interactive voice response (IVR) system is used to trick callers (or people who have called) into giving up information.

TIP

A good way to avoid a vishing call is to never say "yes" as a response to an unknown caller. Your response can be recorded and used to "prove" you ordered something you didn't actually want.

Whaling

Two variations on phishing are directed at personnel in a particular company. One, called "spear phishing," is designed to target individuals who have access to confidential or financial information.

In "whaling," attempts are made to persuade executives or other high-level personnel to authorize wire transfers or other benefits for the attacker under the guise of carrying out important business operations. Millions of dollars have been stolen in recent years by successful whaling attacks.

NOTE

See examples of whaling messages and learn about variations that use SMS messaging, wire transfer, and other methods at www.tessian.com/blog/whaling-phishing-attack.

Impersonation

An impersonation attack is a type of phishing attack in which the sender impersonates an executive or high official and asks you to take an action such as transferring funds or sending sensitive information. Some of the hallmarks of an impersonation attack are as follows:

▶ Contact information that is very similar to the impersonated executive's actual email address.
▶ Urgency: "get this done immediately, or else!"

▶ An attempt to bypass channels: "I can't reach your supervisor, so I am asking you directly to do this . . ."

▶ A request to keep this request confidential: "Keep this to yourself. I will let your supervisor know . . ."

> **NOTE**
>
> See more signs of an impersonation attack and how to prevent them from succeeding at `https://easydmarc.com/blog/ what-is-an-impersonation-attack`.

Evil Twin

Everyone is looking for a Wi-Fi connection, and the evil twin attack is at your *dis*service. An Evil Twin attack uses a fake Wi-Fi access point, and when users connect to it, the information shared with the access point is detoured to a server that copies the desired data before sending it on to the destination. An evil twin has the same name as a legitimate Wi-Fi access point, and it often has a stronger signal than the legitimate access point they're mimicking, which makes getting unwary users to connect even easier.

Avoid evil twin attacks by disabling automatic connection to hotspots in your device's Wi-Fi configuration and have professional wireless site surveys performed to help determine which access points are legitimate and which ones are fake.

> **NOTE**
>
> Learn more about evil twin attacks and countermeasures at `www.purevpn .com/wifi-vpn/threats/evil-twin-attack` and `www.kaspersky .com/resource-center/preemptive-safety/evil-twin-attacks`.

Shoulder Surfing

When someone is watching you log into your system, work on a document, or check your email, you could be a victim of shoulder surfing: someone trying to read what's on your screen or your desk. Shoulder surfing can happen in your office, when you are getting cash from an ATM, or when you're working remotely at a coffee shop.

Here are some tips to block would-be shoulder-surfers: Lock your system when you turn away from it to talk. Keep your office door closed. Use a privacy screen to reduce the viewing angle on your system. Keep confidential documents in a closed folder when not actually being worked on, and lock them up when you're away from your desk. Ask people to sit at an angle where they can't see your screen if you must work and talk.

> **NOTE**
> Shoulder surfing can happen almost anywhere when people use technology carelessly. Learn where it can happen and how to stop it at `www.aura.com/learn/shoulder-surfing`.

Tailgating

When an unauthorized person follows someone into a secure area and grabs the door handle before it closes, that's tailgating. A related security violation is called piggybacking—that's when the authorized person knowingly helps an unauthorized person get into a secure area.

To stop tailgating, don't "help" people who don't have an access card or PIN to get into a secure area. If they're helping someone in the building or the department, ask them to call to be let in. An access control vestibule (also known as a mantrap) can stop tailgating and piggybacking, as you saw in Chapter 12, "Physical Security."

> **NOTE**
> For more insights into what makes tailgating and piggybacking easier to happen and how to stop it, see `www.cybertalk.org/2021/11/12/tailgating-social-engineering-attacks-what-is-tailgating-and-why-it-matters`.

Dumpster Diving

Dumpster diving is a potential threat to an organization. If an organization throws out technology instead of properly recycling it, the devices might contain confidential information. But a bigger threat may be calendars, organization charts, phone lists, or other items that are typically discarded when the information is not completely current.

Make sure that all paper, including junk mail, gets shredded in a cross-cut shredder. Locked recycle bins should be near trash cans so that people will be encouraged not to toss paper into the trash.

To learn about how to obtain certification of destruction/recycling for outdated information and technology, see Chapter 20, "Data Destruction and Disposal."

> **NOTE**
> For more information about the dangers of dumpster diving to organizations, see `https://cyberior.com/dumpster-diving` and `www.social-engineer.org/framework/information-gathering/dumpster-diving`.

EXAM TIP

To prepare for the Core 2 1102 exam, be sure you understand the different types of social engineering and how they threaten computer users and organizations: phishing, vishing, shoulder surfing, whaling, tailgating, impersonation, dumpster diving, and evil twin. Be prepared to deal with these threats in security scenarios.

THREATS

Threats are primarily technology-based (although some also include social engineering), and stopping them relies on both user education and sophisticated countermeasures. Here are some of the major technology threats organizations face and how to deal with them.

Denial of Service (DoS)

A denial-of-service (*DoS*) attack is designed to prevent a computing device from performing its normal tasks because of constant interruptions. A DoS attack is performed by a single computer and typically involves either buffer overflow or flood attacks.

Buffer overflow attacks, in which the attacker is attempting to cause the memory buffer to use up all memory or disk space, cause slow system behavior or crashes. Many of the Patch Tuesday updates issued by Microsoft for Windows or apps are designed to stop buffer overflow attacks.

A flood attack overwhelms a server with more data packets than the server can handle. Typically, a single device can carry out a buffer overflow attack, but a flood attack usually requires multiple devices.

NOTE

Learn more about DoS attacks at www.cloudflare.com/learning/ddos/glossary/denial-of-service.

For an example of how buffer overflows can be exploited, see the notes for the March 2022 Microsoft .NET updates at https://devblogs.microsoft.com/dotnet/march-2022-updates.

Distributed Denial of Service (DDoS)

A distributed denial-of-service (*DDoS*) attack is like a DoS attack, but it involves multiple devices sending attack traffic to the same target. Internet of Things (IoT) devices as well as desktops, laptops, and servers can be used as part of a DDoS attack. Typically, a DDoS attack is preceded by infecting multiple devices with malware that turns them into remotely controlled bots (or zombies) that form a botnet. The DDoS attack is launched by sending commands to the botnet.

Some of the signs that a DDoS attack is in process include:

▶ High levels of traffic that come from a single IP address or range of addresses
▶ High levels of traffic going to the same web page
▶ High levels of traffic that happen at the same time or times

Types of DDoS attacks include:

▶ HTTP floods, in which an attacker floods a website with HTTP requests that overload the server
▶ SYN floods, in which a website receives a lot of initial connection request packets, acknowledges them, but never receives a response
▶ DNS amplification, in which a DNS server is sent a large number of requests from an attacker masquerading as a client and the responses are sent to the client

Some defenses against DoS and DDoS attacks include:

▶ Using an Anycast network of servers instead of a single server to handle traffic
▶ A web application firewall that acts as a reverse proxy
▶ Rate limiting
▶ Using services such as Cloudflare to check inbound connections for attacks

> **NOTE**
>
> To learn more about DDoS attacks and how to mitigate them, see www
> `.cloudflare.com/learning/ddos/what-is-a-ddos-attack` and
> `www.fortinet.com/resources/cyberglossary/ddos-attack.`

Zero-Day Attack

A zero-day attack (also known as a zero-day exploit) is targeted at not-yet-patched vulnerabilities in an operating system or app. The term *zero-day* comes from the attacks often occurring on the same day that the vulnerability is announced or discovered.

Help block zero-day attacks by installing latest patches for your operating system and apps, along with using up-to-date antivirus and firewall apps.

> **NOTE**
>
> To learn more about zero-day attacks and get patches for affected apps and
> operating systems, see www.`zerodayinitiative.com`. For a list of
> best practices to avoid zero-day attacks, visit www.`cybertalk`
> `.org/2022/06/14/`
> `top-10-zero-day-attack-prevention-best-practices-2022.`

Spoofing

Spoofing is a blanket term for any type of an attack that involves the attacker pretending to be someone else. Spoofing can use email, text messaging, Address Resolution Protocol (ARP), domains, caller ID, and other means.

Some of the hallmarks of spoofed messages include:

▶ Unsolicited information, including attachments
▶ Requests for sensitive information
▶ Domains that don't match the alleged origin of the message
▶ Messages addressed to "Customer" instead of a specific person
▶ Bad grammar and spelling
▶ Non-secure links to banking or e-commerce websites (HTTP instead of HTTPS)

To avoid being spoofed, users should be taught to:

▶ Log into websites themselves and not through links in messages
▶ Avoid non-secure connections to banking and e-commerce sites
▶ Never download unsolicited attachments or click unsolicited links

> **NOTE**
>
> To learn more about different types of spoofing attacks and how to avoid them, see www.crowdstrike.com/
> cybersecurity-101/spoofing-attacks and www
> .securitymagazine.com/articles/91980-types-of-spoofing-
> attacks-every-security-professional-should-know-about.

On-Path Attack

An on-path attack places the attacker between two devices (such as a web server and a client) to steal information in the process of going between the ends of the connection. An on-path attack is sometimes referred to as a man-in-the-middle attack.

Some of the ways that on-path attacks are carried out include creating a proxy in the HTTP connection, stealing cookies, and intercepting DNS requests for redirection. On-path attacks often take place on unsecured wireless networks.

To help prevent on-path attacks, avoid unsecured networks unless you are using a VPN and use S/MIME email encryption.

> **NOTE**
>
> To learn more about different types of on-path attacks and how to avoid them, see
> https://cxosjournal.com/on-path-attacker and www
> .cloudflare.com/learning/security/threats/on-path-attack.

Brute-Force Attack

A brute-force attack is directed against password-protected resources, including secure websites, databases, and encrypted wireless connections, by calculating and using every possible combination of characters in login attempts. Given enough time, a brute-force attack will succeed. Use these steps to help stop brute-force attacks:

▶ Adopting a lockout policy that stops logins for a period after a specified number of unsuccessful login attempts are made

▶ Using cryptography techniques such as salting the hash and 256-bit encryption to store passwords

▶ Using CAPTCHA as an additional step before logging in

▶ Using multifactor authentication

▶ Preventing users from repeating old passwords

▶ Using password managers to make complex passwords easier for users to manage and use

Thus, it's a combination of user education and stronger policies for password-protected assets that is the best defense against brute-force attacks. Learn more about using CAPTCHA in Chapter 22, "Browser Security."

> **NOTE**
>
> To learn more about brute-force attacks and how to mitigate them, see www
> .fortinet.com/resources/cyberglossary/
> brute-force-attack and www.upguard.com/blog/
> insider-threat and https://us.norton.com/
> internetsecurity-emerging-threats-brute-force-attack
> .html.

Dictionary Attack

A dictionary attack is a more sophisticated type of brute-force attack. It uses a list of common passwords, such as those that might have been obtained from compromising other systems as well as common passwords such as "12345678" and (you guessed it!) "password." Use the same methods recommended to stop brute-force attacks to stop dictionary attacks.

> **NOTE**
>
> To learn more about dictionary attacks and how to mitigate them, see
> https://nordpass.com/blog/what-is-a-dictionary-attack.

Insider Threat

An insider threat is a blanket term for any type of an attack against technology assets or data by an employee of an organization. Insiders have an advantage over outside attackers because they are in positions where they can easily uncover passwords and other security measures and circumvent existing protections.

Clues indicating possible insider threats include unauthorized remote access hardware or software, changed passwords not authorized by the account holder, unauthorized changes to firewall or antivirus apps, data hoarding, using unauthorized external storage devices, and more.

> **NOTE**
>
> To learn more about insider threats and how to mitigate them, see www.fortinet.com/resources/cyberglossary/insider-threats and www.upguard.com/blog/insider-threat.

SQL Injection

Structured Query Language (*SQL*) is the standard language for locating, changing, and retrieving data from a relational database. SQL injection happens when malicious SQL commands are entered into an online SQL database data entry form. Because SQL databases are used to store customer data, inventories, and other information, SQL injections have been used to steal millions of customer records and large amounts of money over the years.

It's up to SQL database administrators to stop SQL injections by keeping their SQL database software up-to-date with security patches and by upgrading to more secure versions, providing stored procedures instead of allowing web users to enter their own SQL commands, and enforcing the principle of least privilege.

> **NOTE**
>
> To learn more about SQL injection, see www.malwarebytes.com/sql-injection. For examples of SQL injection in action and ways to improve SQL security, see www.geeksforgeeks.org/sql-injection-2.

Cross-Site Scripting (XSS)

Cross-site scripting (*XSS*) refers to a variety of attacks in which malicious script content (often JavaScript, as well as other web content such as HTML) is placed on a website where it can run whenever a web browser opens the website. XSS can transmit cookies to the attacker, redirect a browser to web content, or perform other attacks that appear to be coming from the visited site.

Since HTML can be used to deliver XSS, some interactive websites don't permit any HTML or limit it to appearance tags instead of scripts. From a user standpoint, using add-ons such as NoScript (available for Firefox and Firefox-based browsers as well as Chrome) is very useful for blocking XSS attacks.

NOTE

XSS blockers are considered a type of ad blocker. For reviews of some of the leading ad blockers, see `https://proprivacy.com/adblocker/reviews`.

For a deep dive into how XSS attacks work and what developers can do to prevent their websites from being hacked, see `www.ptsecurity.com/ww-en/analytics/knowledge-base/what-is-a-cross-site-scripting-xss-attack`.

EXAM TIP

To prepare for the Core 2 1102 exam, be sure you understand the different types of threats and how they threaten computer users and organizations: Denial of service (DoS), Distributed denial of service (DDoS), Zero-day attack, Spoofing, On-path attack, Brute-force attack, Dictionary attack, Insider threat, Structured Query Language (SQL) injection, and Cross-site scripting (XSS). Be prepared to deal with these threats in security scenarios. User education regarding common threats is the best defense, so check out Chapter 15, "Malware," for more about this topic.

VULNERABILITIES

Vulnerabilities refer to devices that, for various reasons, are not sufficiently protected against current threats. The following sections discuss typical vulnerabilities and what you can do to lessen the threat they pose.

Noncompliant Systems

A noncompliant system is a system that doesn't have the latest security updates installed, either in the operating system or applications. Many system management apps, such as Microsoft Endpoint Configuration Manager (formerly System Center Configuration Manager) and third-party remote monitoring and management programs, will check for security updates and can install missing ones. Systems that are lacking the latest security patches or are end-of-life (EOL) are very vulnerable to attacks. See "EOL OSs" later in this chapter for more information.

Individuals can use the free Belarc Advisor (www.belarc.com/free_download .html) to check for missing security updates. In Figure 16.2, Belarc Advisor displays several end-of-life (EOL) programs that should be updated or removed and several security updates that need to be installed.

```
Missing Security Updates – for Adobe, Apple, Java, Microsoft and more

Hotfixes from Microsoft Update (agent version 10.0.19041.1865) are turned off.
Last install: 11/30/2022 4:35:09 PM, check: 11/30/2022 11:43:00 AM.

These security updates apply to this computer but are not currently installed (using Advisor definitions version 2022.11.9.1),
according to the 11/08/2022 Microsoft Security Bulletin Summary and bulletins from other vendors. Note: Security benchmarks
require that Critical and Important severity security updates must be installed.

Hotfix Id        Severity      Description (click to see security bulletin)
EOL-Microsoft    End of Life   Microsoft Silverlight is vulnerable and no security updates are provided by the vendor
EOL-Microsoft    End of Life   Microsoft Office 2007 is vulnerable and no security updates are provided by the vendor
EOL-Apple        End of Life   Apple Quicktime 7.7.9 (1680.95.84) is vulnerable and no security updates are provided by the vendor
EOL-Adobe        End of Life   Adobe Shockwave 11.6.8.638 is vulnerable and no security updates are provided by the vendor
APSB20-49        Critical      Adobe Download Manager security update for Download Manager 1.5.2.19
CpuOct2022       Critical      Oracle Java SE Critical Patch Update for Java 8.0.3110.11 32-bit
HT213259         Critical      Apple iTunes security update for iTunes 12.12.2.2
Q4057115         Unrated       Microsoft security advisory (KB4057115)
Q5019959         Critical      Microsoft security update (KB5019959)
Q5020687         Important     Microsoft security update (KB5020687)
```

FIGURE 16.2 Belarc Advisor finds several security vulnerabilities on this system.

Unpatched Systems

An unpatched system is a system that has not been updated to the latest version of the operating system. Windows 10, Microsoft's pioneering software-as-a-service operating system, has released many versions since it was introduced in July 2015. All versions should be updated to the latest release supported by the hardware. Typically, Microsoft alerts users of non-current Windows that updates are available. However, Windows users can also manually download the latest version of Windows supported by their hardware from www .microsoft.com/en-us/software-download/windows10.

Automatic updates are supported by Windows (using Windows Update) and by macOS (using System Preferences ➢ Software Updates ➢ Automatically Keep My Mac Up To Date).

For Ubuntu Linux, recent versions have the Unattended Upgrades feature installed and enabled by default. To verify this, open Terminal and use the following command:

```
systemctl status unattended-upgrades
```

Unprotected Systems (Missing Antivirus/Missing Firewall)

A system might have the most up-to-date operating system and have all security updates installed. However, if it is lacking antivirus or a firewall app, it's still vulnerable to attacks of various kinds.

The Windows Security dialog box (Settings ➢ Update & Security ➢ Windows Security in Windows 10; Settings | Privacy & Security | Windows Security in Windows 11) displays an overview of protection areas, including Windows Defender Firewall and Microsoft Antivirus. In Figure 16.3, this Windows 11 system needs attention to Firewall and Device security settings.

FIGURE 16.3 Windows 11's Windows Security dialog box displays a problem with Firewall and Device security.

Click the problem area(s) to change the setting.

To learn more about Windows Defender Antivirus and Firewall, see Chapter 17, "Windows Security."

EOL OSs

An operating system that has reached end-of-life (EOL) is no longer supported by its vendor with updated security or other updates. Unfortunately, it's often necessary for organizations to continue to use EOL operating systems because upgraded operating systems won't work with existing hardware and software.

Chapter 8, "Operating System Types," provides more about the support challenges EOL operating systems pose.

EOL operating systems aren't necessarily ancient, like Windows XP or macOS 9. In the case of Windows 10, for example, versions 2004 and earlier are at EOL as of the third quarter of 2022 and will no longer be patched by Microsoft. Updating them to version 21H2 or later will keep them current until mid-2024 or later. By October 2025, all versions of Windows 10 will reach EOL.

macOS versions prior to macOS 10.15 Catalina are EOL as of the third quarter of 2022. Older versions of Linux and Unix-like distros have also gone EOL, such as CentOS Linux 8 and 6, Debian 9 and earlier, Fedora Linux 35 and earlier, FreeBSD stable versions prior to 12, Ubuntu .10 releases, and many others.

> **NOTE**
>
> For a list of versions of Linux, Windows, and server apps and their EOL dates, visit `https://endoflife.date`.

To protect EOL OSs, make sure the final updates from the vendor have been installed, be sure to use and update third-party firewall and antivirus apps, and if possible, run them inside a virtual machine (VM). Both the virtual machine manager (VMM) or host OS and the VM themselves should be using up-to-date antivirus and firewall apps.

> **TIP**
>
> EOL versions of Windows still in use are vulnerable to fake antivirus apps, such as those listed at `https://blogote.com/fake-antivirus-softwares`. Remind users not to be tricked by these imitations of actual alerts.

Bring Your Own Device (BYOD)

Bring Your Own Device (*BYOD*) is a policy that allows personal devices to be used for corporate purposes. Although the smartphone, tablet, or laptop is owned by the user, its security and software should be managed by the organization, regardless of where the device is— in the office, on a business trip, or at another remote location (including home).

Some ways to make BYOD usage less risky to organizations are:

- ▶ A BYOD policy for permitted devices, allowed/blocked applications, and what to do if a device is lost/stolen
- ▶ User education teaching best/worst practices
- ▶ Data encryption in the device (at rest) and during email or other information exchange (in motion)
- ▶ Separation of personal and business data

▶ Use of VPNs and other protection levels, including secure web gateways, firewalls, and cloud access security brokers

▶ Customized security that takes into account user behavior, what each user needs access to, and where users are located

▶ Multifactor authentication (MFA) with single sign-on (SSO) to block brute-force attacks

---

NOTE

Learn more about BYOD security at `www.citrix.com/solutions/secure-access/what-is-byod-security.html` and `https://perception-point.io/byod-security-threats-security-measures-and-best-practices.`

EXAM TIP

To prepare for the Core 2 1102 exam, be sure you understand the different types of vulnerabilities and how they threaten computer users and organizations: non-compliant systems, unpatched systems, unprotected systems (missing antivirus/missing firewall), EOL OSs, and bring your own device (BYOD). Be prepared to deal with these threats in security scenarios.

CERTMIKE EXAM ESSENTIALS

▶ One of the biggest threats to computer users and organizations is social engineering. Users and organizations need to be on their guard against in-person or technology-based examples.

▶ People in the executive suite and in IT are just as vulnerable as low-level users to social engineering, threats, and vulnerabilities. If they fall prey to attacks, the costs can be colossal and even fatal to an organization.

▶ Failure to retire EOL software (and hardware) when alternatives are available makes an organization very vulnerable to threats. If EOL devices and software must be used, extra protection is needed.

Practice Question 1

You are staying at a hotel that you've used before and you've complained about the low strength of the Wi-Fi signal. This time, a very strong unsecured Wi-Fi access point with the hotel name is available no matter where you are in the facility. However, you note that the hotel's welcome information didn't say anything about this Wi-Fi access point and the hotel normally requires guests to log in to use Wi-Fi. Which of the following attacks is the *most likely* one in use?

A. Phishing

B. Impersonation

C. Evil twin

D. Dumpster diving

Practice Question 2

You are trying to log into your corporate website to upload the day's activities. The website, normally very speedy, can barely display a login screen. However, when you try other websites, including another division of your company that uses the same login procedure and database, they work properly. Which of the following attacks is *most likely* taking place on the corporate website?

A. DDoS

B. Zero-day attack

C. Brute-force attack

D. XSS

Practice Question 1 Explanation

This question is designed to test your real-world understanding of security issues. Let's evaluate these answers one at a time.

1. The first answer (A, Phishing) is incorrect. A phishing attack is done by sending you an email or other message asking you to connect.

2. The next answer (B, Impersonation) is incorrect. This refers to alleged email or messages from a superior asking you to take action that would actually benefit an attacker.

3. The next answer (C, Evil twin) is correct. Evil twin attacks are often carried out using public Wi-Fi. The high strength of the signal and the fact that the hotel doesn't seem to know about it strongly suggest an evil twin Wi-Fi access point.

4. The last answer (D, Dumpster diving) is incorrect. There's no indication of anyone rooting around in the hotel's trash—or your room's trash.

Correct Answer: C. evil twin

Practice Question 2 Explanation

This question is designed to test your knowledge of threats. Let's evaluate these answers one at a time.

1. The first answer (A, DDoS) is correct. The website is being flooded with requests so that it cannot respond properly.

2. The second answer (B, Zero-day attack), is incorrect. A zero-day attack would probably be evident at the company's other websites since they use the same login procedure and database.

3. The third answer (C, Brute-force attack) is incorrect. This type of attack would not cause the entire website to become unresponsive.

4. The last answer (D, XSS) is incorrect. This type of attack would not cause the entire website to become unresponsive.

Correct Answer: A. DDoS

CHAPTER 17

Windows Security

Core 2 Objective 2.5: Given a scenario, manage and configure basic security settings in the Microsoft Windows OS.

Microsoft Windows includes a variety of security features to protect the operating system itself and the data it manages. However, it's up to users and administrators to set up and properly use these features. In this chapter, you will learn everything you need to know about A+ Certification Core 2 Objective 2.5, including the following topics:

▶ **Defender Antivirus**
▶ **Firewall**
▶ **Users and groups**
▶ **Login OS options**
▶ **NTFS vs. share permissions**
▶ **Run as Administrator vs. Standard User**
▶ **BitLocker**
▶ **BitLocker to Go**
▶ **Encrypting File System (EFS)**

DEFENDER ANTIVIRUS

Windows includes Microsoft Defender Antivirus, also known as Defender Antivirus. You can configure and use Defender Antivirus by selecting Settings, clicking Update & Security, choosing Open Windows Security, and clicking Virus & Threat Protection (see Figure 17.1).

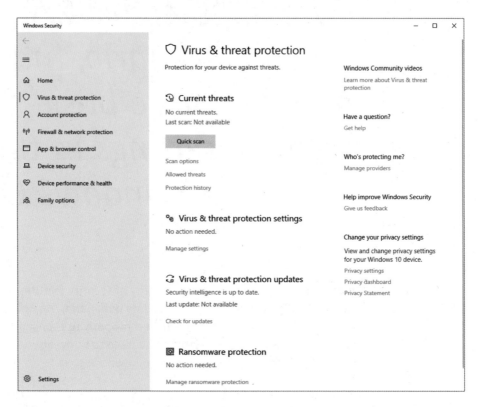

FIGURE 17.1 **Virus & Threat Protection is used to configure scanning, updates, and ransomware protection.**

Activate/Deactivate

Defender Antivirus has several different settings you can activate/deactivate separately: real-time protection, cloud-delivered protection, automatic sample submission, and tamper protection. Click Virus & Threat Protection Settings to access the options shown in Figure 17.2 and make changes.

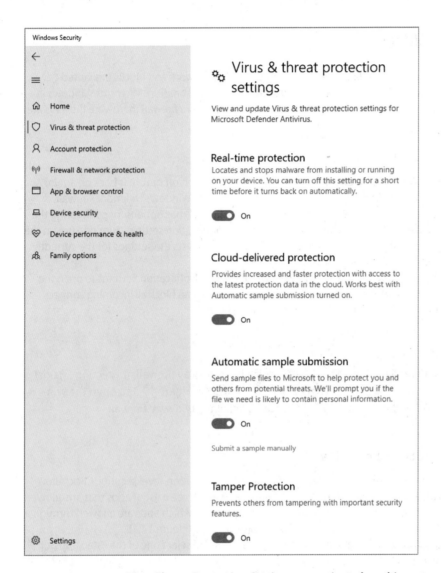

FIGURE 17.2 Virus Threat Protection Settings are activated on this system.

Updated Definitions

Defender Antivirus is updated automatically with Security Intelligence on a daily basis. However, you can update it manually by clicking Check For Updates in the Virus & Threat Protection window shown in Figure 17.1.

FIREWALL

A firewall examines data packets traveling through a network and blocks unwanted packets while forwarding requested information to its destination. Microsoft Windows includes the Windows Defender Firewall, a type of software firewall (hardware firewalls are built into network appliances or routers).

Activate/Deactivate

By default, Windows Defender Firewall is running. To turn it off or turn it back on again, open Control Panel, click System and Security, and select Windows Defender Firewall.

The left pane of Windows Defender Firewall (Figure 17.3) has options for configuring the firewall to permit or block apps or features, change notification settings, turn off/turn on the firewall, and configure advanced settings. The main pane lists the settings for the currently connected network type.

Click Windows Defender Firewall On Or Off or Change Notification Settings to open the Customize Settings dialog box shown in Figure 17.3. You can block all incoming connections, get notified of blocked apps, or turn off the firewall.

> **NOTE**
>
> The standard Windows Defender Firewall is a one-way firewall, protecting against inbound threats. Click Advanced Settings shown in Figure 17.3 to open the Windows Defender Firewall with Advanced Settings, a two-way firewall.

Application Security

Windows Defender Firewall is designed to provide application-level security. Click "Allow an app or feature through Windows Defender Firewall" to see a list of apps that are allowed and the network types each is allowed to use. To change which apps are allowed through a firewall, or to make other changes, click Change Settings (Figure 17.4).

To add an app, click the Allow Another App button and select one of the listed apps, or click Browse to go to the app's location and select the app. Click Network Types to select which networks the app can be used with. Click Add to finish.

To remove an app from the list, highlight it and click Remove.

> **NOTE**
>
> If you are unable to add or remove an app with the normal Firewall dialog box, you can use netsh from the command prompt or PowerShell to make changes. See `www.tenforums.com/tutorials/70903-add-remove-allowed-apps-through-windows-firewall-windows-10-a.html` for details.

FIGURE 17.3 Windows Defender Firewall's main menu and Customize Settings menus

Port Security

Port security is used to permit or block UDP or TCP ports with specific apps, services, or devices. The standard Windows Defender Firewall doesn't support port security, but Windows Defender Firewall with Advanced Security can control traffic at the port level. Click Advanced Settings in the main Windows Defender Firewall window to open Windows Defender Firewall with Advanced Security.

To see the protocol and ports settings for a specific rule, double-click it and click Protocols And Ports. The setting for Microsoft Office Outlook is shown in Figure 17.5.

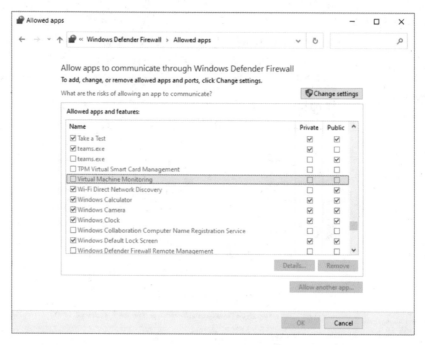

FIGURE 17.4 Preparing to make changes to Windows Defender Firewall's allowed apps

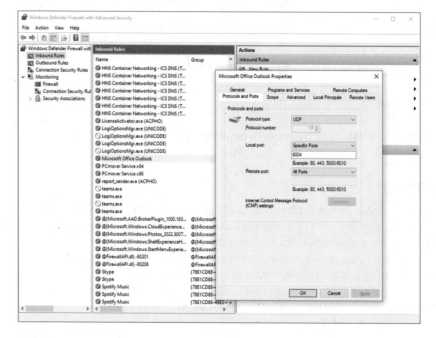

FIGURE 17.5 Reviewing Ports and Protocols settings for Microsoft Office in Windows Defender Firewall with Advanced Security

NOTE

For an introduction to Windows Defender Firewall with Advanced Security, see
`https://learn.microsoft.com/en-us/windows/security/`
`threat-protection/windows-firewall/`
`windows-firewall-with-advanced-security`.

EXAM TIP

Make sure you understand the differences between Windows Defender Antivirus
and Windows Defender Firewall, how to access each of them, and how to change
settings.

USERS AND GROUPS

Groups in Windows have different levels of permissions. Windows supports three types of
groups: Administrators, Standard Users, and Guests. Power Users can be added as a fourth
group by adjusting security policies.

There are also two types of user accounts in Windows: Microsoft Accounts and Local
Accounts. All of these are discussed in this section.

Local vs. Microsoft Account

When a new account is created, the user can choose between a Microsoft account or a local
account. The process encourages users to opt for a Microsoft account. A Microsoft account
uses your email address (from any provider) and a password you provide when you set up
your account. With a Microsoft account you can sync your settings across all devices that
you use, install and use apps from the Microsoft Store, use the Cortana personal assistant,
and automatically sign into OneDrive cloud storage, Microsoft 365, Skype, Xbox, and other
services. A Microsoft account is a good choice for taking advantage of Windows' many
cloud services. However, you sacrifice privacy and security if you don't set up PIN logins on
your devices and rely only on the Microsoft Account password.

When you set up a user with a local user account (an offline account), it uses a name, a
locally stored password, a password hint, and three security questions in case the password
is lost. A local account can also use a password reset disc or USB drive in case the password
is lost and needs to be reset. A local account can be used for an administrator or standard
account on an individual computer. A local account doesn't support Windows cloud services, but it provides a much higher level of privacy and can be more secure than a Microsoft account.

User Account Types Overview

Local User accounts include Administrator, Standard User, and Guest (disabled). Local Groups that you should know include Administrators, Guests, Power Users, and Users. You can access Local Users and Groups by clicking Start, choosing Run, and entering **lusrmgr .msc**. Groups are used to manage privileges for multiple users. You put user accounts into groups with similar interests.

Standard Account

When you set up a user with either a Microsoft or local account on an individual Windows PC, you must also assign the user to either a standard or administrator account. A user with a standard account can make changes to their own desktop, color scheme, and other personal settings. However, a user with a standard account cannot install new hardware or new software or run other tasks that have the Windows security shield identifier in Control Panel. When a standard user tries to perform a task that requires administrator credentials, User Account Control (UAC) prompts the user to enter the administrator's password.

Administrator

An administrator account gives that user full control over all aspects of a PC—software and hardware installations, the ability to access standard users' files, and so on.

> **TIP**
>
> Many security experts recommend that each administrator also have a standard account and use the standard account for everyday operations. Use the administrator account for systemwide changes.

Guest User

A Guest user account is intended to allow temporary users very limited access to computer resources; a Guest user cannot install new hardware or software or access files in shared folders. A Guest account is assigned to the Guests group. However, the Guest account is disabled by default.

As an alternative to enabling the Guest account, you can create an account with a different name (such as Visitor) that is set up as a standard user but without a password. You can then remove the Visitor account from the Users group (used for Standard users) and add it to the Guests group by using net commands.

> **NOTE**
>
> See the steps to create a Guest user account in Windows at www.howtogeek .com/280527/how-to-create-a-guest-account-in-Windows-10.

Power User

The Power Users group is a group that originally was granted permissions greater than a Standard user but lower than an Administrator. Although it is still present in Windows, the Power Users group is present for backward compatibility only. Without creating a custom security template for specific legacy apps, a member of the Power Users group only has the capabilities of a Standard user.

> **NOTE**
>
> Learn more about Local Users and Groups in Windows at www
> .thewindowsclub.com/
> open-local-users-and-groups-on-windows-10.

> **EXAM TIP**
>
> Make sure you understand the differences between standard user and administrator users, how to create a Guest user, and what Power Users is used for. Also make sure you understand the differences between Local and Microsoft accounts.

LOGIN OS OPTIONS

Windows offers a wide variety of login methods, depending on the account type (Microsoft or local) and the capabilities of a particular PC. To change your sign-in options, click Settings, select Accounts, and choose Sign-in Options (Figure 17.6).

> **NOTE**
>
> Learn more about different types of Windows sign-in options and account protection at https://support.microsoft.com/en-us/windows/windows-sign-in-options-and-account-protection-7b34d4cf-794f-f6bd-ddcc-e73cdf1a6fbf.

Username and Password

The default method for logging into a Windows PC is username and password, and this is true for both Microsoft and local accounts. The difference is that a Microsoft account is cloud-based and can be used on multiple PCs, whereas a local account is used only on one specific PC.

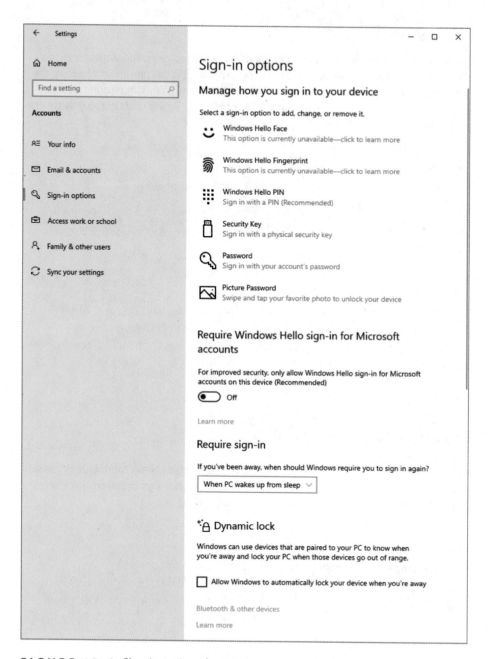

FIGURE 17.6 Sign-in options for Windows

Personal Identification Number (PIN)

Current versions of Windows support the use of a PIN as an alternative to a username and password login. A *personal identification number (PIN)* is a numeric or alphanumeric string that is stored on the local PC. The default PIN type is numeric and must be at least four digits long.

Microsoft refers to a PIN login as a Windows Hello PIN, and it is the preferred way to sign into Windows. When you create a PIN or change it, you have the option to include letters and symbols.

Fingerprint

To use a Windows Hello Fingerprint, your system must have a built-in or USB-connected fingerprint reader. You can teach Windows to recognize more than one fingerprint. You must set up a PIN before you can use Windows Hello Fingerprint.

Facial Recognition

Windows Hello Face uses a 3D or infrared (IR) camera (either built-in or connected via USB). You must set up a PIN before you can use Windows Hello Face.

Single Sign-On (SSO)

A *single sign-on (SSO)* enables users of multiple resources to use a single login credential to access them. SSO is often used on domain networks and other complex networking schemes to provide easier sign-in for users while providing a high level of security.

> **NOTE**
> Learn more about SSO and how it is implemented at www.csoonline
> .com/article/2115776/sso-explained-single-sign-on-
> definition-examples-and-terminology.html.

> **EXAM TIP**
> Make sure you know the requirements for different types of Login OS options and the prerequisites for using Windows Hello. Also understand that with SSO, a user only has to log in once to access multiple apps on a network.

NTFS VS. SHARE PERMISSIONS

There are two types of file and folder permissions in Windows: NTFS and share permissions. NTFS permissions are used only on drives that use the NTFS filesystem (typically hard drives, including SSDs), and share permissions are used on drives shared on networks and apply to network users. When both permissions apply to a specific file or folder, the permission type that is more restrictive is the one used to control access.

NTFS Permissions

NTFS permissions include the following:

- ▶ **Full control:** Complete access to the file or folder's contents. Full control includes all of the following:
  - ▶ **Modify:** Permits changes to file or folder contents.
  - ▶ **Read & Execute:** Permits access of file or folder contents and running apps.
  - ▶ **List Folder Contents:** View folder contents.
  - ▶ **Read:** Access a file or folder.
  - ▶ **Write:** Add a new file or folder to current location.

When an additional user is added to the list of users for a resource, the NTFS permission defaults for that user are Read & Execute, List Folder Contents, and Read.

To see or change NTFS permissions in File Explorer, right-click a file or folder and click Permissions, then select the Security tab. Figure 17.7 illustrates NTFS permissions for the owner and an additional user.

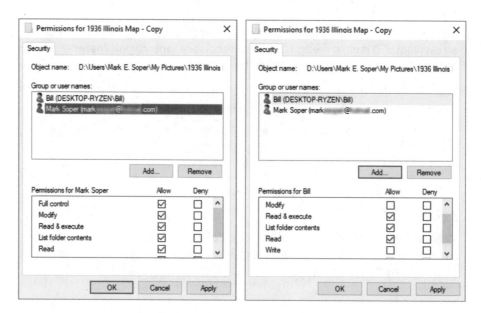

FIGURE 17.7 NTFS permissions for the owner of a file (left) and an additional user (right)

NOTE

Learn more about Share and NTFS permissions and inheritance at www
.sys-manage.com/Blog/
how-share-ntfs-permissions-and-inheritance-actually-work.

Share Permissions

Share permissions are set up when a file or folder is configured as a shared resource. To share a file or folder, right-click it in File Explorer, click Properties, and click the Sharing tab (Figure 17.8). When a file or folder is shared with others, the default setting is Read. The owner can also select Read/Write for other users.

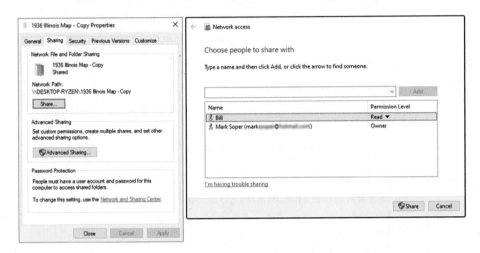

FIGURE 17.8 Setting share permissions for an additional user

To set up advanced permissions, such as the number of simultaneous users (up to 20 on workgroup shares) and Full control for specified users or groups, click Advanced Sharing.

File and Folder Attributes

File and folder attributes change how Windows works with and displays files and folders. To view file or folder attributes in Windows, right-click a file or folder in File Explorer and select Properties. The General tab lists file attributes. Figure 17.9 lists attributes for a folder (left) and a file (right).

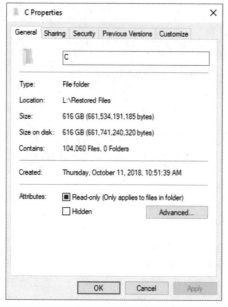
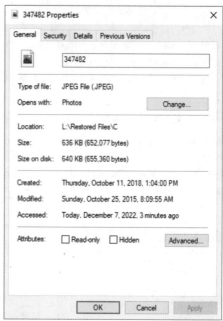

FIGURE 17.9 Typical folder (left) and file (right) attributes

Here are the common file attributes in Windows:

- ▶ **Read-only:** Allows a file to be read, but nothing can be written to the file or changed.
- ▶ **Archive:** Tells Windows Backup to back up the file.
- ▶ **System:** System file.
- ▶ **Hidden:** File is not shown when doing a regular dir from the command prompt.

If you look at the attributes for a folder, the Read-only box is always filled in (not checked). Windows cannot make a folder read-only, so this indicates that the files in the folder might—or might not—be read-only.

To see a hidden file or folder in File Explorer, go to View and click the empty Hidden Items check box (Figure 17.10). To see a hidden file or folder with command prompt or PowerShell, use the **dir /ah** command while referencing the folder or file location.

If a file was downloaded from another computer, you might see an empty Unblock check box in the File Properties dialog box. If you cannot open or edit the file, click the check box. When you change any of these attributes, click Apply afterward to use the changes.

To see file or folder attributes from cmd.exe or Windows PowerShell, use the attrib command (see Figure 17.11).

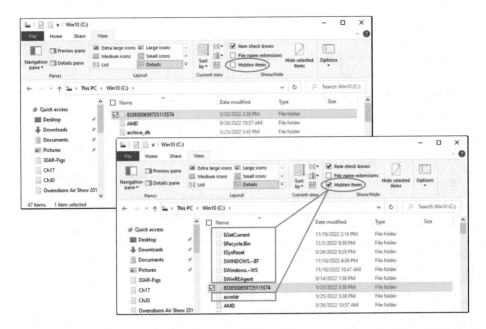

FIGURE 17.10 Comparing the root folder of C: in normal view (left) and with Hidden Files option enabled (right)

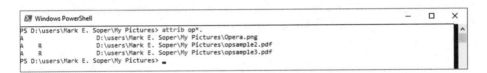

FIGURE 17.11 Listing file attributes for files beginning with op in My Pictures; A = **archive,** and R = **read-only**

Click Advanced Attributes if you want to compress or encrypt the file or folder (you can do one or the other). See "Encrypting File System (EFS)" later in this chapter for details.

The file or folder is marked as ready for archiving (backup) until it is backed up, and the file or folder can be indexed. Clear the check box to turn off the attribute; click the empty check box to turn it on.

Inheritance

By default, permissions for a subfolder of a folder on an NTFS drive are inherited from the parent folder (the folder containing the file or other folder).

This option can be disabled by selecting the Security tab, clicking Advanced, (refer to Figure 17.9) and clicking Disable Inheritance (Figure 17.12)

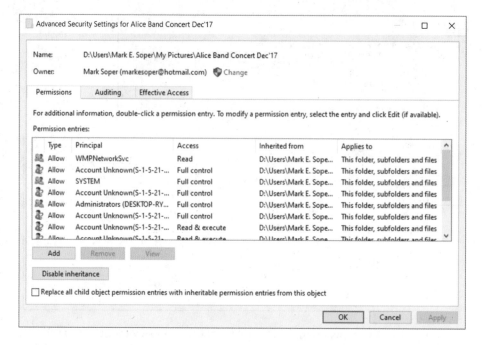

FIGURE 17.12 Preparing to disable permissions inheritance

When a folder is copied, the folder inherits the permissions from the target folder (directory) it was copied to. If a folder is moved to a different location on the same volume, it keeps its original permissions.

> **EXAM TIP**
>
> Be sure you understand the differences between NTFS and Share permissions, how inheritance works, and how to view and change file and folder attributes.

RUN AS ADMINISTRATOR VS. STANDARD USER

Applications that will change the system need to be run as administrator (also called elevated mode). Applications that will not change the system can be run in standard mode. For example, the Windows System File Checker (sfc.exe), which is run from a command prompt or from Windows PowerShell, displays an error message and will not run if the command prompt or PowerShell is running in standard mode. However, you can perform commands such as dir (displaying the contents of a folder or drive) in standard mode.

To open either cmd.exe (command prompt) or Windows PowerShell as administrator, search for the app and select Run As Administrator (Figure 17.13). You can also right-click Start and select Command Prompt (Admin) or Windows PowerShell (Admin). In any case, just click Yes to a User Account Control box if it appears.

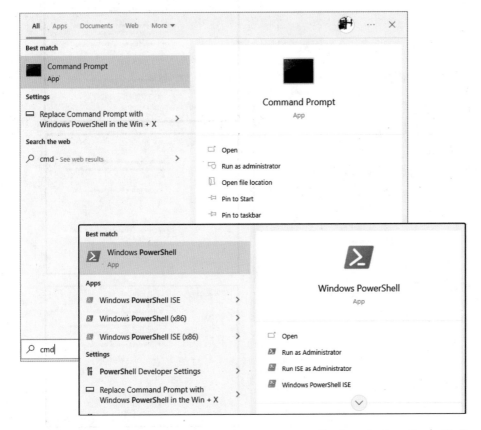

FIGURE 17.13 **Preparing to run Command Prompt (top) or Windows PowerShell (bottom) as an administrator**

Administrator mode is also a compatibility option you can use to help older software to run under current Windows versions.

User Account Control (UAC)

User Account Control (UAC) is an adjustable access control feature built into Windows. It helps prevent potentially harmful apps from running on a system. You manage UAC by opening Control Panel, selecting System And Security, and clicking User Account Control Settings. The default setting notifies the user when apps try to change the computer configuration, but not if the user makes changes to Windows. This and other settings are shown in Figure 17.14.

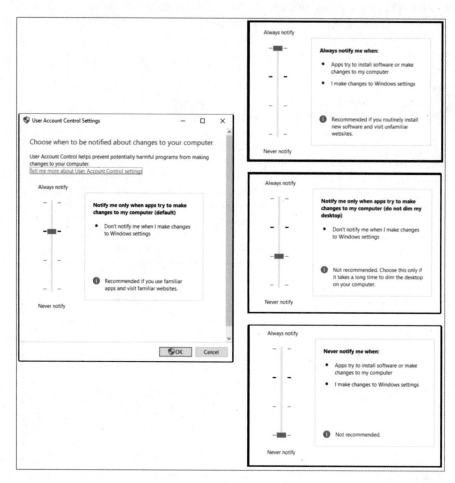

FIGURE 17.14 The default setting (left) for UAC in Windows 10 compared to other settings

When a UAC notification appears, an administrator can click through it, but a standard user must provide administrator credentials to perform the action.

EXAM TIP

Be sure you understand when to use Run As Administrator mode and how to configure UAC settings.

BitLocker

BitLocker is a full-disk encryption tool available in non-Home versions of Windows 10 and 11. The hardware requirements for BitLocker on Windows 10 include a Trusted Platform Module (TPM) chip on the motherboard or a CPU with TPM. Windows 11 requires TPM 2.0 support, so some systems that support BitLocker with Windows 10 might not run Windows 11. This means that if you upgrade from Windows 10 to Windows 11, BitLocker might not be supported.

To enable BitLocker on the system (C: drive) or fixed data drives, open Control Panel, select BitLocker Drive Encryption, and turn on BitLocker for any drives (Figure 17.15). Encryption will take some time. BitLocker's recovery key can be saved to your Microsoft account, to a USB flash drive or a file, or you can print it out. Be sure you make a recovery key backup so that your BitLocker drive can be accessed in the event of hardware changes. See `https://support.microsoft.com/en-us/windows/back-up-your-bitlocker-recovery-key-e63607b4-77fb-4ad3-8022-d6dc428fbd0d` for details.

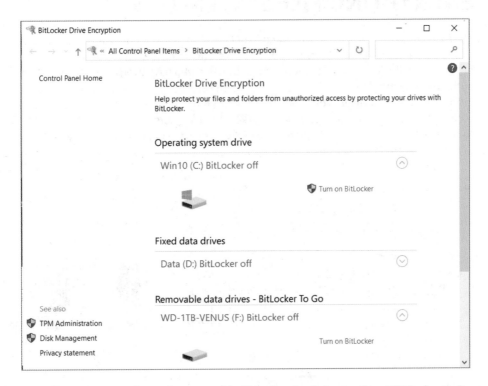

FIGURE 17.15 Preparing to enable BitLocker for C: (system) and BitLocker to Go for F: drive

NOTE

Windows 10 can use BitLocker without a TPM chip by storing the encryption key on a USB flash drive. See `https://techexpert.tips/windows/gpo-enable-bitlocker-encryption-without-tpm` for details.

BITLOCKER TO GO

BitLocker to Go is a version of BitLocker that provides full-disk encryption for removable-media drives. You run it on a selected drive from the BitLocker menu (refer to Figure 17.15). During the process, you specify a password or a smart card to store credentials, depending on your computer's configuration.

ENCRYPTING FILE SYSTEM (EFS)

The *Encrypting File System (EFS)* is a file and folder encryption feature built into non-Home editions of Windows. EFS works only on NTFS drives. Encrypted files and folders can only be opened by the user who encrypted them or by users who have been added to the list of authorized users that is stored in the EFS encryption key.

To enable EFS for a file or folder, right-click it, select the General tab, click Advanced, and click the Encrypt Contents To Secure Data checkbox shown Figure 17.16. Follow the prompts to complete encryption. An encrypted file or folder's icon has a padlock. To unencrypt a file or folder, clear the EFS check box.

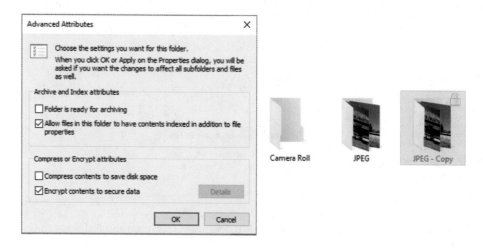

FIGURE 17.16 Encrypting a folder with EFS

The EFS encryption key is stored in the following location: `C:\Users\`*`username`*`\`
`AppData\Roaming\Microsoft\SystemCertificates\My\Keys\Certificates`.
However, you must export a backup of the key to be able to access your files if the current
certificate is corrupted or lost.

NOTE

To back up the EFS encrypted key, see www.`top-password.com/blog/`
`backup-or-export-efs-certificate-in-windows`.

EXAM TIP

Be sure you understand the differences between BitLocker, BitLocker to Go, and
EFS and how to encrypt a drive, file, or folder.

CERTMIKE EXAM ESSENTIALS

▶ To achieve the best balance of security and usability, make sure you use antivirus
and firewall tools; choose the right balance of accounts (administrators and standard users); and use more secure logins such as PIN, fingerprint, or facial recognition, and Encrypting File System (EFS) or BitLocker encryption.

▶ Make sure you understand login OS options, single-sign on, NTFS permissions,
and User Account Control.

▶ Every system should have a local Administrator account in case Internet access fails.

▶ BitLocker and BitLocker to Go encryption keys can be saved to your Microsoft
account or other locations, but EFS keys must be backed up manually.

Practice Question 1

You are preparing a laptop computer that will have confidential information stored on both the system drive (C: drive) and a USB drive. Which of the following will best protect this information from theft?

A. BitLocker on both drives
B. EFS encryption for data folders
C. BitLocker and BitLocker to Go
D. Image backup

Practice Question 2

Your client is concerned about blocking specific UDP or TCP ports from attacks. Which of the following tools provides the best protection from these attacks?

A. Defender Antivirus
B. Defender Firewall with Advanced Security
C. EFS encryption
D. Inheritance

Practice Question 1 Explanation

This question is designed to test your real-world understanding of Windows Security. Let's evaluate these answers one at a time.

1. The first answer (A, BitLocker on both drives) is incorrect. BitLocker works only on system drives.

2. The next answer (B, EFS encryption for data folders) would protect data folders, but it's designed to protect individual files and folders, not drives. This is not correct.

3. The next answer (C, BitLocker and BitLocker to Go) is correct. BitLocker encrypts system drives, and BitLocker to Go encrypts removable drives.

4. The last answer (D, Image backup) is incorrect. An image backup would protect the system drive's contents in case of loss or damage, but not theft, and would probably not back up the USB drive.

Correct Answer: C. BitLocker and BitLocker to Go

Practice Question 2 Explanation

This question is designed to test your knowledge of Windows Security features. Let's evaluate these answers one at a time.

1. The first answer (A, Defender Antivirus) is incorrect. Antivirus apps protect against viruses and malware, not attacks on specific ports.

2. The second answer (B, Defender Firewall with Advanced Security) is correct. This firewall can be configured to block specific ports for both inbound and outbound network traffic

3. The third answer (C, EFS encryption) is incorrect. EFS encryption prevents files or folders from being accessed by users other than the owner.

4. The last answer (D, Inheritance) is incorrect. Inheritance refers to using the same permissions as the parent folder.

Correct Answer: B. Defender Firewall with Advanced Security

CHAPTER 18

Workstation Security Configuration

Core 2 Objective 2.6: Given a scenario, configure a workstation to meet best practices for security.

Each part of a computing environment must be secure to keep the entire computing environment secure. So, security starts with each workstation. In this chapter, you learn the essentials of Core 2 Objective 2.6, including:

▶ **Data-at-rest encryption**
▶ **Password best practices**
▶ **End-user best practices**
▶ **Account management**
▶ **Change default administrator's user account/password**
▶ **Disable AutoRun**
▶ **Disable AutoPlay**

DATA-AT-REST ENCRYPTION

Workstation security starts with protecting the data residing on it. Data that is not being transmitted through a network or being used by an application is referred to as *data-at-rest*. Full-disk encryption provides protection for data-at-rest.

Full-disk encryption is provided by Microsoft BitLocker (supported by Windows editions other than Windows Home), FileVault (macOS 10.13 and later), and a variety of Linux tools such as cryptsetup, ecryptfs, and others.

I covered BitLocker in Chapter 17, "Windows Security" and FileVault in Chapter 10, "macOS."

> **TIP**
>
> To learn more about Linux encryption tools, see `www.tecmint.com/file-and-disk-encryption-tools-for-linux`.

PASSWORD BEST PRACTICES

Workstation passwords can be either formidable barriers to entry or a "welcome mat" to would-be intruders. To make passwords difficult to break, CompTIA recommends that you make sure passwords are complex and replaced periodically, and that BIOS/UEFI setup passwords be used. Following the recommendations in this section will help make sure that passwords do their job of protecting workstations.

Complexity Requirements

Just about everyone understands that a password like "password" is no protection at all, but what does it mean to create a password that meets complexity? The simplest ways to define complexity is in terms of uniqueness, length, and character types.

Uniqueness
Using the same password for multiple accounts puts those accounts at risk. If an account name/password pairing is discovered, an attack known as *credential stuffing* uses known account name/password pairs on other sites. To avoid this, don't use the same password on different sites.

Length
The longer a password is, the harder it is to guess. That's why the minimum password length is typically eight characters. Don't stop at the minimum, though: passwords can be longer. `Cybernews.com`, for example, recommends a minimum of 12 characters, whereas Microsoft recommends a minimum length of 14 in its discussion of recommended security policy settings.

> **NOTE**
>
> For more information about the benefits of longer passwords, see `https://cybernews.com/best-password-managers/how-to-create-a-strong-password`, `https://learn.microsoft.com/en-us/windows/security/threat-protection/security-policy-settings/minimum-password-length`, and `https://resources.infosecinstitute.com/topic/password-security-complexity-vs-length`.

Character Types

Short passwords that use common words or alphanumeric combinations can be easy to guess. However, passphrases that combine four or more random words are practically uncrackable (see www.useapassphrase.com for details) as well as being easy to remember.

Using punctuation marks as part of a password helps increase the amount of time needed to crack a password, and the longer it takes, the more likely it is that a potential attacker may give up and try attacking an easier-to-breach account instead.

The Password Meter website (www.passwordmeter.com) enables you to enter a password to determine how strong it is. In Figure 18.1, we compare the strength of using this author's name (marksoper) as a 9-character password with a version that capitalizes some letters and replaces others with similar-looking numbers, also 9 characters (mArk50P3r). The name alone has a rating of very weak (score 10%), while the version using capitalization and substitution has a rating of very strong (score 81%). Using punctuation marks makes a password even stronger.

You can enforce complexity requirements in Windows by changing settings in Group Policy.

Expiration Requirements

Although current best password practice according to the National Institute of Standards and Technology (NIST), Microsoft, and others, doesn't require users to change passwords, some company policies may still require periodic password changes. You can enforce password expiration requirements in Windows by changing settings in Group Policy.

> **EXAM TIP**
>
> Make sure you are aware of password best practices. Given a scenario, you should know where and how to set requirements for complexity, length, and expiration. Before making any changes, always consider company policy when doing so.

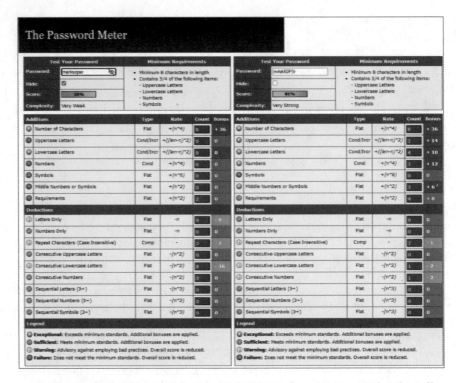

FIGURE 18.1 Make a weak password stronger by mixing capital and small letters and using numbers in place of letters.

Using Group Policy to Improve Password Settings

After starting the Group Policy Editor for your workstation or network, click Computer Configuration, select Windows Settings, click Security Settings, click Account Policies, and select Password Policy, as shown in Figure 18.2.

To require a password change, set Maximum Password Age to the desired number of days before a new password is required. To minimize the reuse of passwords, enter a value greater than 0 for Enforce Password History. For example, enter **5** and the user must use five new passwords before recycling an old one.

To require more complex passwords, enable Password Must Meet Complexity Requirements and set the minimum password length to 8 or more characters.

Basic Input/Output System (BIOS)/Unified Extensible Firmware Interface (UEFI) Passwords

Changes in BIOS/UEFI settings can cause a system to stop booting, be incapable of running Windows 11, or be started with unauthorized operating systems on thumb drives. BIOS (Basic Input-Output System) is the firmware used to configure the motherboard and components built into it, such as RAM, CPU, and built-in ports. It has been replaced by Unified Extensible Firmware Interface (UEFI), which supports hard drives with capacities above 2 TB, a GUID partition table supporting more than four partitions, secure startup, and built-in networking for remote management.

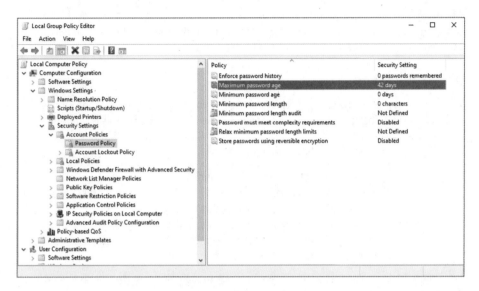

FIGURE 18.2 Use Group Policy to change password settings such as password age (expiration), complexity, and others.

To prevent these and other changes to a system's configuration, you can set up a password to prevent changes to BIOS/UEFI settings (Figure 18.3). This type of password is usually called the Administrator password. A BIOS/UEFI password that must be entered before a system can be started is called a user password, and is configured separately.

FIGURE 18.3 A typical BIOS/UEFI administrator password screen

EXAM TIP

To prepare for the Core 2 1102 exam, make sure you know about the drive encryption programs in Windows, macOS, and Linux, and how to enable and improve password settings.

END-USER BEST PRACTICES

Whether you're using a desktop computer or something that's easier to tote, such as a laptop or a convertible tablet, your device can be a magnet for data thieves when it's in use. Here's how to make it a less attractive target.

Use Screensaver Locks

Make sure you know how to lock your system when you're not using it. Anyone who wants to get to the information on your computer would need to log into it. This is often referred to as a screensaver lock.

To enable the screensaver lock in Windows:

1. Go to Settings, select Personalization, and click Lock Screen.
2. Click Screen Saver Settings (Windows 10) or Screen Saver (Windows 11).
3. Choose a screen saver from the drop-down list.
4. Specify how long to wait before the screensaver lock starts.
5. Make sure the On Resume, Display Logon Screen option is selected.
6. Click Apply, then click OK.

In Windows, you can also lock the screen immediately by pressing the Windows key+L to lock the screen and display the login screen.

On a macOS system, use Command+Control+Q to lock your system.

On Linux, install xtrlock from the software repository. Run **xtrlock** from Terminal.

> **NOTE**
>
> To learn more methods for locking your Mac, including automatic locking after a period of idleness, see www.howtogeek.com/703785/ 8-ways-to-lock-your-mac and https://it.cornell.edu/ device-security/set-your-macs-screen-lock-automatically. To learn how to set up keyboard shortcuts for running xtrlock on Linux, see https://trendoceans.com/how-to-lock-keyboard-on-linux-windows.

Log Off When Not In Use

As an alternative to a screensaver lock, log off your system when not in use. On Windows 10 or 11, click Start, enter your name, and click Sign Out.

Secure/Protect Critical Hardware (e.g., Laptops)

Don't overlook using physical locks to protect easy-to-move hardware such as laptops, portable hard drives, and printers. Many of these devices support the Kensington lock system shown in Figure 18.4.

FIGURE 18.4 A Kensington hardware lock before (left) and after (right) being attached to a 3.5-inch external hard drive

Secure Personally Identifiable Information (PII) and Passwords

Personally identifiable information (PII) is information that can be used to identify an individual, ranging from the full name and Social Security number to financial and medical data.

There are a variety of ways to protect PII, including encrypting files or drives that contain PII and removing PII from documents. With Microsoft Office, for example, choose File ➢ Info, and open the Check For Issues menu in the Inspect Document section of the Info page. Click Inspect Document and click Inspect to use the Document Inspector feature shown in Figure 18.5. If Document Properties and Personal Information are discovered, they are flagged. Click Remove All to remove them from the document.

Don't "store" your passwords on a sticky note attached to the side of your monitor or a filing cabinet in a cubicle. Instead, use secure physical or electronic storage, such as a locked filing cabinet with an anonymous file label, an electronic file encrypted with EFS, or a password management system. Some password management systems are available in both free and paid versions, enabling you to try a system and see if the free version is adequate or if you need more features.

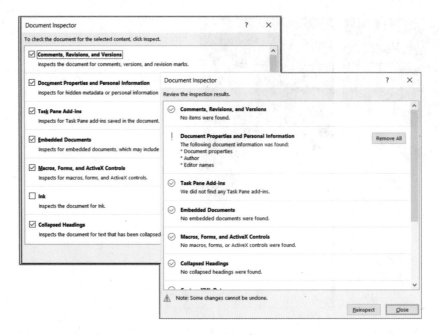

FIGURE 18.5 Preparing to remove personal information from a Microsoft Word document with Document Inspector

NOTE

For reviews of top-rated password managers, see `https://us.cybernews.com/lp/best-password-managers-us` and `www.pcmag.com/picks/the-best-password-managers`.

EXAM TIP

To prepare for the Core 2 1102 exam, make sure you understand the screen-locking processes for Windows, macOS, and Linux; how to use hardware locks; and how to secure PII and passwords.

ACCOUNT MANAGEMENT

Changes to default account settings can also help keep a system secure, as you will learn in this section.

Restrict User Permissions

The principle of "least permissions" should be used when setting up users or groups. Simply stated, the principle of least permissions means determining what a user needs access to and allowing access to only those files, folders, devices, and apps.

When setting up a user on a stand-alone PC or a workgroup, set up users so they only have accounts on devices that they need access to. Don't provide root folder access but only access to specific folders. Use read-only access unless a user needs to make changes to a file. When installing a new app, you can sometimes specify whether to install an app for all users or only for specific users.

When setting up a user on a domain network, you have more control over user permissions. Create groups with different levels of access and assign users to a specific group based on their access needs.

For more information about Active Directory (domain) security and the principle of least privilege, see Chapter 13, "Logical Security."

Restrict Login Times

Another way to apply the principle of privilege is to restrict users' login times to actual work hours. In Windows 10/11, you can use the `net user` command to specify the days and hours a user can log into a system:

1. Open a command prompt as Administrator.
2. Enter this command:

```
net user {username} /times:{days,times}
```

For example, to allow user Bill to log in only on Mondays–Fridays between 8:00 and 17:00 (8A–5P), enter this:

```
net user Bill /times:M-F,08:00-17:00
```

Use **net user Bill /time:all** to reverse this command so that Bill can log in at any time.

On an Active Directory account, you can configure login hours and use Group Policy to force a user or group to log off when time expires.

> **NOTE**
>
> For more information about using Group Policies to control log on hours, see
> `www.rebeladmin.com/2014/06/`
> `use-of-group-policies-to-control-log-on-hours-to-the-network.`

Disable Guest Account

One of the easiest ways to make a computer more secure is to disable the Guest account. This was designed to provide a way for users without an account to log onto a computer, but it lacks effective protection for information.

Guest accounts can be disabled with the Local Group Policy Editor: Computer Configuration | Windows Settings | Security Settings | Local Policies | Security Options | Accounts: Guest account status: Disabled. Guest accounts can also be disabled with Computer Management by typing **Net user guest /active:no** from the command prompt (as Administrator), and from Manage Accounts in Control Panel. These methods work in Windows 10 or 11.

> **NOTE**
>
> For more information about disabling Guest accounts, see `www.isunshare`
> `.com/windows-10/`
> `4-ways-to-enable-and-disable-built-in-guest-on-windows-`
> `10.html`.

Use Failed Attempts Lockout

Setting up effective password policies is only half the battle in stopping unauthorized users from trying to hack into a system. The Account Lockout Policy dialog box shown in Figure 18.6 provides settings that can be used to prevent an uninterrupted stream of attempts to guess a password.

The Account Lockout Duration setting specifies how long (in minutes) a user must wait after being locked out before new login attempts can be made. Microsoft recommends 15 minutes.

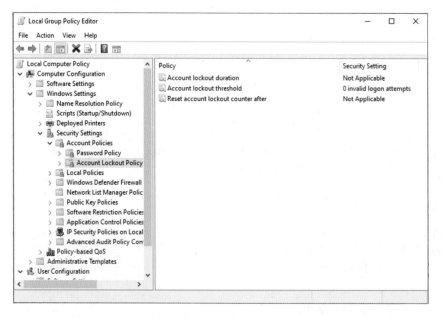

F I G U R E   1 8 . 6   **The Account Lockout Policy settings dialog box in Local Group Policy Editor**

The Account Lockout Threshold setting specifies how many invalid login attempts can be made before the user is locked out. Microsoft recommends 10 as a starting point.

The Reset Account Lockout Counter After specifies how many minutes elapse between the time a user fails to sign in before the counter resets to 0. The value should be less than or equal to the Account Lockout Duration value. Microsoft recommends 15 minutes.

> **NOTE**
>
> For more information about when to use or change recommended values for these settings, see `https://learn.microsoft.com/en-us/windows/ security/threat-protection/security-policy-settings/ account-lockout-policy`.

Use Timeout/Screen Lock

When Windows 10 and 11 shut off the display, you must log back into the computer by waking up the display and entering your credentials at the lock screen. To change the amount of idle time before the display is shut off, select Settings, click System, and select Power and Battery in Windows 11, or select Settings, click System, and select Power and Sleep in Windows 10.

Reduce these values to enable the system to shut off quickly when idle, so if a user walks away from the system for a break, the computer will lock itself, even if the user forgets to lock it manually.

> **NOTE**
>
> To learn how to configure the screen lock to stay on screen longer when the system is locked, see `www.howtogeek.com/267893/ how-to-change-the-windows-10-lock-screen-timeout`.

> **EXAM TIP**
>
> To prepare for the Core 2 1102 exam, make sure you understand the principle of least privilege, how to use timeout and screen lock to safeguard systems, how to restrict login times, how to lock out users after unsuccessful login attempts, and how to disable Guest accounts.

CHANGE DEFAULT ADMINISTRATOR'S USER ACCOUNT/PASSWORD

The default administrator account on Windows is called Administrator, and it does not have a password, which makes this account a relatively easy target for hackers if it's enabled (it's hidden by default but can be enabled in various ways).

This account, created by default in all Windows versions, bypasses User Account Control (UAC), so there's nothing to slow down a hacker from making catastrophic changes to your system unless you change the name of the account and add a password.

To change the name of this account:

1. Open Local Group Policy Editor by searching for it or click Start ➤ Run and enter **gpedit.msc**.
2. Click Windows Settings, Security Settings, Local Policies, Security Options, Accounts, and Rename Administrator Account.
3. Enter a name other than Administrator; do *not* use an existing account name (Figure 18.7).
4. After entering a new name for the Administrator account, click Apply, then OK.

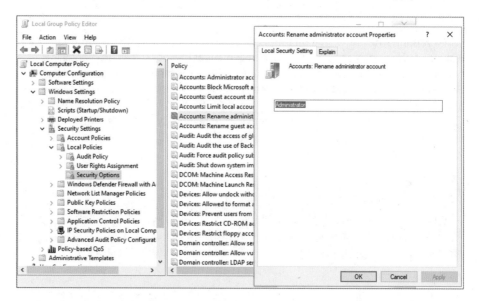

FIGURE 18.7 Changing the name of the built-in Administrator account

To add a password to the built-in Administrator account:

1. Search for **cmd**.
2. Right-click cmd and select Run As Administrator.
3. Enter the command **net user** to see the accounts on the system. You should see the name of the built-in Administrator account listed.
4. Enter the command
   net user *administratoraccount password* to add a password. For example, if the built-in Administrator account has been renamed to Spider-man and the new password is Parker61, the command would be

```
net user Spiderman Parker61
```

NOTE

Lear more about changing the name of the built-in Administrator account at `www.techjunkie.com/change-built-in-administrator-account-name`. Learn more about setting a password for the built-in Administrator account at `https://madestuffeasy.com/find-windows-10-administrator-password`.

DISABLE AutoRun

AutoRun, not to be confused with AutoPlay (see the next section), is a technology used primarily to automatically start applications stored on optical media, but it can also be used on other types of media that can tell the host system that new media has been inserted or connected.

A drive configured to use Autorun will have an `autorun.inf` file in its root directory (root folder) to instruct the computer which file on the media to run. The contents of a typical `autorun.inf` file resemble the following:

```
[autorun]
open=Program.exe
icon=Program.exe,1
```

You can use Notepad to view the contents of an `autorun.inf` file.

Although installations from AutoRun have not been supported since Windows XP, AutoRun can still cause havoc by running malware from an optical disc or other removable media.

To block AutoRun for specific drives, you can change the Registry.

NOTE

For details on how to block AutoRun by changing the Windows Registry, see `www.wikihow.com/Disable-Autorun-in-Windows`.

DISABLE AutoPlay

AutoPlay is a Windows feature that performs a specified action when a removable media drive, a memory card, or a smartphone is connected to a PC. AutoPlay can be configured to perform a wide variety of actions, such as open the drive in File Explorer, run an application that uses the media stored on the card, or ask the user to select an action.

By disabling AutoPlay, you prevent an application or computer that might be compromised by a hacker from accessing content on the device automatically.

AutoPlay can be disabled in Windows in two ways: by turning AutoPlay to Off, or by selecting Take no action for each of the device types it supports. See Figure 18.8 to see a typical AutoPlay dialog box when enabled and both ways to disable it.

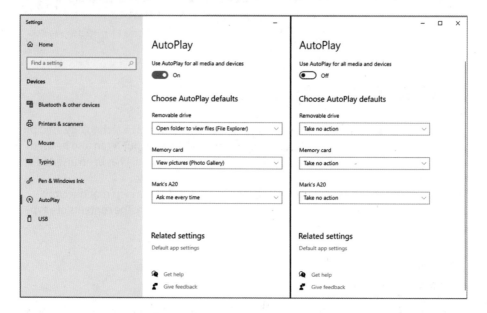

FIGURE 18.8 Typical AutoPlay settings enabled for different types of media (left) and disabled (right)

NOTE

Figure 18.8 (right) shows the AutoPlay switch set to off and "take no action" for each media type. You can use either method; it is not necessary to perform both actions at the same time.

EXAM TIP

To prepare for the Core 2 1102 exam, make sure you understand the process of protecting the built-in Administrator account, disabling Autorun, and disabling AutoPlay.

CERTMIKE EXAM ESSENTIALS

▶ Password, end user, and account management settings should be used together to make it very difficult for unauthorized users to access a system.

▶ Encryption, disabling AutoRun, and disabling AutoPlay help prevent attacks on system contents from malware.

▶ All accounts should be password-protected, including the hidden Administrator account.

Practice Question 1

A user named Smith tries to use Smith12345 as a password. Which of the following is the *most likely* reason the password was rejected?

A. Password is too short.

B. Password complexity requirements are enabled.

C. No alphanumeric passwords are permitted.

D. Password expiration requirements.

Practice Question 2

Your client wants to prevent thumb drives from being opened automatically, but wants to see the photos stored on memory cards. Which of the following AutoPlay settings are the *best* to allow these actions to take place?

A. Disable AutoPlay.

B. Enable AutoPlay.

C. Removable drive: Take No Action; Memory Card: View Pictures with *app*.

D. Smartphone: Ask me every time.

Practice Question 1 Explanation

This question is designed to test your real-world understanding of best password practices. Let's evaluate these answers one at a time.

1. The first answer (A, Password is too short) is incorrect. Most systems require a password of at least 8 characters, and this password contains 10.

2. The next answer (B, Password complexity requirements are enabled) is the *most likely* answer. Password complexity requirements reject repeating the username as part of the password and also reject simple numeric sequences.

3. The next answer (C, No alphanumeric passwords are permitted) is incorrect. Most passwords are alphanumeric.

4. The last answer (D, Password expiration requirements) is incorrect. There is no indication that this password has been used before.

Correct Answer: B. Password complexity requirements are enabled

Practice Question 2 Explanation

This question is designed to test your knowledge of AutoPlay settings. Let's evaluate these answers one at a time.

1. The first answer (A, Disable AutoPlay) is incorrect. Disabling AutoPlay prevents any AutoPlay options from working.

2. The second answer (B, Enable AutoPlay) is incorrect. The client wants to selectively use AutoPlay for certain media types, and this setting by itself has no limitations.

3. The third answer (C, Removable drive: Take No Action; Memory Card: View Pictures with *app*) is the *best* answer. As long as the specified app is installed, the pictures will be displayed.

4. The last answer (D, Smartphone: Ask me every time) is incorrect. The client is not asking about Smartphone AutoPlay settings.

Correct Answer: C. Removable drive: Take No Action; Memory Card: View pictures with *app*

CHAPTER 19

Mobile and Embedded Device Security

Core 2 Objective 2.7: Explain common methods for securing mobile and embedded devices.

Over the last 10 years, mobiles devices and embedded devices have been adopted at a rapid pace by consumers and organizations. The number of devices on the entire planet grew over the course of the pandemic, with much of the planet working from home. Post-pandemic, the workplace looks very different, with mobile and embedded devices creating a balance of work and life. Now more than ever we need to secure these devices to make sure data is not leaked, intercepted, crypto-ed, and ransomed. In this chapter, you will learn what you need to know about the A+ Certification Core 2 Objective 2.7, including the following topics:

► **Screen locks**
► **Remote wipes**
► **Locator applications**
► **OS updates**
► **Device encryption**
► **Remote backup applications**

- ► **Failed login attempts restrictions**
- ► **Antivirus/antimalware**
- ► **Firewalls**
- ► **Policies and procedures**
- ► **Internet of Things (IoT)**

SCREEN LOCKS

Both Apple and Android mobile devices have the ability to lock the screen. You should turn the feature on for privacy, and the operating system encourages you to enable a lock during the initial setup of the device. If your device is ever lost or stolen, the data is safe with a screen lock; the threat actor cannot get past the locked screen without your biometrics, PIN code, or pattern. This means that your device is useless to a criminal if stolen and your data is safe on the device. In this section you will learn about the various types of locks that you can implement to secure your device.

> **NOTE**
>
> In December 2015 a terrible terrorist attack happened that involved two terrorists, and an iPhone was seized in the aftermath of the crime. The FBI needed to unlock the iPhone to attain evidence on future potential terrorist plots. Apple was petitioned by the FBI to unlock the device, but even Apple didn't have a master key for the screen lock. The government then demanded that Apple add a law enforcement backdoor in all Apple products. However, Apple declined, saying they would not undermine the security of their customers. The letter to their customers remains online at www.apple.com/customer-letter.

Facial Recognition

The facial recognition feature on phones is a biometric lock that uses your front-facing camera to unlock your device by comparing features of your face to a previously stored copy. Facial recognition may experience false positives when an imposter potentially matches someone else's facial features. Most phones today have front-facing cameras, and most laptops also have cameras built into the screen. Apple, Android, and Microsoft all support face lock technology. On Apple devices, this technology is called Face ID. Android devices call this technology facial recognition and Microsoft supports face locks with Windows Hello.

> **EXAM TIP**
> Facial recognition is a biometric feature on phones that uses the front-facing camera to unlock the devices with your facial features.

PIN Codes

A personal identification number (PIN) is another common way to unlock your device. The PIN works by entering a 4-to-6-digit numeric passcode. The PIN code does not need to be solely a numeric number; it can also be alphanumeric, depending on the device. Most devices require you to set up a PIN before you can turn on biometrics. The device will use the PIN as a fallback method in case your camera breaks. The disadvantage to a PIN code is that it's something that you know and others can learn by shoulder surfing. Your PIN number can even be guessed by looking at the fingerprints on your screen.

> **EXAM TIP**
> A PIN code lock is a way to unlock your devices with a passcode.

Fingerprint

A fingerprint lock is another type of biometric that uses your fingerprint to secure the device. The fingerprint lock is probably the most secure biometric method to secure your device. You place your finger on an optical sensor on the device, and the sensor will then read and compute the point of your fingerprint and compare it with previously stored values. On Apple devices, the fingerprint recognition is called Touch ID. Android devices call this fingerprint recognition, and Microsoft supports fingerprint locks with Microsoft Hello.

> **Exam Tip**
> A fingerprint lock is a biometric lock that uses your fingerprint to unlock the device.

Pattern

The pattern lock is a visual passcode that allows you to unlock your device. Swipe lock functions by displaying nine dots in a matrix of 3×3. You can then unlock the device by swiping, connecting the dots in a pattern with your finger. The result will then be compared with the registered pattern to unlock the phone. The swipe lock is the least secure of any locking methods. An oil trail from your fingers can allow someone to derive the swipe pattern.

Swipe

The swipe lock is not considered a security lock, but it is a screen lock. Turning it on will allow your phone to lock so that your phone does not pocket-dial a person. However, it will unlock by simply swiping your finger across the screen to unlock an on-screen slider. Therefore, this is not really a security measure.

> **EXAM TIP**
>
> A swipe lock is not a secure lock—it is only used to prevent an accidental key press.

LOCATOR APPS AND REMOTE WIPES

Modern smartphones, tablets, and other devices provide remote location features that allow the owner (or someone else with access to the account) to pinpoint where the device is located. Apple products will allow you to find a multitude of devices, such as iPhones, iPads, Apple Watches, MacBooks, and AirPods. The MacBook needs to be powered on and connected to the Internet (via cellular, Wi-Fi, Ethernet, and so on). The app allows the device to be controlled remotely to lock it, play a sound (even if audio is off), display a message, or wipe it clean. To find an Apple product, it is as simple as browsing to www .icloud.com/find or opening the Find My app on another device and locating your device. From the website or the app, you can play a sound on the device, see a map location of where the device is, or even remotely wipe the device.

Within a newer iPhone's Settings screen, you can find an iCloud settings page and select the Find My iPhone switch. If this switch is off, the Find My iPhone app and iCloud web page will be unable to find your device, as shown in Figure 19.1.

Android devices also have a feature to locate mobile devices, such as tablets and phones. The website Google Find My Device located at www.google.com/android/find allows you to see your device on a map, locate the device, sign out of your Google account, and in the worse scenarios, erase the device. Just like the Apple site, you will need to be logged into your Google account to use the locator.

In addition to Apple and Android, Microsoft has a device location service that is built into the operating system of Windows 10/11. If you lose your laptop and it is still connected to the Internet, you can locate the device or lock the device. Unfortunately, remote device wipes will require enrollment in a mobile device management suite, such as Intune. However, if you encrypt the drive, remotely lock the device, and change your password on your account, the data is relative safe.

FIGURE 19.1 The Find My iPhone settings

> **EXAM TIP**
>
> Locator apps allow you to locate your mobile devices if they are missing or lost. You can also remote-wipe a device if it is stolen.

OS UPDATES

Not keeping up with software updates creates an environment of known weaknesses (exploits) and unfixed bugs. Mobile devices and embedded devices operate on a tight tolerance of hardware and software performance, and this can be a bad reflection on the vendor of the device. Therefore, many vendors have methods to force updates on to the end user. Some of the methods that vendors use to force an installation are mandatory scheduled installations, nag screens, and countdowns to the inevitable installation.

For the iPhone and iPad, you can check for updates by tapping Settings ➢ General ➢ Software Update. For the Android operating system, there are multiple updates that can be checked for manually. All of them are accessible by following Menu ➢ Settings ➢ System Updates.

DEVICE ENCRYPTION

As a best practice, device encryption should be used on mobile devices to protect your data in the event of device theft. Apple devices are automatically encrypted whenever the phone is locked with a passcode, Touch ID, or Face ID. Android devices now ship with encryption enabled by default, and just like with Apple you will need to set up a lock screen. Older Android operating systems will require you to manually encrypt the operating system from the Settings menu.

Laptops can also benefit from device encryption. BitLocker greatly enhances security on Microsoft laptops by encrypting the data on drives. Apple FileVault uses AES-XTS data encryption to protect data on Mac computers. Both of these technologies prevent data leakage in the event of the laptop becoming lost or stolen.

Some encryption best practices are as follows:

▶ Full-drive encryption should be turned on any mobile device that could be lost or stolen.

▶ The devices should be backed up on a consistent basis, using automated tools in the operating system or cloud-based tools.

▶ If the operating system has an option to exclude removable media such as SD cards, this should be avoided and the entire device should be encrypted along with the removable storage. When Android devices are configured for full-device encryption, the SD card is automatically encrypted.

REMOTE BACKUP APPLICATIONS

Automated remote backup is a best practice that should be used whenever possible. If the backup requires your intervention, it might not get done and you'll realize that when it's too late. Thankfully, every mobile device vendor also has their own free built-in remote cloud backup application to protect their customers. Apple iOS devices can automatically back themselves up to the configured iCloud account associated with the device. Android devices can back themselves automatically up to the associated Google account on the device. Microsoft also features a built-in backup-to-cloud feature on the Windows 10/11 operating system called Microsoft OneDrive.

These remote backup applications require an Internet connection so that your mobile device can back itself up. However, with the megapixel size of pictures and movies today, your precious cellular data can be eaten up quickly. So most applications are set to back up the big files only when you are connected to Wi-Fi. The backup applications will typically back up Wi-Fi passwords, phone logs, app settings, contacts, messages, pictures, and other related files.

FAILED LOGIN ATTEMPTS RESTRICTIONS

On Apple devices, after you've set a passcode or Touch ID, the device will wipe data after 10 failed attempts. You can access these settings by tapping Settings, then tapping either Face ID & Passcode or Touch ID & Passcode depending if the iPhone has Face ID or a Home button, as shown in Figure 19.2. Apple will impose a cooling-off timeout period of increasing duration, even if the Erase Data feature is disabled and the code is repeatedly entered wrong over multiple lockouts. Ultimately, after the 10th wrong passcode entered, your data will be erased. You will then need to restore your device from an iCloud backup or set it up again as a new device.

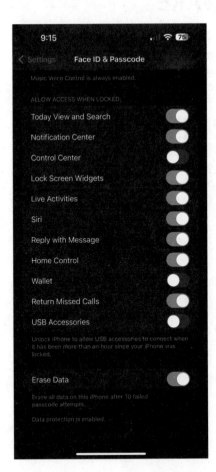

FIGURE 19.2 Apple setting for Face ID & Passcode

After a passcode, pattern, or fingerprint is set on an Android, the device will erase after 10 failed attempts. As on Apple devices, there is a cooling-off timeout period of increasing duration. After the 10th attempt the device will erase your data. The phone can be restored from backup or set up as a new device if this happens.

On Windows 10/11 operating systems, after 5 failed attempts to enter the password, the 6th attempt will begin to slow your entries down. However, by default the operating system will not lock the account out.

> **NOTE**
>
> Account lockouts and the use of timeout/screen locks were covered in Chapter 18, "Workstation Security Configuration."

ANTIVIRUS/ANTIMALWARE

The effect of the malware installed on mobile and embedded devices is typically ads from the Internet spammed on your device. However, some malware can expose your personal information and even subject your device to the control of a malicious individual. Viruses, on the other hand, will use your email application to send copies of itself or turn your device into a zombie.

The outcome of the damage from the installation of malware or a virus is hard to estimate and can be quite extensive. The installation of an antivirus or antimalware can prevent an infection or installation of antimalware. All the leading vendors, such as AVG, Norton, and Avast, just to name a few, have a product to protect your mobile device from viruses and malware. Most installations of these apps are free, and other services or features can be purchased within the apps.

FIREWALLS

Mobile devices and desktop operating systems both have vulnerabilities, no matter how secure the operating system is touted by the vendor. When a mobile operating system boots up, it obtains an IP address via the Wi-Fi radio or the internal cellular radio. Once an IP address is configured on the operating system, it becomes vulnerable to attack. A firewall can protect the device by preventing unauthorized inbound access to the device.

Firewalls also monitor and control outbound network communication to prevent malicious apps from communicating with the systems on the Internet that control them and collect stolen data. In addition to the firewalls built into operating systems, third-party firewall apps can be downloaded from either Apple's App Store, Google Play, or the Microsoft Store to provide additional protection.

POLICIES AND PROCEDURES

As employees are hired by the organization, the IT department is typically required to have some initial interaction with the new employee. This interaction, called the onboarding procedure, is often coordinated with the Human Resources (HR) department hiring procedures. During the onboarding procedure, an IT representative will assist the new employee with logging in for the first time and setting up their security, including changing their initial password. During onboarding, several policies are also reviewed.

Although most of the policies are discussed during the onboarding procedure, the bring-your-own-device (BYOD) policy is usually discussed with HR at the time of hiring if an organization has one. The password policy is often discussed with the user as they change their password for the first time. The password policy will detail how long their password needs to be, how complex the password needs to be, and how often the user has to change it. Other policies—such as the acceptable use policy (AUP), nondisclosure agreement (NDA), and information assurance—should also be discussed during the onboarding procedure. Each organization will have a different set of criteria that make up the onboarding procedures.

When people leave the organization, the offboarding procedure ensures that all information access is terminated when the employment of the user has ended. This procedure might be a manual procedure, or it could be automated if the organization has an employee management system. Regardless of how the system is implemented, the access to organizational information should be removed as soon as possible.

> **NOTE**
> Common policies are covered in Chapter 28, "Documentation."

BYOD vs. Corporate Owned

During the pandemic, organizations adopted a BYOD and remote access strategy for their workers out of practical need. When employees were unable to access their organizations' physical workplaces, they used any mobile devices available to them or that they could purchase from local retailers. This rapid adoption of BYOD devices kept businesses moving in a productive direction.

As employees have come back, they have returned to a very different workspace and many workers have returned with their BYOD devices. Some organizations have allowed workers to select the corporate-owned device that they prefer from an approved list. This strategy is called choose-your-own-device (CYOD). Other organizations have also allowed personal data on corporate devices under corporate-owned, personally enabled (COPE) policies.

> **EXAM TIP**
> Expect to see a lot of acronyms on the A+ exam. Be sure that you understand the differences between bring-your-own-device (BYOD), choose-your-own-device (CYOD), and corporate-owned, personally enabled (COPE) policies for mobile devices.

Profile Security Requirements

BYOD or corporate devices must be adopted and managed in a uniform fashion. Typically, you will build profile security policies when you implement an MDM solution to manage the mobile devices. The profile security policy might require passcodes or biometrics to lock the device, since the device will contain organizational data that must be secured in the event it is lost or stolen. The profile security policy in this case should apply to both BYOD and corporate devices, uniformly.

As an administrator, you can choose settings for mobile devices under your purview and enforce security policy requirements in various ways. In a given scenario, you may want to enforce settings for the entire organization, whereas in other scenarios you may want to adjust the settings based on organizational unit, role, or another group type. Among the settings you may want to enforce are those requiring the encryption of drives and the use of complex passwords.

INTERNET OF THINGS (IoT)

The Internet of Things (IoT) has changed our daily life and continues to be a growing industry. Every embedded device has an IP address today, from BBQ grills to thermostats. Any device that can be controlled and/or monitored via the Internet falls into the category of IoT. IoT devices might be joined to a wireless network, or they may contain a subscriber identity module (SIM) card that joins them to a cellular network. The downside to connecting things to the Internet is that they must be patched so that they are not vulnerable to exploit. IoT vendors will often use off-the-shelf components in the hardware, such as Wi-Fi modules or microcontrollers. Some of these components never receive a firmware update for the life of the product. This of course becomes a major security consideration for organizations adopting these devices.

In the past, attackers have harvested compromised IoT devices for distributed denial-of-service (DDoS) attacks. The bandwidth from botnets can be hundreds of gigabits per second. One way you can mitigate your IoTs being used in a DDoS attack is by placing the devices in an isolated network. This isolated network should also be firewalled so that the outbound bandwidth can either be policed to a maximum bandwidth or restricted outbound to only the networks they are intended to contact.

CERTMIKE EXAM ESSENTIALS

▶ Screen locks prevent unauthorized use of mobile devices. Facial recognition uses biometrics of a person's face to unlock the device. PIN codes use a numeric password to unlock the device. Fingerprint is another biometric screen unlock method that uses your fingerprint. Patterns allow for a unique swipe pattern to unlock the device. A swipe screen lock is not a security measure and only prevents the device from pocket dialing.

▶ Locator apps are built into modern mobile devices to allow the owner to locate a missing device. In addition, the macOS and Windows operating systems also have location apps built in for locating missing laptops. In the event a mobile device cannot be found, remote wiping capabilities can be used. Remote backup applications should be used to back up personal data in the event a device is lost or stolen and must be remotely wiped. Most mobile devices and operating systems have built-in remote backup software that can protect personal files.

▶ The security of mobile devices begins with their OS updates that typically patch known weaknesses and bugs in the operating system. Device encryption assures that data will be encrypted in the event the mobile device is lost or stolen. Antivirus/antimalware software should also be installed on the mobile device to ensure that it does not become infected. A firewall should also be installed on the mobile device to prevent unauthorized network activity from malicious software.

▶ Many organizations will have employee policies, such as a password policy, nondisclosure agreement (NDA), acceptable use policy (AUP), and bring-your-own-device (BYOD) policy to set the expectations of employment. In an effort to support these policies and security, an administrator can employ profile security requirements on BYOD devices with the help of mobile device management (MDM) software.

▶ IoT devices must be evaluated for functionality versus the inherent risk. The devices should be firewalled when applicable, and supported devices should be purchased and maintained.

Practice Question 1

You have been tasked to create a security profile that will require all BYOD devices to have the most secure method for unlocking the devices. Which method should you choose?

A. Face lock
B. PIN code
C. Pattern
D. Fingerprint

Practice Question 2

You need to assure users have access to files on their Windows laptops in the event the device is stolen or lost. Which software should you configure to protect your users?

A. OneDrive
B. FileVault
C. iCloud
D. Google

Practice Question 1 Explanation

This question is designed to test your knowledge of screen locks on mobile devices.

1. The first answer (A, Face lock) is incorrect. The face lock is not the most secure method because of the number of false positives.

2. The next answer (B, PIN code) is incorrect. The PIN code is not the most secure method because the passcode can be shoulder surfed or learned by another person.

3. The next answer (C, Pattern) is incorrect. The pattern lock method is not the most secure because the pattern can be shoulder surfed or learned by another person.

4. The last answer (D, Fingerprint) is correct. The fingerprint lock is the most secure method because it has the least number of false positives.

Correct Answer: D. Fingerprint

Practice Question 2 Explanation

This question is designed to test your knowledge of backup for mobile devices.

1. The first answer (A, OneDrive) is correct. To ensure files are accessible in the event a device is stolen or lost, OneDrive should be configured; it is Microsoft's primary cloud-based backup method.

2. The next answer (B, FileVault) is incorrect. FileVault is an encryption technology for macOS.

3. The next answer (C, iCloud) is incorrect. iCloud is the primary cloud-based backup method for Apple devices.

4. The last answer (D, Google) is incorrect. Google cloud-based backup is the primary method for Android mobile devices.

Correct Answer: A. OneDrive

CHAPTER 20

Data Destruction and Disposal

Core 2 Objective 2.8: Given a scenario, use common data destruction and disposal methods.

When a hard drive, tape library, or flash memory device is no longer needed, keep in mind that it still contains information that could be a problem if it falls into the wrong hands. Erasing files or using normal data formatting routines won't eliminate data, but this chapter shows you the methods that will. In this chapter, you will learn everything you need to know about A+ Certification Core 2 Objective 2.8, including the following topics:

▶ **Physical Destruction**
▶ **Recycling or Repurposing Best Practices**
▶ **Outsourcing Concepts**

PHYSICAL DESTRUCTION

When media and drives have reached the end of their useful life, the data they contain should be eliminated beyond any possibility of recovery. Some organizations prefer to wipe the contents of drives and donate them to nonprofits or schools, but if your organization prefers not to or has data in media types that have no reuse potential, it's destruction time! The following sections discuss typical physical destruction methods and what media types are most suited to a particular method.

Drilling

Ordinary drills are great for destroying flash memory cards, USB flash memory drives, and hard drives (mechanical and SSD). Be sure to use eye protection and a mask because this method creates a lot of metal and plastic dust. This do-it-yourself process can take place on-site.

Drill several holes through the platters of hard disk drives and the controller board on the bottom of the drive (Figure 20.1).

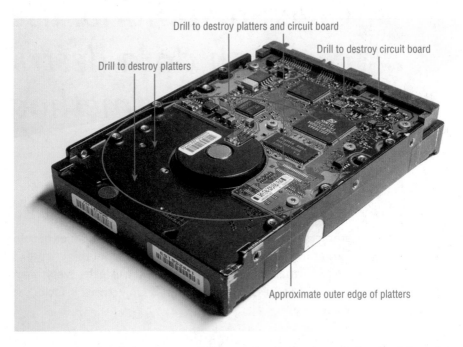

FIGURE 20.1 **Make sure you drill one or two holes through the circuit board on the bottom of a hard disk drive as well as the platters.**

TIP

See www.mypctechs.com/techclub/
destroy-a-hard-drive-the-cheap-and-easy-method for more information about using a drill to wipe out data.

For SATA SSDs, drill through the memory chips and controller chip. They are generally located nearer the SATA power and data interfaces shown in the lower left of Figure 20.2.

For USB flash memory drives (Figure 20.3) and memory cards (Figure 20.4), a couple of holes, one through the controller chip and one through the flash memory, will do the trick.

FIGURE 20.2 A typical SATA SSD with its bottom cover removed showing the locations of memory and controller chips

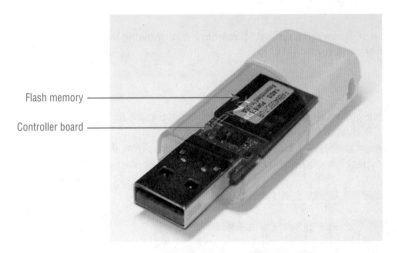

FIGURE 20.3 Cutaway of a typical USB flash memory drive showing the approximate locations of the flash memory and controller board

> **TIP**
>
> As an alternative to drilling USB flash memory drives and memory cards, you can use a Dremel or similar rotary cutter with a grit wheel to cut through chips and boards.

Memory Controller Chip

Flash Memory Chip(s)

FIGURE 20.4 Cutaway of a typical SD memory card showing the approximate locations of memory and controller chips

Shredding

If you have an office-grade shredder with an optical disc slot (Figure 20.5), you can destroy obsolete data on CD, DVD, or Blu-ray media.

Electronics recyclers have heavy-duty shredders that can turn drives, flash memory, tape, floppy, and other types of media into tiny bits. Shredding can take place on-site or off-site.

FIGURE 20.5 An optical disc shedder built into an office-grade paper shredder

Degaussing

Degaussing is the process of using powerful magnets to erase magnetic media such as hard disk drives, tape media, or floppy disks; degaussing does *not* work on SSD or flash memory. Although degaussers can be purchased for in-house use, they can cost thousands of dollars each and might not achieve the results of degaussing services that use National Security Agency (NSA)-approved degaussers.

A properly degaussed drive has not only all of the data removed in the process but also all of the sector markings and other partitioning information. The drive is completely useless and unrecoverable. Degaussing can take place on-site or off-site.

Incinerating

Incinerating old optical, floppy, hard drive, and tape media is another method for safely destroying data. However, unlike other methods, this cannot be performed on-site and produces a lot of potentially hazardous waste.

> **NOTE**
> For a comparison of the environmental impact and effectiveness of various methods of physical destruction of media, see www.bitraser.com/knowledge-series/data-destruction-methods-and-techniques.php.

RECYCLING OR REPURPOSING BEST PRACTICES

If you or your organization wants to donate old hard disk drives, USB drives, or SSDs, physical destruction is off the table, but the need to securely destroy the data on the drives is still paramount. In the following sections, we'll look at three methods that are used for this purpose to determine which one works the best.

Standard Formatting

If you were to ask a typical office worker how to clear the contents of a drive before donating it, you would probably get the answer, "Format it!" After all, when you format a drive using the normal Quick Format option in Windows (Figure 20.6), whatever was on there before seems to be gone (Figure 20.7).

Unfortunately, "Format it!" without changing any options is the wrong answer. Although the operating system can't find the data, it's still there. Here's why.

F I G U R E   2 0 . 6   The default format option in Windows is Quick Format.

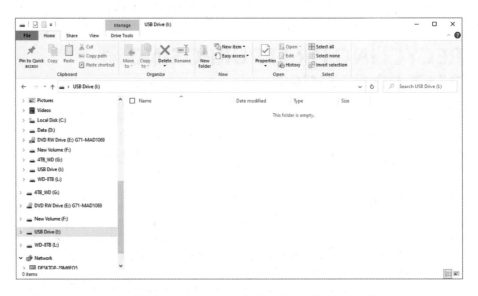

F I G U R E   2 0 . 7   An SD flash memory card after the default quick format appears to be empty

When a drive is quick formatted, the record of where data is stored is what is erased, but the data itself is still on the drive. It can be easily retrieved with a data recovery app (Figure 20.8). The default format routine in macOS is also a quick format.

FIGURE 20.8 Locating "lost" photos from the card shown in Figure 20.7 by using an evaluation version of a data recovery app. To complete the recovery process, buy a license for the data recovery app.

Low-Level Formatting

A low-level format (also known as a physical format), unlike a quick format, also rewrites all of the sector markings on a drive. If you clear the Quick Format check box in Windows when you format a drive, you are performing a low-level format (Figure 20.9).

A low-level format takes significantly longer than a quick format, and it can also be performed with third-party tools. A physical (low-level) format in Windows overwrites data in such a way that it cannot be retrieved by data recovery software programs. However, data might be recoverable by data recovery firms, which use more powerful tools than those available to the public.

FIGURE 20.9 The Quick Format option is not checked, so the drive will receive a physical (low-level) format in Windows.

> **NOTE**
>
> Two popular free low-level formatting utilities are the SD Association's free SD Memory Card formatter (for SD-type cards only; www.sdcard.org/downloads/formatter) and the HDDGuru's HDD LLF Low Level Format Tool (for almost any type of mechanical or flash drive; http://hddguru.com/software/HDD-LLF-Low-Level-Format-Tool). A faster version of the HDD LLF Low Level Format Tool is also available for a fee.

Erasing/Wiping

Although a low-level (physical) format overwrites data by re-creating sector markings, data might still be recoverable by using the services of a data recovery firm. If you are concerned about data privacy but want to reuse or donate drives with data, the best precaution to take is to wipe them instead of formatting them, or to wipe them after formatting them.

Drive wiping refers to the overwriting of all data areas with meaningless information. Drive wiping options are built into current versions of Windows, macOS, and Linux, as well as third-party apps.

The Format command in Windows performs a zero-fill operation (which writes zeros across the entire disk surface) when you disable Quick Format, and by opening a command prompt and using `format` with the `/P:`*number* option, it also overwrites the disk with random numbers. For example, to overwrite drive F: with zeros and four passes of random numbers during the format process, open the command prompt and enter **`format f: /P:4`**.

> **NOTE**
>
> Learn more about Windows's built-in disk wiping feature at www
> `.techrepublic.com/article/perform-a-secure-disk-`
> `wipe-with-windows-10s-format-command.`

In macOS, use Disk Utility. Select the drive you want to format, click Erase, and click Security Options (Figure 20.10).

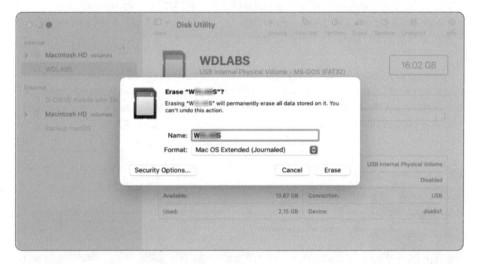

F I G U R E 2 0 . 1 0 Selecting Security Options to access more secure formatting/ disk wiping options with macOS Disk Utility

The default Fastest option works the same way as the Windows Quick Format. Drag the slider to the right to select wiping plus formatting options; the setting all the way to the right uses formatting plus a 7-pass random disk wiping process (Figure 20.11) to eliminate your data. Click OK after making your selection.

In Linux, you can use various utilities to wipe specific files as well as drives. Some of these include dd, shred, and wipe. Some require installation from your distro's app store.

FIGURE 20.11 Selecting Fastest (no wiping) to Most Secure (format plus 7-pass random overwrite) in the Security Options Erase menu

NOTE

Learn more about these and other Linux disk wiping utilities and how to install them at `https://linoxide.com/ delete-files-permanatly-linux/` and `https://opensource .com/article/21/10/linux-tools-erase-data`. The second website includes special commands for NVMe SSD drives.

Some vendor-supplied disk utility programs can perform a zero-fill operation, which writes zeros across the entire disk surface, while many commercial and freeware programs can perform a wide variety of disk wiping processes. Figure 20.12 shows a typical example of disk wiping options.

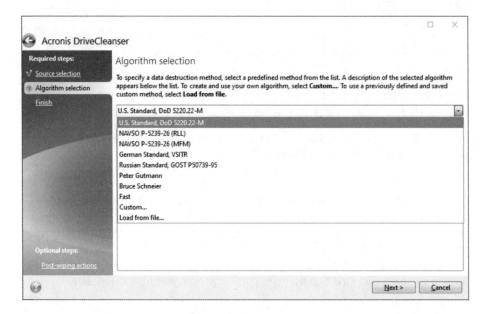

FIGURE 20.12 Disk wiping options available in Acronis Cyber Protect Home Office tools

NOTE

Many of the most complete selections of data wiping methods are those offered by the KillDisk commercial disk wiping program. Read about the methods and how they work at www.`killdisk.com/`
`KillDisk-Industrial-manual/index.html#erase-methods`
`.html`.

How many disk wipes are needed to make data unrecoverable? That depends on who you ask. Older recommendations of up to 35 passes with different junk data patterns such as Peter Guttman's method were developed years ago for far less sophisticated drives than we have now. The U.S. Department of Defense's DoD 5220.22-M data wipe method involves the following passes: Pass 1: Writes a zero and verifies the write. Pass 2: Writes a one and verifies the write. Pass 3: Writes a random character and verifies the write. With recent drives, many experts believe that this three-pass method is more than enough, and a single zero-fill or similar is sufficient sanitation of drive contents in almost every case.

EXAM NOTE

Make sure you understand the methods of data destruction: physical destruction, drive formatting, erase/wiping, the use of third-party vendors, and certificates of destruction or recycling. Be prepared to specify which would be best in a particular scenario on the Core 2 1102 CompTIA exam.

OUTSOURCING CONCEPTS

Although a do-it-yourself approach to data destruction might seem to save you money, it takes time, and if you need to prove legally that data has been destroyed, your solemn promise that the drives or media are unrecoverable isn't much good. For these reasons, consider outsourcing data destruction and recycling.

Third-Party Vendor

There are many third-party vendors who use many of the methods we've discussed in this chapter. Search for "data destruction" or "data shredding" to find some in your area. Here are some questions to ask based on your requirements:

- ▶ What type of media do they work with?
- ▶ Do they recycle drives, destroy drives, or offer you options?
- ▶ What methods of data overwriting or destruction do they offer?
- ▶ Will they provide a list of recent satisfied users?

▶ Do they have memberships in organizations such as the National Association for Information Destruction (NAID)?

▶ Do they perform data destruction for federal agencies and the Department of Defense (DoD)?

Get these answers along with pricing before you make a decision.

Certification of Destruction/Recycling

Whichever company you choose to destroy or overwrite your data, be sure to get a certificate of destruction or recycling. Typically, a certificate of destruction indicates the owner of the data, the company and technician who destroyed the media or drives, the type(s) of materials destroyed, and when. A certificate of recycling will indicate the owner of the drive(s), the drive(s) by serial number, the overwrite technique, the dates of overwriting, and the recycling company and technician responsible.

These certificates are extremely important if your organization or industry requires this information as part of its information retention and destruction policies. Make sure these certificates are complete and accurate and store them in a safe place, such as digital copies in backup and cloud storage.

> **NOTE**
>
> If you prefer to recycle drives in-house but want to have a certificate of erasure to prove it, the Active KillDisk Professional application offers this option. Learn more at www.killdisk.com/killdisk-pro.htm.

CERTMIKE EXAM ESSENTIALS

▶ You can physically destroy unwanted hard drives, flash memory drives, and SSDs yourself with ordinary hand tools by performing drilling, but if you need to provide proof of destruction, using a third-party data destruction organization that will provide you with a certificate of destruction is better. These organizations can use methods such as shredding, degaussing, and incinerating.

▶ If you want to recycle used drives, keep in mind that the default quick format option (also known as standard formatting) does not protect data from being recovered.

▶ The physical format (low-level format) feature in Windows or the Security Options format settings in macOS Disk Utility provide overwrite options. For additional protection, use data wiping (also known as erasing/wiping), which is also available in Linux).

Practice Question 1

Your client is donating three Windows computers with 250 GB hard disk drives that contained confidential information. Which of the following processes will thoroughly wipe out the data and allow the drives to be safely included in the donation?

A. Use a drill on the hard disk drives.
B. Use the standard Quick Format on each hard disk drive.
C. Boot from a USB drive and run **`format c: /p:4`**.
D. Right-click the C: drive in File Explorer and select Format.

Practice Question 2

Your client remembers that he once received an obsolete computer running an old version of Windows from his employer and was surprised to discover he was able to undelete the files from the system drive after the drive had been formatted with the Quick Format option disabled. He is understandably hesitant to have this happen with the computers referred to in Practice Question 1. What is different about the way Windows Format works in Windows 10 than in older versions?

A. Windows Format in Windows 10 includes disk wiping options not available in old versions of Windows.
B. Windows Format is a program that must be downloaded separately from the rest of Windows.
C. Windows Format works only from File Explorer in Windows 10.
D. The `format` command in the old version of Windows was corrupted.

Practice Question 1 Explanation

This question is designed to test your real-world understanding of how to remove data on storage devices. Let's evaluate these answers one at a time.

1. The first answer (A, Use a drill on the hard disk drives) is incorrect. The drives are to remain working so that they can be included in the computer donations.

2. The next answer (B, Use the standard Quick Format on each hard disk drive) is incorrect. Quick Format does not overwrite data so that it can be easily recovered with data recovery software available to the public.

3. The next answer (C, Boot from a USB drive and run **format c: /p:4**) is correct. This `format` command overwrites the data on the drive with zeros and then does four additional passes of random data so that the data cannot be recovered.

4. The last answer (D, Right-click the C: drive in File Explorer and select Format) is incorrect. Windows will not permit the system drive to be formatted.

Correct Answer: C. Boot from a USB drive and run `format c: /p:4`

Practice Question 2 Explanation

This question is designed to test your knowledge of the improvements in Windows 10 versus older versions. Let's evaluate these answers one at a time.

1. The first answer (A, Windows Format in Windows 10 includes disk wiping options not available in old versions of Windows) is correct. This is the *best* answer.

2. The second answer (B, Windows Format is a program that must be downloaded separately from the rest of Windows) is incorrect. Windows Format is included in both versions of Windows.

3. The third answer (C, Windows Format works only from File Explorer in Windows 10) is incorrect. Windows Format can be run from the command prompt or from File Explorer.

4. The last answer (D, The `format` command in the old version of Windows was corrupted) is incorrect. The `format` command in old versions of Windows was not designed to perform any type of a disk wipe when Quick Format was disabled, unlike the Windows 10 `format` command.

Correct Answer: A. Windows `format` in Windows 10 includes disk wiping options not available in old versions of Windows

CHAPTER 21

Network Security

Core 2 Objective 2.9: Given a scenario, configure appropriate security settings on small office/home office (SOHO) wireless and wired networks.

Security implications should be fully understood and security settings should be configured appropriately to mitigate security threats. Network security is so crucial because the threat actor doesn't even need to be in the same zip code as your network. Also, unlike application security or operating system security, your network is always on, and if there is a vulnerability, it is ever present. This chapter will focus on the small office/home network (SOHO) wireless and wired networks you will encounter as an A+ technician. In this chapter, you will learn what you need to know about the A+ Certification Core 2 Objective 2.9, including the following topics:

▶ **Home router settings**
▶ **Wireless specific settings**
▶ **Firewall settings**

HOME ROUTER SETTINGS

The most common device you will set up as an A+ technician is the home router. The home router connects the small office/home office (SOHO) to the Internet. This connection to the Internet doesn't come without considerations for security. This section explores the common settings as well as the best practices that accompany the various settings on a home router.

Change Default Passwords

When installing a network device, such as a router, the very first thing you must do is log into the device. There is often a wizard that will require you to change the default password when you first access the device. Other devices require you to enter a vendor-standardized default username and password custom to the product. Therefore, a best practice to setting up home routers is to change the default password to a complex password.

If the wizard does not guide you on the initial login to change the default username, you can always browse to the setting in the router and change it manually. Every router will be different, but the admin username and password are generally located on the System or Administration tab, as shown in Figure 21.1.

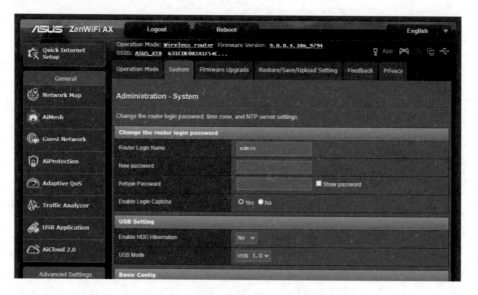

FIGURE 21.1 Manual password update on a home router

Firmware Updates

Most hardware vendors will automatically update the firmware when the device is connected to the Internet for the first time. Future updates may be scheduled via an email notification, or they may just be forced onto your device in the middle of the night. On some devices you may be able to manually check for the update on the System or Administration tab, as shown in Figure 21.2. Some devices will also allow you to manually upload a firmware update, to upgrade or in some cases downgrade a router's firmware.

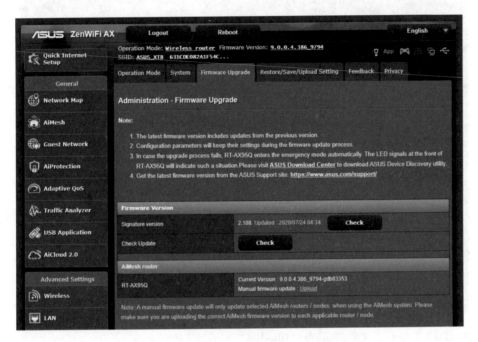

FIGURE 21.2 Manually check for updates on a home router

IP Filtering

A common feature of modern routers is the ability to filter the management traffic for the local area network (LAN) with IP filtering. Typically, you don't want all clients in your SOHO network to be able to access the administration web page of the router. With IP filtering you can filter only the clients that should administer the router; all the other clients will be denied access. By default, this feature is generally not turned on, but by enabling it and configuring it you can harden the security of the network. These settings are usually under the System or Administration tab on the router, as shown in Figure 21.3. In this example, you would simply add an access restriction for the admin computer.

Content Filtering

Content filtering is a method of restricting content to the end user, based on keywords, uniform resource locators (URLs), IP addresses, or content categories, just to name a few. Content filtering is really useful in preventing children from viewing inappropriate content on a home network. It can also be used in small offices and organizations to restrict employees from viewing questionable content.

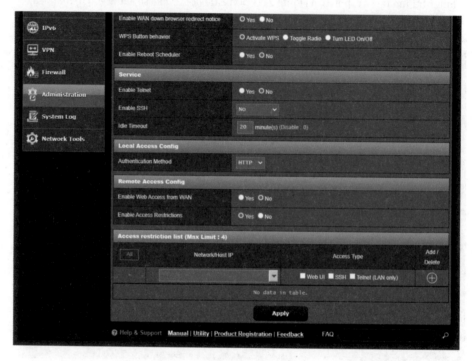

FIGURE 21.3 Configuring IP filtering

The content filter operates by watching content and requests from web browsers and other applications. The content filter functions in two ways. The first is content-based; when images and text are requested from a website, the content filter can use rules to filter the content according to the content policies. The second method is URL-based, which is much more common since many websites now use SSL/TLS (encryption) and the traffic is encrypted.

Content filters settings on the router can generally be found on the URL Filter tab or Firewall tab, as shown in Figure 21.4.

EXAM TIP

Content filtering is useful to restrict content for both home and office, where certain content categories should not be accessed. For larger organizations, solutions can be software-based or hardware-based in the form of an appliance.

FIGURE 21.4 The Firewall – URL Filter screen for a typical router

Physical Placement/Secure Locations

If the network equipment is physically accessible, an employee or threat actor can potentially reset the device and gain unauthorized access. In the extreme circumstances, the equipment can even be stolen. The network equipment should be placed in a secure location to prevent tampering, but you should also consider the physical placement of the equipment. You should install the network router close to the Internet connection and to the clients it will service. Both the physical placement and the overall security of the location should be considered when deploying network equipment.

> **EXAM TIP**
> The placement of network equipment is a balance between accessibility to connecting devices and the overall physical security of the network equipment.

Dynamic Host Configuration Protocol (DHCP)

Dynamic Host Configuration Protocol (DHCP) is responsible for the automatic configuration of IPv4 IP addresses and their accompanying subnet masks on hosts. The DHCP server will serve clients from a pool of IPv4 addresses called a DHCP scope. The DHCP scope can also have options configured that are sent along with the IP address, such as the default gateway, DNS server addresses, and many other IP-based servers. DHCP performs the automatic configuration of the client with a series of network broadcasts and unicast messages.

The DHCP server can be configured on SOHO routers from either the DHCP tab or the LAN tab, as shown in Figure 21.5. The DHCP server process can only be configured for the LAN side of the connection.

FIGURE 21.5 DHCP configuration

Reservations

DHCP automatically serves clients the next IP address in the pool of IPv4 addresses. However, sometimes you need a specific IP address to be assigned every time to the client. Creating a reservation allows the DHCP server to automatically serve the same IP address every time the device requests an IP address. The reservation is created by assigning the MAC address of the client to the IP address you want to statically assign. When an IP address is requested by the client, the client's MAC address is referred to the reserved address.

> **EXAM TIP**
>
> DHCP reservations are useful for devices that require the same IP address every time they start up. Printers are common devices that are set statically with reservations.

Static Wide Area Network (WAN) IP

The wide area network (WAN) connection side of the router faces your Internet service provider (ISP). ISPs typically serve a public IP address to the subscriber based on the DHCP process, similar to how you would manage clients on your own private network. The difference is that the ISP serves a public IP address that is world accessible.

There are instances where you might need a static WAN IP address—for example, if you are hosting a server or have services that need to be accessible over the Internet, such as a camera surveillance system. In such instances, you would need to contact the ISP and request a static IP address. The ISP will furnish a static IP address, along with a default gateway. After obtaining the static IP address from the ISP, you would configure the SOHO router from the WAN tab, as shown in Figure 21.6.

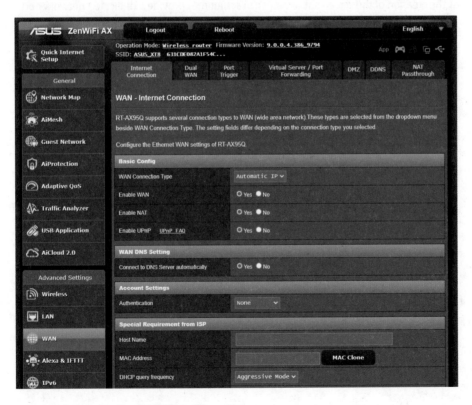

FIGURE 21.6 Static WAN configuration

Universal Plug and Play (UPnP)

Port forwarding is the method of allowing traffic from a computer on the Internet to be forwarded to a computer on your private network. One of the inherent problems with port forwarding is that you need to understand what you are doing to configure it properly. Universal Plug and Play (UPnP) solves this problem by automatically configuring a port forwarding rule to allow clients on the Internet to reach the destination computer. The SOHO router will automatically configure the connection from the WAN IP address to the network device that needs connectivity. This functionality is useful for video games that allow the creation of a server for friends to connect. However, it can be used for other productive services as well.

UPnP can be configured from either the Firewall tab or the WAN configuration tab. It will vary from vendor to vendor and can also be found on the LAN tab.

Screened Subnet

The screened subnet is also known as the demilitarized zone (DMZ). It is a screened (firewalled) subnet that sits between the exterior and the interior segments of the network. Hosts that serve Internet clients are placed in the screened subnet. SOHO routers will allow for the creation of the screen subnet and can sometimes provide a dedicated network port for the screen subnet computer. The logical representation of a screen subnet is shown in Figure 21.7.

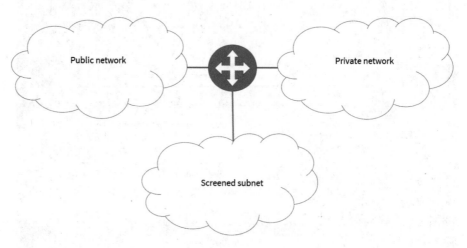

FIGURE 21.7 Logical screened subnet diagram

The screen subnet or DMZ is typically configured from either the Firewall tab or the WAN tab on SOHO routers, as shown in Figure 21.8.

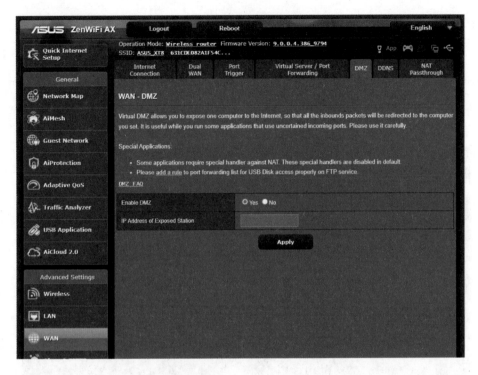

FIGURE 21.8 **DMZ configuration**

EXAM TIP

The screened subnet is a network segment that exists between the public (Internet) and private network segments. It is primarily used for servers and services that need to communicate between the Internet and private network.

WIRELESS SPECIFIC SETTINGS

Wired SOHO routers were the first SOHO routers released to market almost 25 years ago. They set the benchmark for router services, such as WAN/LAN ports, NAT, and DHCP. Wireless routers eventually became the standard for SOHO routers, so now every SOHO router has wireless services built-in. It just makes sense because of the explosive growth of mobile devices over the past decade.

Wireless communications will never be as secure as wired communication, but it is convenient and that is why we choose to use it in the small office/home office. In this section you will learn how to make some configuration changes to make wireless a little more secure.

Changing the Service Set Identifier (SSID)

Changing your service set identifier (SSID) is the simplest configuration change you can make on your SOHO router. Changing it will serve two purposes. First, you will no longer announce the make or model of your router to anyone in proximity to your wireless equipment. Often the SSID is initially configured as your router's vendor and model. The SSID can be changed on the Wireless tab of your router, as shown in Figure 21.9.

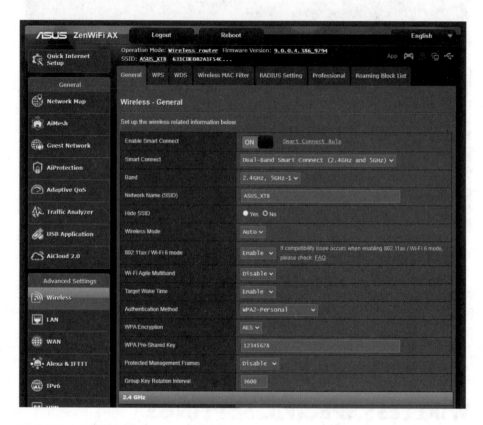

FIGURE 21.9 Wireless configuration

The second reason to change the SSID of your SOHO router is to make it yours. Your clients should be able to quickly identify your wireless network over a neighboring wireless network that is in the same proximity. This makes it easier to allow your family or coworkers to join the proper network.

Disabling SSID Broadcast

All radio frequency (RF) signals can be passively monitored and eavesdropped on. To eavesdrop on wireless traffic, all you need is a PC with an appropriate 802.11 wireless card installed and some open source software. One way to evade someone from eavesdropping is to hide. The 802.11 wireless protocol will periodically advertise the SSID via a management broadcast. On most SOHO routers, you can configure the SSID to be hidden.

> **NOTE**
> While this tactic of hiding the SSID will not deter a true threat actor, it will prevent someone from trying to connect to your network. A consideration to hiding the SSID is that some network devices will not be compatible with the setting.

Encryption Settings

The easiest way to secure your wireless network traffic is to enable encryption. You should always choose the highest level of wireless encryption that your wireless clients can support. The following are some wireless protocols that you might encounter when securing wireless communications.

Open
Open security is just that—open with no passphrase or authentication protocol. Open security was originally how all wireless access points (WAPs) were shipped to the customer. Open security still has its uses when used in conjunction with guest wireless access.

Wired Equivalent Privacy
Shared passphrases are used with Wired Equivalent Privacy (WEP). WEP provides 64- or 128-bit encryption via the shared passphrase. WEP is extremely insecure, as the passphrase can easily be cracked with tools. WEP is not typically an option when setting up modern SOHO routers.

Wi-Fi Protected Access
Wi-Fi Protected Access (WPA) uses 256-bit keys and operates in two modes for security: personal mode (also known as preshared key [PSK]) and enterprise mode. Personal mode is the most common mode, because it can easily be implemented with a mutual agreed-upon passphrase. Enterprise mode, also called WPA-802.1X, requires a certificate server infrastructure. Enterprise mode uses the 802.1X protocol, RADIUS or TACACS+, and EAP; it is often used in corporate environments.

Wi-Fi Protected Access 2 (WPA2)

WPA2 uses the Advanced Encryption Standard (AES) encryption algorithm to protect data. The WPA2 protocol is the successor to WPA and, just like WPA, operates in both personal mode (PSK) and enterprise mode.

Wi-Fi Protected Access 3 (WPA3)

The WPA3 encryption protocol is the successor to WPA2 and addresses weaknesses in the encryption algorithms. WPA3 introduced 192-bit cryptographic strength in WPA3 enterprise mode. The most significant improvement is the use of Simultaneous Authentication of Equals (SAE) exchange that replaces the preshared key (PSK) exchange use with WPA and WPA2 personal mode.

The wireless encryption settings can be configured on the Wireless tab of the SOHO router. Typically, when set it applies to both the 2.4 GHz and 5 GHz radios on the router.

> **NOTE**
>
> For more detailed information on wireless encryption, see Chapter 14, "Wireless Security."

Disabling Guest Access

The guest network, also known as the guest access feature, for your SOHO wireless router allows guests to connect to your wireless network and obtain Internet access. The guest access will restrict the guest from accessing the private network. It is a best practice to disable guest access unless it is needed for guest users.

The guest wireless network can be configured on either the Wireless tab or the Guest Network tab, as shown in Figure 21.10.

Changing Channels

Changing the channels that a wireless router operates on doesn't make it any more secure. However, changing the channel does allow better performance and higher bandwidth. You can improve performance in the 2.4 GHz range by selecting a nonoverlapping channel of 1, 6, or 11. In the 5 GHz range you can improve performance by selecting a non-bonded channel.

The channel can be configured for both the 2.4 GHz radio and the 5 GHz radio from the Wireless tab, as shown in Figure 21.11. These settings can typically be controlled independently on the two frequency bands.

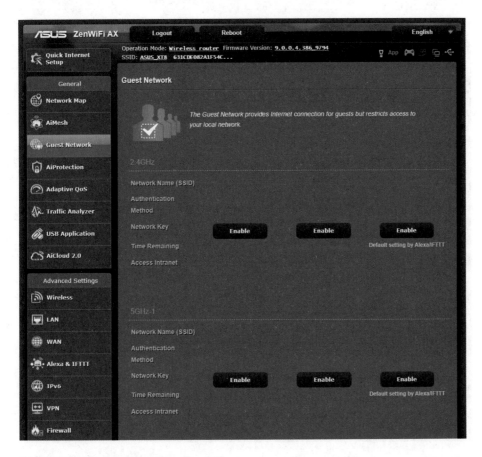

FIGURE 21.10 Guest configuration

EXAM TIP

When your router operates on the same channel as another neighboring router, performance and bandwidth is impacted. Changing the operating channels will enhance performance and allows for higher bandwidth by removing the interference.

FIGURE 21.11 Channel configuration

FIREWALL SETTINGS

The main purpose of a SOHO router is the ability to route network traffic to the Internet; this is done with the use of Network Address Translation (NAT). Although NAT provides some basic functionality in protecting clients from the Internet, by itself it is not a firewall. The true strength of the SOHO router is its ability to act as a firewall, which is a feature that has been implemented over the past decade as a standard feature.

The addition of a firewall feature in the SOHO router means that it can protect you from DDoS attacks or log packets that have been dropped or allowed. Some routers will allow you to configure advanced firewall features, such as configuring an intrusion prevention system (IPS), intrusion detection system (IDS), or custom rules for wired networks versus wireless.

The firewall settings can typically be configured on the Firewall tab, as shown in Figure 21.12.

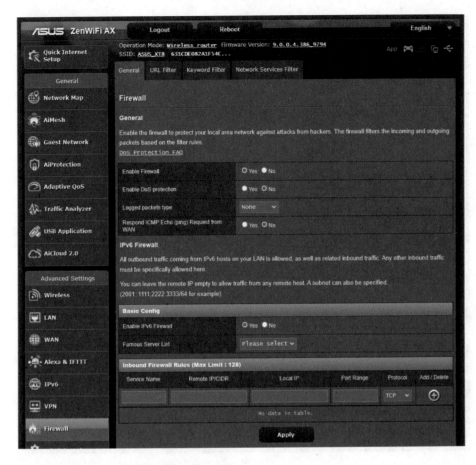

FIGURE 21.12   Firewall configuration

Disabling Unused Ports

A best practice when configuring any network device is to disable any unused TCP or UDP ports. By doing this, you will strengthen the security of the device. Depending on how often you upgrade the firmware, an exploitable vulnerability can exist in one of the unused network services, such as Telnet or SSH. Therefore, if you are not actively using the network service provided by the router or network device, you should disable the port.

Disabling services can disable unused ports and can be configured in a number of places on the router. The first place to always check is the System tab or Administration tab, as shown in Figure 21.13. Typically, you can configure Telnet, SSH, and external WAN access from this tab. However, you may also be able to configure external access from the WAN tab on some routers. These settings will vary from vendor to vendor.

FIGURE 21.13 Administration configuration

Port Forwarding/Mapping

Firewalls restrict external traffic inbound to the private network. This is one of the main functions of a firewall, which is to keep you safe from threat actors. However, there are times when we want traffic to be accepted from the external network and delivered to an internal host. Universal Plug and Play (UPnP) can help automatically configure port forwarding. However, configuring a manual port forwarding entry is a pretty common task for an A+ technician, because UPnP is not compatible in all situations.

In order to properly configure port forwarding, you will need a few things. The first is the port and protocol that the service responds on. For example, a web service will respond on 443 for HTTPS and the protocol is TCP. The next piece of information you will need is the internal IP address you will map the requests to. You can then configure the port mapping for the external IP address port number and protocol on the router to the internal IP address port number and protocol.

Typically, you can configure port forwarding on the Firewall tab or the WAN tab, as shown in Figure 21.14. This is such a common task that entire websites have been dedicated to port forwarding, such as https://portforward.com.

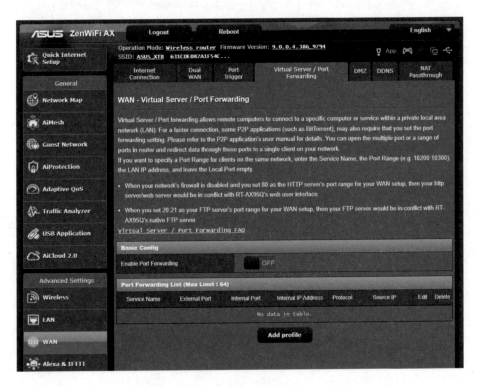

FIGURE 21.14 Port Forwarding configuration

CERTMIKE EXAM ESSENTIALS

▶ Changing certain router settings will strengthen your router security and overall security posture for the network. Changing default passwords and vendor username and password combinations is a best practice. Upgrading firmware will patch vulnerabilities that can exist in the router's code. Disabling guest access is another best practice that protects you from misuse of your wireless. Disabling unused ports and employing encryption are best practices to harden the security of your SOHO network.

▶ SOHO routers have slowly implemented firewall functionality, and from vendor to vendor their features will differ. IP filtering allows you to restrict ranges or specific IP addresses from accessing the administrative interface on the router. Content filtering can restrict what users can access the network through the router. A screen subnet, also known as DMZ, creates a segment between the private and public interfaces for servers. Port forwarding allows you to forward an incoming port request to a specific computer. Universal Plug and Play (UPnP) automatically configures port forwarding for the end user.

▶ Wireless security can be tightened by disabling SSID broadcasting. This will make it more difficult for a threat actor to compromise wireless. Changing the default wireless SSID will protect you from threat actors because the SSID typically is set to the vendor and model of the router by default. Changing the SSID also allows your users to find it easier if there are neighboring SSIDs.

▶ DHCP is responsible for the automatic configuration of IPv4 addressing for clients. By default, it will serve clients an IP address and subnet mask. It can be configured to serve additional options, such as router, DNS, and other settings. DHCP reservations can be configured to ensure the same IP address is configured on the client computer day to day.

Practice Question 1

You are configuring a printer that is extremely difficult to configure with a static IP address. What should you use to allow for the automatic configuration of the same IP address every time the printer is rebooted?

A. DHCP reservation

B. UPnP

C. Content filtering

D. IP filtering

Practice Question 2

You are tasked with configuring a wireless encryption protocol for your wireless clients. Which wireless encryption protocol has the ability to operate in personal mode and has the highest level of encryption?

A. WPA

B. WEP

C. WPA2

D. WPA3

Practice Question 1 Explanation

This question is designed to test your knowledge of home router settings.

1. The first answer (A, DHCP reservation) is correct. The Dynamic Host Configuration Protocol (DHCP) is responsible for the automatic configuration of IP addresses and options on clients. A DHCP reservations reserves a specific IP address to the MAC address of the printer.

2. The next answer (B, UPnP) is incorrect. The Universal Plug and Play (UPnP) protocol is responsible for configuring the port forwarding configuration on SOHO routers.

3. 3.The next answer (C, Content filtering) is incorrect. Content filtering is the method of restricting content based on keywords, URLs, IP addresses, or content categories.

4. The last answer (D, IP filtering) is incorrect. IP filtering is used to protect the administration of the SOHO router.

Correct Answer: A. DHCP reservation

Practice Question 2 Explanation

This question is designed to test your knowledge of wireless encryption options.

1. The first answer (A, WPA) is incorrect. The WPA protocol was created to address problems with WEP security. It does operate in personal mode, but it does not have a high level of encryption.

2. The next answer (B, WEP) is incorrect. The WEP protocol is considered extremely insecure and has the weakest security.

3. The next answer (C, WPA2) is incorrect. The WPA2 protocol operates in personal mode and is more secure than WEP and WPA, but it's not as secure as WPA3.

4. The last answer (D, WPA3) is correct. WPA3 operates in personal mode and has the highest level of encryption compared to the prior versions of WEP, WPA, and WPA2.

Correct Answer: D. WPA3

CHAPTER 22

Browser Security

Core 2 Objective 2.10: Given a scenario, install and configure browsers and relevant security settings.

The web browser is the most popular application to be used in the operating system. With today's Web 3.0 apps, you really can't tell the difference between a web application and a desktop application. The web browser is how we learn, work, bank, and relax to engaging content. It should be no shock that threat actors linger in the dark. In this chapter, you will learn what you need to know about the A+ Certification Core 2 Objective 2.10, including the following topics:

▶ **Browser download/installation**
▶ **Extensions and plug-ins**
▶ **Password managers**
▶ **Secure connections/sites – valid certificates**
▶ **Settings**

BROWSER DOWNLOAD/INSTALLATION

The Microsoft Edge browser is the successor to Internet Explorer (IE) and comes preinstalled in the Microsoft Windows 10/11 operating systems. There are a number of other web browsers freely downloadable on the Internet that you might want to download and install on your Windows 10/11 OS. Each web browser has different advantages and disadvantages to their platform. Chrome and Edge web browsers are all based on the Blink browser engine developed as part of the Chromium project. Chrome is a popular browser that has become the dominant web-based browser in market share on the Internet. Firefox is also a popular browser that is based off the Mozilla engine.

In addition to the major web browsers there are quite a few other less-known niche browsers. These web browsers have their own user base and features. However, when choosing a browser to download and install, always consider the developers' attentiveness to security. This can usually be measured in patch cycles and security-related features periodically introduced.

Trusted vs. Untrusted Sources

Installing a web browser might seem like a trivial task, but threat actors would love for you to download their web browser in lieu of your web browser of choice. Threat actors often use search engine optimization (SEO) and misspellings to promote their download links, and these are considered untrusted sources.

Whenever you download a web browser, make a valid attempt to spell it correctly and verify the link you are about to click in the search results. As you can see in Figure 22.1, the first ad directs to `https://www.chromeenterprise.google`. This is actually a valid link, but not the link you would need to install Google Chrome. The second link is an ad as well, and it too directs to a valid link. The actual result you are looking for is the third link down in the results and is considered the trusted source. If the first and second links were malware, you could easily click on them. Another way to ensure that you are going to the right place is clicking on the URL in the knowledge pane on the right side. This link will take you to Google and from there you can download Google Chrome.

Search engine results are not the only way you can be tricked into installing a malware-laced web browser. Misspelt domains can also get you into trouble. By typing a wrong letter, you might find yourself downloading malware. Other untrusted sources are file repositories such as FileHippo, Softpedia, CNet Download, and Softonic, just to name a few. These file repositories are not malicious—they are just not the original source of the application and therefore should not be trusted in the same way.

> **EXAM TIP**
>
> A trusted source for the web browser download is the software publisher's site; an untrusted source is often a file repository.

Hashing

One way to verify that the installer has not been manipulated is to compare the current hash of the executable to the originally published hash. A *hash* is a one-way numeric value or calculation derived from the executable or file. The developer has also performed the hashing and both hashes should match; if they don't, that means the file has been tampered with. The most common hashing today is SHA256. Other hashing algorithms are MD5 and SHA512. In Figure 22.2, you see the various hashes for Firefox installation executables.

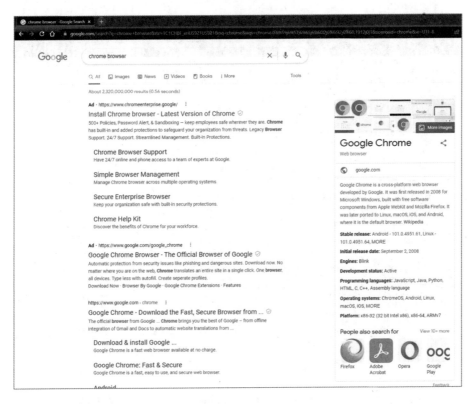

FIGURE 22.1 Typical search engine result

NOTE

You can get a hash from a file using the PowerShell cmdlet
Get-FileHash *filename*. Always use a SHA512 hash because MD5 is
considered a weak hashing algorithm.

EXAM TIP

Be sure you can identify trusted vs. untrusted browser sources and know that
hashing is used to verify the integrity of downloaded files.

Extensions and Plug-Ins

Sometimes you need more functionality than the web browser came with, such as PDF
editing, grammar checking, or ad blocking. This is where extensions and plug-ins come to
the rescue. Most web browsers support extensions and plug-ins to extend the functionality
of the browsers.

FIGURE 22.2 A hash list

The definition of an extension is that it modifies the core functionality of the web browser, whereas a plug-in provides extra functionality without modifying the core functionality of the browser. In any case, add-ons extend the functionality of the web browser. Add-ons are usually how an end user chooses their favorite web browser. Typically, the user will browse to a web page where trusted add-ons can be downloaded, as shown in Figure 22.3. The user can read reviews about the add-on, both good and bad. The user can then choose to install the add-on by clicking the install button.

Trusted vs. Untrusted Sources

Some add-ons contain malicious code that can enable a threat actor to take control of your web browser, direct you to malicious pages, steal your search history, and ultimately steal your private information. Therefore, it is important for you to install add-ons only from a trusted source, such as the Chrome Web Store, the Microsoft Edge Add-ons site, or the Firefox Add-ons site. Add-ons found with these trusted sources are usually vetted by the web browser developers and are malware-free.

Some add-ons are only available from outside the ecosystem of the web browser's add-on site. This is because those add-ons typically violate the policy of the ecosystem of the web browser's add-on site. This could be because they download videos or pictures from

FIGURE 22.3 Edge Add-ons

protected sites, or they contain malicious code that violates policies of the ecosystem of the web browser. These add-ons should not be trusted since the risk is your personal data.

Password Managers

Password managers allow you to store all these unique username and password combinations in a digital vault. When the website requests the login information, the password manager fills in the blanks so you don't have to remember it all. Most web browsers have password managers built in so there is nothing to install. Microsoft Edge and Internet Explorer both use the Microsoft Credential Manager. In Figure 22.4, you can see web credentials stored by Microsoft Edge. Credential Manager can be accessed in Windows 10/11 by navigating to the Start menu, typing **Control Panel**, selecting Credential Manager in the results, and then clicking Credential Manager.

Web browsers such as Google Chrome and Mozilla Firefox have password managers built in. These third-party web browsers do not use the built-in Credential Manager. Third-party web browsers save passwords inside the browser and typically sync them to their own cloud storage so that subsequent installations can share the saved passwords. In addition to the built-in Credential Manager and embedded password manager in modern web browsers, stand-alone password managers can be used. KeePass `https://keepass.info` is an example of a stand-alone password manager, and there are several other stand-alone passwords managers that are freely available on the Internet.

> **NOTE**
>
> macOS also contains a password manager; see the discussion on FileVault in Chapter 10, "macOS."

FIGURE 22.4 Microsoft Credential Manager

Secure Connections/Sites – Valid Certificates

The Hypertext Transfer Protocol over Secure Sockets Layer (SSL) protocol, also known as HTTPS, is a protocol that secures websites from eavesdropping. SSL is a cryptographic suite of protocols that use public key infrastructure (PKI) and Transport Layer Security (TLS) to provide secure data transfer between your web browsers and the destination web server. You can tell if the HTTPS protocol is securing a website by looking at the address bar; a lock will be displayed to the left of the address. If you want to view the certificate used to secure the web page, you can click the lock and view the certificate.

The public/private key pairs facilitated by PKI will aid in securing the transmission between the client and the website. However, an initial level of trust needs to exist between the public/private key pair and the web browser. The beginning of the trust chain will always start with the root CAs. Every operating system comes with an initial list of trusted root CAs, as shown in Figure 22.5. However, some web browsers maintain a list of their own trusted root CAs. See our discussion of the Windows Certificate Manager in Chapter 3, "Windows 10 Operating System Tools."

Every key pair has an issued date and expiration date, and the root certificates are no different. The root certificates issued from the root CAs have an expiration date as well. Therefore, the list of trusted root certificate authorities must be updated periodically. The Microsoft Windows platform does this with routine Windows Updates, but browsers may update their own list with updates of their own.

FIGURE 22.5 Trusted root CAs

NOTE

The SSL suite is a suite of protocols that includes the current standard of Transport Layer Security (TLS) 1.3. TLS 1.3 is used for securing websites as of this writing. SSL is also a protocol that is part of the SSL suite of protocols, but it has been deprecated and is no longer used for encryption.

EXAM TIP

Be sure you are familiar with password managers such as Windows Credential Manager and FileVault in macOS. You should also know if a website connection is secure and if the website has a valid digital certificate.

SETTINGS

Once you've decided on your web browser of preference, downloaded and installed the web browser from a trusted source, and installed your favorite add-ons, it's time to adjust settings in the web browser. In this section you will learn about the most common settings as they relate to the security of the web browser. The settings that follow are listed on the CompTIA Core 2 exam objectives, but in no way are they a complete list of security settings. The web browser is the most used application for accessing data, and new settings are introduced all the time to combat threat agents and adjust the web browser for the end user.

Pop-Up Blocker

Pop-up blockers are built into modern web browsers to prevent a web page from spawning another web page as a pop-up or pop-under. The use of pop-ups in web pages was popular in the early days of the World Wide Web. These pop-ups were used to grab the user's attention and were typically an ad of some sort. The use of a pop-under is a fairly new technique in which a web page will spawn a web page under the page you are currently viewing. Older browsers did not incorporate an option to block pop-ups. Most current browsers, including the latest versions of Edge and Chrome, have that capability built-in.

The pop-up blocker feature is enabled on all sites globally on modern web browsers. There are some instances where a pop-up is required; for example, banking websites might need to pop up a web page to show a check that has been cashed. When this happens, the address bar will notify you that an attempted pop-up occurred. You can then click to allow the specific site to use pop-ups. If you want to view a site's permission for pop-ups, click the lock at the left of the address bar and choose Permissions For This Site, as shown in Figure 22.6.

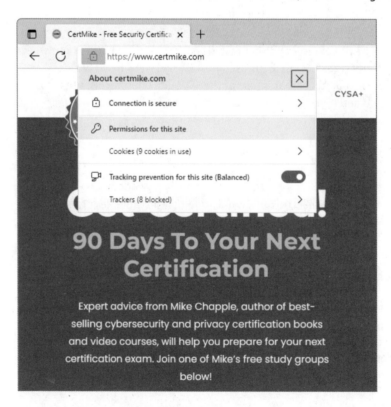

FIGURE 22.6 Permissions for a site

Clearing Browsing Data

Browsing data tends to be a broad concept used to describe any data collected by the web browser while visiting websites. This might include browsing history, download history, cookies, image and file cache, passwords, autofill form data, and site settings, just to name a few.

There are a number of reasons you may want to clear browsing data; typically, the reason is data privacy. Clearing browser data is extremely handy when you are trying to replicate a problem with the web browser. You can clear the browsing data by clicking the three dots in the upper-right corner of the Edge web browser. Then click Settings, choose Privacy, Search, And Services, and scroll down to Clear Browsing Data Now and select Choose What To Clear. You will be presented with a dialog box similar to Figure 22.7. You can choose the time period Last Hour, Last 24 Hours, Last 7 Days, Last 4 Weeks, or All Time.

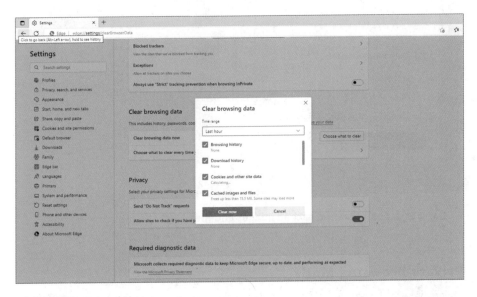

FIGURE 22.7 Clearing browsing data

Clearing Cache

The web browser cache is a temporary location that stores images and files as you surf web pages in the browser. If you visit the web page again, the browser cache is used for the images and files that make up the contents on the web page. The webmaster of the site can control how long the files exist in the cache. This caching mechanism speeds up the web browser and reduces unneeded trips to the website, overall improving the end-user experience.

When you are developing a web page, your changes may not be seen right away in your web browser. The browser cache will interfere with what you are seeing and what is actually being served. If an end user browses a site and gets a different result from what is expected, the browser cache can be the culprit. In these circumstances, the web browser cache will need to be cleared to see the proper rendering of the web page. The cached images and files are part of the web browsing data that can be cleared. The process is similar to the previously described process for clearing browsing data, except only the cache images and files will be cleared, as shown in Figure 22.8.

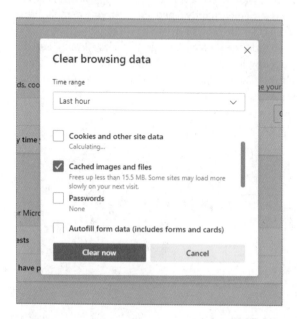

FIGURE 22.8 Clearing cached images and files

Private Browsing Mode

Private browsing mode was created to address data privacy concerns while you are browsing the Internet. Private browsing mode does not store web browsing data when it is in use. This is useful if the intent is to prevent your activity from being recorded in the web browsing history. Any browsing data collected in memory during your private browsing session is discarded when you close out of private browsing mode.

Every web browser supports some form of private browsing mode. On the Edge web browser, it is called InPrivate Browsing; Chrome calls it Incognito mode. You can enter InPrivate mode on the Edge web browser by clicking the three dots in the upper right-hand corner of the window, then selecting New InPrivate Window. A quicker way to enter private browsing mode is to press Ctrl+Shift+N. When you use either of these methods, the InPrivate window will open, explaining that you are InPrivate browsing mode and what InPrivate does and doesn't do, as shown in Figure 22.9.

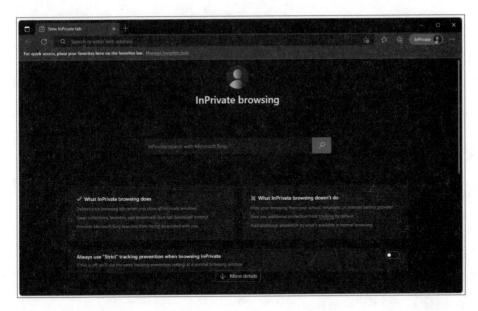

FIGURE 22.9 InPrivate browsing

EXAM TIP

When you use InPrivate browsing mode, none of the browsing data is saved, even history.

Sign-In/Browser Data Synchronization

You will find that you access the web browser on several devices, such as on a work laptop, on your home computer, and on mobile devices. As you are using these various devices, it is really handy to have your web browsing data follow you as well. Many modern web browsers have solved this problem by supporting a feature called *browser data synchronization*. After you log into the web browser, the data synchronization feature will automatically sync the content of your shared browsing data. This means all your passwords, browsing history, cookies, download history, and site settings, just to name a few, will be synced to the browser.

To sync your device, you just need to make sure that you have signed in and acknowledged that you want to synchronize browsing data. You can verify this by clicking your account in the upper-right corner of the Edge or Chrome web browser. Your account details will be displayed and show that Sync is on, as you can see in Figure 22.10. If you are not syncing, you can click Turn On Sync.

FIGURE 22.10   Sync is on.

Ad Blockers

Ad blockers are typically add-ons for most modern web browsers. An ad blocker is useful for stopping annoying ads and spammy ads that might be part of a web page. Many different websites subsidize their income with marketing ads, such as new websites, weather websites, and video websites. If you don't have a paid subscription, then you have to allow marketing ads in order to enjoy their content; it seems a pretty fair trade. Most of these sites will have directions for exempting their site from the ad blocker.

Ad blockers are not very useful on many websites that require you to exempt their website, such as the aforementioned. However, you should still install an ad blocker add-on to insulate yourself from threat actors. Threat actors will typically not go through the trouble of educating you to turn it off, since many of their websites are misspelt domains and provide no service to the end user. Ad blockers when used for security reasons provide two benefits: they block malicious ads, and they allow you to judge whether the site is legitimate before you exempt the website.

CERTMIKE EXAM ESSENTIALS

▶ Many different browsers can be downloaded and installed for operating systems. Care should be taken to only download the web browsers from a trusted source, such as the developer's website. If the developer furnishes a hash, the hash should be checked against the downloaded installer to ensure it has not been altered.

▶ Extensions and plug-ins can be installed on the web browser to extend the browser's functionality. Extensions and plug-ins should only be installed from a trusted source, such as the ecosystem in the web browser. Extensions and plug-ins should be avoided if they are outside of these trusted sources, since they can contain malicious software.

▶ Password managers help keep track of username and password combinations for websites. Many modern web browsers include a password manager to assist the user. Password managers will typically sync to all other devices that the user signs into.

▶ Pop-up blockers prevent pop-ups and pop-unders on web pages. The pop-up blocker is enabled on most modern web browsers. From time to time you may need to adjusted the pop-up blocker for legitimate sites that require the user to receive a pop-up in the web browser.

▶ Private browsing mode allows the user to browse without being recorded in the browsing data. When the user exits private browsing mode, all browsing data is erased.

▶ The web browser can synchronize web browsing data between devices if the user signs in. This allows all the user's passwords, browsing history, cookies, download history, and site settings to be synced between devices.

Practice Question 1

You need to install a web browser for several computers in your organization. How can you verify that you have a legitimate download for a web browser that has not been altered?

A. Check the file hash.

B. Download from a file repository.

C. Make sure you have an SSL/TLS connection when downloading.

D. Use a password manager.

Practice Question 2

An end user calls in and explains the web page they see has old data. How can you direct the user to remedy the issue with the minimal amount of disruption?

A. Adjust the pop-up blocker.

B. View the page with an ad blocker.

C. Clear the web browser data.

D. Clear the web browser cache.

Practice Question 1 Explanation

This question is designed to test your knowledge of trusted and untrusted sources for downloading a web browser.

1. The first answer (A, Check the file hash) is correct. By checking the file hash you can validate that you have downloaded a legitimate web browser and that it has not been altered.

2. The next answer (B, Download from a file repository) is incorrect. The web browser should only be downloaded from a trusted site such as the publisher's site and not from a file repository.

3. The next answer (C, Make sure you have an SSL/TLS connection when downloading) is incorrect. The encryption of the connection will not guarantee that you have a legitimate web browser downloaded.

4. The last answer (D, Use a password manager) is incorrect. The use of a password manager will not guarantee you have a legitimate web browser downloaded.

Correct Answer: A. Check the file hash

Practice Question 2 Explanation

This question is designed to test your knowledge of settings in the web browser.

1. The first answer (A, Adjust the pop-up blocker) is incorrect. The pop-up blocker is typically not responsible for old data.

2. The next answer (B, View the page with an ad blocker) is incorrect. Viewing the page with an ad blocker will not make the content fresher.

3. The next answer (C, Clear the web browser data) is incorrect. Although clearing the web browser data will fix the problem, it will also clear cookies and passwords, disrupting the end-user experience.

4. The last answer (D, Clear the web browser cache) is correct. Clearing the web browser cache is the best option and will cause minimal disruption for the user.

Correct Answer: D. Clear the web browser cache

Domain 3.0: Software Troubleshooting

Software troubleshooting is the third domain of CompTIA's A+ Core 2 exam. In this domain, you'll learn about the ways that IT professionals troubleshoot Microsoft Windows operating systems, personal computers, malware issues and mobile devices. This domain has five objectives:

3.1 Given a scenario, troubleshoot common Windows OS problems.

3.2 Given a scenario, troubleshoot common personal computer (PC) security issues.

3.3 Given a scenario, use best practice procedures for malware removal.

3.4 Given a scenario, troubleshoot common mobile OS and application issues.

3.5 Given a scenario, troubleshoot common mobile OS and application security issues.

Questions from this domain make up 22% of the questions on the A+ Core 2 exam, so you should expect to see approximately 20 questions on your test covering the material in this part.

CHAPTER 23

Troubleshooting Windows

Core 2 Objective 3.1: Given a scenario, troubleshoot common Windows OS problems.

When Microsoft Windows goes down, not much computing will be happening in the typical office or home office. So, it's essential to get Windows working again. In this chapter, you will learn what you need to know about A+ Certification Core 2 Objective 3.1, including the following topics:

▶ **Common Symptoms**
▶ **Common Troubleshooting Steps**

COMMON SYMPTOMS

Although we speak of Microsoft Windows as a single entity, it's actually made up of many software components. Consequently, it's no wonder that problems happen from time to time.

> **TIP**
> Keep in mind that similar symptoms can have more than one cause. Make sure you consider the "big picture" as you develop a hypothesis in your trouble-shooting.

Blue Screen of Death (BSOD)

A Windows STOP error, better known as the Blue Screen of Death (*BSOD*) occurs when Windows has a fatal error: an error that prevents Windows from continuing (Figure 23.1).

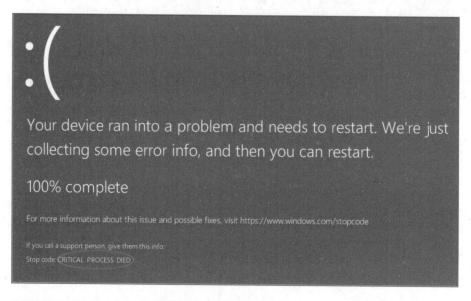

FIGURE 23.1 A typical BSOD (Windows STOP error) in Windows 10. Look up the circled error code to start the troubleshooting process.

BSODs can take place at any time when Windows is running, and have many causes, including:

- ▶ Incompatible hardware
- ▶ Incompatible software
- ▶ Registry problems
- ▶ Viruses/malware

To start the troubleshooting process, record the STOP error and look it up at `https://support.microsoft.com` or by searching for the STOP error text or error code number in your favorite search engine. Be prepared to try several solutions before you find the one that works.

Some common BSOD/STOP errors and typical causes include:

- ▶ IRQL_NOT_LESS_OR_EQUAL (corrupted system files, incompatible device drivers, incomplete software installation, bad graphics drivers)
- ▶ PAGE_FAULT_IN_NONPAGED_AREA (bad RAM or incompatible antivirus application, device drivers)
- ▶ SYSTEM_SERVICE_EXCEPTION (device drivers, recent hardware/software changes, corrupted system files)

The easiest way to solve a BSOD/STOP error is to review the possible causes and to work backward. Determine what was the last change made to the system (new hardware, Windows Update, new application) and go back to the previous condition; remove the hardware, undo the changes made with Windows Update, and uninstall the application. You can use System Restore to help reset Windows to its previous state.

> **TIP**
>
> For an interactive guide to solving the most common BSOD/STOP errors, go to `https://support.microsoft.com` and search for **Troubleshoot blue screen errors**.

Preventing Immediate System Startup After a BSOD

The default setting in Windows is to restart the system immediately after a BSOD, so you would need to check system logs to find the error. A restart is helpful for systems that might fail when no one is around to record a STOP error, but it's a lot easier to solve the problem if you can see and record the BSOD yourself. To prevent immediate restart after a STOP error:

1. Click Start.
2. Click Search.
3. Type **Advanced System Settings**.
4. Click the View Advanced System Settings – Control Panel application.
5. Click the Settings button in the Startup And Recovery section of the System Properties Advanced tab.
6. Deselect Automatically Restart (Figure 23.2). The system will not restart until you press the spacebar or other key after a BSOD, giving you time to record the STOP error.

Low Memory Warnings

A low memory warning (Figure 23.3) can be displayed by Windows or by an application if there's not enough physical RAM installed or not enough paging file space available.

For an immediate workaround, open Task Manager and close unneeded apps. Until more RAM can be installed, increase the size of the paging file (see "Sluggish Performance," next, for details).

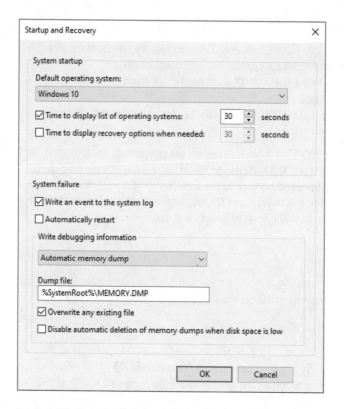

FIGURE 23.2 Deselecting the Automatically Restart option in System Properties' Startup And Recovery

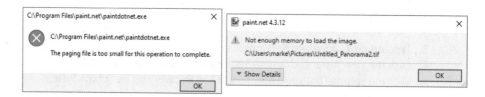

FIGURE 23.3 Too-small paging file (left) and low memory (right) errors displayed by the `Paint.net` program

Sluggish Performance

Long before Windows or applications display "out of memory" errors, sluggish performance is a clue that Windows is short of physical or virtual memory or running too many programs. Use Resource Monitor in Administrative Tools (Windows 10) or Windows Tools (Windows 11) to see the programs consuming memory and CPU resources at a deeper level than Task Manager. Figure 23.4 shows a system with 100 hard faults/second in memory.

> **NOTE**
> A hard fault results when there isn't enough physical memory for the programs in data and memory and the system must swap to virtual memory (paging file). A high number of hard faults/second indicates it's time to check virtual memory size or install more RAM.

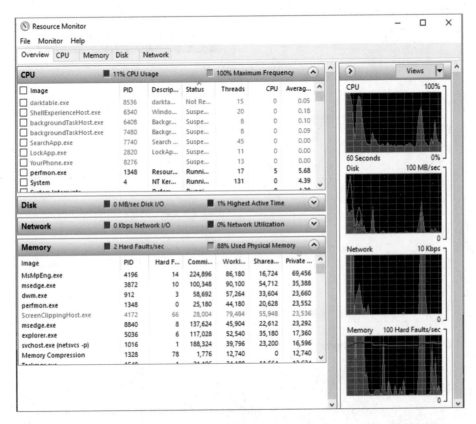

FIGURE 23.4 A high number of hard faults/second in the memory display in Resource Monitor indicates that more physical RAM or virtual memory is needed.

To check the size of the paging file:

1. Click Start.
2. Click Search.
3. Type **Advanced System Settings**.
4. Click the View Advanced System Settings – Control Panel application.
5. Click the Settings button in the Performance section of the System Properties Advanced tab.

6. Click the Advanced tab (Figure 23.5).
7. Note the size of the paging file. If it is too small, click Change.
8. Click the System Managed Size radio button, then click Set.
9. Click OK, then click Apply and click OK again. Restart Windows to put the new paging file size into effect.

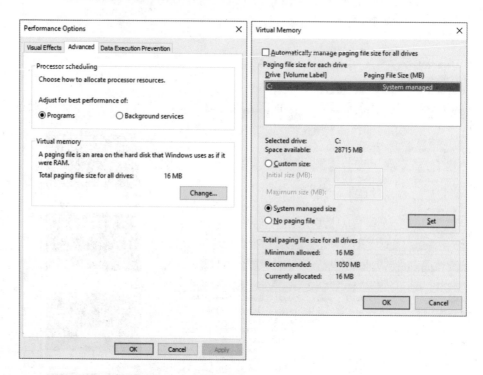

FIGURE 23.5 Changing the size of the paging file

TIP

If the system drive is short on space, other hard drives (not removable drives) can be used for the paging file. To learn more about determining the paging file size, see https://docs.microsoft.com/en-us/windows/client-management/determine-appropriate-page-file-size.

No OS Found

Errors such as "No boot device found," "No boot media," and so on indicate that the BIOS/UEFI firmware configuration can't locate the operating system (*OS*); the operating system is the software that controls the computer and provides an interface between the computer and applications. To access the system configuration, restart the system and press the appropriate function key if the system is not in Secure Boot mode. If it is configured to start in Secure Boot mode (the default for Windows 10/11), follow these instructions for Windows 10:

1. Click Start ➤ Settings.
2. Click Update & Security.
3. Click Recovery.
4. Click Restart Now.
5. Click Choose An Option.
6. Click Troubleshoot.
7. Click Advanced Options.
8. Click UEFI Firmware Settings.

For Windows 11:

1. Click Start ➤ Settings ➤ Advanced Startup.
2. Click Startup.
3. Click Troubleshoot.
4. Click Advanced Options.
5. Click UEFI Firmware Settings.

After opening the BIOS/UEFI settings screen, go to the Boot Options menu and confirm that the correct boot drive is selected. If the system is configured to use an OS other than Windows 10, the boot drive is typically a physical drive. If the system is running in Secure Boot mode, the boot drive is controlled by Windows Boot Manager (Figure 23.6). If the boot drive is not listed, change settings to display the boot drive, save the changes, and restart the system.

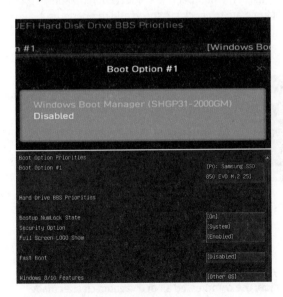

FIGURE 23.6 Correct boot device settings for Secure Boot and non-Windows 10/11 boot configurations

> **EXAM TIP**
>
> Incorrect boot settings can be caused by a dead or dying motherboard battery. If you suspect the battery is dead or dying, check the date and time listed in BIOS/UEFI settings. If the time is way off, replace the motherboard battery.

Boot Problems

If the boot sequence is correct in BIOS/UEFI settings but the system won't boot, it's time to repair the startup files. In Windows 10/11, follow the steps listed above until you open the Advanced Options menu; click Startup Repair.

After Windows performs startup repairs, it restarts the system. If it is unable to repair startup files automatically, open a command prompt and enter the following commands in this order:

```
bootrec /fixmbr
bootrec /fixboot
bootrec /scanos
bootrec /rebuildbcd
```

Restart the system after making these changes.

Frequent Shutdowns

If your system frequently shuts down by itself, the number one suspect is overheating components. You can access BIOS/UEFI firmware to check fan speed and temperature (Figure 23.7). If the temperature is too high and the fan speed is too low or has stopped, replace the fan.

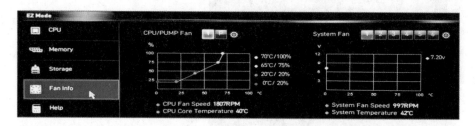

FIGURE 23.7 Checking temperature and fan speeds in a typical recent UEFI system

If the fan speeds are normal, check system ventilation. Clogged intake or exhaust locations will prevent fans from doing their job. Use compressed air or a vacuum cleaner made for computer use to clean dirty CPU, case, and GPU fans and ventilation holes in the case.

Services Not Starting

A service that doesn't start prevents the Windows function the service provides from working. Typically, services that aren't running will display an error when they are needed (Figure 23.8).

FIGURE 23.8 An error message triggered by trying to print when the printer is not installed or the correct service (usually Print Spooler) isn't running

You can use a Windows troubleshooter to check the status of what the service does (for example, use the audio troubleshooter if audio isn't working, the printer troubleshooter if the print spooler has stopped, and so on). You can also use the System File Checker (covered later in this chapter) or check the configuration of a component such as networking.

> **TIP**
>
> Dig deeper into the differences between Windows services and regular apps by reading www.coretechnologies.com/blog/windows-services/windows-service-vs-regular-application.

Applications Crashing

Applications can crash for a variety of reasons, including corrupted installation files, errors in the application's Registry entries, incompatibility with the current version of Windows, insufficient RAM, a CPU that is too slow, or a GPU that is not powerful enough.

First, determine if there were any changes to the computer prior to the application's crashing, such as Windows updates, a new version of Windows being installed, or new hardware. If the application was just installed, check to see if the system meets or exceeds the application's requirements. If it was written for an older version of Windows, compatibility is a concern. See Chapter 7, "Application Installation and Configuration," for more information about compatibility issues.

USB Controller Resource Warnings

A USB Controller Resources Exceeded error message means that you have too many devices connected to a USB hub connected to your system. This can happen if you have a USB hub connected to another hub (also known as daisy-chaining hubs) or if you use bus-powered hubs instead of self-powered hubs. Avoid daisy-chaining hubs, use a different USB port on the computer for each hub, and use self-powered hubs (hubs that use AC adapters) if you are using the hub to connect to portable USB drives and other devices that use bus power to run.

System Instability

System instability, including frequent system crashes, system restarts, incorrect colors and shapes onscreen, and failure of USB devices to work properly, can have several causes:

▶ Overheating CPU, GPU, or RAM
▶ Overclocking without adequate CPU or GPU cooling
▶ Fan failure or poor system airflow
▶ Power supply not adequate for system requirements

To work around these issues:

▶ Stop overclocking and run all components at normal clock speeds and memory timings.
▶ Check speed and function of CPU, GPU, and system fans.
▶ Check power supply fan.
▶ Test power supply voltages under load.
▶ Replace power supply if system or wattage requirements are near or exceed the power supply rating (especially with 12V wattage requirements).

Slow Profile Load

If a user profile (account) stored on a local computer is loading a lot slower than usual, it's probably corrupted. This is certainly the case if other accounts on the same system are loading normally. Here are some ways to deal with the problem.

To fix slow profiles due to corruption, create a new user profile and move files and preferences to the new profile.

A user profile created from a default profile can contain a copy of a different user's profile, causing slowdowns. To solve this problem, delete hidden files and folders from the previous user. For details, see `https://docs.microsoft.com/en-us/troubleshoot/windows-server/performance/performance-issues-custom-default-user-profile`.

Users with a roaming user profile (typical of large networks) with a slow network connection will have slow profile loads. If the connection is too slow, Windows automatically loads a local copy of the user profile from the user's PC.

If domain users with Group Policy Objects (GPOs) and login scripts have slowdowns, there are probably too many GPOs and scripts being loaded. Look for more efficient ways to load this information, such as using third-party solutions. To learn more about login scripts, see Chapter 13, "Logical Security."

Time Drift

Time drift is the term for systems that lose time gradually in service. For PCs on a small network, you can use the Settings menu's Date & Time submenu to periodically sync time using the Windows Time Server. Click Sync Now if your clock appears to be off. Also note the last time the sync was performed (it's usually daily).

On a domain network, a Group Policy Object might use a different time server. In either case, if the problem recurs, check the motherboard battery used to maintain BIOS/UEFI settings and clock timing and replace if it is dead or dying.

> **EXAM TIP**
>
> Prepare for the Core 2 1102 exam by researching each of the problems listed here and looking up the appropriate troubleshooting steps that follow. Install a VM of Windows 10 or 11 and use it to practice solutions.

COMMON TROUBLESHOOTING STEPS

Windows offers a wide variety of troubleshooting steps you can follow to fix the common symptoms discussed in the previous section, from restarting the computer to upgrading hardware and looking for damaged Windows system files.

Reboot

Rebooting a Windows system with problems is a good first step with most issues. When you reboot, any transient problems are resolved by reloading Windows. This author has a saying: "Once is a glitch, twice is a problem." If an issue goes away after a reboot, it's a glitch. However, if it recurs, it's a problem and it's time to dig deeper for solutions.

Restart Services

Open Services in Computer Management and make sure the service mentioned in the error message is running. If it is not running, right-click the service and click Start (Figure 23.9). To see other settings for the service, click Properties.

To open Services in Computer Management in Windows, use one of these methods:

- ▶ Open Computer Management in Windows. Click Services And Applications in the left pane to expand it. Click Services to open it.
- ▶ Press Windows key+R, type **services.msc** in the Run dialog box, and press Enter to open it.
- ▶ Click Start or the Cortana Search Box, type **services**, and click the best-matched result to open the Windows Services application.

▶ Click the Start menu and scroll down the list to find Windows Administrative Tools to expand it. Click Services to open it.

▶ Open Control Panel, click System And Security in the Control Panel window, and click Administrative Tools (Windows 10) or Windows Tools (Windows 11). Find the Services shortcut in the list and double-click it to open it.

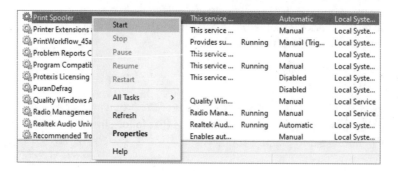

FIGURE 23.9 Preparing to start the Print Spooler service

Make sure services that are needed at all times, such as Print Spooler, are using Automatic for Startup Type. Services that only run under certain circumstances are set as Manual.

> **TIP**
>
> You can speed up Windows by configuring services you don't need to use Manual startup. The ASKVG website has a listing of nonessential services for most users at `www.askvg.com/`
> `beginners-guide-to-configure-windows-10-services`.

Uninstall/Reinstall/Update Applications

If the application ran normally before but is now crashing and there haven't been any changes to the computer, run a repair (change) installation from Apps in Settings or Control Panel. This can fix missing or corrupted installation files and Registry entries. If this doesn't work, uninstall and reinstall the application.

If the app was originally written for an older version of Windows, try settings on the Compatibility tab for the program's executable file or use the compatibility checker on the same tab to test settings that Windows determines are the best (Figure 23.10). If possible, update to the latest version of the app.

Check hardware compatibility issues, such as recommended RAM, paging file size, CPU type and performance, and GPU type and performance using tools such as MSInfo32, CPU-Z (`www.cpuid.com`), or GPU-Z (`www.techpowerup.com`). If the application requires more hardware than your system offers, change apps or upgrade your computer.

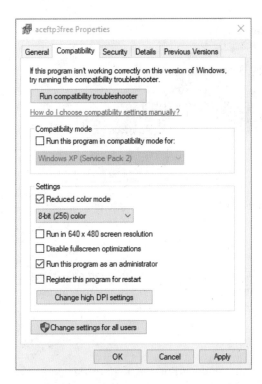

FIGURE 23.10 Using the Compatibility tab to configure an old program to run properly on Windows 10

Add Resources

Adding hardware resources might seem like an odd way to deal with Windows issues, but Windows controls both the hardware and the software. So, here are ways to make Windows work better with better hardware.

RAM

While you can work around some memory problems by adjusting the size of your virtual memory paging file, there's nothing like the real thing. Use the interactive memory tools available at major memory vendors such as Crucial.com to identify onboard memory and suitable upgrades.

USB Ports

If you are short of USB 3.0 ports on a desktop computer, check to see if there's an unused USB 3.0 header on the motherboard and connect a USB 3.0 header cable to it (Figure 23.11). You can then connect a USB device or hub to each port. Similarly, unused USB 2.0 headers can become functional USB ports by connecting a USB 2.0 header cable. Add a USB 3.0 card with Type-A or Type-C ports to a PCIe x1 or wider slot for even more ports.

FIGURE 23.11 **A USB 3.0 dual-port header cable and the matching motherboard header (inset)**

Storage

If you have unused 2.5-inch or 3.5-inch SATA or M.2 SATA or NVMe drives left over from previous upgrades, convert them into external drives with USB enclosures. You can use them for storage and free up the entire system drive for more apps.

> **TIP**
>
> Learn how to use a different drive for your Windows libraries/folders (Documents, Photos, and so on) at www.zdnet.com/article/windows-10-tip-move-your-default-data-folders-to-a-different-drive.

Verify Requirements

It's frustrating to download or purchase a new app only to discover that it won't run on your system because it lacks the processor power, GPU performance, RAM, or available disk space. Use `MSInfo32.exe` (System Information) to check out essential facts about your system's Windows version, CPU, and physical and virtual memory size (Figure 23.12). Need to learn more? Download CPU-Z from www.cpuid.com for detailed CPU information (accurate core count, clock speed, and so on); download GPU-Z from www.techpowerup.com for detailed GPU information, including accurate video RAM size, component clock speeds, and more.

System File Checker

System File Checker (SFC) is a command-line utility you can run to replace missing or damaged Windows system files. Microsoft recommends that you use SFC along with the Deployment Image Servicing and Management (DISM) tool using this procedure:

1. Open a command-prompt session as administrator, and enter this command:

```
DISM.exe /Online /Cleanup-image /Restorehealth
```

   2. After DISM has completed, enter this command to replace any corrupted system files:

```
sfc /scannow
```

   3. SFC will report its findings.

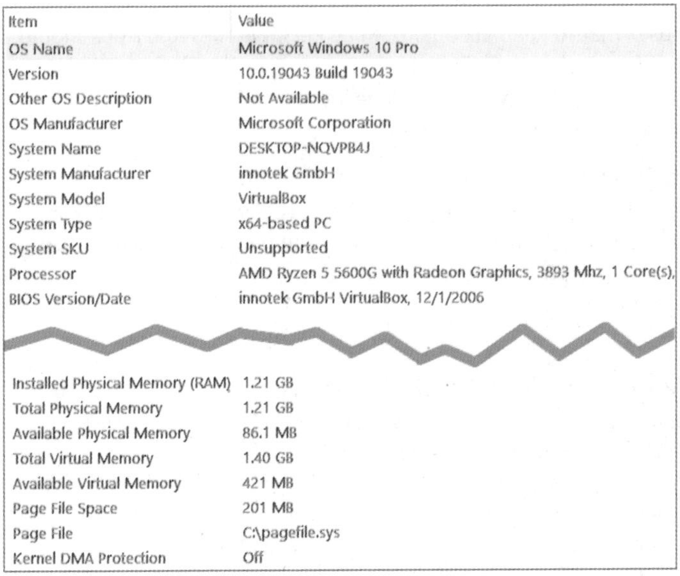

Item	Value
OS Name	Microsoft Windows 10 Pro
Version	10.0.19043 Build 19043
Other OS Description	Not Available
OS Manufacturer	Microsoft Corporation
System Name	DESKTOP-NQVPB4J
System Manufacturer	innotek GmbH
System Model	VirtualBox
System Type	x64-based PC
System SKU	Unsupported
Processor	AMD Ryzen 5 5600G with Radeon Graphics, 3893 Mhz, 1 Core(s),
BIOS Version/Date	innotek GmbH VirtualBox, 12/1/2006
Installed Physical Memory (RAM)	1.21 GB
Total Physical Memory	1.21 GB
Available Physical Memory	86.1 MB
Total Virtual Memory	1.40 GB
Available Virtual Memory	421 MB
Page File Space	201 MB
Page File	C:\pagefile.sys
Kernel DMA Protection	Off

FIGURE 23.12 Details from MSInfo32 of a system's Windows version and physical/virtual memory sizes

---

NOTE

For details, including steps to take if DISM or SFC can't run with the current system configuration, see http://support.microsoft.com/kb/929833.

Repair Windows

If you have tried several repair options for Windows and it still isn't working, a reinstallation may be in order. Some reinstallations can wipe out non-Microsoft Store apps or even your data. If you want to keep all of your installed apps but want to reinstall Windows, it's time for a repair installation. A repair installation is officially referred to by Microsoft as an in-place upgrade.

1. Download the same or later version of your same Windows edition (Windows 10 Home, Pro, etc.; Windows 11 Home, Pro, etc.) as an ISO file.
2. Remove any optical media in internal or external drives.
3. Open File Explorer and mount the ISO you created in step 1.
4. Open Setup.
5. Click Yes to continue.
6. Click Next to start installation.
7. Click Accept to accept license terms.
8. In the Choose What To Keep dialog box, Keep Personal Files And Apps should be selected. If not, select it. Click Next.
9. Make sure your version of Windows will be installed and that your personal files and apps will be kept. Click Install.

Your system should be working better when the installation is finished.

If you suspect that corrupted applications are the problem, consider using Settings ➢ Recovery ➢ Reset This PC. You can keep your personal files (but not your applications) and reinstall Windows, or remove everything and reinstall Windows.

Restore

The System Restore feature in Windows is designed to help you reverse changes made to Windows, Windows apps, or hardware drivers. It must be enabled before it can be used to revert Windows to a previous configuration.

Create a Restore Point

Follow these steps to create a restore point:

1. Click Start and type **system restore** in the Search box.
2. Click Create A Restore Point.
3. If Protection is turned off for the C: drive (the default), click Configure. If protection is turned on, skip to step 7.
4. Click Turn On System Protection (Figure 23.13).
5. Adjust the slider to specify the amount of space used for system protection. About 5–10 percent of your system is recommended for most users.
6. Click Apply, then click OK.
7. Click Create to create a restore point.
8. Type a description, then click Create.
9. Click Close.

Revert Windows to a Restore Point

To restore Windows to a particular restore point:

1. Click Start and type **system restore** in the Search box.
2. Click Create A Restore Point.

3. Click the System Restore button.
4. Click Next.
5. Click the restore point you want to use.
6. To see what programs and drivers will be affected, click Scan For Affected Programs.
7. Click Close after reviewing the deleted items (top pane) and those that will be restored (bottom pane).
8. Click Next to continue.
9. Review the changes that will be made, and click Finish (Figure 23.14). Windows will reboot and run the process.

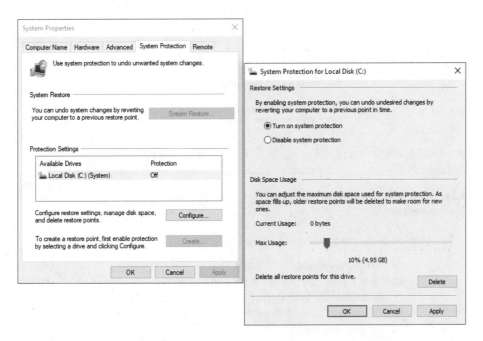

FIGURE 23.13 **Enabling System Restore and creating a restore point**

Reimage

A more thorough method of restoring your system to its earlier configuration is to create a disk image when your system is working properly and restore the image, a process known as *reimaging*. You can create an image with the Control Panel Backup and Restore (Windows 7) app (included in Windows 10) or with a variety of third-party programs such as Macrium Reflect and Acronis True Image, among others.

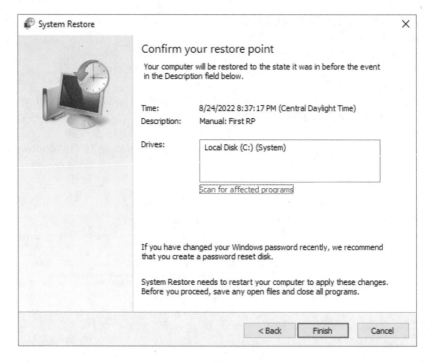

FIGURE 23.14 **Preparing to revert Windows to an earlier configuration with System Restore**

To restore an image made with the Backup and Restore (Windows 7) app:

1. Create the image with Backup and Restore (Windows 7) and store it on your choice of media. You can get to Backup and Restore (Windows 7) from Settings ➤ Update & Security ➤ Backup. Backup also allows you to back up files to OneDrive cloud storage and with File History. Use Search in Windows 11 to find Backup and Restore (Windows 7).

2. Create a system repair disc (CD or DVD) with the link on the Backup and Restore (Windows 7) app.

3. If you can't boot Windows, use the system repair disc to start the restore process.

4. If you can boot Windows, open Settings ➤ Update & Security ➤ Recovery and click the Restart Now button (Windows 10) or Settings ➤ System ➤ Recovery and click Restart Now (Windows 11).

5. In the Choose An Option dialog box, click Troubleshoot ➤ Advanced Options ➤ System Image Recovery.

6. Follow the prompts to connect your image media to the computer to complete the process.

Roll Back Updates

Sometimes updates backfire; they can cause Windows or devices to fail. To solve problems caused by updates, you need to know how to roll them back.

To roll back updates to Windows 10 or 11:

1. Open Programs and Features in Control Panel.
2. Click View Installed Updates.
3. Click the update you want to remove.
4. Click Uninstall.

To roll back a driver update in Windows 10 or 11:

1. Open Device Manager.
2. Click the + sign next to the category where the device is listed.
3. Open the device listing.
4. Select the Driver tab.
5. Click Roll Back Driver.
6. Select the reason for the rollback and click Yes.
7. Close the dialog box and close Device Manager.

Rebuild Windows Profiles

An error message stating "The User Profile Service failed the logon. User Profile cannot be loaded" means that the user profile is corrupted. A typical cause is that the `NTUSER.DAT` file in the `C:\Users\Default` folder has become corrupted.

To fix the issue, replace the `NTUSER.DAT` file in the `Default` folder with a copy from another user profile. See `www.technipages.com/windows-10-fix-user-profile-cannot-be-loaded-error`. Other methods include using Regedit (Registry Editor) or using DISM and SFC to repair Windows problems including the user profile. If possible, back up your system before using these methods.

> **NOTE**
>
> For step-by-step instructions on Regedit or DISM/SFC repair methods, see `www.easeus.com/computer-instruction/fix-a-corrupted-user-profile-windows-10.html`.

CERTMIKE EXAM ESSENTIALS

▶ Capturing details of Windows errors from BSODs to pop-up messages is critical to troubleshooting Windows. Use a smartphone or digital camera if screen captures are not possible.

▶ Many symptoms have multiple possible causes, so don't rule out anything until you dig deeper.

▶ "Bad" software and "bad" hardware are both possible causes for Windows errors, but both can be solved by updates.

Practice Question 1

You see an error message stating that the application doesn't have enough virtual memory to run. What is the most likely cause for this error?

A. Corrupted user profile
B. Disk error
C. Memory shortage
D. Too many programs in the Start menu

Practice Question 2

You have received a call from a user who has received a USB controller resource warning. You remember purchasing a new self-powered USB 3.0 hub for this user just a week ago but you let the user install it. Which of the following installation errors did the user most likely make?

A. Connected the hub to another hub
B. Connected USB 2.0 devices to the USB 3.0 hub
C. Connected self-powered and bus-powered devices to the hub
D. Used a USB Type-C to Type-A adapter for one of the devices connected to the hub

Practice Question 1 Explanation

This question is designed to test your real-world understanding of memory types in Windows. Let's consider each of these answers.

1. The first answer (A, Corrupted user profile) is incorrect. User profiles have nothing to do with memory.

2. The next answer (B, Disk error) is incorrect. A disk error would cause other types of error messages.

3. The next answer (C, Memory shortage) is correct. Windows uses virtual memory when actual RAM is not large enough for running programs.

4. The last answer (D, Too many programs in the Start menu) is incorrect. The number of programs here has nothing to do with memory.

Correct Answer: C. Memory shortage

Practice Question 2 Explanation

This question is designed to test your knowledge of USB errors. Let's evaluate these answers one at a time.

1. The first answer (A, Connected the hub to another hub) is correct. This can cause the system to run out of USB resources. The hub should have been plugged into a different USB port on the computer.

2. The second answer (B, Connected USB 2.0 devices to the USB 3.0 hub) is incorrect. USB 3.0 hubs can work with any type of USB device.

3. The third answer (C, Connected self-powered and bus-powered devices to the hub) is incorrect. A self-powered hub supports either type of device, including a mixture of bus-powered and self-powered devices.

4. The last answer (D, Used a USB Type-C to Type-A adapter for one of the devices connected to the hub) is incorrect. A Type-C device might run more slowly when connected to a USB 3.0 hub, but it will certainly work.

Correct Answer: A. Connected the hub to another hub

CHAPTER 24

Troubleshooting PC Security

Core 2 Objective 3.2: Given a scenario, troubleshoot common personal computer (PC) security issues.

Troubleshooting common PC security issues is just one of the many daily tasks for an A+ technician. When troubleshooting a problem, an A+ technician should investigate the security related to the problem first. Most of the troubleshooting should be common sense to an A+ technician, but it may not be common sense to the average end user. In this chapter, you will learn what you need to know about the A+ Certification Core 2 Objective 3.2, including the following topics:

▶ **Common symptoms**
▶ **Browser-related symptoms**

COMMON SYMPTOMS

As an A+ technician, you will find that the operating system is the largest surface area of attack for a threat actor, compared to the network or even the end user.

Each application that is installed can weaken the security of the operating system, if a vulnerability exists in the application. A threat actor can use this weakness in the application to elevate privileges in the operating system.

> **NOTE**
>
> Elevated privileges allows for administrative access to the operating system. To learn more about privileges, refer back to Chapter 13, "Logical Security."

Unable to Access the Network

Computers will undoubtably be connected to a network through wireless or a wired connection. From time to time, the network might not function properly. In most cases, it is attributed to a bad physical connection or a corrupted device driver. A Symptoms that there is a problem with the network are: you can't log into the network, access any network services, or access the Internet. These problems are sometimes obvious and can often be fixed by repairing physical connections or by reinstalling correct or new device drivers.

In some situations, the symptoms might be related to a security-related threat. If you still do not have network connectivity after verifying the physical connection and reinstalling the device driver, you should suspect the problem to be malware-related. Malware installed on the computer could crash and prevent network access, creating the symptoms similar to a bad physical connection or bad device driver.

Some security concerns can be external of your network. If your network is being attacked externally with a denial-of-service (DoS) or distributed DoS (DDoS) attack, this could cause a slow browsing experience similar to that caused by malware or other network problems.

> **NOTE**
>
> DoS and DDoS were covered in Chapter 16, "Social Engineering and Security Threats."

Desktop Alerts

Desktop alerts are normal notifications or dialog boxes that pop up in the operating system to alert you of an event. In Windows 10/11 these notifications are called *toast notifications*, because they pop up like a piece of toast in the lower-right corner of the desktop. Most of these are normal desktop alerts like a Window Defender Antivirus status message, as shown in Figure 24.1. In fact, any application can use toast notifications to display a message, such as a new piece of mail that was delivered to your mailbox.

FIGURE 24.1 Toast notification

It is important to be able to identify a toast alert from a piece of malware. You can always click the lower-right corner of the screen where the message status box is located. This will open all the toast notifications on Windows 10/11 and detail which application created the alerts, as shown in Figure 24.2. If a program is unidentified and it creates a security-related alert, you should investigate it further to isolate the security issue.

FIGURE 24.2 Toast notification summary

NOTE
Windows Security Settings were covered in Chapter 5, "Windows Settings."

False Alerts Regarding Antivirus Protection

Threat actors will craft a desktop alert with either a web page and JavaScript or a piece of malware that is downloaded to your computer. If a malicious application is running on your operating system, it can create toast notifications. The desktop alert will look like it came from the operating system with some urgent message, such as a virus was detected. Then the threat actor will coerce the end user to download a piece of malware, call a tech support scam, or visit a website. This is a type of social engineering; the threat actor creates a problem with urgency and offers a swift solution. This is nothing more than a trap.

Typically, a desktop alert attack will not be as sophisticated as a toast notification. This is because web pages are limited in how they can render and where they can place a child window. When these desktop alert attacks are launched from a web browser, you will most likely see a dialog box that appears over the web page, as shown in Figure 24.3. The tactics are the same: create a problem, create urgency, and direct the user to the solution.

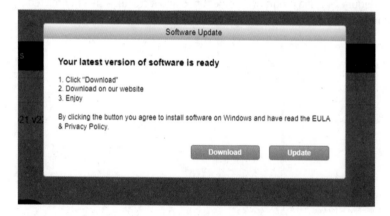

FIGURE 24.3 Web page generated download alert

EXAM TIP
False alerts regarding antivirus is a form of social engineering to make the user take a false action.

Altered System or Personal Files

Once a threat actor has compromised your operating system, their first priority is typically creating persistence between reboots and elevating privileges. Creating persistence allows

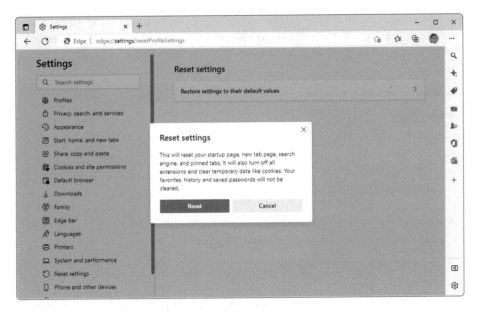

FIGURE 24.7 Resetting the web browser settings

If you continue to receive pop-ups, pop-unders, or overlays, then you may be infected with malware. You might even have a malicious web page that is minimized serving the pop-ups/overlays. You can use Task Manager in Windows to end all web browsers' tasks or reboot the operating system to remove the malicious web page from RAM. If this fixes the problem and it is a malicious web page, it is a good idea to scan your operating system with antivirus/antimalware software.

Certificate Warnings

Certificates aid in the encryption of web pages and certify that you are browsing the website that you intended to browse. Certificates are fickle, and there are a few issues that surround the technology. The first is related to time and date; certificates have a defined start date and end date as to when they are valid. The time on the end user's computer should always be checked first when diagnosing a problem with certificates. If the end user's computer accessing the web page has an inaccurate time and date, it could cause problems with the certificate and subsequent SSL/TLS encryption. If the certificate itself is expired, then there is not much you can do other than notify the owner of the website. The owner of the website will need to reenroll and obtain a current certificate for the website. You can check the certificate validity period by clicking the lock next to the URL in the address bar, then selecting Connection Is Secure or Your Connection To This Site Isn't Secure, then clicking the certificate icon in the dialog box. The certificate information will be displayed, as shown in Figure 24.8.

A second common problem is a faulty or untrusted SSL/TLS certificate. When encountered you will be alerted that the connection isn't private, as shown in Figure 24.9. The address bar will also display a caution triangle and the words Not Secure. The problem could arise from a multitude of reasons. One such reason could be misconfiguration by the website owner. Another issue could be the chain of trust is broken on the certificate.

Certificate Viewer: www.certmike.com ✕

| General | Details |

Issued To

Common Name (CN)	www.certmike.com
Organization (O)	<Not Part Of Certificate>
Organizational Unit (OU)	<Not Part Of Certificate>

Issued By

Common Name (CN)	RapidSSL Global TLS RSA4096 SHA256 2022 CA1
Organization (O)	DigiCert, Inc.
Organizational Unit (OU)	<Not Part Of Certificate>

Validity Period

| Issued On | Sunday, July 24, 2022 at 5:00:00 PM |
| Expires On | Friday, August 25, 2023 at 4:59:59 PM |

Fingerprints

| SHA-256 Fingerprint | 1A 8B F7 9D 33 81 9B 1A CB AA 46 DB 85 65 2A 83 BD D2 B9 3B A2 6B 27 65 66 30 CF B9 42 85 BB 8C |
| SHA-1 Fingerprint | F9 A9 9A 0E 77 39 2F 36 C5 A9 A9 04 49 E1 87 51 04 73 06 03 |

FIGURE 24.8 **Certificate information**

The first step to diagnosing the problem is to check that the hostname in the address bar matches the certificate common name (CN). The hostname in the certificate must match the hostname in the address bar or it will be invalid. You can encounter this problem if you visit the website by the IP address. If the hostname in the certificate matches the address bar, then the certificate should be inspected closer for a broken chain of trust. You can check the certificate's chain of trust by following these steps:

1. Click the Not Secure message next to the URL in the address bar.
2. Select Your Connection To This Site Isn't Secure.
3. Click the certificate icon in the dialog box.
4. Select the Details tab, as shown in Figure 24.10. You can quickly see that the chain of trust is fine, that DigiCert Global Root CA is the trusted CA, and that no errors exist in the chain. If an error existed, it would be highlighted where the chain was broken.

A common misconfiguration problem is the use of a self-signed certificate; this is where the root trust is also the hostname (common name). This type of configuration is very common in the initial website development. You will find self-signed certificates used for management web pages on network equipment.

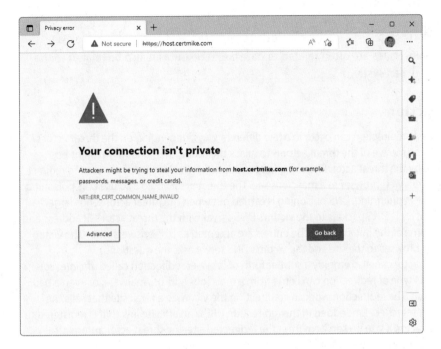

FIGURE 24.9 A connection that isn't private

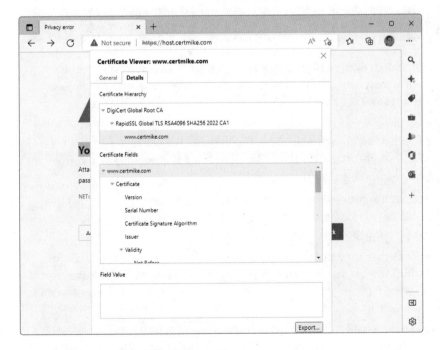

FIGURE 24.10 Details for a certificate

> **EXAM TIP**
>
> Certificate issues are often related to date and time but can also be related to the trust between systems.

Redirection

Web browser redirection can occur in a few different ways, depending on the threat actor's motive. If the motive of the threat actor is to hijack the traffic, then pharming might be employed by the threat actor. Pharming is a technique in which pop-ups are used to redirect the end user's web browser to a malicious site. The threat actor could also use DNS poisoning to accomplish pharming. DNS poisoning is carried out when the threat actor sends large amounts of reply DNS packets to the victim's DNS server with the threat actor's IP address and the hostname of the initial server. The entries are accepted as DNS answers when the victim eventually browses to the site and the victim's DNS server asks the question.

A threat actor can also employ a subtler form of browser redirection called *affiliate redirection*. This type of redirection can come from a malicious add-on, malware, or even a bad search result. The redirection works by redirecting the victim to a retail site that sells the item being searched. Embedded in the redirection URL is an affiliate link that is registered to the threat actor. If you buy an item from the redirected site, the threat actor automatically gets a commission.

CERTMIKE EXAM ESSENTIALS

▶ Desktop alerts are typically normal alerts in the Windows operating system, also known as toast notifications. In some circumstances, a threat actor can disguise malware to look like a desktop alert in an attempt to direct the end user.

▶ After a threat actor has compromised an operating system, the threat actor will alter system files in an attempt to create persistence through reboots. Therefore, unusual system files that are altered are typically a sign of malware or that a root kit has been installed by a threat actor.

▶ Threat actors will use ransomware to encrypt or delete personal files so that the files can be held for ransom. Typically, a text file will accompany the encrypted files with instructions on how to pay the ransom.

▶ Certificates are used to encrypt and sign web pages to assure the end user of security. Therefore, warnings should not be ignored; a threat actor could eavesdrop or the traffic might not be encrypted, depending on the circumstances of the warning.

▶ Browser redirection can be executed by the threat actor in multiple ways, depending on the threat actor's motive. Regardless of the tactics used, browser redirection is the act of redirecting an end user's web browser to a malicious site.

Practice Question 1

A security-related notification has popped up on the desktop stating an urgency to click a download link; which security concern could this be?

A. OS update failure
B. False desktop alert
C. Altered system files
D. Redirection

Practice Question 2

What do you call an unwanted web page that opens in a new browser window in the background?

A. Pop-up
B. Toast notification
C. Pop-under
D. Overlay

Practice Question 1 Explanation

This question is designed to test your knowledge of common symptoms related to security.

1. The first answer (A, OS update failure) is incorrect. An OS update failure will not display a security-related alert.

2. The next answer (B, False desktop alert) is correct. A false desktop alert could be a sign of a security issue.

3. The next answer (C, Altered system files) is incorrect. Altered system files will not display a desktop alert.

4. The last answer (D, redirection) is incorrect. Redirection is a threat actor tactic with web browsers.

Correct Answer: B. False desktop alert

Practice Question 2 Explanation

This question is designed to test your knowledge of common browser security issues related to pop-ups.

1. The first answer (A, Pop-up) is incorrect. A pop-up is an unwanted web page that opens in the foreground.

2. The next answer (B, Toast notification) is incorrect. A toast notification is an operating system notification.

3. The next answer (C, Pop-under) is correct. A pop-under is an unwanted web page that opens in a new browser window in the background.

4. The last answer (D, Overlay) is incorrect. An overlay is a web page that opens over the current web page and looks like part of the original web page.

Correct Answer: C. Pop-under

Troubleshooting Malware

Core 2 Objective 3.3: Given a scenario, use best practice procedures for malware removal.

As a technician, you will encounter malware on an operating system and need to remove it. The seven steps in this section are not only listed in the CompTIA A+ exam objectives, but they are best practices that you should memorize and apply in the field. The steps are in no way a guide to remove *all* malware, but they serve as solid baseline. In this chapter, you will learn what you need to know about A+ Certification Core 2 Objective 3.3, including the following topics:

▶ Step 1. Investigate and verify malware symptoms.
▶ Step 2. Quarantine infected systems.
▶ Step 3. Disable System Restore in Windows.
▶ Step 4. Remediate infected systems.
▶ Step 5. Schedule scans and run updates.
▶ Step 6. Enable System Restore and create a restore point in Windows.
▶ Step 7. Educate the end user.

STEP 1. INVESTIGATE AND VERIFY MALWARE SYMPTOMS

The first step to removing malware is investigating and verifying that malware exists on the operating system. This can be accomplished by monitoring the symptoms that were covered in Chapter 24, "Troubleshooting PC Security." There are also some common tools in the operating system that can aid in investigating and verifying the malware. One such tool is the Resource Monitor, as shown in Figure 25.1. Resource Monitor can be used to isolate performance problems that are typical symptoms of malware infections. Resource Monitor allows you to identify the specific process that is overutilizing the resource. The resources that you can examine with Resource Monitor are CPU, Memory, Disk, and Network. Task Manager can also be used to identify performance issues as they relate to malware infection. The Details tab in Task Manager, as shown in Figure 25.2, allows you to identify the processes running, memory allocated, and the user the process is running as.

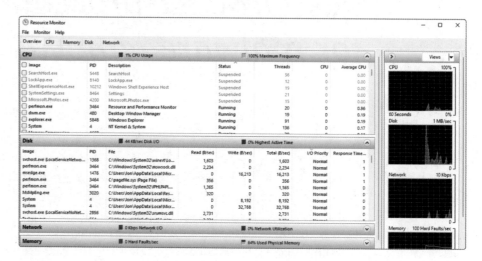

FIGURE 25.1 Resource Monitor

> **NOTE**
>
> You should always follow your organization's incident response plan as it relates to malware. Also ensure that you have a backup of the system before making any changes.

Signs of malware infection are high resource utilization, such as CPU, memory, disk and network activity. A tool such as Resource Monitor will help locate the culprit that is overutilizing the resource. There are several other tools, such as Process Explorer from Windows Sysinternals, that allow you to view the processes running on the operating system.

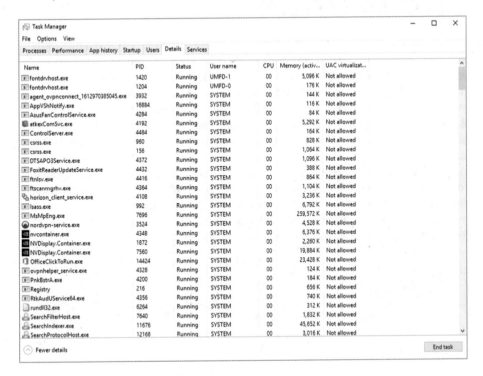

FIGURE 25.2 Task Manager

Resource Monitor and Process Explorer require some experience and assume you know what you are looking for. The use of Microsoft Defender Antivirus is also useful when you're trying to identify malware. Microsoft Defender Antivirus takes some of the guesswork out of identifying malware, provided it is known malware and there are virus definitions to identify the malware.

NOTE

Chapter 17, "Windows Security," covered Microsoft Defender Antivirus in detail.

EXAM TIP

Malware symptoms can be investigated and verified with built-in operating system tools for monitoring performance and processes, but you will need experience in malware hunting. Microsoft Defender Antivirus is useful for identifying malware.

STEP 2. QUARANTINE INFECTED SYSTEMS

After you have verified that the malware exists on the operating system, you must swiftly quarantine the infected system. Malware can spread to the rest of the computers in the network if not swiftly quarantined. Malware typically spreads through network connections, email, files, and a number of other insidious ways. Another important reason to swiftly quarantine the malware is to prevent the exfiltration of data; this is the main tactic of ransomware. Computers with wired connections should be unplugged and wireless devices should be placed in Airplane mode, or the network card should be disabled in the operating system.

If an infected system is identified and needs to be remediated, it should be quarantined from the immediate network and put into an isolated network. The isolated network is usually a place where the malware can be further studied and potentially remediated. Some endpoint detection and response (EDR) software, such as Microsoft Defender for Endpoint, can automatically isolate a client when malware is discovered.

> **EXAM TIP**
> An infected system should be quarantined as soon as possible to prevent the spread of malware or the exfiltration of data.

STEP 3. DISABLE SYSTEM RESTORE IN WINDOWS

Once you have quarantined the infected system, the next crucial step is to disable System Restore in Windows. This is a critical step to prevent a remediated operating system from reinfecting itself from a restore point that may contain infected or corrupted files. Threat actors will often use the Windows Task Scheduler to restore from a restore point in the event of remediation.

System Protection in Windows 10/11 is turned off by default. You can check and/or disable System Protection with these steps:

1. Click the Start menu.
2. Type **Recovery** and select it from the results.
3. Choose Configure System Restore.
4. Select the system drive and click Configure.
5. Select Disable System Protection.
6. Click Delete (Disk Space Usage).
7. Click Continue, then Close, OK, and finally Yes.

The System Protection dialog box can be seen in Figure 25.3.

> **NOTE**
> Ransomware will often clear your restore points to prevent you from recovering data.

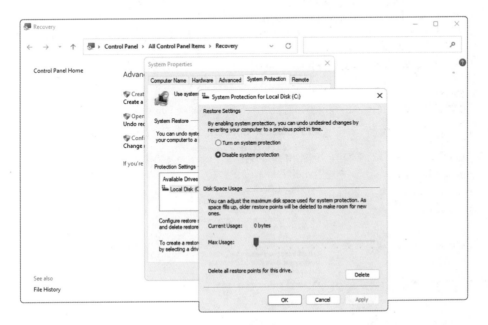

FIGURE 25.3 System Protection

STEP 4. REMEDIATE INFECTED SYSTEMS

Remediating the infected system or systems will largely depend on the malware that has infected the operating system. If it is simple malware that redirects you when you search websites, then it will be relatively easy to remediate the operating system. If the malware is advanced and uses a command and control (C&C) server, then you might consider reinstalling the operating system. In either case, you will need to remediate the operating system to retrieve your files.

A. Update Antimalware Software

New malware comes out every day, and because of that, you will need to update your antimalware software by downloading the latest definitions. This operation should be done prior to scanning the operating system to remediate from the malware. Microsoft Defender can be updated on Windows 11 with the following steps:

1. Click the Start Menu.
2. Click the Settings gear.
3. Select Privacy & Security.
4. Select Windows Security.
5. Click Virus & Threat Protection.
6. Under Virus & Threat Protection Updates, click Protection Updates.
7. Click Check For Updates.
8. Verify the Last Update date and time, as shown in Figure 25.4.

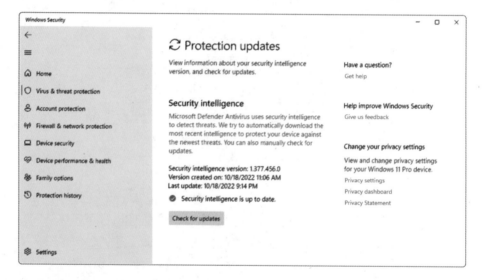

FIGURE 25.4 Updating Microsoft Defender definitions

EXAM TIP

Antimalware definitions should always be updated prior to scanning and the very latest updates should be installed. Typically, the definitions will have been created within the past few hours.

B. Scanning and Removal Techniques (e.g., Safe Mode, Preinstallation Environment)

Once you have gotten the operating system to a stable point and the virus definitions are updated, it is time to identify the malware with a scan and remove it. The most complete way to scan your operating system is performing a full scan. You can perform a full scan of the operating system by following these steps:

1. Click the Start menu.
2. Click the Settings gear.
3. Select Privacy & Security.
4. Select Windows Security.
5. Click Virus & Threat Protection.
6. Click Scan Options.
7. Click Full Scan.
8. Click Scan Now, as shown in Figure 25.5.

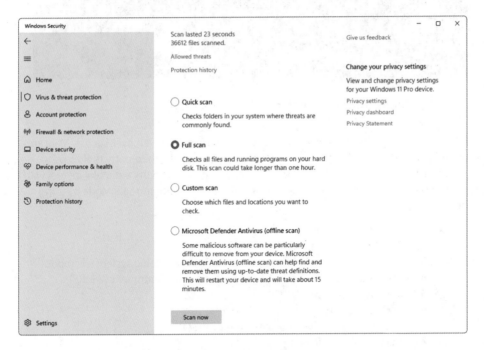

FIGURE 25.5 Performing a Microsoft Defender scan

Depending on how difficult the malware is to remove from your operating system, you may need to perform an offline scan. In lieu of selecting a full scan with the previous procedure, you will select Microsoft Defender Antivirus (Offline Scan). After clicking Scan

Now, a confirmation box will remind you to save your work. You will then be prompted with a User Account Control (UAC) prompt and the operating system will reboot into a scaled-down version of Windows, called Windows Preinstallation Environment (PE). Microsoft Defender Antivirus will run within Windows PE, as shown in Figure 25.6.

FIGURE 25.6 A Microsoft Defender offline scan

There are plenty of third-party tools that can perform malware removal, such as Malware-bytes, Avast, Webroot, and ZoneAlarm, just to name a few. Most third-party tools have a personal edition that can be used for free. In many cases a third-party antimalware tool will require you to boot into Safe Mode and run a scan. You can boot into Safe Mode by using the following process:

1. Click the Start menu.
2. Click the Power icon.
3. Click Restart and hold down the Shift key (the operating system will reboot).
4. Click Troubleshoot from the Windows Recovery Environment (WinRE).
5. Click Advanced Options.
6. Click Startup Settings.
7. Click Restart (the operating system will reboot).
8. Select 4 Enable Safe Mode.

The operating system will reboot into Safe Mode and you can launch your preferred anti-malware tool, as shown in Figure 25.7. In Safe Mode basic drivers are loaded. Unless you selected Safe Mode With Network, you will have no network connectivity. This is the perfect condition to run antimalware software to remove the malware.

FIGURE 25.7 Windows Safe Mode

EXAM TIP
When performing an offline Microsoft Defender scan, the operating system will reboot into a minimal version of Windows to perform the scan.

In many cases your files may have been encrypted by the malware, as in the case of ransomware. If this happens to you, then you should remediate the malware first. After the operating system is clean, you will need to restore files.

STEP 5. SCHEDULE SCANS AND RUN UPDATES

If you are successful in removing the malware, then it's time to harden your operating system. The best approach is to run updates and schedule periodic scans for malware. Most antimalware applications will allow for scheduled scans and frequent updates. Microsoft

Defender is scheduled to automatically scan the operating system during idle times. However, if you want to schedule a scan, you can use the Task Scheduler:

1. Click the Start menu.
2. Type **Task Scheduler** and then select Task Scheduler from the results.
3. Open the Task Scheduler Library.
4. Select Microsoft, then Windows.
5. Select Microsoft Defender, and double-click Microsoft Defender Scheduled Scan.
6. Select the Triggers tab.
7. Click New on the Triggers tab, then select Weekly and choose the day of the week in the New Trigger dialog box.
8. Click OK, as shown in Figure 25.8.
9. Click OK again after the New Trigger dialog box closes.

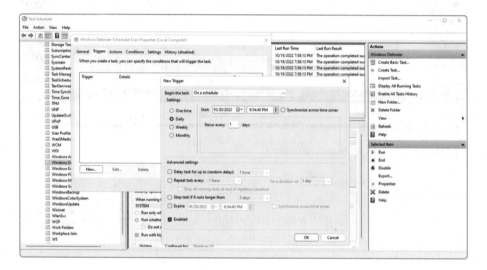

FIGURE 25.8 Creating a Microsoft Defender scheduled scan

Microsoft Defender is scheduled to automatically download updates during the periodic Windows Update check, which is daily. If you want to manually get the latest updates, you can either use the Check For Updates option in the Windows Update settings or the Check For Updates option in the Microsoft Defender Security Center. Alternately, you can manually set a trigger for more frequent checks for Windows Update via the Task Scheduler, using a similar process as described for malware scans.

EXAM TIP

Microsoft Defender periodically scans the operating system and the Windows Update periodically checks for antimalware updates.

STEP 6. ENABLE SYSTEM RESTORE AND CREATE A RESTORE POINT IN WINDOWS

Now that you have a stable operating system again, it is time to create a restore point. This will ensure that if you have a problem in the future, you can revert back to a time where the operating system was healthy and malware-free. You can enable System Protection by following these steps:

1. Click the Start menu.
2. Type **Restore** and select Create A Restore Point from the results.
3. Select the System drive and click Configure.
4. Click Turn On System Protection, and click OK.

Once System Protection is turned back on, you can create a restore point with the following process:

1. Select Create in the main System Protection dialog box.
2. Type a description for the restore point in the Create A Restore Point dialog box and click Create.
3. Click Close in the Restore Point Was Successfully Completed dialog box.
4. Click OK to close System Protection.

> **NOTE**
>
> Windows 10 and 11 no longer have System Protection enabled by default. With Windows 10/11 you can reinstall the operating system and keep your user files. You can achieve this via the Reset This PC feature in Settings.

STEP 7. EDUCATE THE END USER

The end user is always going to be the greatest risk to security. Therefore, the last step to malware removal is the education of the end user. You should brief the end user on what led to the malware infection and what to avoid. The ultimate goal is to have the end user educated to the point where they can prevent malware installation in the future.

The training can be formal training, such as a classroom setting, or it can be online training that engages the user to participate and answer questions. However, the best way to educate the end user after a malware infection is to engage the person in a conversation. You should explain the ramifications and how they can avoid malware, phishing, and other security pitfalls.

When new employees are hired, they typically go through an onboarding process. During this onboarding process, they should be educated to identify phishing and malware, as well as other social engineering threats.

EXAM TIP

You should educate the user to avoid potential malware installation in the future. Remember, proper user training against malware threats is the best defense!

CERTMIKE EXAM ESSENTIALS

▶ The first step to troubleshooting malware is to investigate and verify the malware symptoms. This can be accomplished with operating system built-in tools and third-party support tools to identify the infection.

▶ The second step is to quarantine the infected operating system to stop the malware from spreading to other systems. If the operating system is connected via a wire, it should be disconnected. If the operating system is connected via wireless, it should be placed into Airplane mode or disabled.

▶ The third step is to disable System Restore so that the malware does not create a reinfection in the operating system. This can be performed by verifying and turning off System Protection in Windows 10/11.

▶ The fourth step is to remediate the operating system by updating antimalware definitions and scanning the operating system for removal. The antimalware should have the latest updates before scanning in order to be current on the latest malware signatures. The removal process can be performed with Microsoft Defender or third-party products.

▶ The fifth step is to make sure the operating system periodically downloads updates and scans for malware. This step will ensure that the antimalware engine is up-to-date and scans for malware at a predetermined interval.

▶ The sixth step is to enable System Restore and manually create a restore point so that you have a healthy point-in-time backup. This step ensures that you have a known good restore point and that restore points function as expected in the future.

▶ The seventh and final step is to educate the user to prevent future security implications. Training can be formal or informal, but the underlying theme should be to engage the user and educate them.

Practice Question 1

You have just identified and verified that an operating system contains malware. What is the next step to perform to remediate the operating system?

A. Quarantine the infected system.
B. Disable System Restore.
C. Remediate the infected system.
D. Educate the end user.

Practice Question 2

Which Microsoft Defender scan allows you to boot into a trusted environment and run a scan?

A. Offline scan
B. Quick scan
C. Full scan
D. Custom scan

Practice Question 1 Explanation

This question is designed to test your knowledge of identifying malware on the operating system.

1. The first answer (A, Quarantine the infected system) is correct. After you have identified an infected operating system, you should quarantine the infected system so that the infection does not spread.

2. The next answer (B, Disable System Restore) is incorrect. After you have quarantined the infected system, you should then disable System Restore.

3. The next answer (C, Remediate the infected system) is incorrect. Remediating the infected system should be done after disabling System Restore.

4. The last answer (D, Educate the end user) is incorrect. Educating the end user is the last step in removing malware in an operating system.

Correct Answer: A. Quarantine the infected system

Practice Question 2 Explanation

This question is designed to test your knowledge of remediating operating systems.

1. The first answer (A, Offline scan) is correct. An offline scan is used to remove stubborn malware by booting into the Windows Preinstallation Environment and running a Microsoft Defender scan.

2. The next answer (B, Quick scan) is incorrect. A quick scan will scan user files and common locations on the operating system.

3. The next answer (C, Full scan) is incorrect. A full scan will scan the entire operating system.

4. The last answer (D, Custom scan) is incorrect. A custom scan will allow you to select a folder to scan.

Correct Answer: A. Offline scan

CHAPTER 26

Troubleshooting Mobile Device OS and Applications

Core 2 Objective 3.4: Given a scenario, troubleshoot common mobile OS and application issues.

Over the past decade, the number of mobile devices has grown tenfold. During the pandemic, anyone who had not fully adopted mobile devices found that their entire life focused on mobile devices. Just like full operating systems, mobile OSs and applications have their issues from time to time. In this chapter, you will learn what you need to know to master A+ Certification Core 2 Objective 3.4, including the following topic:

▶ **Common symptoms**

COMMON MOBILE OS AND APPLICATION SYMPTOMS

This chapter will focus on many of the common symptoms for mobile operating system problems, as well as their possible solutions. The two major mobile operating systems that will be covered in this chapter are Apple iOS and Google Android. Both of these operating systems have variations of the initial operating system over various models (Apple) and vendors (Android). However, most of the symptoms will be common to both variations of the operating system and vendors, as well as the applications that are installed.

Application Fails to Launch

When an application fails to launch, there could be a number of reasons why it fails. The most common reason is that the application is already running in the background. The first solution to this symptom is to force-quit the application. Here are the steps to force-quit on Android or Apple:

Android
1. Press the tab view (usually the leftmost soft button).
2. Swipe left or right to find the application.
3. Selectively close the application by swiping it upwardly.
4. Press the middle soft button to exit this mode.

Apple
1. Double-tap the Home button if equipped or swipe up from the bottom of the screen.
2. Swipe left or right to find the application.
3. Selectively close the application by swiping it upwardly.
4. Click a blank area to exit this mode.

If you have completely quit the application and it is still not loading, you can try to clear the cache associated with the application. It is common for cache to become corrupted, typically after an update of the application. Clearing the cache will not affect the application's data such as login information.

You can clear the application cache by doing the following:

Android
1. Tap Settings.
2. Tap Apps.
3. Choose the application.
4. Tap Storage.
5. Tap Clear Cache.

Apple

1. Tap Settings.
2. Tap General.
3. Tap iPhone Storage.
4. Choose the application.
5. Tap Reset Cache On Next Launch.

Sometimes you will need to uninstall and reinstall the application, which will require you to log back in. You can remove applications by following these steps:

Android

1. Tap Settings.
2. Tap Apps.
3. Choose the application.
4. Tap Uninstall.
5. Visit the Google Play Store and reinstall the application.

Apple

1. Tap and hold on an icon until all the icons dance back and forth.
2. Tap the X displayed in the upper-left corner of the application.
3. Visit the Apple App Store and reinstall the application.

EXAM TIP
Applications failing to launch can be remedied by applying a force-quit to the application, clearing the cache of the application, and uninstalling and reinstalling the application.

Application Fails to Close/Crashes

Another common problem with applications is that they crash or close unexpectedly. The solutions for crashing or closing applications are similar for applications failing to launch. You should first understand the series of events that lead to a crash or unexpected close. Then try to fix it with the following steps and retest to see if one of the steps has solved the issue:

1. Force-quit the application.
2. Clear the application cache.
3. Clear the application data.
4. Uninstall the application.
5. Reboot the device.
6. Reinstall the application.

If these steps do not solve the issue, then it is time to check with the vendor. Vendor support might be paid, community forums, or case by case. Describe the issue, detail the mobile device make and model, and the steps to reproduce the crash.

Application Fails to Update

The Google Play Store and the Apple App Store allow for the purchase, installations, and update of applications. The update of applications happens automatically in the background, without the end user being aware of it. Updates are important because most applications interface with a back-end website, such as your favorite retail application. If the application does not update along with the expected back-end updates, the system may crash, provide inaccurate data, or cease to function entirely.

When applications fail to update, you should try to manually update the application from the Google Play Store or the Apple App Store. If the application will not manually update, then you should try these steps:

1. Force-close the application.
2. Reboot the mobile device.
3. Temporarily disable any antivirus or antimalware software.
4. Try to upgrade the application manually from the store.

Make sure that you are connected to the Internet via Wi-Fi since the app store typically treats cellular data as a metered connection. Metered connections don't allow for updates due to data restrictions.

If none of these solutions work, then you can try to uninstall the application and reinstall it from the app store. Be sure to check the version before and after installation to verify it has been updated.

> **EXAM TIP**
>
> Symptoms that an application is not properly updated include erratic behavior, crashes, and inaccurate data, or it may cease to function entirely.

Slow to Respond

The issue of a mobile device that is slow to respond is almost always related to CPU performance issues, RAM usage, or a combination of both. Mobile devices, just like their cousin the PC, have a finite amount of CPU and RAM. When too many applications are open, the CPU and RAM utilization will increase. This in turns makes the device slow to respond. The following steps should be taken to remedy the symptom of slow response; test at each step for improvement of response:

1. Close all applications on the device.
2. Reboot the mobile device.
3. Factory-reset the device.

If the mobile device responds fine after closing all the applications or after a reboot, then it may be a CPU or RAM usage issue. If after a reboot the mobile device is slow to respond, the next step is to factory-reset the mobile device. In some rare cases, the system upgrades exceed the performance of the device; this is typical in lower-end models. Depending on the age of the mobile device, it may be time for a new one.

> **EXAM TIP**
> Slow response of mobile devices is typically due to CPU or RAM utilization.

OS Fails to Update

The operating system could fail to update on the mobile device. There could be a number of reasons for this symptom. However, the troubleshooting steps are no different than those for any other application on the mobile device:

1. Reboot the mobile device.
2. Check compatibility of the OS upgrade.
3. Make sure you have enough free storage.
4. Check connectivity to a Wi-Fi connection.

If none of these suggestions allow you to successfully update the mobile device, then you can try to manually install the operating system update with a computer. Every Android vendor and model will have a different procedure to manually update the software. Apple mobile devices can be manually updated with a macOS computer and the Finder application.

Battery Life Issues

The battery in your mobile device is probably the most important resource. Without power, your phone is nothing more than a fragile piece of glass in your pocket. Battery life could mean two different things: the life span of the battery before it needs replacement or the amount of battery life left before the device requires recharging. Apple defines battery life as the latter of the two, and that is the focus of this section.

Battery life can be shortened by a number of factors with a mobile device. Battery life will typically be shortened by the device's use. Here is a list of other possible reasons for shortened battery life:

- ► Power-saving features turned off
- ► Turning on precision location-based services
- ► Connecting peripherals
- ► Poor cellular signal
- ► Environmental factors of excessive heat or cold
- ► Brightness setting too high
- ► Too many apps open

In addition to the preceding list, battery life is often attributed to a performance problem. High CPU usage by applications and high RAM usage by applications can lead to battery life issues. If you suspect this is the cause, use the battery monitor built into the mobile device operating system to view the consumption of battery life by the application, as shown in Figure 26.1. Then uninstall the application that uses the most battery and monitor battery life.

F I G U R E 2 6 . 1 Battery usage

EXAM TIP

Excessive use of CPU and RAM by applications can lead to shortened battery life.

Random Reboots

Mobile devices can randomly reboot for any number of reasons, just like any other symptom related to mobile device operating systems. The following is a list of common reasons for random reboots with mobile devices:

- ▶ Poor battery health.
- ▶ A pending system update.
- ▶ Low available storage.
- ▶ Applications with high utilization.
- ▶ The Android auto restart feature is turned on, as shown in Figure 26.2.

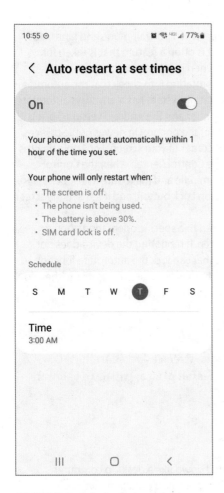

FIGURE 26.2 Auto restart

If you have checked the preceding common issues and random reboots continue to be a problem, you can try to factory-reset the mobile device. A factory reset will reset the operating system back to a known good working state. You can then apply applications and settings back on the device and monitor its behavior.

> **NOTE**
> Before performing a factory reset on your device, be sure that you have a backup of your data.

Screen Does Not Autorotate

The autorotate function allows a phone to switch between portrait mode and landscape mode by sensing how you are holding the phone. It is often a feature that is taken for granted when it works, but it is very inconvenient when it doesn't work at all.

The most common solution to the screen not autorotating is to check that the autorotate feature is not turned off or locked. The Android operating system has many ways autorotate can be locked or turned off, all dependent on the vendor and the Android version. So, it is best to check with the vendor of the specific model of the phone. On newer Apple devices, you can check by swiping down from the top-right corner of your screen. For Apple devices with a Home button, you must swipe up to open the Control Center. When the Control Center opens, look for the circle with the lock in the middle and make sure it is not enabled, as shown in Figure 26.3. This is the Portrait Orientation Lock button, and if it is set, the screen will not autorotate.

If the autorotate function is not turned off or locked to a specific orientation, then a reboot of the mobile device is the next diagnostic step. If rebooting the device does not remedy the issue, check applications on the device that can lock the autorotate function, such as the camera app. If none of these possible solutions remedies the problem, then you should suspect a hardware issue.

> **EXAM TIP**
> The screen not autorotating may be because the screen is locked by the operating system (Settings), or it could be the result of an app issue or hardware failure.

Connectivity Issues

Mobile devices are mobile because they are not tied down like a desktop computer with wires. The Internet and voice network are connected via a cellular network provider, such as Verizon, T-Mobile, or AT&T, just to name a few. The Internet can even be connected via Wi-Fi communications. Peripherals are connected via Bluetooth, and other

FIGURE 26.3 Apple autorotate

communications can facilitate Bluetooth as well. With so many different connectivity methods, it is inevitable that problems crop up occasionally. This section will explore the various connectivity issues and their associated solutions.

Bluetooth

Bluetooth connectivity is used to connect peripherals such as earbuds, a watch, and even a vehicle. Bluetooth connectivity distance is limited to about 30 feet. So peripherals should be in a close proximity to the mobile device, or they will not be able to connect. Other common reasons connectivity can be interrupted are as follows:

▶ Airplane mode is on (Android).
▶ Bluetooth is off.
▶ The device requires repairing.

When Airplane mode is turned on for an Android device, all wireless connectivity is turned off, including Bluetooth. So, Airplane mode should be checked first on an Android device. On Android and Apple devices, you can swipe down or swipe up if the device has a Home button, then make sure the Airplane icon is not lit up. This menu will also show the status of Bluetooth; if Bluetooth is off, you obviously won't be able to use it, so make sure the Bluetooth icon is lit up, as shown in Figure 26.4.

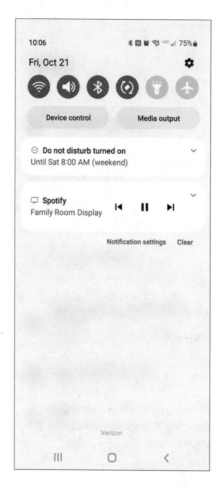

FIGURE 26.4 Wireless connectivity options

NOTE

On newer Apple devices, such as iPhones, Bluetooth is not turned off when you enter Airplane mode.

A device might not be able to connect if it is not paired anymore or there is a problem with the current pairing. The easiest way to check the pairing is to repair the device. This can be accomplished with the following procedure:

Android
1. Tap Settings.
2. Tap Connections.
3. Tap Bluetooth (the phone will immediately start scanning for discoverable devices).
4. Select the available device.
5. Enter the passcode from the vendor's documentation.

Apple
1. Tap Settings.
2. Tap Bluetooth.
3. Tap the device name.
4. Enter the passcode from the vendor's documentation.

Wi-Fi

Wi-Fi connectivity problems can occur for a number of reasons, but the two most common are a lack of signal strength and interference. Increasing the number of wireless access points (WAPs) for coverage, or being closer to them, can address the lack of a good signal.

Interference can be avoided by selecting a wireless channel that does not overlap with other nearby WAPs. This setting is made on the WAP serving the clients. Interference can also come from external sources, such as microwave ovens or Bluetooth devices operating on the 2.4 GHz frequency band.

Most interference can be avoided by using a WAP that is dedicated to the 5 GHz frequency band. Using this band won't guarantee no interference, but you will have more channels that can avoid interference.

The 6 GHz frequency band has been opened up to Wi-Fi communications. The new 802.11ax wireless standard was ratified by the Wi-Fi alliance in July 2020. It offers faster connectivity for clients, but it does not offer better interference avoidance or distance over 802.11b/g/n. It does, however, offer better distance when compared to 802.11ac.

> **NOTE**
>
> Chapter 14, "Wireless Security" covers the various wireless protocols and their capabilities.

Another common problem with Wi-Fi communications is using the improper SSID name, along with the incorrect encryption settings. This was covered in detail Chapter 14, "Wireless Security." Mobile devices have an auto-reconnection feature for SSIDs. When your device goes into sleep mode, it disconnects from the SSID. When it wakes back up, it must reconnect. If the auto-reconnection feature is not enabled for the wireless network, you will never associate back to the SSID. This can be verified with the following procedure:

Android

1. Tap Settings.
2. Tap Connections.
3. Tap Wi-Fi.
4. Tap the current SSID.
5. Tap Edit.
6. Verify Auto Reconnect is selected.

Apple

1. Tap Settings on your Home screen.
2. Tap Wi-Fi.
3. Tap the blue circled i next to your current SSID.
4. Verify that Auto-Join is on.

> **EXAM TIP**
>
> Wi-Fi problems are often caused by interference, signal strength, or improper SSID settings.

Near-Field Communication (NFC)

Near-field communication (NFC) is used as a very short-distance wireless communication protocol. NFC requires 4 centimeters or less to operate. NFC is enabled on mobile devices for payment systems, such as Google Pay and Apple Pay. NFC can also be used to exchange data between mobile devices; this feature is typically used when upgrading phones. You will tap the new phone with the old phone and settings will be transferred over.

If NFC is not working, check the following:

- ▶ NFC is turned on.
- ▶ Airplane mode is turned off.
- ▶ The phone is less than 4cm from the other device.

If all of these items have been checked, then you should suspect interference or the mating device. Interference can happen if the mobile device is in a protected case. Removing the device and trying NFC is a quick way to verify that interference is not a problem. The mating device can also be the issue. If the mating device is a payment terminal, be sure your mobile device is directly over its sensor. Also, ask the retail staff if other people have had problems.

AirDrop

AirDrop is Apple's proprietary protocol to quickly transfer files between iPhones, iPads, and Macs. The AirDrop protocol uses Bluetooth and Wi-Fi to create a connection. Bluetooth is used to negotiate the communications. Wi-Fi is used to actually transfer the files. Because AirDrop uses Bluetooth and Wi-Fi, most of the diagnostics discussed in this section should be checked. The following is a list of items to be checked:

- ▶ Airplane mode is turned off.
- ▶ Both devices have Bluetooth turned on.

▶ Both devices have Wi-Fi turned on.

▶ Both devices have Personal Hotspot turned off.

▶ Both devices are within 30 feet of each other.

If you have checked these items and the problem persists, then verify that you have the other person in your contacts. By default, you can only send files to people in your contacts. Temporarily you can set the AirDrop to receive files from anyone with the following steps:

1. Go to Settings.
2. Tap General.
3. Tap AirDrop.
4. Choose Everyone.

CERTMIKE EXAM ESSENTIALS

▶ Applications can fail to launch for a number of reasons. The most common is that the application is running in the background. One common solution for fixing launch issues with an application is force-quitting the application. If that doesn't fix the problem, you can try to either clear the application cache or uninstall and reinstall the application.

▶ Mobile devices that exhibit slow responsiveness are almost always related to CPU performance, RAM usage, or a combination of both. Steps to solve the issue are closing all applications on the device, rebooting the device, and if the problem persists, then factory-resetting the device.

▶ Battery life for a mobile device is the most important resource. When a mobile device suffers from battery life issues, the possible reasons are power-saving features have been turned off, precision location-based services have been turned on, peripherals are directly connected, cellular signals are poor, the device is experiencing excessive heat or cold, the display brightness setting must be adjusted, or too many apps are open.

▶ The autorotate function allows a mobile device to switch between portrait mode and landscape mode. When the autorotate function stops working, issues are typically caused by the locking of portrait mode by an application, such as the camera application. The operating system can also lock the orientation of the screen.

▶ Connectivity issues with mobile devices are typically attributed to signal strength of the wireless access point or cellular signal. If a Bluetooth device is experiencing connectivity issues, the proximity to the mobile device should be checked. The device could also be accidentally placed into Airplane mode, which could cause Wi-Fi and Bluetooth connectivity issues.

Practice Question 1

What should you try first when an application fails to launch on a mobile device?

A. Reinstalling the application
B. Force-quitting the application
C. Charging the mobile device
D. Clearing the data storage for the application

Practice Question 2

If you are having problems with Bluetooth connectivity on an Apple device, which icon should be lit up in the connection screen?

A. Bluetooth icon
B. Wireless icon
C. Cellular icon
D. Airplane icon

Practice Question 1 Explanation

This question is designed to test your knowledge of common symptoms of mobile operating systems.

1. The first answer (A, Reinstalling the application) is incorrect. Reinstalling the application is the most obtrusive step, since data will be lost.

2. The next answer (B, Force-quitting the application) is correct. Force-quitting the application is the easiest first step to launching the application successfully.

3. The next answer (C, Charging the mobile device) is incorrect. Charging the mobile device will not affect the launching of applications.

4. The last answer (D, Clearing the data storage for the application) is incorrect because clearing the data for the application is very obtrusive, since data will be lost.

Correct Answer: B. Force-quitting the application

Practice Question 2 Explanation

This question is designed to test your knowledge of connectivity issues with mobile devices.

1. The first answer (A, Bluetooth icon) is correct. The Bluetooth icon should be lit for Bluetooth communications to work properly.

2. The next answer (B, Wireless icon) is incorrect. The wireless icon will have no effect on Bluetooth communications.

3. The next answer (C, Cellular icon) is incorrect. The cellular icon will have no effect on Bluetooth communications.

4. The last answer (D, Airplane icon) is incorrect. If the Airplane icon is lit, then Airplane mode is turned on, but Bluetooth communications is unaffected.

Correct Answer: A. Bluetooth icon

CHAPTER 27

Troubleshooting Mobile Device Security

Core 2 Objective 3.5: Given a scenario, troubleshoot common mobile OS and application security issues.

In Chapter 26, "Troubleshooting Mobile Device OS and Applications," we covered common problems with mobile devices as it pertains to functional problems. This chapter will focus on security-related problems with mobile devices. In this chapter, you will learn what you need to know to master A+ Certification Core 2 Objective 3.5, including the following topics:

▶ **Security concerns**
▶ **Common symptoms**

SECURITY CONCERNS

Mobile devices contain data from our lives more now than ever. Our mobile devices are used for work and leisure in our lives. Therefore, they contain a lot of personal information and sensitive information, which makes them prime targets for security concerns. In this section we will explore the various security concerns you should have as they relate to mobile devices.

Android Package (APK) Source

Applications on the Google Android operating system are typically developed on desktop operating systems within a development environment such as Android Studio. When a developer packages up the installation, the package is saved as an Android Package (APK).

The developer will then upload the APK to the Google Play Store. The Google Play Store is considered Google's ecosystem for distributing, installing, and updating applications. This allows Google to evaluate applications and remove any malicious ones. If the application does something malicious or violates Google Terms of Service (ToS), it will be removed. Subsequent violations and the developer account could be canceled.

A security concern with APKs is the trustworthiness of the source. APKs that are downloaded from the Internet do not provide an assurance of trustworthiness. They also typically do not allow for automatic updating since they are not part of the Google Play ecosystem. There are some applications that violate the Google ToS and find themselves without an ecosystem for installation. What you will need to consider is the value of the app versus the potential security concern. These APKs should be largely avoided.

> **EXAM TIP**
> An APK is an installable stand-alone package application for Android operating systems.

Developer Mode

Mobile application developers will typically use an emulator that imitates the functions of the device for course testing and debugging. Nothing replaces real hardware for testing and debugging. The developer mode on Android and Apple devices allow a developer to connect to the device via a USB connection to upload their application for testing and debugging.

When developer mode is turned on with Android devices, the developer can view running services, set a mock GPS location, and perform USB debugging, just to name a few. The developer mode will allow a number of security tweaks for the application, which is why there is a security concern. If the GPS location was manually set, you could trick the phone into thinking it is someplace that it isn't physically located. This of course could avert a geo-location or geofence for security purposes.

The development mode on Android can be turned on with these steps:

1. Tap Settings.
2. Tap About Phone.
3. Tap Software Information.
4. Tap Build Information seven times.

The Development menu will be on the parent menu under About Phone.

Apple's latest iOS does not have a stand-alone developer mode like Android. When you connect with the Apple development environment (called Xcode) from a Mac computer, you'll have the option to turn on development mode.

> **NOTE**
> Xcode is a development environment for Apple that allows development of apps on all Apple products.

> **EXAM TIP**
> Developer mode allows you to change settings in the operating system that could be used for malicious purposes.

Root Access/Jailbreak

Root access is a term that describes the highest privilege access in a Linux/Unix operating system, also known as the *superuser* access. The mobile Android operating system is based on the Linux kernel. The Android operating system does not allow you to directly attain root access. There are exploits that allow you to elevate privilege to attain root access. Once you attain root access in the Android operating system, you can change low-level security. This can allow malicious applications to attain root privilege access. Therefore, a mobile device that is "rooted" is an extreme security concern.

Jailbreak access is a term that is used with Apple iOS products. Jailbreak access is identical to root access on Android devices. Jailbreaking is a security concern because you have similar abilities to modify the Apple iOS. This means that malicious software can take advantage of the new level of access and can hide itself.

It is highly debated whether root access and jailbreak access pose much of a security concern. However, many organizations prevent phones that have been "rooted" or jailbroken from accessing their networks, since it presents major security concerns. Obtaining root access or jailbreaking a device can void manufacturer warranties for the device.

EXAM TIP

Illegally gaining administrative privileges on Apple iOS is known as *jailbreaking*, while performing a similar action on Android devices is called *rooting*.

Bootleg/Malicious Application

A bootleg application is a premium application that has been cracked to remove the digital rights management (DRM). A bootleg application is usually downloaded from questionable sources, such as torrent sites, forums, and web pages that look suspicious, just to name a few places. The bootleg software will be downloaded and installed in the form of an APK. This means there is no trustworthiness for the application, as previously discussed. Typically, bootleg applications are malicious in intent and contain some form of malware. This makes bootleg software a security concern. Licensing is covered in Chapter 33, "Privacy, Licensing, Policy, and Incident Response."

Malicious software will appear in the Google Play Store or Apple App Store from time to time. You can identify a malicious application by reading the application's reviews and examining its install base of users. If an application only has an install user base of 5,000 and users complain of ads popping up, then it might be malicious and a security concern. You should also always scrutinize the permissions an application requires compared to its operation or function. If you download a camera app and it requires access to your contacts, it may be malicious software.

Application Spoofing

Application spoofing is the act of developing an application that is named the same or similar as a familiar application or brand. The intent is that the end user mistakenly installs the application in lieu of the intended application. Application spoofing can be observed on both Apple and Google mobile platforms.

The security concern is the same for application spoofing as it is with bootleg and malicious applications. An application disguising itself as a legitimate application is malicious in intent and therefore cannot be trusted. Always verify the developer of the application with the application name and make sure you are only downloading the application from a trustworthy source.

Exam Tip

Bootleg applications are typically malicious in intent, along with applications that are spoofing legitimate applications.

COMMON SYMPTOMS

This section covers the common symptoms that are related to mobile device OS and application security. Keep in mind that not all symptoms are security-related; many of these symptoms indicate a mobile device issue such as poor battery life or overheating. Until they are deemed security-related issues, then they should be treated as mobile device issues. These are the common security symptoms outlined in the CompTIA A+ objectives. You are likely to see many others throughout your career as a technician.

High Network Traffic

Network traffic on a mobile device is typically metered and expensive if attained through a cellular network. When network traffic is higher than normal on a mobile device, it may be indicative of a security issue. For example, large amounts of traffic from your mobile device could be data being exfiltrated to a threat actor, or perhaps your device is being used as a pawn in a bigger threat. The high traffic could also be caused by an application that is misbehaving.

On mobile devices, it is very easy to view and identify the culprit. Many vendors include network usage tools that identify high network activity among the applications installed. In Figure 27.1, you can see an example of cellular data usage. Third-party apps are also available that allow you to identify high network traffic on wireless devices.

You can view mobile network usage on mobile devices by following these steps:

Android
1. Tap Settings.
2. Tap Connections.
3. Tap Data Usage.
4. Tap Mobile Data Usage.

iOS
1. Tap Settings.
2. Tap Cellular.

High network utilization on a mobile device can be mitigated with two methods:

▶ The first method is watching the normal usage of data from month to month. Identifying a normal baseline of usage can alert you when data usage is abnormal.

▶ The second method is to use a mobile firewall, which limits the traffic leaving the mobile device.

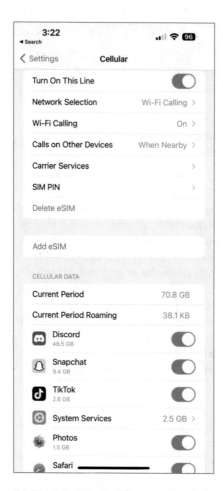

FIGURE 27.1 iPhone network data usage

> **EXAM TIP**
>
> Higher-than-normal network traffic can indicate a security problem or a misbe-having application.

Sluggish Response Time

Sluggish response time on mobile devices was covered in Chapter 26, "Troubleshooting Mobile Device OS and Applications." As it pertains to sluggish response time, this could be a symptom of a security issue. Checking the RAM and CPU usage is one way to identify a security-related problem. A malicious application might use CPU resources for cryptomining or some other nefarious purpose. Keep in mind that sluggish response time could be related to a legitimate reason, such as an application that is just poorly written.

Data-Usage Limit Notification

Typically, every cellular plan has a data cap or limit. Mobile device operating systems can track mobile data usage, as discussed in the previous section "Security Concerns." Android can warn you when you approach a data limit so that you don't exceed these data caps. It will help you catch a problem before you "run out of data." Data-usage limit notifications are not set by default, but if you have data-usage limits set, your device could alert you before a problem arises. You can set data-usage limit notifications on Android devices with this procedure:

1. Tap Settings.
2. Tap Connections.
3. Tap Data Usage.
4. Tap Billing Cycle and Data Warning.
5. Select the slider for Set Data Warning.
6. Tap Data Warning.
7. Adjust Data Warning and tap Set, as shown in Figure 27.2.

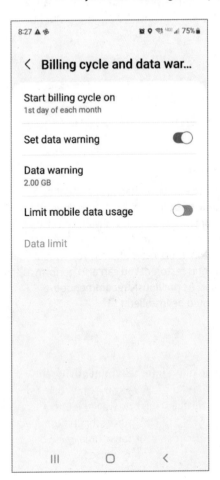

FIGURE 27.2 **Setting Data Warning**

Apple mobile devices do not allow for data-usage notification. You must manually track your data usage in the Settings ⇨ Cellular section of your phone. Therefore, you'll want to set up a third-party mobile firewall application if you desire this function.

Limited Internet Connectivity

Limited Internet connectivity does not automatically equate to a security symptom. There are plenty of other reasons for limited Internet connectivity that are unrelated to a security issue. Mobile devices are very susceptible to limited Internet connectivity because of their small transceivers for cellular and wireless communications.

The first potential solution is the move to a known good area where service has been used. If that does not solve the problem, then a simple reboot might take care of the issue. After verifying the basics, you might consider that the problem is security-related. A malicious application could be the cause of limited Internet connectivity.

Malicious applications can send traffic through a threat actor's endpoint in an effort to passively collect information, such as usernames and passwords. Malicious applications can also change DNS entries for the redirection of traffic. If you suspect a malicious application is to blame, you should factory-reset the mobile device, and then install a mobile device firewall and antimalware software.

> **EXAM TIP**
>
> Limited Internet connectivity is a common problem for mobile devices and does not always indicate a security issue.

No Internet Connectivity

No Internet connectivity on a mobile device is easier to diagnose than intermittent or limited Internet connectivity. Malware can send traffic through a threat actor's endpoint in an attempt to steal username and passwords, as previously stated. Malware can also change network settings, such as DNS servers. These changes can cause limited Internet connectivity or no Internet connectivity. If the symptom is no Internet, then you should uninstall questionable applications until your Internet is restored. You can also perform a factory reset on the device and add applications back. As previously recommended, a mobile device firewall and antimalware software should be installed.

> **EXAM TIP**
>
> If basic troubleshooting has not solved the issue of no Internet connectivity, the problem is most likely security-related.

High Number of Ads

A high number of ads being displayed on a mobile device is a symptom of adware. Adware is a category of malware that pops up ads on the device to entice the user to click on them or purchase something. Adware is often the result of a malicious application that is installed on the mobile device.

You can troubleshoot the problem in two ways. The first is to perform a factory reset of the device and add applications back until the symptoms reappear. The second option is to leave the operating system in its current state and remove applications one by one until the problem goes away. The second option is typically quicker since recently installed applications should be suspected first. Antimalware software should be installed to prevent future malware infections.

> **EXAM TIP**
> A high number of ads on a mobile device is directly related to adware installed on the mobile device.

Fake Security Warnings

Fake security warnings on mobile operating systems are typically the result of an adware infection. The "security warning" will pop up on the device in an attempt to convince the user to download malware. These fake security warnings are similar to their PC counterparts discussed in Chapter 24, "Troubleshooting PC Security."

When fake security warnings are encountered, you can remedy the problem with the same two options used with other typical adware: perform a factory reset of the device and add applications back until the ads appear or leave the operating system in its current state and remove applications until the problem goes away.

Unexpected Application Behavior

Unexpected application behavior is common on mobile devices and can happen for a number of reasons—typically, because updates are not being applied in a timely fashion, the application cache is corrupted, or a number of reasons covered in Chapter 26, "Troubleshooting Mobile Device OS and Applications." Unexpected application behavior is not always an indication that you have been infected with malware or have a symptom of a security issue. Basic troubleshooting should be performed first.

If a newly installed application starts to behave in an erratic way, this could be a sign of a security problem with the application. You should immediately check the trustworthiness of the application. This can be done by reading the reviews and examining the user install base. As an example, if the install base consists of 19 people and everyone says the application is great, you probably don't have a sufficient sample. A small user base should be a warning sign that the app might be a security concern.

If you believe an application is a security concern, most mobile antimalware software will allow you to perform a scan of the application to see if anything is detected. If malware is detected, perform a factory reset on the device and only reinstall applications from a trusted source.

Leaked Personal Files/Data

The worst outcome of an encounter with malware is leaked personal files and data. Leaked data refers to data that is leaked publicly; it is also known as data loss. Depending on the sensitivity of the data, such a data breach can cost an organization millions, or even billions, of dollars.

Ransomware is a type of malware that will ransom your files one of two ways:

▶ By encrypting all the documents so that you cannot continue your everyday business

▶ By posting your files publicly for other criminals and people to download

To combat this threat, mobile security should be applied in layers. Antivirus and antimalware software should be installed on the mobile device to protect it from malicious applications. Additionally, a mobile firewall should be installed along with the antivirus and antimalware software. There are third-party security suites that can protect you from all these threats. The device should be encrypted to protect against accidental physical loss or theft.

Depending on how you use the device, mobile device management (MDM) software should be used to enforce organization policies and settings. MDM software was covered in Chapter 13, "Logical Security." An MDM solution can require passcodes, encryption, updates, installation of antimalware and mobile firewall software, as well as a number of other settings. One of the most important facets of MDM software is the ability to wipe data remotely if, for instance, an employee is terminated or a device is lost or stolen.

CERTMIKE EXAM ESSENTIALS

▶ The Google Play Store is a trusted ecosystem where applications are vetted by Google. The Play Store will typically be free from malware. Android packages known as APKs can be downloaded from outside of the Play Store and installed manually. These APKs are typically applications that violate the terms of service of the Play Store or that cannot be trusted.

▶ Mobile devices can be placed into developer mode so that developers can test their applications. Developer mode should not be enabled unless you are actively developing an application. Placing a mobile device into developer mode can weaken its security, because of the tweaks and security controls that can be changed.

▶ Root access on an Android device and jailbreaking an Apple device can give you control over the entire mobile operating system. It also gives a threat actor the same level of control over the device. Therefore, root access and jailbreaking mobile devices should be avoided. The act of gaining root access or jailbreaking the device can also void manufacturer warranties.

▶ Bootleg applications are premium applications that have been cracked to remove the digital rights management (DRM). The person or persons removing the DRM will often embed malware in the bootleg application. Therefore, these applications should be avoided and should be considered untrusted installations.

▶ Many of the common security symptoms you will encounter can also be considered typical mobile device issues and unrelated to security. When troubleshooting a symptom, you should not immediately suspect the symptom is security-related. For example, high network traffic will not always be related to a security concern— the high network traffic can result from a faulty application using too much data.

▶ A high number of ads being displayed on a mobile device is typically a result of adware. Adware is a form of malware that pops up ads on the mobile device in an attempt to advertise products or services to the end user. A factory reset of the device and selectively adding back only the trusted applications is one way to rectify adware installations. Alternately, you can uninstall applications recently added to the device just before the ads started to appear.

▶ Ransomware is a type of malware that will ransom your data by encrypting it so that you cannot use it, or the threat actors will threaten to publicly disclose your data. Mobile devices can combat ransomware with a layered approach. A mobile firewall and antimalware software should be installed on the mobile device you need to protect. In addition, mobile device management (MDM) software can be used to manage the device in the event it is lost or stolen.

Practice Question 1

Which of the following terms refers to removing software restrictions imposed by Apple on the iOS operating system?

A. APK
B. Root access
C. Jailbreak access
D. Developer mode

Practice Question 2

Which security software implementation can require and enforce the use of passcodes, encryption, updates, and the installation of antimalware software?

A. Mobile firewall
B. MDM
C. Data-usage limit notifications
D. Malware proxy

Practice Question 1 Explanation

This question is designed to test your knowledge of security concerns for mobile devices.

1. The first answer (A, APK) is incorrect. An APK is an Android packaged application.

2. The next answer (B, Root access) is incorrect. Root access, also known as superuser access, is the result of a permissions escalation on an Android device.

3. The next answer (C, Jailbreak access) is correct. Jailbreak access is the result of a permissions escalation on an Apple device that removes software restrictions.

4. The last answer (D, Developer mode) is incorrect. Developer mode allows a developer to test an application during the initial coding of an application.

Correct Answer: C. Jailbreak access

Practice Question 2 Explanation

This question is designed to test your knowledge of common symptoms for the security of mobile devices.

1. The first answer (A, Mobile firewall) is incorrect. A mobile firewall can protect you against a network-based threat.

2. The next answer (B, MDM) is correct. The implementation of mobile device management (MDM) software allows you to require and enforce the use of passcodes, encryption, updates, and the installation of antimalware software.

3. The next answer (C, Data-usage limit notifications) is incorrect. Data-usage limit notifications is a feature specific to the Android operating system.

4. The last answer (D, Malware proxy) is incorrect. A malware proxy is a tactic of a threat actor in an attempt to steal usernames and passwords.

Correct Answer: B. MDM

Domain 4.0: Operational Procedures

Operational Procedures is the fourth domain of CompTIA's A+ Core 2 exam. In it, you'll learn how IT professionals follow standard operating procedures for everything from safety and environmental protection to security incident response. This domain has nine objectives:

4.1 **Given a scenario, implement best practices associated with documentation and support systems information management.**

4.2 **Explain basic change-management best practices.**

4.3 **Given a scenario, implement workstation backup and recovery methods.**

4.4 **Given a scenario, use common safety procedures.**

4.5 **Summarize environmental impacts and local environmental controls.**

4.6 **Explain the importance of prohibited content/activity and privacy, licensing, and policy concepts.**

4.7 **Given a scenario, use proper communication techniques and professionalism.**

4.8 Identify the basics of scripting.

4.9 Given a scenario, use remote access technologies.

Questions from this domain make up 22% of the questions on the A+ Core 2 exam, so you should expect to see approximately 20 questions on your test covering the material in this part.

CHAPTER 28

Documentation

Core 2 Objective 4.1: Given a scenario, implement best practices associated with documentation and support systems information management.

As an A+ technician, you will be responsible for working with end-user issues and equipment problems. Some of the typical tasks you will encounter are identification of problems and implementation of solutions, asset management, and most important, documentation associated with support systems information management. In this chapter, you will learn what you need to know to master A+ Certification Core 2 Objective 4.1, including the following topics:

▶ **Ticketing systems**
▶ **Asset management**
▶ **Types of documents**
▶ **Knowledge base/articles**

TICKETING SYSTEMS

The ticketing system is used to receive incoming requests, track progress, and assure that problems and requests are solved and completed in a timely fashion. The ticketing system also serves other purposes that might not be obvious, such as accountability, collaboration, reporting, and escalation of problems, just to name a few.

Helpdesk tickets are either entered by the end users or by helpdesk staff. Typically, end users will enter tickets by filling out a form on the helpdesk website. Depending on the system, users can sometimes email problems to the ticketing system. Helpdesk staff will enter tickets when users call into the helpdesk.

The following section will cover the various elements of a helpdesk ticket. In this section we will assume that a user has called into the helpdesk and a ticket is manually being entered by helpdesk staff.

> **EXAM TIP**
> Ticketing systems receive issues from end users and are the main communication mechanism for technicians.

User Information

When a ticket is created, the user information is important because it shows how to contact the end user to obtain more information on the problem and ultimately resolve it. User information can be in the form of email address, phone number, or location on a campus. The user information is also useful for reporting and satisfaction follow-up.

> **EXAM TIP**
> The user information element of a ticket will contain the contact info, so a technician can contact the end user.

Device Information

The device information is equally important to the user information. If the device information is populated in the ticket, the technician can collect details to assist with solving the problem without the user's assistance. This information might consist of age, make and model, warranty information, software patch level, and any number of trackable attributes for the asset. In addition, this information is also useful for reporting and identifying problem devices.

> **NOTE**
> Asset management is covered later in this chapter.

Description of Problems

The description of the problem states why the user is opening a helpdesk ticket. The description should contain the symptoms, steps to re-create the problem, any user observations, system(s) affected, and any directions for the technician. This field is typically not reported on as criteria but may be included in reports as details.

> **EXAM TIP**
> The description of the problem should contain the symptoms, steps to solve the problem, observations, and directions for the technician.

Categories

The use of categories in a ticket helps get a problem to the right technician to work on the issue. Common categories largely depend on your helpdesk responsibilities:

- ▶ Password resets
- ▶ Networking issues
- ▶ Application errors
- ▶ Hardware issues
- ▶ Email issues

Categories are also used for reporting, such as showing how many password problems your helpdesk encountered compared to networking issues.

Severity

The *severity* of the problem is how quick it needs to be solved by the technician. Typically, this field has a value of high, medium, or low. Your severity levels can also be critical, major, or minor. The field value can even be a number representing severity. This field is also used for reporting so that you can view how many critical problems your users had in a period of time.

Escalation Levels

Escalation levels is the process of passing the ticket to a more knowledgeable technician while shielding your more advanced technicians from troubleshooting day-to-day common issues that may be more suitable for less experienced techs. A helpdesk will be typically structured in a hierarchical fashion with tiers. As a helpdesk technician exhausts their knowledge, the ticket will be passed to a higher tier. Tiers might be arranged as shown here:

▶ **Tier 0:** Self-service, knowledge base articles, chatbots
▶ **Tier 1:** Technicians who can troubleshoot basic problems
▶ **Tier 2:** Technicians who have a more in-depth knowledge of a particular system or subject matter
▶ **Tier 3:** Developers or engineers who have expert knowledge of your systems and subject matter

This field is also commonly used in reporting to identify how many tickets reach Tier 2 and Tier 3 personnel.

> **EXAM TIP**
>
> When a technician exhausts their knowledge of a system while trying to solve a problem, the ticket needs to be escalated.

Clear, Concise Written Communication

Tickets can be entered by the end user or the helpdesk support staff on behalf of an end user when they call in. Although you won't always have control over the user's submission, you should promote clear, concise communications with users and support staff.

> **EXAM TIP**
>
> The communication should be clear and concise for the end user as well as other technicians working on the problem.

Problem Description

It is extremely important that the problem description be clear and concise. If an end user states that they can't access a system, it could mean either they can't get to it or they can't log into the system. Therefore, once the problem is understood by the technician, the problem description should be edited/updated to reflect the actual problem the end user is trying to communicate.

Keep in mind that other support staff might have to read through the problem if the ticket is escalated to them. A clear and concise description of the problem is also useful for technicians in the future who might search for a previous problem to understand the resolution.

Progress Notes

The progress notes are crucial for both detailing the path to resolving the problem and keeping the end user current on the progression of the problem. These notes are especially crucial if the problem needs escalation to another technician, as it will help them understand the troubleshooting steps taken.

It is common in helpdesk systems to have both staff notes and end-user notes. Staff notes are only viewable by other support staff and are typically used for information that is not relevant for the end user, such as logging information or system-related information. End-user notes will be updated in the ticket and sent to the user as an email to update them on the progress of the problem.

Problem Resolution

The resolution to the problem should be communicated in clear and concise language for the end user so that they understand the problem has been solved. The language should also be clear and concise for other technicians who might search for prior solutions to the same problem.

The problem resolution might be different for the end user than for the support staff, depending on the sensitivity and depth of information for the resolution. It is common to make the last staff progress note the support staff resolution and the problem resolution dedicated to communicating to the end user.

ASSET MANAGEMENT

Technicians will work with various assets on a day-to-day basis, such as printers, laptops, servers, and desktop computer, just to name a few. These assets are considered property of the organization. They add to the monetary value of the organization and must be tracked and managed from procurement of the assets to their retirement. Every IT department will adopt a different strategy based on their size and complexity of assets. This section will cover the various elements and ideology of asset management.

> **EXAM TIP**
> Assets must be managed from cradle to grave because they have monetary value for the organization.

Inventory Lists

Inventory lists are the simplest form of asset management. An inventory list is nothing more than a list of the inventory that the IT department manages. These systems are the simplest and offer the least amount of scalability. Therefore, inventory lists are usually reserved for unused assets, such as how many printers or laptops an IT department has available to assign to users.

Database System

Database-driven asset management systems are much more common when a large number of assets must be tracked across the enterprise. Typical systems are often part of enterprise resource planning (ERP) systems that track both people and assets, as well as business processes.

It is also common for ticketing systems to contain a list of your assets so that a technician has insight when diagnosing a problem regarding the age of a system, the length of the warranty, resources on the asset, and many other attributes.

Asset Tags and IDs

Part of an asset management system is the ability to track assets during their useful life in the organization. In order to track the asset, you assign the asset a tag with an ID that is unique to the organization. The asset tag is often a permanent, indestructible tag that states the asset is the property of the organization, along with an ID number that is often in bar-code form, as shown in Figure 28.1.

Property of
XYZ Corporation

012-1234-000-01

FIGURE 28.1 Asset tag and ID number

Procurement Life Cycle

The typical life cycle for IT systems consists of procurement, deployment, management, and retirement. Procurement is the process of purchasing the asset. It is also where the asset is introduced to the life cycle process in the organization. The asset is then deployed to the end user in the form of an upgrade or initial assignment to the user. Throughout the life of the asset, the IT department will manage the device, providing operating system updates, upgrades patches, software, and so forth. When the asset is no longer useful to the organization, it is retired. Retirement is when the asset is upgraded to a newer asset and the process starts all over again for the newer asset, as shown in Figure 28.2.

> **EXAM TIP**
>
> The asset life cycle is a cyclical cycle that starts with procurement and ends with retirement.

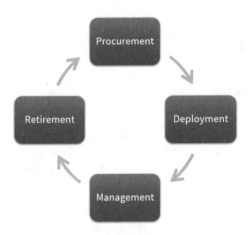

FIGURE 28.2 An asset life cycle

Warranty and Licensing

A component of asset management is the management of the warranty on hardware, as well as the licensing of applications installed on the assets. The end date of the warranty should be defined in the asset management system. This allows a technician working on a ticket to query whether the asset is under warranty.

Software can also be considered an asset for the period you have licensed the product. Software licensing is typically purchased a year at a time, and during that year, you own the right to use the software. Therefore, the software/licensing is considered an asset to the organization. Purchases of software/licensing should be recorded in the asset management system, just like any other asset. This provides two functions: budgeting for the next year and identifying end-user allocations of software.

> **NOTE**
> Licensing is covered in Chapter 33, "Privacy, Licensing, Policy, and Incident Response."

> **EXAM TIP**
> Licensing can be considered a tangible asset to the company for the term of the license.

Assigned Users

When an asset is deployed in the organization, it is assigned to a user and the user takes custody of the asset. This deployment can be part of the onboarding (hiring) process or a simple upgrade. The assignment to a user should be tracked in the asset management system or ERP system, depending on the organization's policies. It also allows for a clear concise list of assets in the event of offboarding (leaving/termination) of an employee.

TYPES OF DOCUMENTS

You will encounter various types of documents as a technician. These documents are used to establish procedures, policies, reporting, checklists, and documentation. In the following section we explore the various documents you will work with day-to-day and need to be familiar with for the A+ exam.

Acceptable Use Policy (AUP)

An acceptable use policy (AUP) is an internal policy used to protect an organization's resources from abuse by employees or guests. New employees are often required to sign an AUP during the onboarding process. The policy typically details the acceptable use of email, copy services, phone calls, the Internet, as well as other services specific to the organization. For example, the policy might restrict the use of email for religious, political, or personal causes; illegal activities; or commercial use outside of the organization's interest.

> **EXAM TIP**
> An AUP prevents abuse of an organizational resource by defining the acceptable use of company assets.

Network Topology Diagram

Network topology diagrams are used by technicians for troubleshooting networking issues. They are maps of how data flows and how systems are connected.

When implementing a new network system, the technician should create documentation in the form of a network topology diagram. The initial documentation is called *scratch documentation*, usually because it is scratched out on a whiteboard or notepad. The final documentation is called *finish documentation* and is typically created at the finish line of a project.

There are two main types of network topology diagrams:

Logical Diagrams   These diagrams are used to understand the flow of information in a network or system. They are considered high-level documents, because they explain how the network functions. Logical diagrams will focus on the flow of information, without the details of how everything is specifically connected.

Physical Diagrams   These diagrams are used to understand how a network is physically connected. They are considered low-level documents, because they detail only how everything is connected together. You typically detail switchport port locations and IP addresses in physical diagrams, as shown in Figure 28.3.

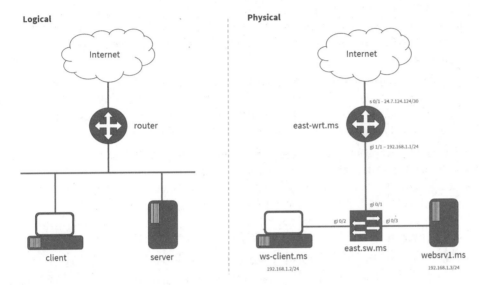

FIGURE 28.3 Logical vs. physical diagrams

> **EXAM TIP**
> Network topology diagrams can be logical diagrams that depict the flow of information for a network system, or a physical diagram that depicts how everything in the network system is connected.

Regulatory Compliance Requirements

Every organization will have different regulations imposed on them by various regulatory bodies. The regulations that apply will depend on the sector(s) that the organization does business in. Some of the regulations will be imposed at the federal, state, and local government levels, as well as industry. The following are some common regulations organization must comply with, but this is not a complete list; compliance changes often.

The Sarbanes–Oxley Act (SOX) This regulation affects publicly traded companies. The Securities and Exchange Commission (SEC) enforces how companies maintain financial records and how they protect sensitive financial data.

The Health Insurance Portability and Accountability Act (HIPAA) This regulation affects health-care providers and providers that process health records. The

Department of Health & Human Services (HHS) enforces how a patient's information is secured and processed during the patient's care.

The Family Educational Rights and Privacy Act (FERPA)   This regulation affects education providers and organizations that process student records. The Department of Education enforces the handling of student records, such as grades, report cards, and disciplinary records.

The Gramm–Leach–Bliley Act (GLBA)   This regulation affects providers of financial services. The Federal Trade Commission (FTC) requires that financial institutions that offer products and services, such as loans, investment advice, or insurance, safeguard customer information and detail the practices for sharing consumer information.

Payment Card Industry Data Security Standard (PCI DSS)   This regulation affects merchants that handle credit card transactions, as well as the service providers that aid merchants with these transactions. The banks and credit card companies enforce these regulations on any merchant or service provider.

> **EXAM TIP**
> There are many different regulatory bodies that organizations must comply with based on their industry.

Splash Screens

The use of splash screens is a common documentation method to help detail a problem, the solution of a problem, or the installation of software. You can manually copy and paste screenshots into Microsoft Word using a tool like the Snipping Tool. Windows 10/11 also contains a built-in tool called Steps Recorder that can record screenshots as steps, shown in Figure 28.4. In addition to the built-in tools, there are third-party tools such as Camtasia that allow for screen recording.

The term *splash screen* can also refer to a screen that pops up and warns a user. These can commonly be found on systems that might splash their AUP up on the screen for the user to acknowledge before continuing. They are typically found on captive portals for wireless connectivity.

Incident Reports

Incident reports are used to document events that are unusual or outside of the normal processes. There are several different incidents that might need to be reported on, such as network security incidents, network outage incidents, and even customer service incidents. The following are common elements of a network incident document:

- ▶ Date and time the incident happened
- ▶ Summary of the incident
- ▶ Root cause of the incident

- ▶ Actions taken during the incident
- ▶ Remediation of the incident
- ▶ Services impacted during the incident
- ▶ Recommendations to prevent the incident

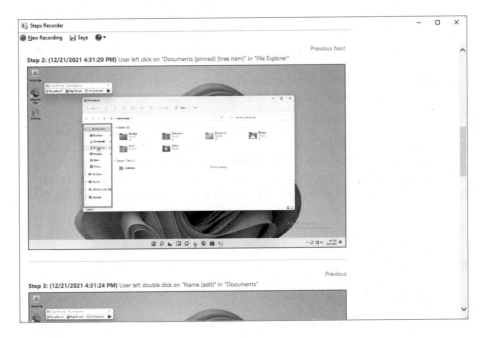

FIGURE 28.4   Steps Recorder

EXAM TIP
Incident reports detail unusual or outside of the normal events.

Standard Operating Procedures

Standard operating procedures (SOPs) are defined at the organizational level so that new employees can be guided on how to complete a particular process. A process may contain several different SOPs that must be completed in a certain order. The SOP contains repeatable steps to a procedure, so an expected outcome is derived every time.

An example of a process is the installation of a new Windows operating system. The SOPs might be procurement of the installation media, installation of the OS, renaming the OS, updating of the OS, setting the time and data, and this list can go on. Each of these would be an SOP that must be finished to complete the overall process of installing a new Windows operating system.

Procedures for Custom Installation of Software Package

When new software is purchased for the organization, the installation process should be documented step-by-step. By documenting the procedures for the initial installation of the software package, you can ensure that future installations are standardized and conform to prior installations. Creating procedures for custom software installation packages also enables other technicians to be able to install and troubleshoot the installations.

New-User Setup Checklist

It is common practice to follow a checklist of the tasks you need to perform when setting up a new user. The setup of a new user is also called the onboarding process by Human Resources (HR).

A checklist assures everyone that, in the process of onboarding the new user, everything is completed and covered. New users are anxious to ask many questions during the onboarding process, and a checklist helps keep the technician on task so that nothing is missed. A checklist ensures that every new employee gets the same treatment and that the same topics are covered with every new employee. A typical checklist might have the following:

- ▶ Assigning a user ID
- ▶ Permissions to files
- ▶ Security access cards
- ▶ Tokens
- ▶ Mobile device issued
- ▶ Laptop issues

End-User Termination Checklist

It is common practice to follow a checklist of tasks that are required to be performed when an end user is terminated. The process of a user being terminated by the organization is called *offboarding*.

A checklist ensures that all tasks related to the end-user termination are performed. Some of these tasks are crucial to the overall process of termination, such as removing organization data from bring-your-own-device (BYOD) devices via mobile device management (MDM) software, retrieving organizational assets, terminating access to systems, and providing access to email for management. These are just some of the common tasks; every organization will have a different list of tasks to be performed. A typical checklist might have the following:

- ▶ Disabling user IDs
- ▶ Revoking permissions
- ▶ Collecting security access cards
- ▶ Collecting tokens
- ▶ Collecting mobile devices
- ▶ Collecting laptops

KNOWLEDGE BASE/ARTICLES

A knowledge base (KB) is a grouping of articles that explain the symptoms and solutions to problems. The knowledge base allows a technician or user to search articles to self-service their problems. Most helpdesk and ticketing solutions allow for the creation of a knowledge base article from the resolution of a problem. A knowledge base can become very large, so many knowledge bases also allow keyword searches.

Here are common elements of a typical knowledge base article:

Title   Represents the key symptom of the problem

Introduction   Explains what the rest of the article will cover

Symptom   Explains how to identify the symptoms of the problem

Solution   Contains the steps to fix the issue outlined in the introduction

More Information   Contains a list of resources that were used to formulate the solution

Date   Gives the article creation date

Author   The original technician who created the article

Although these are the most common elements for a knowledge base article, there are many other elements that you can include, depending on the software used.

> **EXAM TIP**
> A knowledge base allows end users and technicians to solve common problems in a self-service model.

CERTMIKE EXAM ESSENTIALS

▶ Ticketing systems are used by end users to submit problems and requests to technicians. The ticketing system allows the technician to track progress and solve tickets in a timely fashion. The most important elements of a ticket are the user and device information and the description and severity of the problem. In addition, the technician can assign categories and escalation levels to the ticket.

▶ Technicians are responsible on a day-to-day basis to manage the organization's assets. There are several different strategies for asset management; it can be a manual process or it can be automated with software. The simplest approach for small organizations is the use of inventory lists. As the organization grows, a database-driven system can be adopted that ties into enterprise resource planning (ERP) systems.

▶ There are various types of documents in an organization that support the documentation, policies, and procedures. The acceptable use policy (AUP) defines the acceptable use of organization resources. Network topology drawing help technicians understand the flow of information (logical) and how devices are wired (physical). There are documents that the technician will need to prepare, such as incident reports, standard operating procedures, and new-user setup checklists.

▶ A knowledge base is a collection of articles that contain the symptoms and solutions to common problems. The knowledge base article will typically contain a title, introduction, symptom, solution, information about the solution, date, and author. Knowledge base articles are instrumental in allowing users to self-service.

Practice Question 1

You are working on a ticket for an end user, and you have exhausted your knowledge. What should you do as a next step?

A. Escalate the problem.
B. Direct the user to the knowledge base articles.
C. Check the asset management system.
D. Review standard operating procedures.

Practice Question 2

You are alerted to an incident in the organization in which an employee is sending spam from the email system to promote their own business. Which document should you use to report this?

A. Incident report
B. SOP
C. AUP
D. Regulatory compliance requirements

Practice Question 1 Explanation

This question is designed to test your knowledge of ticketing systems.

1. The first answer (A, Escalate the problem) is correct. When a technician exhausts their knowledge of a subject, they should escalate the problem to a more senior technician.

2. The next answer (B, Direct the user to the knowledge base articles) is incorrect. Knowledge base articles are typically a self-service option for end users.

3. The next answer (C, Check the asset management system) is incorrect. Checking the asset management system will only verify the assets assigned to the user.

4. The last answer (D, Review standard operating procedures) is incorrect. Standard operating procedures are used to detail day-to-day operations and are not typically used for diagnosing problems.

Correct Answer: A. Escalate the problem

Practice Question 2 Explanation

This question is designed to test your knowledge of the various types of documents.

1. The first answer (A, Incident report) is correct. Incident reports are used to document events that are outside normal processes. In this case the incident is the abuse of an organization resource.

2. The next answer (B, SOP) is incorrect. Standard operating procedures are used to establish procedures and processes for the organization.

3. The next answer (C, AUP) is incorrect. The acceptable use policy is a policy used to prevent abuse of resources in an organization. This document is helpful in outlining acceptable use for devices.

4. The last answer (D, Regulatory compliance requirements) is incorrect. Regulatory compliance requirements can encompass a number of regulations such as SOX, HIPAA, and GLBA, just to name a few.

Correct Answer: A. Incident report

CHAPTER 29

Change Management

Core 2 Objective 4.2: Explain basic change-management best practices.

When implementing changes to an organization's existing systems or implementing new systems, there is a risk to operations. To mitigate the risks, many organizations have adopted change management practices, such as documenting business processes and change management controls. Both of these allow the organization to have a plan if operations are affected and to foresee any effects to operations before they happen. In this chapter, you will learn what you need to master the A+ Certification Core 2 Objective 4.2, including the following topics:

▶ Documented business processes
▶ Change management

DOCUMENTED BUSINESS PROCESSES

Documented business processes contain all the necessary steps to complete a particular process. Each of these steps should be standard operating procedures (SOPs) that you learned in Chapter 28, "Documentation." The documented business process provides an overview of the business process so that a change in the business process can be evaluated as part of the change management process.

The documented business process defines the exact flow of process in the organization and also defines *who* interacts with the process, *how* they interact with the process, *why* they interact with the process, and *when* they interact with the process. Because the document details all the procedures of a process for the organization, it also explains how to deal with changes. The document might include instructions for the elements discussed in this section.

Rollback Plan

The rollback plan details the steps for rolling back a failed change to a business process. The rollback plan is also known as the backout plan. The rollback plan will detail the steps to restore the functionality for a business process if the initial primary change plan fails.

For example, if your primary plan was to upgrade a router with new firmware, that requires newer configuration as well. Your primary plan will outline the steps to upgrade the firmware and configuration. The rollback plan will detail how to downgrade the firmware and restore the original configuration.

EXAM TIP

The rollback plan is a plan that is used to roll back changes in the event there is a failure executing the primary plan.

Sandbox Testing

A sandbox is a lab environment where you can make changes that will not affect production. Technicians will find it extremely useful to perform sandbox testing when proposing a change that can affect production. It allows a technician to detail their primary plan, as well as the rollback plan in the event of failure of the primary plan. It will also help the technician determine the total time of an outage during the proposed changes, in addition to identifying any problems that could arise during the change.

Many organizations that implement change control practices require sandbox testing before proceeding with the change. It is typically integrated into the development process for applications used by an organization.

EXAM TIP

Sandbox testing is a lab environment where the technician can perform the change without affecting production.

NOTE

A sandbox can be a server, virtual machine, or container, depending on the type of testing.

Responsible Staff Member

The responsible staff member is the person who is responsible for a particular process in the organization. This person will be detailed in the documentation for the business process. They will be designated by the manager of the department that the process impacts. Any modifications or changes to the process should be communicated to the responsible staff member.

The responsible staff member can typically identify problems the change could impose. Therefore, this person should be included in the decision for the change as a stakeholder of the change to be implemented.

CHANGE MANAGEMENT

Change management is the process of controlling changes for organizations. It is common in any organization that cannot afford downtime due to a proposed change. It is also required in organizations that are restricted by regulations, such as publicly traded organizations, or medical offices, just to name a few.

The main purpose of change management is to standardize the methods and procedures used to facilitate changes in the organization. Changes to be controlled by change management can be policy-based changes for personnel or technical changes of network services and systems.

The following section will describe the various elements for change management control. Every organization will be different, but these are the most common elements.

Request Forms

When a change is proposed for an organization, it is formally submitted with a change request form. The request form can be simple or complex. However, the request form itself will contain the same elements adopted by the organization.

The change request form is used throughout the entire change control process. Well after the changes are implemented, the document will serve as a historic record in the event of an audit. The document also helps a technician determine when a change occurred, as problems might not be found until long after a change has been implemented.

The following are the common elements found in a change request form. The exact elements will differ slightly depending on an organization's requirements.

Item to Be Changed   The request form asks this item to be changed.

Reason   This explains the reason for the change.

Priority   This is the urgency, or priority, of the change.

Change Description/Plan   The description or plan for the change is documented in this section.

Change Rollback Plan The rollback plan describes the steps to roll back from a change.

Technical Evaluation This is the reason the primary plan will succeed. Any sandbox testing should be explained.

Duration of Changes This is the estimated duration of the change process. Any service outages should be described in this field.

> **EXAM TIP**
>
> The request form is used to submit the request for change and acts as a historical document after the change has been made.

Purpose of the Change

The purpose of the change is the reason for the change. The change can be a simple one, such as a change to a policy that will affect personnel. These are also known as *soft* changes, as they don't affect an IT system directly. The change can also be an upgrade or replacement of equipment, firmware, software, or applications, just to name a few. These are also known as *hard* changes, because they directly impact IT systems and are probably the bulk of changes that as a technician you will submit.

This section will also explain why the change is necessary for the organization. It should include any documentation from third-party vendors detailing the change. One of the most common reasons for a change is the necessity of security patches. Other reasons might be legal, performance, capacity, or software bugs, just to name a few.

> **EXAM TIP**
>
> The purpose of change is the reason for the change, as well as any third-party vendor documentation.

Scope of the Change

The scope of the change element details how the change will affect the organization as a whole. This element also lists which specific system, people, or applications the change will affect. In addition, this element should detail what will be affected if the change fails or goes wrong in some way.

The scope of the change element should answer the following questions:

▶ Who will the change affect?
▶ What will the change affect?

Date and Time of the Change

The data and time of the change element will detail when the change is proposed to start and end. This will be when the technician performs the change. If there is any pre- and post-change work, it should be detailed in this element. In addition, this element should detail how long any of the systems will be offline.

The date and time of the change element should answer the following questions:

▶ When is the proposed change?
  ▶ Date and time of the change
  ▶ Duration of the change

Affected Systems/Impact

The affected systems/impact element will coincide with the scope of the change element. All systems that will be affected or impacted by the change should be detailed in this element. The details of how the systems will be affected during the change and after the change should be found in this element. Any system outages should be detailed in this element.

The affected systems/impact element should answer the following questions:

▶ What will be impacted during the change?
▶ What will be impacted after the change?

Risk Analysis

The risk analysis element of the change request should document any known risks for the change. If a system is to be patched, then the potential failure of the system should be perceived as a potential risk.

In many cases the perception of risk might be narrow from an IT aspect. Therefore, risk analysis as it is related to the change management process is more than just an element of a form. An analysis of the overall risk to other systems and processes should be performed by a group of key stakeholders that the change might affect. As an example, the change could be successful but might inadvertently cause problems elsewhere in the business process.

Risk Level

An outcome from the risk analysis process is the likelihood of a risk precipitating into an issue, otherwise known as the *risk level*. The risk level can be as simple as green, yellow, and red to signify low, medium, and high-risk levels. However, it is more common to find a five-level system to depict the risk levels of highly unlikely to highly likely or five to one (respectively). The definitions of the five-point risk level is as follows:

▶ **Highly Likely**—Risks at this level are almost certain to occur.
▶ **Likely**—Risks at this level have a better than average chance of occurring.
▶ **Possible**—Risks at this level may happen about half the time.
▶ **Unlikely**—Risks at this level have a relatively low chance of occurring.
▶ **Highly Unlikely**—Risks at this level are not likely to occur and have a less than 10 percent chance of occurring.

Every organization will adopt a different risk-level system, depending on their requirements.

> **EXAM TIP**
>
> The risk level is an outcome from the risk analysis process in the form of a number or word representing the perceived risk.

Change Board Approvals

The *change board*, also known as the *change advisory board*, is a group of people who will evaluate and then approve or deny the change proposed via the change request. Their goal is to reduce the impact of day-to-day operations by evaluating any changes. Meetings are typically at a certain time every week to allow other key stakeholders to join.

Keep in mind that the change board consists of managers and key stakeholders throughout the organization. The change request documents are the focus of these meetings, and the requests need to be clear and concise.

The board will typically perform a deeper risk analysis from the one submitted by the authors of the change request. The board often has a better insight of overall operations. Only approved changes can be executed. If additional changes need to be made, outside of the original request, additional approvals must be acquired by the board.

> **EXAM TIP**
>
> The change board is a group of managers and stakeholders who review change requests as applied to day-to-day operations.

End-User Acceptance

End-user acceptance is the process of the end-user testing changes to applications and/or systems to validate functionality. End-user acceptance has been widely adopted in the change management process, although it is synonymous with application development.

When a change is made in which the user's interaction is impacted, the technician should obtain end-user acceptance. This is also commonly known as *user testing*. You can obtain end-user acceptance in two different ways:

▶ **In-Person Testing**—The user performs testing in person with the technician.
▶ **Self-Paced Testing**—The user performs testing in their own environment.

Regardless of which method is used to obtain end-user acceptance, once obtained, it should be documented in the change management document. The method of testing and users involved in testing should be documented as well.

EXAM TIP

End-user acceptance is a method to validate that a change has not impacted the user's interaction.

CERTMIKE EXAM ESSENTIALS

▶ The documented business process will define the standard operating procedures (SOPs) used to complete a defined business process for the organization. The documented business process will define who interacts with the process, how they interact with the process, why they interact with the process, and when they interact with the process.

▶ A documented business process might include a rollback plan. The rollback plan will detail any steps required to roll back or back out any changes if the initial primary change plan fails.

▶ Sandbox testing allows changes to be tested prior to production. A sandbox consists of a lab environment, virtual machine, or container depending on the type of testing to be performed. Some organizations require sandbox testing prior to making the change(s) in production.

▶ Change management processes are used to reduce the amount of risk to the organization for a change in the organization. Change management will begin with the request form that will document the item to be changed, the reason for the change, the priority of the change, the change plan or description, the rollback plan, and the technical evaluation and duration of the change. The request for the change will then be evaluated by a change advisory board.

▶ End-user acceptance is a method used to validate that a change has not impacted the user's interaction with an application and/or system. End-user testing can consist of in-person testing or self-paced testing to validate functionality. The outcome of the testing should be documented in the change management document.

Practice Question 1

You are submitting a change management request to the change advisory board. Which element of the change management request will assist the board in identifying potential outage time for the change to the business process?

A. SOP
B. Rollback plan
C. Sandbox testing
D. Primary plan

Practice Question 2

You are responsible for a line-of-business application that was just modified by the developers. What should be done before deployment of the application for your users?

A. End-user acceptance
B. Risk level
C. Impacted systems
D. Scope of change

Practice Question 1 Explanation

This question is designed to test your knowledge of documented business processes.

1. The first answer (A, SOP) is incorrect. A standard operating procedure details the steps for a procedure within a business process.

2. The next answer (B, Rollback plan) is incorrect. A rollback plan is used to roll back changes in the event of failure in executing the primary plan.

3. The next answer (C, Sandbox testing) is correct. Sandbox testing is used to identify potential problems during the change and to determine the outage time for the change.

4. The last answer (D, Primary plan) is incorrect. The primary plan contains the steps for carrying out a change.

Correct Answer: C. Sandbox testing

Practice Question 2 Explanation

This question is designed to test your knowledge of change management.

1. The first answer (A, End-user acceptance) is correct. You will want to obtain the end users' acceptance so that your users can acknowledge that changes made to a system have not impacted functionality.

2. The next answer (B, Risk level) is incorrect. The risk level is an outcome of the risk analysis process.

3. The next answer (C, Impacted systems) is incorrect. An impacted system is outlined as an element of the change request.

4. The last answer (D, Scope of change) is incorrect. The scope of change details what systems or people a change will affect.

Correct Answer: A. End-user acceptance

CHAPTER 30

Workstation Backup and Recovery

*Core 2 Objective 4.3:
Given a scenario,
implement workstation
backup and
recovery methods.*

Computer workstations are used to create vast amounts of data, but everything from user error to system failure can wipe out years of work in an instant. That's why workstation backup is essential. In this chapter, you will learn what you need to know about A+ Certification Core 2 Objective 4.3, including the following topics:

► **Backup and recovery**
► **Backup testing**
► **Backup rotation schemes**

BACKUP AND RECOVERY

Backup is the process of creating copies of files and folders, and recovery is the process of retrieving files and folders for reuse. A backup that can't be recovered is a colossal waste of space, time, and money.

There are several different types of backups. The most common are full, incremental, and differential. For a quick reference, take a look at Table 30.1. The following sections discuss these in more detail.

TABLE 30.1   **Backup types quick reference**

Backup type	Attributes
Full Backup	Amount of Storage Space: High
	Speed to Backup: Slowest
	Speed to Restore: Fastest
	Recovery Media Required: Most recent backup
	Reset Archive bit: Yes*
Incremental Backup	Amount of Storage Space: Low
	Speed to backup: Fastest
	Speed to Restore: Slowest
	Recovery Media Required: Most recent full backup + all incremental backups since full backup
	Reset Archive bit: Yes*
Differential Backup	Amount of Storage Space: Medium to High
	Speed to Backup: Fast
	Speed to Restore: Fast
	Recovery Media Required: Most recent full backup + most recent differential backup
	Reset Archive bit: No*

*   The Archive bit is a file attribute that is used to determine if files have been previously backed up. The bit is set if a file is modified.

Full

A full backup backs up everything on your system: the system drive (the drive where the operating system and apps are installed and run from, typically the C: drive) and connected data drives. Backup and Restore (Windows 7), which is also available in Windows 10, is an example of a program that can create a full backup. This is also true of almost all backup programs, both free and commercial (a few free backup programs make image copies only).

The File History backup shown in Figure 30.1 backs up data files only. To access Backup and Restore (Windows 7), click the link.

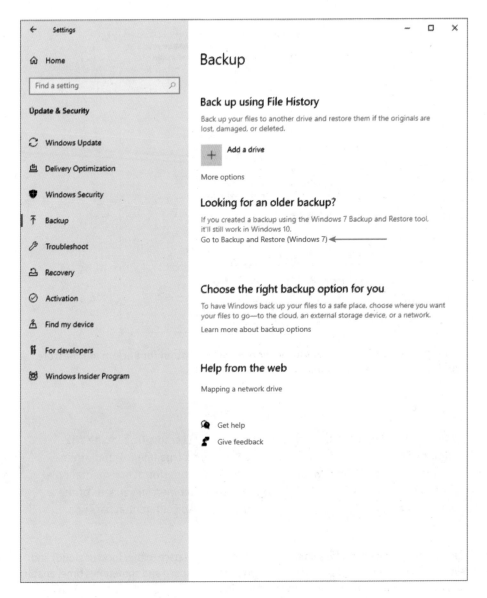

FIGURE 30.1 Backup options in Windows 10

A full backup might incorporate a separate disk image for the operating system as well as backups of user files (Figure 30.2).

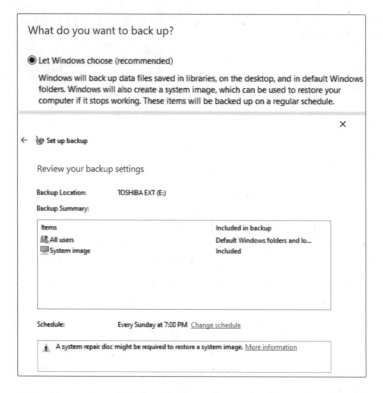

FIGURE 30.2 The Let Windows Choose backup option for Backup and Restore (Windows 7) includes a disk image.

> **NOTE**
> Some free backup utilities, such as Western Digital (Acronis True Image WD Edition), Seagate (DiscWizard, also based on Acronis True Image), and others perform full backups and image backups but cannot perform incremental or differential backups (see the following sections). Commercial versions of these and other backup utilities can perform incremental or differential backups.

Performing full backups frequently uses a lot of storage space (either local or cloud) and takes the most time of all standard backup types. To save space and sometimes time, enable data compression if your backup software supports it.

Incremental

A full backup is not necessary every time a system is backed up. An incremental backup backs up only new and changed files. So, if you create a full backup and incremental backups between full backups, you have captured the latest versions of your files as well as the files that have not changed (Figure 30.3).

To restore a system from an incremental backup, you restore the full backup and all of the incremental backups made afterward. Keep in mind that if one of the incremental backups is damaged or lost, it could prevent recovery of some of your data. To reduce the number of incremental backups that must be retained between full backups, create full backups periodically, as with the Grandfather-Father-Son backup scheme covered later in this chapter.

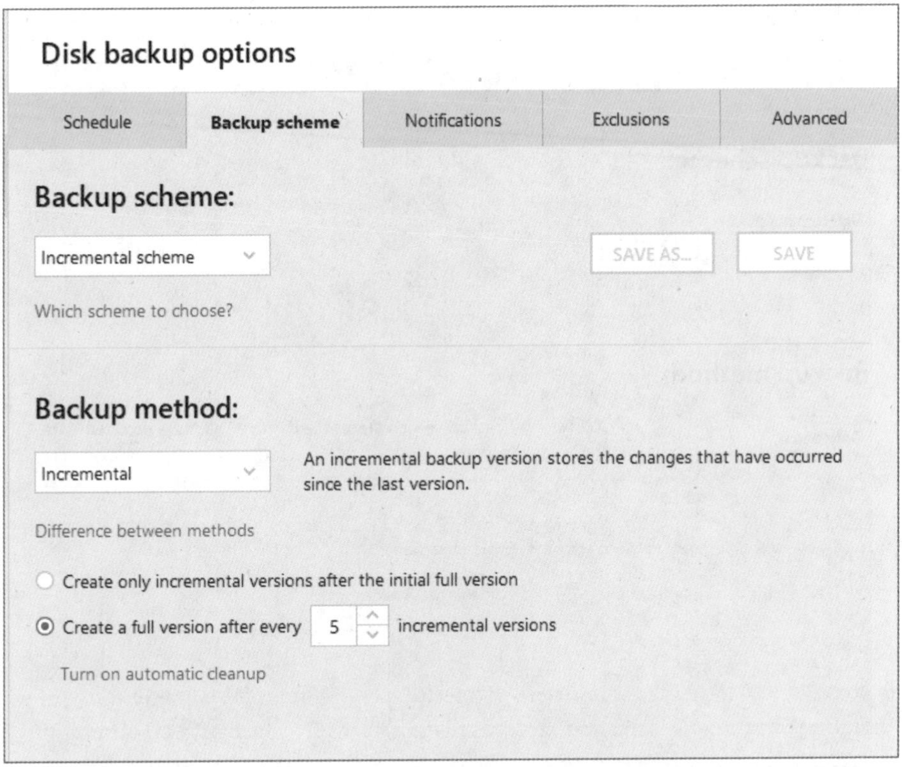

FIGURE 30.3 Selecting an incremental backup with Acronis

Differential

A differential backup is similar in some ways to an incremental backup. A differential backup backs up only the files that have changed since the last full backup (Figure 30.4) but adds them to its backup repository, so the differential backup file gets larger over time. Differential backups are recommended for databases such as SQL but use more disk space than incremental. Typically, a full backup is performed periodically, with differential backups performed between full backups.

NOTE

Some backup utilities that perform incremental or differential backups have cleanup options that will remove outdated backups. Before enabling this option, consider your working style to determine if enabling this option is a good choice for you.

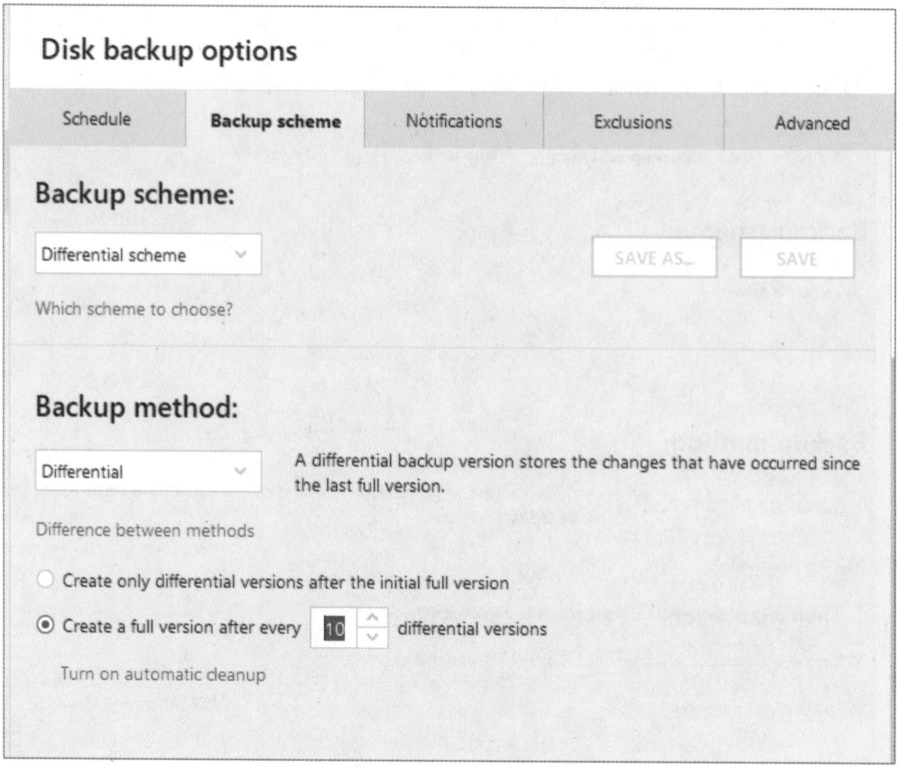
Disk backup options
Schedule
Backup scheme
Notifications
Exclusions
Advanced
Backup scheme:
Differential scheme
SAVE AS...
SAVE
Which scheme to choose?
Backup method:
Differential
A differential backup version stores the changes that have occurred since the last full version.
Difference between methods
Create only differential versions after the initial full version
Create a full version after every
10
differential versions
Turn on automatic cleanup

FIGURE 30.4 Selecting a differential backup with Acronis

TIP

To learn more about backup types, see "Basic Concepts" at www.acronis.com/en-us/support/documentation/ATI2022/index.html.

Synthetic

The most recent type of backup is the synthetic backup. It starts with a full backup, adds incremental backups, and creates a synthetic full backup periodically from a combination of full backup and incremental backups. While both local and cloud storage backups can perform full, incremental, and differential backups, only certain cloud and virtual machine backup providers offer synthetic backups.

> **NOTE**
>
> To learn more about synthetic backup compared to other types, see www
> .backblaze.com/blog/whats-the-diff-full-incremental-
> differential-and-synthetic-full-backups and www.nakivo
> .com/blog/what-is-synthetic-backup.

> **EXAM TIP**
>
> Make sure you understand the differences between full, incremental, differential, and synthetic backups. Be prepared to select a backup type to meet a requirement in a scenario.

BACKUP TESTING

Backup testing is the process of making sure that a backup can be restored, preferably to both the original computer and a different computer.

To make sure that a backup can be restored successfully, make sure that you do the following:

- ▶ Have installable media for the backup application; copy it to a USB flash drive or an optical disc.
- ▶ For an image backup of a system drive, make sure you create a startup USB drive or optical disc using the backup application's utility. Because you might be restoring an image backup to a different computer, be sure to follow the instructions to create media for a restoration to different hardware (Figure 30.5).
- ▶ Create a new version of installable media or startup media whenever the backup application is updated.

To safely test a backup on the original computer, create a new folder on a drive that has sufficient room for the backup and restore a folder tree to it, rather than just a couple of files. For example, after backing up a folder containing the company payroll or archival photographs you've scanned, select files and folders and restore them to a different drive or folder. Make sure the files restored successfully. In the example in Figure 30.6, error messages revealed that a number of files did not restore.

To test a disk image, use a drive that is at least as large as your original disk and restore the image to it. If you made an image of a bootable drive, make sure the restored image boots and check the most important apps for proper operation.

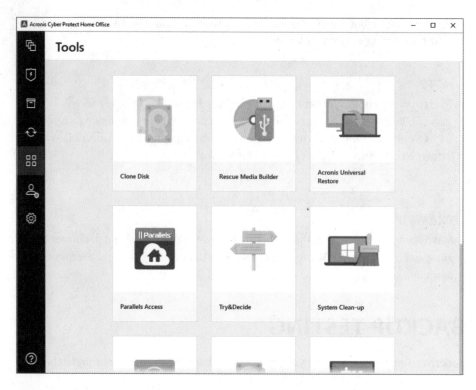

FIGURE 30.5 In this example from Acronis, the Rescue Media Builder is used to create restore media for the current system; the Universal Restore option is used to create restore media for a computer with different hardware.

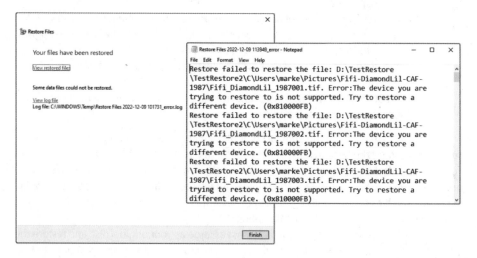

FIGURE 30.6 Not all files were restored; be sure to save the log file so you can find out why.

Frequency

Backup testing should be performed at least monthly or more frequently if backups are performed frequently. By testing backups on a regular basis, you can determine whether your backup process is working or if settings need to be adjusted or the backup program needs to be updated or replaced.

> **TIP**
>
> To learn more about backup testing, visit `https://solutionsreview` `.com/backup-disaster-recovery/` `a-step-by-step-guide-to-backup-testing` and `www.msp360` `.com/resources/blog/how-to-test-your-backups-` `comprehensive-guide`.

BACKUP ROTATION SCHEMES

Backup rotation schemes are designed to create multiple backups that can be stored in different locations to avoid the loss of backup information. When considering backup rotation schemes, take into account the recovery time objective (RTO), which is the amount of time it takes to return your workstations or servers to use after a disaster. Don't confuse RTO with recovery point objective (RPO), which refers to the amount of data loss that can be tolerated.

   RTO affects your choices of backup location (local, network, cloud), backup types (full, incremental, differential, synthetic), and where additional backups are stored. For example, if a system crashed on Friday, what amount of time or how may backups (full, incremental, or differential) would be required to restore the system to use and how quickly could this happen?

> **TIP**
>
> To learn more about RTO and RPO, see `www.msp360.com/resources/` `blog/rto-vs-rpo-difference`.

On-Site vs. Off-Site

For personal and small-business users, storing a backup off-site can be as simple as using a cloud-based backup service along with local or network backups. However, you should keep in mind that if the cloud-based backup service can only restore data via an Internet connection, data restoration could take many days. Consider using both off-site and on-site backups following the 3-2-1 backup rule (which we cover in a moment). Restore the most critical data from the fastest backup medium and other data from online backups.

Larger organizations should consider using data vaulting. *Data vaulting* refers to backup storage that is protected from ransomware or data extortion in one of two ways: a physical or logical "air gap" that blocks network access from normal systems and first-level backup operations or an active archive that is read-only and accessible only by authorized users and applications. As an A+ technician, you are not likely to be involved in the decision to use data vaulting, but you should be familiar with the process as you will likely need to make network and hardware changes to enable it.

> **NOTE**
>
> To learn more about data vaulting, visit `www.techtarget.com/searchdatabackup/tip/What-is-data-vaulting-and-how-does-it-shape-modern-backups` and `https://learn.microsoft.com/en-us/azure/backup/backup-vault-overview`.

Grandfather-Father-Son (GFS)

The *grandfather-father-son* (GFS) backup strategy combines full and incremental backups to help make data recovery as quick as possible while enabling backup data to be stored for an extended period.

A typical implementation could work like this:

▶ The Grandfather backup – full backup – run monthly or yearly
▶ The Father backup – full backup – run weekly or monthly – stored on local media; rotate to Grandfather status
▶ The Son backups – incremental backups – run daily or weekly – stored on local media; have multiple sets for rotation

The Father and Son backups provide a month's or week's worth of restore points for a quick RTO. A GFS backup strategy works best with backup software that is explicitly designed to support it.

> **NOTE**
>
> To learn more about GFS backups, see `https://backup.ninja/news/grandfatherfatherson-gfs-backup-strategy` and `https://vitanium.com/best-backup-practices-the-grandfather-father-son-backup-strategy`.

3-2-1 Backup Rule

The 3-2-1 backup rule is simple to understand:

▶ Create at least three copies of data.
▶ Keep these copies on two or more different media types.
▶ Keep one of the media types in off-site data storage.

However, it provides for a great deal of flexibility. You can decide how to make backups (file copies, drive imaging, dedicated local or network file/folder backup apps and hardware, cloud storage); what to save data on (local or network drives, removable media, file sync services, cloud backup, and so on); and which type of off-site data storage to use.

Although many discussions of 3-2-1 backup examine this topic at an enterprise level, it can also be applied to backups at any level. For example, a home or small-business user can use two different local or network drives and a cloud storage backup to satisfy this rule. Enterprise backups could use local or LAN hard drive storage, tape libraries, and data vaulting to satisfy this rule.

NOTE

To learn more about the 3-2-1 backup rule, see www.seagate.com/blog/ what-is-a-3-2-1-backup-strategy and https://it.wisc.edu/ news/3-2-1-backup-strategy.

EXAM NOTE

Although GFS and 3-2-1 backup strategies vary widely from each other, both stress the need to create both on-site and off-site backups in case of disaster. Be sure to keep this in mind as you deal with backup questions.

CERTMIKE EXAM ESSENTIALS

▶ Backups are designed to protect your computer's operating system and the data stored on it. A full backup includes all files and settings on a system, including the operating system. Incremental and differential backups are two different ways to save only changed files. To protect your system, use a combination of full and either incremental or differential backups. A synthetic backup combines full and incremental backups.

▶ Backup testing is an essential part of the backup process to discover and replace defective backups before data loss occurs. Backup testing should include full backup testing to verify that an installation can be restored to a new system and used to start and run it as well as file backup testing to verify that files and settings can be restored and used.

▶ Backup rotation methods will help make the data to be restored as recent as possible while also protecting backup data from being stored in a single location. Two popular backup rotation methods are Grandfather-Father-Son (GFS) and 3-2-1 (three copies of data, two or more media types, and one stored off-site).

Practice Question 1

A workstation cannot boot. Which of the following should you restore from?

A. Image backup
B. Incremental backup
C. Cloud backup
D. Differential backup

Practice Question 2

Your client is calling in a panic because the Grandfather backup from a monthly backup strategy is not working. After checking your notes on the client's backup strategy, which of the following best describes the issue?

A. Very serious – The Grandfather backup is the only full backup of the system performed in the last month.
B. Moderately serious – The Grandfather backup is the most recent full backup of the system.
C. Very serious – The Grandfather backup is the most recent incremental backup of the system.
D. Not very serious – Father backups are full backups performed weekly.

Practice Question 1 Explanation

This question is designed to test your real-world understanding of backup types. Let's evaluate these answers one at a time.

1. The first answer (A, Image backup) is correct. An image backup backs up the operating system and all data.

2. The next answer (B, Incremental backup) is incorrect. An incremental backup stores only changes to the system since the previous backup. Bootable operating system files would not be backed up.

3. The next answer (C, Cloud backup) is incorrect. Cloud backup is for data files, not for operating system files.

4. The last answer (D, Differential backup) is incorrect. A differential backup backs up only changes made since the last full backup.

Correct Answer: A. Image backup

Practice Question 2 Explanation

This question is designed to test your knowledge of the GFS backup strategy.

Let's evaluate these answers one at a time.

1. The first answer (A, Very serious) is incorrect. The Grandfather backup is not the only monthly full backup – a Father full backup is performed weekly.

2. The second answer (B, Moderately serious), is incorrect. Father backups are full backups performed weekly.

3. The third answer (C, Very serious) is incorrect. Son backups, not Grandfather backups, are performed daily.

4. The last answer (D, Not very serious) is correct. A Father full backup is performed weekly, so the Grandfather backup is not the only full backup in a month's time.

Correct Answer: D. Not very serious

CHAPTER 31

Safety

Core 2 Objective 4.4: Given a scenario, use common safety procedures.

Whether you're upgrading a computer, moving it into place, plugging it into power, or storing leftover parts from the upgrade, there are plenty of potential hazards waiting for you. In this chapter, you will learn what you need to know about A+ Certification Core 2 Objective 4.4, including the following topics:

▶ **Electrostatic Discharge (ESD) Straps**
▶ **ESD Mats**
▶ **Equipment Grounding**
▶ **Proper Power Handling**
▶ **Proper Component Handling and Storage**
▶ **Antistatic Bags**
▶ **Compliance with Government Regulations**
▶ **Personal Safety**

ELECTROSTATIC DISCHARGE (ESD) STRAPS

Electrostatic discharge (*ESD*) is the discharge of static electricity buildup from an object carrying a high electrostatic charge to one with a lower charge. Look at your hands, and you're looking at one of the biggest dangers to computers and their components.

As you move around your workspace, you tend to build up electrical potential compared to your surroundings. Touch a doorknob in the winter, and you can feel the spark as an ESD of about 2000V takes place to equalize the electrical potential between you and the doorknob.

As relative humidity drops from the ideal 55–65 percent range, ESD generation and discharge becomes a greater risk. According to the European Space Agency (http://escies.org/escc-specs/published/23800.pdf), common activities such as walking across carpet, walking over a vinyl floor, and picking up a polybag off a workbench can generate tens of thousands of electrostatic volts just waiting to be discharged under low-humidity conditions (20 percent or less). Although you can't feel most ESD events, it takes less than 1000V of ESD (sometimes as little as 10V) to damage or destroy a motherboard, RAM, or other internal components.

ESD should not be confused with radio frequency interference (RFI). Also known as electromagnetic interference (*EMI*), this is interference with electrical signals from natural or artificial sources causing a loss of clarity and information. AM radio static and auroras (Northern Lights, Southern Lights) are a few examples of EMI.

To help prevent ESD by equalizing electrical potential, put on an ESD strap, also called a wrist strap (Figure 31.1). The metal plate goes against your skin, and you adjust the elastic or hook-and-loop band for a comfortable, yet snug, fit. A flexible cable with a 1 megohm resistor snaps to the wrist strap. The other end of the cable has an alligator clip used to connect the wrist strap rap to a computer case or other metal object providing a ground near your work area (Figure 31.2).

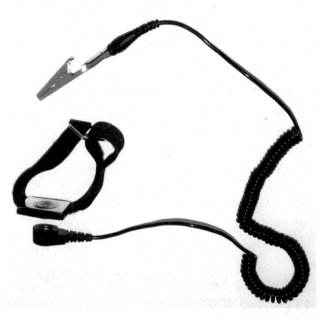

F I G U R E 3 1 . 1 **An ESD strap showing the components (wrist strap with metal plate, coiled wire with alligator clip, 1 megohm resistor at other end of coiled wire)**

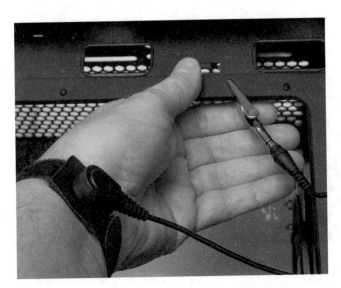

FIGURE 31.2 Connecting the ESD strap to a computer case before assembling the computer

NOTE

To learn more about the dangers to electronic equipment from ESD, see `https://desco-europe-esd-protection.blog/2020/10/20/an-introduction-to-electrostatic-discharge-esd`.

ESD MATS

For additional protection against ESD, use ESD table or floor mats. The ESD mat shown in Figure 31.3 is designed to be portable, so a technician can unfold it at a work area, connect the ESD strap to it, and connect the alligator clip on the mat to a ground such as a metal table or the computer chassis. ESD floor mats are made of thick material and often use a metal loop that can be connected to a ground with a metal bolt.

NOTE

To learn more about ESD straps, mats, and other ESD protective devices, visit `www.electronicsdesignhq.com/electrostatic-discharge-esd-protection`. The term "heal strap" on the website is a misspelling of "heel strap."

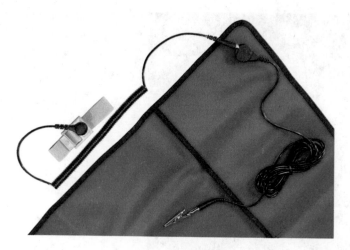

FIGURE 31.3 This ESD table mat includes a resistor and an alligator clip for connection to a suitable ground.

EQUIPMENT GROUNDING

Surge suppression depends, in part, on having a proper ground to plug into. Don't use a three-prong to two-prong "cheater" plug (Figure 31.4) if you don't have a grounded outlet unless you can attach a wire to the loop and connect the wire to a ground.

FIGURE 31.4 A three-prong to two-prong converter "cheater" plug that doesn't have a ground wire attached to it is dangerous to electrical equipment that needs to be grounded.

Does that mean that an outlet with a ground connector outlet is safe to use? Don't assume that a "grounded" outlet has a proper ground or is wired correctly. This author has had to rewire several AC outlets because hot and neutral wires were reversed. Some surge suppressors have signal lights to warn users of wiring problems, but the best way to find out is to use an outlet tester (Figure 31.5) to check outlet wiring before you plug in a surge suppressor or any other electronic device.

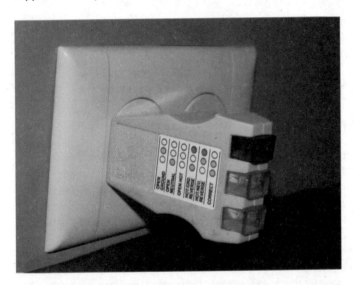

FIGURE 31.5 **Plug the outlet tester in, observe the signal lights, and quickly learn whether the outlet is properly wired (as this example is).**

PROPER POWER HANDLING

Electrical power can be dangerous, so take precautions when working around computers and peripherals that use power, especially AC current. Proper power handling practices include the following:

- ▶ When a power supply fails, replace it. Do not open it, since it contains capacitors that can store very high voltages after the power is disconnected.
- ▶ When a CRT monitor fails, replace it. Do not open it, because it contains capacitors and other components that will store very high voltages until discharged.
- ▶ When an LCD display that uses a fluorescent backlight has a bad inverter, keep in mind that the inverter is a high-voltage component. If you decide to replace the inverter rather than the display, be sure to disconnect power from the display and then the inverter before removing it. Inverters on laptops are typically inside a protective plastic enclosure; don't remove the enclosure.

▶ When you need to check AC or DC voltage levels, be sure to use voltage testers made for the type of voltage and set them to the correct voltage type and power level. Contact experienced repair people to replace defective outlets.

▶ If you install a UPS battery backup, check volt-amps or wattage rating against the power needed to run connected equipment for at least 10–15 minutes. Don't use an undersized UPS unit, and replace its batteries when they wear out.

▶ Before working with electricity, check the relevant portions of the OSHA regulations for electrical safety at www.osha.gov/electrical.

PROPER COMPONENT HANDLING AND STORAGE

If you upgrade computers, you are likely to accumulate extra parts over time. If you want these parts to be usable in the future, they need to be handled and stored properly. Use ESD protection when handling parts and reuse purpose-built packaging whenever possible. For example, keep the box, cradle, and antistatic bag from a hard drive upgrade to store the old one for reuse. Keep the box and antistatic bag from a motherboard upgrade to store the old one for reuse.

If you are storing a device that has additional parts, such as charger, cables, brackets, screws, or other components, make sure you store them with the device. You can use cardboard boxes or antistatic bags for this purpose if they'll fit into the box intended for the device. If not, get a larger box.

Mark boxes or antistatic bags with labels so it's apparent what is stored inside.

ANTISTATIC BAGS

Several types of antistatic bags and wraps are available for protecting computer and network parts. Silvery antistatic bags provide the best ESD protection (Figure 31.6).

To provide both ESD protection and limited protection against physical damage, you can also use pink antistatic bubble wrap (Figure 31.7). To hold the wrap in place, you can use antistatic tape. Pink antistatic foam sheets can also be used to help provide ESD protection and protection against physical damage.

COMPLIANCE WITH GOVERNMENT REGULATIONS

Be sure to comply with government regulations regarding disposal of computer parts containing mercury (laptops and LCD panels that use fluorescent backlights), rechargeable batteries, and items containing lead or other toxic chemicals. The easiest way to comply with government regulations is to use registered electronics recycling centers for hardware and batteries and registered chemical disposal facilities for toxic chemicals.

FIGURE 31.6 Close up an antistatic bag to provide maximum protection from the electronics inside the bag.

PERSONAL SAFETY

Staying safe when working on PCs and related technologies requires you to pay attention to several potential dangers, including electrical, weight, fire safety, eye protection, and lung protection. Keep reading for details.

Disconnect Power Before Repairing PC

Today's PCs have some power flowing through them even when they appear to be turned off. If you don't completely cut power to a PC, it can hurt—or even kill—you if you work on its interior. It's a three-step process:

1. Run the shutdown process in the operating system.
2. Turn off the power supply (if it has a switch).
3. Disconnect the power supply cable from the power supply (Figure 31.8).

FIGURE 31.7 Antistatic bubble wrap protecting a DVD rewriteable drive

FIGURE 31.8 A typical PC power supply after being turned off and its AC power supply cord disconnected

After disconnecting power from the PC, wait about a minute before you open it up and start working on it. It takes a little while for capacitors on the motherboard to lose all power. Some motherboards have signal lights that shut off after all power has left the system.

Lifting Techniques

Lift with your legs, not your back. It's good advice whether you're lifting a desktop PC, a desk, a bulky flat-screen display, or a hulking multifunction printer-copier-fax device. Specifically, follow this method: stand close to the item, bend the knees to get down to the item, and keep your back straight as you lift with your legs. Turn your body by moving your legs instead of twisting your back, and keep the item close to your body.

If a boxed item is marked "team lift" or "back support required," don't act like your favorite superhero—get someone to help you, put on a back brace, or take whatever other steps are required to safely carry and move the item. Don't break yourself!

Even if a box is not marked with specific safety warnings, pay attention to the gross weight of the box (box plus contents). For example, if you're comfortable with lifting 30 pounds but the box has a gross weight of 45 pounds, get help! Similarly, lifting lightweight but bulky objects like flat-panel HDTVs should be a two-person job.

Electrical Fire Safety

Forget Type A and Type B fire extinguishers if you're facing an electrical fire: fire extinguishers marked with a Type C rating are the only type of fire extinguishers that can safely and effectively put out an electrical fire. Type C fire extinguishers typically use carbon dioxide, which doesn't leave a messy residue.

A Type ABC fire extinguisher works on electrical fires and also works on Type A (wood, paper, cloth, most plastics, and other ordinary flammables) and Type B (flammable liquids, solvents, and so on) fires. A fire in an office or technology workspace could involve one, two, or all three types of fire sources, so the ABC fire extinguisher is the most versatile fire extinguisher type to have on hand. However, a typical ABC fire extinguisher uses nonconductive ammonium dihydrogen phosphate (ADP) that leaves a messy residue.

For protecting computer rooms and large technology spaces, consider using FM-200 fire suppression systems. This type of fire suppression system can be used safely where people are present and doesn't damage electronic components, plastics, common metals, or rubber.

When considering potential fire sources, keep in mind that the popular lithium-ion rechargeable batteries used in computers, mobile devices, digital cameras, and electric and hybrid vehicles are flammable and hard to extinguish. When calling 911 to report a fire, be sure to let the operator know if lithium-ion batteries might be involved.

> **NOTE**
>
> Learn more about the different types of ABC fire extinguishers at `https://selectsafety.net/what-is-an-abc-fire-extinguisher`. Learn more about Janus FM-200 fire suppressant systems at `www.janusfiresystems.com/products/fm-200`.

Safety Goggles

Working on computers and technology can lead to many types of risks for your eyes, from dust and dirt when cleaning out a PC, to metal fragments when using a cutting device to alter a part of the chassis, to errant screws or bolts flying off the end of a tool during component installations. Look for eye protection that meets the ANSI Z87.1 standard (the most recent one is Z87.1-2020). For protection against high-impact dangers, get Z87+ rated goggles.

> **NOTE**
>
> For details about Z87 special markings, including D4 (protection from dust particles), X (fogging resistance), and more, see `https://blog .safetyglassesusa.com/what-does-ansi-z87-1-certified-mean`.

Air Filtration Mask

With the COVID-19 pandemic, face mask usage has become widespread in many localities. However, COVID or no COVID, air filtration masks make sense for anyone working with dirty computers that are being cleaned with compressed air or vacuum cleaners.

The N95 disposable mask, easily recognizable because most versions include flexible metal or plastic nose pieces for a better seal, is the best type of disposable mask for most techs. Don't mistake it for the KN95, which folds in half and lacks the nose pieces of the N95.

For technicians who are working in very dusty environments, with solvents, paints, or other chemicals, respirators are recommended for better protection. Respirators have assigned protection factors (APFs), indicating the level of protection against different types of inhalable materials.

> **NOTE**
>
> For details about respirator APF ratings and what they mean, visit `https:// selectsafety.net/apf-for-respirators`.

> **EXAM TIP**
>
> To prepare for the Core 2 1102 A+ Certification exam, make sure you know both the threat categories and the protection you must use. ESD: ESD straps and mats. Equipment grounding and power handling: grounded outlets with correct wiring. Component handling and storage: reuse purpose-made boxes and bags, antistatic bags. Potentially dangerous items: follow government regulations. Personal safety: disconnect power before servicing equipment, proper lifting techniques, use Type C or ABC fire extinguishers on electrical fires, protect eyes with Z87.1 or Z87+ safety goggles, use N95 or other recommended air filtration masks or respirators.

CERTMIKE EXAM ESSENTIALS

► To help minimize the threat of ESD, check the relative humidity of locations with computers in use as well as repair/build workstations. A relative humidity level of about 55–65 percent is ideal for avoiding corrosion and ESD.

► To avoid problems with unreliable AC sources, use outlet testers before connecting computers or other tech devices, including surge suppressors.

► Technicians need to protect themselves from workplace risks with both protective gear and intelligent behavior.

Practice Question 1

You are evaluating a potential workstation location for use in repairing, upgrading, and building computers. You notice that some of the outlets have two-prong outlet adapters and others have surge suppressors with warning lights lit up. Which of the following categories' recommendations is being *directly* violated?

A. Proper component handling
B. ESD
C. Equipment grounding
D. Fire safety

Practice Question 2

You have just completed upgrading several desktop computers and you have spare parts that will be saved for future projects. Which of the following procedures should be followed to store these parts?

A. Stack motherboards on top of each other with clear bubble wrap between the boards.
B. Use aluminum foil as antistatic shielding material for boards and cards.
C. Store spare RAM in plastic shoeboxes.
D. Reuse motherboard boxes and antistatic bags for motherboards or large add-on cards.

Practice Question 1 Explanation

This question is designed to test your real-world understanding of workplace safety issues. Let's consider each of these answers.

1. The first answer (A, proper component handling) is incorrect. This category is indirectly affected by deficiencies.

2. The next answer (B, ESD) is incorrect. We have no information about relative humidity ranges in the location, and any deficiencies in the location indirectly affect this category.

3. Next answer (C, equipment grounding) is correct. The use of two-prong adapters indicates some outlets are ungrounded and when the warning lights on surge suppressors are lit, the lights indicate some type of wiring problem.

4. The last answer (D, fire safety) is incorrect. Fire safety direct violations would include the lack of ABC or Type C fire extinguishers.

Correct Answer: C. Equipment grounding

Practice Question 2 Explanation

This question is designed to test your knowledge of proper parts storage. Let's evaluate these answers one at a time.

1. The first answer (A, Stack motherboards on top of each other with clear bubble wrap between the boards) is incorrect. Clear bubble wrap can create static electricity buildup instead of preventing it.

2. The second answer (B, Use aluminum foil as antistatic shielding material for boards and cards) is incorrect. If there are batteries on any of the boards, they could short out and catch on fire. Aluminum foil does not protect against ESD.

3. The third answer (C, Store spare RAM in plastic shoeboxes) is incorrect. Plastic shoeboxes can create static electricity.

4. The last answer (D, Reuse motherboard boxes and antistatic bags for motherboards or large add-on cards) is correct. If used antistatic bags are not torn, they will continue to provide excellent ESD protection for their contents, and the motherboard boxes also help protect against ESD and impact damage.

Correct Answer: D. Reuse motherboard boxes and antistatic bags for motherboards or large add-on cards

CHAPTER 32

Environmental Protection

Core 2 Objective 4.5: Summarize environmental impacts and local environmental controls.

The office space, server rooms, and switch closets are just a few environments where equipment is located. We must ensure that environments are a safe place for equipment as well as for the technicians who must service and support the equipment. In this chapter, you will learn what you need to know about the A+ Certification Core 2 Objective 4.5, including the following topics:

▶ Material safety data sheet (MSDS): documentation for handling and disposal
▶ Temperature, humidity-level awareness, and proper ventilation
▶ Power surges, under-voltage events, and power failures

MATERIAL SAFETY DATA SHEET (MSDS): DOCUMENTATION FOR HANDLING AND DISPOSAL

Material safety data sheets (MSDSs), also known as safety data sheets (SDSs), include information such as physical product data (boiling point, melting point, flash point, and so forth), proper storage, potential health risks, disposal recommendations, and spill/leak procedures. The MSDS documentation allows a technician to know how to handle the product safely, as well as respond in the event of an emergency. Any potentially hazardous material will have associated MSDS documentation and some hazardous chemicals ship with their own specific MSDS.

The Occupational Safety and Health Administration (OSHA) mandates that MSDS sheets be supplied for the following types of products:

▶ Products that pose a physical or health hazard
▶ Products that are "known to be present in the workplace in such a manner that employees may be exposed under normal conditions of use or in a foreseeable emergency"

The MSDS documents must be in a location with "ready access" for any employee who could handle the materials. Typically, MSDS documents will be found in a binder near the products or posted on the wall by the product.

NOTE

More information about the OSHA standard for material safety data sheets can be found here: www.osha.gov/laws-regs/regulations/standardnumber/1910/1910.1200.

EXAM TIP

Material safety data sheets detail how to handle and respond to emergencies with hazardous materials.

Proper Battery Disposal

Batteries contain toxic ingredients and several heavy metals, including alkaline, mercury, lead acid, nickel–cadmium, and nickel–metal hydride. The Mercury-Containing and Rechargeable Battery Management Act (aka the Battery Act) was passed in 1996 with two goals:

▶ Phase out the use of mercury in disposable batteries.
▶ Provide collection methods and recycling procedures for batteries.

Five types of batteries are typically used with computers and electronic devices:

Alkaline Batteries   These batteries contained high levels of mercury prior to 1996. Today they contain little or no mercury, but they still contain toxic materials. These batteries create power through a reaction of zinc, manganese, and an alkaline electrolyte.

Nickel–Cadmium (NiCd)   This is a popular format for rechargeable batteries and contains high levels of nickel and cadmium. These types of batteries are categorized by the Environmental Protection Agency (EPA) as hazardous waste and must be recycled.

Nickel–Metal Hydride (NiMH)   These batteries are used in high-drain devices such as cameras. The batteries are most noted for a significant self-discharge rate over other batteries. These batteries are not considered hazardous waste, but they do contain toxic materials and should be disposed of properly.

Lithium-Ion (Li-ion)   These batteries are typically used for laptops. They cannot be overcharged and/or overheated or they present a risk of fire. They are not considered hazardous waste but should be disposed of properly.

Button Batteries   These batteries look like a button and are typically used in calculators and watches as well as computers. They often contain mercury and silver (and are environmental hazards due to the mercury) and must be recycled.

> **NOTE**
> Not all button batteries are the same. The most common button style battery used on motherboards to keep time and date in the BIOS/UEFI is the CR2032. It might look like a button battery, but it has a Lithium composition and is non-rechargeable.

> **EXAM TIP**
> Most batteries contain heavy metals and toxic material and therefore they should be recycled and disposed of properly following local regulations and EPA guidelines.

Proper Toner Disposal

Toner is considered a carcinogen, and it can contain heavy metals that are bad for the environment. Therefore, toner cartridges should be recycled properly. Toner cartridges can often be recycled at recycling centers, and many retailers will accept them for recycling.

There are a number of toner refurbishing companies that sell refurbished toner cartridges. They will then take your toner cartridge and refurbish and refill it. These companies typically provide service to small to large organizations, along with a basic service of laser printer and multifunction copiers.

Proper Disposal of Other Devices and Assets

Outside of batteries and toner, there are many other devices that must be properly disposed of. The Restriction of Hazardous Substances (RoHS) Directive originated in the European Union (EU) and has been adopted worldwide. It restricts hazardous materials in electronic devices, such as lead. Prior to the adoption of the RoHS many electronic devices had a high level of heavy metals and other toxic materials. Therefore, anything electronic is considered hazardous waste and must be recycled appropriately.

Most smaller devices, such as mobile devices, can be recycled at retailers. The retailers will typically have recycling bins for batteries, mobile devices, toner cartridges, and many other items. If the device is still useful and current, you can trade in your device when you purchase a new one. There are even kiosks where you can sell your device and payment is in the form of cash or gift card. The old devices are then refurbished and sold.

For organizations, a recycling program is typically adopted so the organization can dispose of assets properly. A recycling company will pick up the electronics and dispose of them properly, as per environmental laws.

TEMPERATURE, HUMIDITY-LEVEL AWARENESS, AND PROPER VENTILATION

Poor environmental conditions can shorten the life of equipment and can be uncomfortable for personnel. Temperature, humidity, and proper ventilation needs to be adequately adjusted for equipment longevity and comfort.

High temperatures can lead to overheating of equipment and equipment failure. Too low of a temperature can condense water on the equipment and create shorts in the electronics.

A humidity level below 40 percent in the environment can lead to electrostatic discharge (ESD) from static electricity. A humidity level above 60 percent can lead to shorting in the electronics, but also means a lesser chance of ESD.

Proper ventilation of equipment is important to keep the components cooled so they do not overheat. Ventilation should be filtered so that dust does not accumulate on or around the fans and internal components.

The combination of temperature, humidity, and proper ventilation are all equally important for the longevity of equipment, as well as the comfort of workers in the environment.

> **NOTE**
>
> The American Society of Heating, Refrigerating and Air-Conditioning Engineers (ASHRAE) has published standards for temperature and humidity for equipment. You can learn more at www.dataaire.com/how-to-use-ashrae-data-center-cooling-standards. OSHA also has published recommendations for temperature and

humidity for office workers here: www.osha.gov/laws-regs/
standardinterpretations/2003-02-24.

EXAM TIP
Temperature, humidity, and proper ventilation all contribute to the environmental factors for equipment and personnel.

Location/Equipment Placement

The proper placement of equipment is critical for its planned operation. The location should not be in direct sunlight, since that would have a heating effect. Equipment should also not be placed near ventilation shafts—it could be too hot or too cold, depending on the season. Outside of the environment concerns, you also have to consider the safety and security of both the device and the workers.

Dust Cleanup

Dust collects when fans blow against surfaces, and these surfaces are typically the surfaces you need to cool. When dust collects, it creates an insulating effect and traps the heat, thus making the cooling fans ineffective. The increased heat will make the equipment break down faster. If the environment has a high humidity level, the water in the air will mix with the dust to make a conductive surface.

EXAM TIP
Excess dust and humid conditions can cause a conductive mixture that can lead to shorts in the equipment.

Compressed Air/Vacuums

Compressed air can be used to clean dust from computer components. The compressed air can come from an air duster can, or the air can be supplied from an air compressor. If using an air duster can, be sure to keep it upright; if it is turned upside-down, it will release a stream of cold liquid. This cold liquid could damage electronic components when the shock of the cold stream hits it. If an air compressor is to be used, the air pressure should not exceed 15 PSI or you can risk damaging components.

Dust and debris can be cleaned with a vacuum. However, most vacuums create static electricity from the motion of the hose on the carpet and the bristles on the components. Therefore, only a specialized electrostatic discharge (ESD) safe vacuum cleaner should be used on electronic components.

POWER SURGES, UNDER-VOLTAGE EVENTS, AND POWER FAILURES

Electronic devices require adequate power that is free of transients in order to operate without failure. Power surges are an event that happens when the voltage exceeds the nominal voltage for over 3 nanoseconds or more. A power surge can climb to several hundred volts. Surges can occur for common reasons such as lightning strikes and power company grid transitions.

Under-voltage events (brownouts) happen when the voltage drops below the nominal voltage for the equipment. A power sag is an under-voltage event that can happen for 1/2 second to 3 seconds. A brownout is also an under-voltage event that can happen for more than 3 seconds. Both sags and brownouts are related to demand issues on the power grid.

Power failure (blackout) events happen because of external conditions, such as weather, transformer failure, or accidents that involve power poles. A power failure can last minutes or several days, depending on the reason for the failure.

Battery Backup

A battery backup also known as an uninterruptible power supply (UPS) can protect you from transient power problems. During a power failure, a UPS is used to carry the load of the equipment until the generator warms up and produces consistent power.

There are several different types of UPSs depending on use and budget. The following are common battery backup types:

Standby UPS   This operates by transferring the load from the AC line to a battery-supplied inverter with the use of a transfer switch and capacitors. These UPSs are often used to protect home electronics and personal computers.

Line-Interactive UPS   This operates by supplying power from the AC line to the inverter. When a power failure occurs, the line signals the inverter to draw power from the batteries. The inverter transitions the load better than a transfer switch. These UPSs are typically found in network closets and server rooms.

Online UPS   This operates by supplying AC power to a rectifier/charging circuit; this maintains a charge for the batteries. The batteries then supply the inverter with a constant DC power source. The inverter converts the DC power source back into an AC power circuit again, which supplies the load. These UPSs are typically found in data centers because of the seamless transition of the load.

EXAM TIP
Battery backups, also known as UPSs, can deal with a wide array of power transients, including power failure.

Surge Suppressor

Surge suppressors, also known as surge protectors, are used to protect equipment in the event of surges in the electrical voltage. A typical surge of voltage can be upward of 500 volts for several nanoseconds. A surge suppressor will absorb a surge in voltage to protect the electronics connected.

A surge protector will look similar to a power strip. The difference is that power strips do not protect electronics from surges in voltage. A surge suppressor will have a rating of how many joules of energy it can absorb; this is printed on a label on the surge suppressor. Typically, joule ratings for surge suppressors are around 500 to 600 joules of energy.

Some surge suppressors can protect an entire building. These devices are called service entrance surge protection or transient voltage surge suppressors (TVSSs). The devices can absorb over 1,000 joules of energy.

EXAM TIP
Surge suppressors absorb a surge of electricity to protect the connected electronics.

CERTMIKE EXAM ESSENTIALS

▶ Material safety data sheets (MSDSs) describe how to handle harmful materials for day-to-day operations as well as emergencies. OSHA requires that MSDS are supplied for products that pose a physical or health hazard or products that are "known to be present in the workplace in such a manner that employees may be exposed under normal conditions of use or in a foreseeable emergency." The MSDS documents must be in a location with "ready access" for employees who could handle materials.

▶ Batteries can contain toxic materials and heavy metals, such as mercury; therefore, they should be recycled in a safe manner, according to local regulations and EPA guidelines. Other electronic devices must be disposed of properly, since they can also contain heavy metals. Recycling can be performed at retailers for smaller devices, while larger devices must be recycled through a recycling company.

▶ Temperature and humidity must be adjusted appropriately to keep components properly cool and dry. If the temperature is too low, you have the risk of condensation, and if the temperature is too high, you risk overheating. Humidity that is too low can attribute to electrostatic discharge (ESD), whereas humidity that is too high can cause shorting conditions.

▶ Power surges happen when the voltage exceeds the nominal voltage for over 3 nanoseconds or more. A surge protector can be used to mitigate power surges. Under-voltage events happen when the voltage drops below the nominal voltage, and power failures are a complete loss of power. Under-voltage events and power failures can be mitigated with battery backup systems.

Practice Question 1

During severe thunderstorms, you notice that your computer reboots when the power flickers off. Which device can you use to prevent these reboots?

A. Power strip
B. Surge suppressor
C. TVSS
D. UPS

Practice Question 2

You notice that walking across the floor frequently builds up static electricity. What can be adjusted to prevent the buildup of static electricity?

A. Raise the humidity.
B. Lower the humidity.
C. Clean out dust.
D. Provide better ventilation.

Practice Question 1 Explanation

This question is designed to test your knowledge of power failure events.

1. The first answer (A, Power strip) is incorrect. A power strip does not protect anything and only allows multiple devices to be connected.

2. The next answer (B, Surge suppressor) is incorrect. A surge suppressor protects devices plugged in from power surges.

3. The next answer (C, TVSS) is incorrect. A transient voltage surge suppressor protects an entire building from power surges.

4. The last answer (D, UPS) is correct. A UPS can protect you from short-term power failures and under-voltage events.

Correct Answer: D. UPS

Practice Question 2 Explanation

This question is designed to test your knowledge of temperature, humidity, and ventilation.

1. The first answer (A, Raise the humidity) is correct. Raising the humidity above 40 percent can reduce static electricity.

2. The next answer (B, Lower the humidity) is incorrect. Lowering the humidity below 40 percent can create an environment where static electricity is possible.

3. The next answer (C, Clean out dust) is incorrect. Cleaning out dust will not reduce static electricity; dust can create an overheating issue and in some cases a short.

4. The last answer (D, Provide better ventilation) is incorrect. Poor ventilation will create overheating issues with the equipment but will not reduce the potential for static electricity.

Correct Answer: A. Raise the humidity

CHAPTER 33

Privacy, Licensing, Policy, and Incident Response

Core 2 Objective 4.6: Explain the importance of prohibited content/ activity and privacy, licensing, and policy concepts.

Prohibited content is any content that is restricted by the organization. When prohibited content is encountered, an incident response must be followed. Licensing is something that every technician must deal with on a day-to-day basis. Dealing with regulated data is another facet of being a technician. In this chapter, you will learn what you need to know about the A+ Certification Core 2 Objective 4.6, including the following topics:

► Incident response
► Licensing/digital rights management (DRM)/end-user license agreement (EULA)
► Regulated data

INCIDENT RESPONSE

An *incident* is any undesirable event that is outside of the normal policy or processes of the organization. Incidents can be as simple as someone viewing questionable content or as complex as data loss. The person who responds to an incident is called the first responder. The first responder is typically part of the Computer Emergency Response Team (CERT). The CERT is responsible for executing the incident response plan and begins with the collection of evidence in the order of volatility, as follows:

Memory Contents   RAM is the most volatile and should be collected with a memory dumper tool and saved to removable media.

Swap Files/Virtual Memory   Swap files and virtual memory files are RAM contents that have been saved to a file.

Network Processes   Part of a network process, such as a browser redirection, spam, or active network communication.

System Processes   A rouge system process, such as an exploit that has been rooted into the operating system.

Filesystem Information   Files on a hard drive that contains the files related to the incident.

> **EXAM TIP**
>
> When an incident occurs, the first responder is responsible for acquiring data in the order of volatility.

Chain of Custody

Once the evidence is collected by the first responder, it must be secured and damage to evidence should be prevented. The material should be locked in a safe or file cabinet to prevent evidence spoliation. The person controlling the access is then the beginning of the chain of custody. A chain of custody document should be created that describes the nature of the evidence, as well as the following:

- ▶ Who obtained the evidence
- ▶ Who secured the evidence
- ▶ Who controlled the evidence during the entire process

If the evidence is moved, the chain of custody documentation should reflect the following:

- ▶ The reason why it was moved
- ▶ Who moved it
- ▶ How it was secured
- ▶ Who controlled it

A chain of custody should be maintained at all times. Evidence might not be admissible in a court of law if the chain of custody is not maintained and evidence is damaged.

> **EXAM TIP**
> The chain of custody prevents evidence from being inadmissible in a court of law.

Inform Management/Law Enforcement as Necessary

After the evidence has been collected and a chain of custody has been established, it's time to report the incident. Informing management of the incident is the next step; management can then make decisions as to how the incident has impacted operations. If the impact is severe, data loss has occurred, or theft of data has happened, then management will involve law enforcement and further data can be collected.

Before reporting the incident to management, create a report that details the following. The answers should be as clear and precise as possible, because this report might be submitted to management, law enforcement, insurance, and any other number of third parties.

- ▶ What happened?
- ▶ When did it happen?
- ▶ How did it happen?
- ▶ Who made it happen?
- ▶ Why did it happen?

Law enforcement will work at filling in any blanks by using the evidence they collect. The evidence will be used to locate and charge the threat agent. The ultimate goal of law enforcement is to stop a future incident from happening to other victims.

> **EXAM TIP**
> After you know basic information about the incident, report it to management and potentially to law enforcement.

Copy of Drive (Data Integrity and Preservation)

Part of the evidence collection process is to copy any hard drives involved in the incident with forensic copy software. The evidence collection from hard drives will be in the form of a block-level copy of the data. This will maintain the order of data to the sectors on the disk.

During the copy process, a special tool should be used to prevent damage to evidence. Called *write-blockers*, these tools make the media read-only by preventing writes to the original drive during the copy process. Write-blockers promote data integrity and preservation. Something as simple as a timestamp that is changed on a file during the copy operation could be considered spoliation of evidence.

Documentation of Incident

The documentation of the incident should start immediately. A log of events should be recorded, before, during, and after the incident. You should collect as much information as possible during the documentation of the incident. You learned about the incident report that details unusual events outside of the normal in Chapter 28, "Documentation." These elements should be contained in the documentation:

- ▶ Date and time
- ▶ Summary
- ▶ Root cause
- ▶ Actions taken
- ▶ Remediation
- ▶ Services impacted
- ▶ Recommendations

EXAM TIP

The documentation of an incident should start as the incident is reported and continue until the incident is completely over.

LICENSING/DIGITAL RIGHTS MANAGEMENT (DRM)/END-USER LICENSE AGREEMENT (EULA)

Licensing is term used to describe the conditional use of software or services that are set forth by the developer. A license might be free of charge or cost money. The terms in the license agreement will define what can be done and what cannot be done with the software.

The *end-user license agreement (EULA)* sets the terms and conditions that an end user must abide by. The EULA is typically presented during the installation of an application. The EULA is a non-monetary agreement between the application developer and the end user. The agreement will define the terms of liability, fair use, copyright, and many more stipulations.

If the software costs money to use, it is common for the developer to employ *digital right management (DRM)*. The DRM will restrict the use of software or media to someone possessing a valid license. The DRM will require a valid license key or cloud-based license to run or unlock its features.

> **NOTE**
> DRM is not solely used in applications—it can also be used to protect music, media, photos, or any other downloadable content.

Valid Licenses

A valid license is any licensed issued that is current within its service period. Typically, licenses are issued as perpetual or term-based. If the license is perpetual, then there is no expiration of the license. If the license is term-based, it is valid for a given period of time, typically a year in length. DRM is used with the license to restrict use after the term expires.

Nonexpired Licenses

A nonexpired license is a perpetual license that is issued for the software. A typical example of a nonexpiring license is the Windows operating system license. Once the license is activated, it does not expire for the useful life of the operating system. Applications that are paid for are not the only ones that have nonexpiring licenses; freeware applications come with a nonexpiring license.

Personal Use License vs. Corporate Use License

A person license is sold via retail channels to any noncommercial entity. Personal licensing is the most expensive of all the licensing models, since it is generally a single license. The license can be perpetual or term-based, depending on the software.

Corporate use licenses are typically sold via a reseller to businesses in large quantities. Because the licenses are purchased in bulk, the license is often discounted compared to personal licenses. Bulk license purchasing is also called volume licensing. Volume licensing is typically sold per-computer or per-user. When the license is sold per-computer, anyone logging onto the computer can use the software. When the license is sold per-user, only the user named on the license can use the software.

> **EXAM TIP**
> Personal licenses are typically sold via retail channels, and corporate licensing is sold via reseller channels, which allows for bulk purchasing.

Open Source License

Open source software is any software package in which the software source code is open and freely downloadable to anyone. Although open source software is typically free, not all open source software is free. Some open source software packages provide a community license that is free and more sophisticated features that require licensing and support.

> **NOTE**
> Examples of open source license agreements are the Apache license, the BSD license, and the MIT license.

REGULATED DATA

Regulated data is any data that a local, state, federal, or controlling body deems is applicable to their rules and regulations. The regulations can be legal regulations such as under federal mandate. The regulations can also be voluntary with the expectation that you will adhere to compliance guidelines, such as the storage of credit card data. If you violate the regulations and fall out of compliance you might be barred from future service. The following is a list of regulated data that you should know for the exam.

Credit Card Transactions

Credit card transactions are regulated by the Payment Card Industry Data Security Standard (PCI DSS). PCI DSS compliance is not enforced by government entities; it is actually enforced by banks and creditors. Merchants must comply with the PCI DSS standard to maintain payment card services. If you are found in violation of the PCI DSS, banks will not be permitted from doing business with your organization.

Personal Government-Issued Information

Personal government-issued information is regulated at the local, state, and federal levels. Any document issued by a government that contains personal information is considered personal government-issued information. This category of information is very broad and can overlap with other types of protected data, such as protected health information (PHI) or other PII.

PII

Personally identifiable information (PII) is anything that can be used to identify an individual person on its own or in context with other information. This includes someone's name, address, other contact information, the names of family members, and other details that people would consider private. This category of regulated data is broadly regulated by a number of regulatory bodies both government and private.

Healthcare Data

Protected health information (PHI) is protected by the Health Insurance Portability and Accountability Act (HIPAA) and refers to any information used in the healthcare industry to describe a patient or aliment. Electronic health records (EHRs) are PHI and contain the patient's history. EHRs contain vital information about each interaction with healthcare providers. PHI can be used to statistically track larger groups of people, but data must be anonymized first.

Data Retention Requirements

Data retention refers to the length of time data will be stored according to regulatory bodies. Each type of data will have a different data retention requirement, such as legal documents, financial documents, or any transactional documents. Organizations may also have internal requirements for data retention, depending on their needs.

Data retention can be a manual process or automated based on internal requirements to shield organizations from lengthy eDiscovery in the event of a law suit. Each document must be classified with a document type called the *document profile*. If the process is automated, the document profile will contain a validity period. Once the validity period has expired, the document will be deleted or destroyed automatically.

EXAM TIP

Data retention requirements can be imposed by external regulatory bodies or internal regulations.

CERTMIKE EXAM ESSENTIALS

▶ Incident response is the process of responding, collecting, and securing evidence; informing management/law enforcement; and documenting the incident. The order of volatility guides the collection process, with memory contents being collected first and filesystem data last. Chain of custody secures the evidence so that it is admissible in a court of law. Documenting the incident should be performed along the process.

▶ Licensing is the legal right to use an application or service, based on an agreement between the developer and yourself. Licensing can be in the form of term-based or nonexpiring licenses. Personal use licensing is typical end-user licensing, whereas corporate use licensing is volume-based. Open source licensing is downloadable by anyone and typically free to use.

▶ Regulated data is any data in which there is a regulation created by a regulatory body. Credit card transactions are regulated by the Payment Card Industry Data Security Standard (PCI DSS) regulations. Personal government-issued information is any information that is issued by the government and considered confidential. Personally identifiable information (PII) is any specific information that can identify a person. Protected health information (PHI) is protected by the Health Insurance Portability and Accountability Act (HIPAA) and refers to any information used in the healthcare industry to describe a patient or aliment.

Practice Question 1

You want to make sure that the spoliation of evidence will not occur during an incident. Which concept should you pay close attention to during the incident?

A. Chain of custody
B. Incident response
C. Informing management
D. Order of volatility

Practice Question 2

You are responsible for securing credit card transactions on the network. Which regulation should you investigate to make sure you comply with regulations?

A. PHI
B. PII
C. EHR
D. PCI DSS

Practice Question 1 Explanation

This question is designed to test your knowledge of incident response management.

1. The first answer (A, Chain of custody) is correct. The chain of custody is created so that spoliation of evidence does not occur.

2. The next answer (B, Incident response) is incorrect. The incident response is the initial response to an incident.

3. The next answer (C, Informing management) is incorrect. Informing management is the next step after collecting evidence and creating a chain of custody.

4. The last answer (D, Order of volatility) is incorrect. The order of volatility is the order in which evidence should be collected.

Correct Answer: A. Chain of custody

Practice Question 2 Explanation

This question is designed to test your knowledge of regulated data.

1. The first answer (A, PHI) is incorrect. Protected health information (PHI) is any information that identifies a patient and their ailment.

2. The next answer (B, PII) is incorrect. Personally identifiable information (PII) is anything that can be used to identify an individual person.

3. The next answer (C, EHR) is incorrect. Electronic health records (EHR) are patient health records in an electronic form.

4. The last answer (D, PCI DSS) is correct. Payment Card Industry Data Security Standard (PCI DSS) applies to how merchants transact credit card payments.

Correct Answer: D. PCI DSS

CHAPTER 34

Communication and Professionalism

Core 2 Objective 4.7: Given a scenario, use proper communication techniques and professionalism.

As an aspiring IT professional, you should know there are certain qualities that will allow you to stand out from others. By properly using communications techniques and adopting overall professionalism, you ensure that others will identify you as a professional. In this chapter, you will learn what you need to know about the A+ Certification Core 2 Objective 4.7, including the following topics:

▶ Professional appearance and attire
▶ Use proper language and avoid jargon, acronyms, and slang, when applicable
▶ Maintain a positive attitude/project confidence
▶ Actively listen, take notes, and avoid interrupting the customer
▶ Be culturally sensitive
▶ Be on time (if late, contact the customer)
▶ Avoid distractions
▶ Dealing with difficult customers or situations

▶ **Set and meet expectations/time line and communicate status with the customer**

▶ **Deal appropriately with customers' confidential and private materials**

PROFESSIONAL APPEARANCE AND ATTIRE

Your professionalism starts with your appearance, as others see you. Your overall appearance should be clean cut and polished. This means that any facial hair should be groomed and your hair combed, and you should be clean in appearance and odor free. Attire will vary depending on the environment, but professional should always be the overall objective for your appearance and attire.

Match the Required Attire of the Given Environment

Although you should always wear professional attire, there are situations where you should match your attire to the given environment. If you are underdressed, it might make you look unprofessional. If you are overdressed, it might make you look unapproachable or "above the task at hand," so to speak. There are also situations where you may need to "dress down" in the event you must help move an office or equipment. However, many normal situations require you to dress as formal or business casual.

Formal

Formal attire is typical in professional environments such as law firms or corporate offices. Formal attire for males typically consists of a dress shirt, suit jacket, dress pants, and dress shoes. Formal attire for a female is typically a suit or dress, pants suit, or skirt suit; dresses and skirts should be knee-length. Conservative colors are typical and dark colors are usually best, including black, navy, brown, or gray.

> **NOTE**
>
> Although these are the "norms" of formal attire, you may find that gender does not constrain a person to a particular attire.

Business Casual

As the world embraces a work/life balance post-pandemic, the business casual dress attire is replacing formal attire environments. The business casual attire consists of a collared shirt, slacks, khaki pants, blouse, or polo. Typically, business attire means no tie and no jeans. Also wear appropriate footwear, such as flats, loafers, dress shoes, or heeled shoes, but no sneakers.

> **NOTE**
> When you're interviewing for a new job or position, it is advisable to default to formal attire, unless the interviewer instructs you on attire for the interview. Every organization will have a dress code for both interviews and day-to-day.

USE PROPER LANGUAGE AND AVOID JARGON, ACRONYMS, AND SLANG, WHEN APPLICABLE

Communications should be clear and concise when speaking with others in the workplace. You should use proper language that describes the issue or solution clearly. For example, if a cursor does not move on the screen, avoid saying the cursor is frozen.

Also avoid jargon, acronyms, and slang. It's very common for a technician to speak with another technician in these terms. However, when speaking with end users, this language is intimidating and confusing.

> **EXAM TIP**
> You should speak in plain language when dealing with a customer.

MAINTAIN A POSITIVE ATTITUDE/ PROJECT CONFIDENCE

Maintaining a positive attitude is a form of professionalism. When you project negativity, others may be less likely to speak with you about their IT issues. You can also affect morale with others and contribute to them having a bad day. Therefore, even if you don't feel positive, you should appear positive to others.

As it applies to projects, you should maintain confidence and positivity. If you have a negative view on a project, others may view this as acknowledging a project will fail as well as signifying your distrust in the project's leaders. Never underestimate your influence on others, as many of your peers will look up to you and solicit your opinion, verbally and nonverbally.

> **EXAM TIP**
>
> You should maintain a positive attitude when dealing with projects and people—it is a reflection on how others see you.

ACTIVELY LISTEN, TAKE NOTES, AND AVOID INTERRUPTING THE CUSTOMER

If you don't listen, you cannot learn ,and in situations where you must learn the underlying conditions of a problem, not listening can prolong the solution. In addition, listening is how you learn new ideas and concepts. Careful listening will allow you to pick up on clues to a problem before others who don't listen and to pay attention to the verbal clues.

Another best practice is to take notes; as you listen, you should write down important idea, concepts, and clues. Although the human brain is amazing in its ability to store information, pen and paper or phone apps like Evernote allow a visual reference of the information. This allows review of the ideas, concepts, and clues well after the conversation.

When listening to the customer, avoid interrupting so that the customer can focus on their thoughts. When the customer is focused on the issue, they will be more likely to remember important details. It is also common courtesy and an attribute of professionalism.

> **EXAM TIP**
>
> Actively listening, taking notes, and avoiding interrupting the customer are all signs of professionalism.

BE CULTURALLY SENSITIVE

Cultural sensitivity is a part of being professional. You should be culturally sensitive to others in your organization as well as to culturally diverse people you may come in contact with. Although this follows the golden rule of treating others as you want to be treated, when you are culturally sensitive it allows you to be effective in your communications.

Always use clear concise language when appropriate, avoid shortcuts in explaining concepts, and always use appropriate punctuation. Another person might take offense to you asking a question with a period versus a question mark. The difference is a demand versus a question.

Use Appropriate Professional Titles When Applicable

Always use the appropriate professional titles when addressing a person or persons. Professionals expect the proper salutation, and they have often worked hard to attain the title. Not using the appropriate titles could be misconstrued as disrespectful or inconsiderate.

BE ON TIME (IF LATE, CONTACT THE CUSTOMER)

Being on time is a sign of professionalism. When you set an appointment with a customer, the customer will anticipate your arrival and the expectation that their problem will be solved. The customer might even set aside time so that they can speak with you about the problem.

If you are going to be late, you should always contact the customer and communicate the reason. Keep in mind that the customer might be impatiently waiting for your arrival. Being on time and communicating any delay helps maintain your professionalism with the customer.

AVOID DISTRACTIONS

When working with a customer, you should avoid all distractions. The customer will expect your undivided attention to their issues. In turn, you should expect the customer to give you the same courtesy while they work with you. Avoiding distractions helps you effectively communicate with the customer while maintaining professionalism.

Personal Calls

Personal calls are distractions that cannot be completely avoided. Family and friends might call you while you're with a customer. If that happens, you should let the call go to voicemail and then call them back when you are not with the customer. You can also establish some rules with family and friends, such as they only call you at work for emergency situations. You should never initiate a personal call when with a customer or working on a customer's issues.

Texting/Social Media Sites

Texting is just as bad as making personal calls while with a customer. It is unprofessional and, in many cases, disrespectful, because the customer does not have your undivided attention.

Visiting social media sites is considered a leisure activity and therefore deemed unprofessional and disrespectful when you're in the presence of a customer. Browsing social media sites should be restricted to your own personal time, such as lunch or when you are done for the day. Many companies have policies that prohibit personal texting and accessing social media content while on company time.

Personal Interruptions

Personal interruptions should be limited to a minimum when working with a customer. Examples of personal interruptions might be smoke/vape breaks, coffee breaks, or deviating from the problem at hand. You should be considerate of the customer's time in either working with you or being inconvenienced with the problem you are working on.

DEALING WITH DIFFICULT CUSTOMERS OR SITUATIONS

As a technician, you will deal with customers on a daily basis. Arguably, your technical skill will need to be second to your customer service skills. From time to time you will need to deal with difficult customers or situations. Every customer will be different, and no matter how you deal with the customer, the customer may be difficult or may just be having a bad day. This section offers recommendations for dealing with difficult customers and situations.

Do Not Argue with Customers or Be Defensive

When you argue with a customer, you escalate the situation and typically there is no way to deescalate the situation created. Therefore, it is a best practice to not argue with a customer. The customer wants to know that they have been heard and that you understand their issue. The customer will be more apt to listen if they feel you understand the situation.

Sometimes you don't need to directly argue with a customer to cause a situation. If you are defensive with a customer's comments, it could lead to an argument. As silly as it sounds, when you are defensive with a customer this behavior can automatically put the customer on the offensive.

Avoid Dismissing Customer Problems

You should avoid dismissing a customer problem, because doing so is generally viewed as disrespectful by the customer. The customer took the initiative to report the issue and it is obviously making an impact on the customer's productivity. As technicians, we must take equal initiative to investigate the problem and address it with the customer. You should avoid closing a problem ticket without speaking with the customer, since doing so is considered the same as dismissing the customer's problem. If a customer brings up other problems while you are working on a primary problem, constructively inform the customer that you will address each of their problems one at a time.

Avoid Being Judgmental

As technicians attain experience, they will tend to shortcut the diagnostic process and cast a judgment about the customer's problem or situation. It is common for a customer to include bleak details in a problem ticket when they initially submit it. Becoming judgmental about a problem or situation can be avoided by speaking with the customer and understanding more about the problem or situation.

Clarify Customer Statements (Ask Open-Ended Questions to Narrow the Scope of the Problem, Restate the Issue, or Question to Verify Understanding)

After a problem is submitted to the ticketing system or helpdesk, you should contact the customer to clarify the problem and gather symptoms. Often customers will submit vague details about the problem and its accompanying symptoms. Restate the issue with the customer to clarify the actual issue to be discussed, because the customer could have reported several different issues.

Ask open-ended questions to allow the customer to elaborate without leading the customer to a conclusion. As you ask questions, the aim is to narrow the scope of the problem, such as identifying the problem as a computer issue, software issue, or user issue. Once the problem is narrowed down, continue to ask questions to verify your understanding of the issue.

Do Not Disclose Experience via Social Media Outlets

Never disclose any experiences with a customer or the details of an issue with anyone else not directly involved with the problem. This includes social media outlets and other public forums. A customer experience should remain private within the organization. Many organizations will have policies about posting details of interaction on social media, as it is not considered professional and is conduct not fitting for an employee.

SET AND MEET EXPECTATIONS/TIME LINE AND COMMUNICATE STATUS WITH THE CUSTOMER

As a technician working with customers, you have the control to set expectations with the customer. When you begin working with a customer on an issue, you should present them with a time line for the solution. For example, after the initial gathering of information, you should explain that you will look into the information and get back to them at a certain time of the day.

When diagnosing the problem, make sure that you communicate your status on the issue. Any expectations that you have made with the customer should be met or at least communicated as to why you cannot meet them.

Offer Repair/Replacement Options as Needed

If you determine the problem is related to hardware, offer to repair the device if possible or replace the hardware if necessary. If the problem is related to a device, such as a keyboard or mouse, the device should be replaced. If the problem is related to a laptop or printer, you should try to repair the device and, if it cannot be repaired, it should be replaced. Also, if the customer will be without the device while it is being repaired, an arrangement for loaner equipment should be made.

> **EXAM TIP**
>
> By offering the replacement, repair, or loan of equipment, you are treating a customer how they expect to be treated.

Provide Proper Documentation on the Services Provided

As you progress through the life cycle of a problem, set expectations and follow through with them. When you reach the conclusion of the problem and a solution has been found, you should document how the solution was attained. If any services were rendered to come up with a solution, those should be documented as well. Examples of solutions might be defragmenting a hard disk or cleaning debris from a fan making noise.

Follow Up with Customer/User at a Later Date to Verify Satisfaction

Once a problem is solved, follow up with the customer at a later date to verify that the problem has not resurfaced. If anything was originally overlooked, this will give the customer an opportunity to speak with you. By simply following up with the customer, you can meet or exceed their expectations.

DEAL APPROPRIATELY WITH CUSTOMERS' CONFIDENTIAL AND PRIVATE MATERIALS

As a technician, you will occasionally come into contact with confidential information while working with a customer. You should avoid paying attention to anything confidential or private when working with the customer. However, if you identify private material that violates the organization's policies, you should report it promptly to Human Resources (HR).

Located on a Computer, Desktop, Printer, Etc.

If you discover private material located on a computer, desktop, printer or other media, do not snoop or pry. Just because you may have privileges does not mean that you are allowed to investigate. If the private or confidential materials violate organization policy, you still do not have the authority to investigate. The proper department, such as HR, is appropriately staffed to deal with policy infractions. If the material is just questionable and may be related to the customer's job, it may be appropriate to discuss matters with a manager.

CERTMIKE EXAM ESSENTIALS

▶ You should dress as it is appropriately expected for the situation. If you dress down. you may not look professional, and if you overdress, you may look above the task at hand. Formal attire typically consists of a dress shirt, suit jacket, dress pants or dress skirt, and dress shoes. Business casual typically consists of a collared shirt, slacks, khaki pants, blouse, or polo.

▶ Cultural appropriateness should be assumed when working with others. Always treat others as you want to be treated, and this will allow you to be effective in your communications. Use clear, concise language; avoid shortcuts in explaining concepts; and avoid slang.

▶ Distractions such as texting and personal calls should be avoided when you're working with customers. Personal calls should go to voicemail if possible, and you should never initiate a personal call. Texting and using social media sites while you're working with a customer is also unprofessional and can be considered disrespectful.

▶ Dealing with difficult customers or situations should be avoided if possible. Make sure the customer knows that they have been heard and that you understand their issue; it the customer will be more apt to listen to you. Always address customer issues and problems, no matter how obvious or simple the solution might be; make sure the customer knows you've addressed them. Do not disclose any experience with a customer on social media or public forums; always consider these interactions private.

▶ As a technician, you should appropriately set and meet expectations with customers. Always explain the time line for a solution, and keep the customer abreast of where you are when diagnosing the problem. If the problem is related to a piece of equipment, offer replacement options if you have spare equipment or repair the existing equipment. Follow up with customers at a later date to verify that they are satisfied with your solution and that any equipment is working fine.

▶ Confidential information or private information should not be viewed by a technician. If something is questionable, report it for further investigation. Always consider the customer's information as private and privileged, regardless of the location or access level you have.

Practice Question 1

You are currently working with another customer and realize that you will be late for your next appointment. What should you do if you are going to be late to a customer's appointment?

A. Continue on your way.
B. Take notes.
C. Make sure that you have formal attire.
D. Call the customer.

Practice Question 2

As you are listening to a customer's issue, your phone rings. What should you do?

A. Answer the call.
B. Text the person back.
C. Let the call go to voicemail.
D. Excuse yourself and call the person back.

Practice Question 1 Explanation

This question is designed to test your knowledge of professionalism.

1. The first answer (A, Continue on your way) is incorrect. Continuing to be late without calling the customer will waste their time waiting for you.

2. The next answer (B, Take notes) is incorrect. Taking notes will not make up for the fact that you will be late.

3. The next answer (C, Make sure that you have formal attire) is incorrect. The attire you dress in will not make up for the fact that you will be late.

4. The last answer (D, Call the customer) is correct. Calling the customer will improve the situation by communicating with them why you're late.

Correct Answer: D. Call the customer

Practice Question 2 Explanation

This question is designed to test your knowledge of professional behavior.

1. The first answer (A, Answer the call) is incorrect. While working with customer and listening to their issue, you should not answer the call.

2. The next answer (B, Text the person back) is incorrect. While actively listening to the customer, avoid texting or other distractions.

3. The next answer (C, Let the call go to voicemail) is correct. It is best to let the call go to voicemail while you are listening to a customer's issue.

4. The last answer (D, Excuse yourself and call the person back) is incorrect. Excusing yourself to call the person back while listening to the customer's issue could be considered rude.

Correct Answer: C. Let the call go to voicemail

CHAPTER 35

Scripting

*Core 2 Objective 4.8:
Identify the basics
of scripting.*

As a technician, you will have many tasks that have to be repeated over and over again. Scripting a solution allows you to repeat a task with an expected outcome every time. In this chapter, you will learn what you need to know about A+ Certification Core 2 Objective 4.8, including the following topics:

▶ **Script file types**
▶ **Use cases for scripting**
▶ **Other considerations when using scripts**

SCRIPT FILE TYPES

There are several different script file types that are associated with scripting languages. Each scripting language will have its own nuances and syntax. All scripting languages are high-level interpreters, which means that the scripts are not compiled into machine code. This allows the script to be altered and refined with a simple text editor.

The following are some common scripting languages you will encounter as a technician.

BAT

Windows batch scripts have been around since the release of Microsoft's Disk Operating System (MS-DOS). The file extension .bat is associated with the command-line interpreter cmd.exe. Both BAT and CMD files can be used to initiate a batch script, as they are both associated with the command-line interpreter.

You can create a simple batch script using Windows Notepad and saving it with the `.bat` or `.cmd` extension. The following is an example of a simple batch script that will print Hello World! and pause until the user presses a key:

```
@echo off
echo Hello World!
pause
```

PS1

Windows PowerShell scripts have become extremely popular for scripting today on the Windows platform. PowerShell is built upon the .NET Framework of the Common Language Runtime (CLR).

PowerShell uses cmdlets, which are verb-noun commands such as `Get-Disk`, which returns all the information on the disks the operating system is aware of. The most notable feature is PowerShell object-oriented language, and this gives you greater control when scripting.

> **EXAM TIP**
>
> PowerShell is the currently supported scripting language for Windows environments.

VBS

Visual Basic Scripts (VBS), also known as VBScripts, are based off the Microsoft Visual Basic language. VBS is slowly being replaced by PowerShell scripting. VBS is based off the Component Object Model (COM) and is extensible using older COM-based applications.

The language is still widely used for basic tasks. A VBScript will have the extension of `.vbs`. The VBScript interpreter is Windows Scripting Host (WSH), `wscript.exe`, or the command-line version of WSH, `cscript.exe`.

> **EXAM TIP**
>
> Visual Basic scripts (VBScripts) are slowly being replaced with PowerShell scripts. However, Visual Basic is still a supported language on the Windows operating system but is no longer supported in the web browser Internet Explorer.

SH

Bash stands for the Bourne Again Shell, and it is compatible with its predecessor, the Bourne shell (or sh). It is a common scripting language typically only found on Linux/Unix systems. And since the core of Apple macOS is Unix, you can find it being used on Mac computers as well.

The following is an example of a simple Bash script that will print Hello World! and then terminate:

```
#!/bin/bash
echo "Hello World!"
```

Not all Bash scripts will end with an .sh file extension. When a script is run, the interpreter is selected by the operating system as specified by the first line using the *hashbang* operator (#!), as shown in the previous example. The script will have a character combination of #! followed by the path of the script interpreter, typically /bin/bash. The file also needs to be marked for execution by the filesystem. You can do so using the chmod command, as covered in Chapter 11, "Linux."

JS

JavaScript is similar in syntax to the Java programming language. However, JavaScript is an interpreted language and Java applications require compiling for the Java runtime. JavaScript is mainly used in web pages to create interactive web pages, but with the runtime called Node.js JavaScript can run as independent code. JavaScript can be created with a simple text editor and scripts typically have the .js file extension.

EXAM TIP

JavaScript is primarily used in web pages to create interactive content.

PY

Python is a scripting language that has gained popularity in the past decade. Python was created to be an easy scripting language to learn, and it is very forgiving with syntax. Like VBScript and PowerShell, Python is extensible and can use external libraries. This means the script language can perform functions it was never originally designed for, such as machine learning or interfacing with cloud resources, just to name a few.

Python is interoperable with Windows, Linux/Unix, and macOS. Python scripts typically end with the .py extension, so the Windows operating system can associate the Python interpreter with the script. On Linux/Unix and macOS systems, however, the hashbang defines the interpreter and generally looks something like #!/usr/bin/python3.

EXAM TIP

Be sure you can identify the script file types by extensions. Windows batch files use .bat, PowerShell .ps1, VBScripts .vbs, Linux/Unix shell scripts .sh, JavaScript .js, and Python .py.

USE CASES FOR SCRIPTING

As a technician there will be plenty of opportunity to use your scripting skills, and no one scripting language will fit all situations. Scripting a solution is a huge investment of time up front. However, the reward is a script that will repeat a function with a predictable output. This section discussed several different use cases for scripting.

Basic Automation

Basic automation is the most common use case for scripting. Scripting allows you to automate basic tasks, such as file copy jobs or automated backups. By scripting an automated task, you can remove a person from the task. This means that there is less chance of error and no delays; that the task will be completed as fast as the computer it is processing on is capable of; and that the script will always perform the same basic task.

Restarting Machines

You may need to restart a machine or a group of machines for a number of reasons. There may be updates that require a restart, security patches, application updates, or part of a maintenance routine. You can even delay a restart with a script by scheduling it later in the day when people do not rely on the machine.

Remapping Network Drives

Remapping of a network drive is another great use case for a scripted solution. As workers log into their corporate account each day, they must reestablish access to file servers via a login script that maps drive letters to network locations. Remapping network drives via a script might also be used to automate software updates from a network location.

> **NOTE**
> Chapter 2, "Microsoft Command-Line Tools," contains more information about the `net use` command. Chapter 13, "Logical Security," explores login scripts.

Installation of Applications

The installation of the same application over and over again is a daunting repetitious task that fits the perfect use case for scripting. Many applications allow for an automated installation process by using command-line switches with the setup program. Scripts can be created to install applications on several computers so that the manual process does not need to be repeated. You can create automated scripts that install the application with these steps:

1. Map the drive where the installer is located.
2. Install the application unattended.
3. Delete the mapped drive.
4. Restart the computer.

Automated Backups

You can create a script to automate the backup process since most backups happen late at night. A script might copy all the important data into one location in order for the rest of the backup process to succeed. Scripting these tasks will eliminate the need to manually copy files while waiting for the task or tasks to complete.

Gathering of Information/Data

Gathering of information and data is another great use case for scripting. Scripts can be used to collect information about devices in the network, such as network interface utilization or application utilization. Scripting can be used to verify an application or that the system is operating properly. Inventory management can be performed with scripting, such as collecting hardware and software data. Vulnerability and security checks can also be performed with scripts to identify systems that need the latest patches.

Initiating Updates

Installing updates is a constant challenge because everything needs to be updated. Initiating updates for the operating system to installing new features or security patches is a task for scripting. Device drivers occasionally need to be updated for bugs and security patches; this too can be scripted. Applications always need updating for the next version and this task can be scripted as well.

> **EXAM TIP**
> You should be familiar with the various use cases for scripting basic automation, restarting machines, remapping network drives, installing applications, creating automated backups, gathering information/data, and initiating updates.

OTHER CONSIDERATIONS WHEN USING SCRIPTS

Scripting methods allow you to quickly affect thousands of operating systems in a short period of time. Typically, technicians have elevated privileges on the organization's network. This combination of scripting and privileges means that there are many considerations that should be weighed before deploying a script to an organization's network.

Always remember the saying that "with great power, comes great responsibility"; scripting gives you this "great power."

Unintentionally Introducing Malware

When you're creating a script that installs software or performs some other function that requires elevated permissions, there is the chance of installing malware. This can happen two different ways: voluntarily and involuntarily. If you elect to script using an untrusted source, you could voluntarily install malware without even knowing it. Depending on how the script is crafted, you could easily install an untrusted application on every system in the organization's network.

If you create a script that is scheduled to run as a privileged user, you can involuntarily allow the installation of malware if the system is compromised by a threat actor. Because scripts are editable, a threat actor can easily change the script to install their malware. When the schedule runs as the privileged user, any processes spawned from the script will execute as that privileged user.

> **NOTE**
>
> When you're using scripts with a privileged user account, scripts should be secured with the appropriate NTFS permissions to prevent users from changing the contents of the files. More information can be found in Chapter 8, "Operating System Types," and Chapter 17, "Windows Security."

Inadvertently Changing System Settings

When scripting, you can inadvertently change system settings, because typically you will have elevated privileges and sometimes scripts work differently than intended. This, coupled with deploying the script to multiple systems, can create big problems in a short period of time.

Consider testing your scripts rigorously on many different systems; this should be done one at a time. If you have access to a virtual machine or another type of testing sandbox, creating a snapshot of the operating system and performing controlled testing is advisable. If there are ill effects, you can always revert to the snapshot. If you are deploying the script on an organization's network, begin by using a small group of computers as your sample test group before fully deploying the script.

Another best practice is to track changes to your scripts. If further down the line a problem occurs, you can look at your change log and identify what you did wrong.

NOTE

Using a version control system (VCS) such as GitHub allows for change tracking of your scripts. Just keep in mind the free versions of many VCSs allow the world to read your scripts; private VCSs usually require a monthly cost.

Browser or System Crashes Due to Mishandling of Resources

As stated throughout this section, scripts can misbehave and have ill consequences. Some problems are very evident, such as inadvertently deleting a file or Registry setting. Some problems are not so evident and can impact browser or operating system performance and even stability.

These problems can be identified by testing the web browser or operating system before and after the implementation of a script. Use Resource Monitor or Performance Monitor to record a baseline before implementing a script. This will allow you to compare the performance after implementing a script and identify any problems related to resource mishandling.

Always create backups of the system just in case resource mishandling is not identified in testing. A script can quickly delete key files on a system, and that might only be observed when the script is executed in a production environment.

EXAM TIP

You should be aware of the considerations when implementing scripts, such as unintentionally introducing malware, inadvertently changing system settings, and causing browser or system crashes due to mishandling of resources.

NOTE

You can learn more about Resource Monitor and Performance Monitor in Chapter 3, "Windows 10 Operating System Tools."

CERTMIKE EXAM ESSENTIALS

▶ There are many different scripting types, and script languages should be selected according to personal preference and the scripting language limitations. Windows batch scripts are simple scripts that use the extension of .bat or .cmd. Windows PowerShell scripts use cmdlets that consist of verb-noun commands; they are associated with .ps1 extensions. VBScripts are widely used for basic tasks in the operating system and are associated with the .vbs extension. Bash is a common scripting language for Linux/Unix and files are identified by the .sh extension. JavaScript is similar in syntax to the Java programming language and files are identified by the .js extension. Python is a popular scripting language that is interoperable with all popular operating systems, and files are identified by the .py extension.

▶ There are many different use cases for scripting. Basic automation is the most common use for scripting basic tasks. Restarting machines with scripting helps initiate the update or patching process, in addition to finishing the update process. Remapping network drives with a script automates the login process. Scripting can be used for the installation of applications where a repetitive process must be maintained. Information gathering can be automated with scripting when you must gather information from several machines.

▶ When you're scripting, you must weigh several factors. You can unintentionally introduce malware by scripting with an untrusted application source. Scripting can inadvertently change system settings or create system crashes. A script can also make web browsers unstable depending on how the script is implemented and how resources are handled.

Practice Question 1

You need to develop a script that can interoperate on several different operating systems. Which scripting language should you choose?

A. Batch scripts
B. PowerShell scripts
C. VBScript
D. Python

Practice Question 2

Which scripting use case is typically implemented in the end user's login script?

A. Automating backups
B. Restarting machines
C. Remapping network drives
D. Initiating updates

Practice Question 1 Explanation

This question is designed to test your knowledge of script file types.

1. The first answer (A, Batch scripts) is incorrect. Batch scripts are based on the command interpreter and used to automate tasks on Windows operating systems.

2. The next answer (B, PowerShell scripts) is incorrect. The PowerShell script language is based on the .NET Framework and primarily works on Windows.

3. The next answer (C, VBScript) is incorrect. The VBScript language is based on the Component Object Model (COM) and primarily used on Windows.

4. The last answer (D, Python) is correct. Python is a common scripting language that is based on the Python interpreter and is compatible with many different operating systems.

Correct Answer: D. Python

Practice Question 2 Explanation

This question is designed to test your knowledge of scripting use cases.

1. The first answer (A, Automating backups) is incorrect. Automating backups is not implemented in login scripts.

2. The next answer (B, Restarting machines) is incorrect. Restarting machines is performed for maintenance purposes and not implemented in login scripts.

3. The next answer (C, Remapping network drives) is correct. Remapping network drives via a login script will allow users to access their files.

4. The last answer (D, Initiating updates) is incorrect. Initiating updates with a script helps keep the machine up-to-date, but that process is not performed in a login script.

Correct Answer: C. Remapping network drives

CHAPTER 36

Remote Access

Core 2 Objective 4.9: Given a scenario, use remote access technologies.

Businesses of all sizes have become more reliant on remote access technologies than ever before. So, it's more important than ever to understand how remote access technologies work and to make sure remote access is secure access. In this chapter, you will learn what you need to know about A+ Certification Core 2 Objective 4.9, including the following topics:

▶ **Methods/Tools**
▶ **Security Considerations of Each Access Method**

METHODS/TOOLS

In the following sections, you will learn about RDP, VPN, Virtual Network Computing (VNC), Secure Shell (SSH), remote monitoring and management (RMM), Microsoft Remote Assistance (MSRA), and third-party tools. Which one is the best choice for your organization's needs? Let's find out.

RDP

RDP (Remote Desktop Protocol) is a remote access tool built into Windows. In all versions of Windows, RDP enables a Windows computer (known as the RDP client) to connect to a computer running the RDP server so that users can work remotely.

The RDP server is built into non-Home editions of Windows, so users running Windows Pro or higher editions can configure their computers for remote access. (See Chapter 1, "Microsoft Windows Editions," for more information.) RDP clients are also available for Android, macOS, and iOS from the device's app store.

RDP is convenient to use because a user can log into the remote computers using the same password as when at the computer in person. To enable a connection into an RDP server, the computer needs to enable Remote Desktop.

In Windows 10, select Start ➤ Settings ➤ System ➤ Remote Desktop ➤ Enable Remote Desktop - On.

In Windows 11, select Start ➤ Settings ➤ System ➤ Remote Desktop ➤ Remote Desktop - On ➤ Confirm.

Then, in Windows 10/11:

1. Note the name of the RDP server.
2. Connect to the server. To connect to an RDP server with Windows:

   a. Search for **Remote Desktop Connection**.

   b. Click the link.

   OR

   a. Click Start ➤ Run.

   b. Type **mstsc** and press Enter.

   c. Enter the name of the PC you want to connect to (see Figure 36.1).

   d. To see additional options, click Options.

   e. Click Connect.

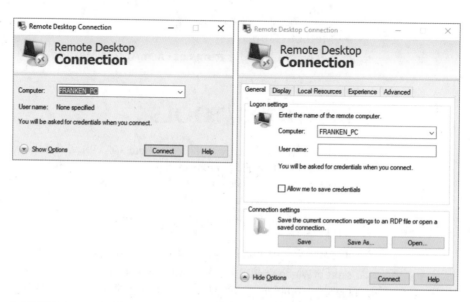

FIGURE 36.1 The initial RDC dialog box (left) and the RDC dialog box with options enabled (right)

Figure 36.2 shows a typical full-screen RDC connection. Figure 36.3 shows a typical RDC connection in a window. Because the remote computer is using a window to show the connection, the remote computer user might need to use scroll bars to view other parts of the remote screen.

FIGURE 36.2 A typical full-screen RDC session. Note the banner across the top of the remote computer's screen.

EXAM TIP

You can access a remote computer anywhere with Remote Desktop. Know how to enable it in Windows Settings and remember that it uses the Remote Desktop Protocol (RDP) and enables remote connections over TCP port 3389.

NOTE

Learn more about Remote Desktop Protocol at www.twingate.com/blog/what-is-rdp.

FIGURE 36.3 A typical RDC session in a window on the remote computer

VPN

A *VPN* (virtual private network) creates an encrypted connection between a VPN server and a client over the public Internet. A VPN connection is often referred to as a *VPN tunnel* because encrypted data is "tunneling" between the endpoints that are part of the unsecured Internet.

Using a VPN makes a normally insecure public Internet connection a secure connection. To set up a VPN in Windows 10, select Start ➢ Settings ➢ Network & Internet ➢ VPN ➢ Add A VPN Connection. To set up a VPN in Windows 11, select Start ➢ Settings ➢ Network & Internet ➢ VPN ➢ Add VPN.

> **EXAM TIP**
>
> Remember that a VPN extends a private network across a public network such as the Internet and allows users to securely send and receive data.

NOTE

Dig deeper into VPNs at www.kaspersky.com/resource-center/
definitions/what-is-a-vpn.

VPN benefits include:

▶ Highly secure encryption is used to set up the connection.
▶ The user's actual location is concealed from would-be snoops (Figure 36.4).
▶ The ability to restore access to blocked content on VPNs that support VPN
  location spoofing, in which users appear to be in a different location than they
  physically are.
▶ Secure file transfers.

Internet Protocol Security (*IPsec*) is the basis for the security features in a VPN. IPsec
includes protocols for authenticating both sides of a connection, negotiating cryptographic
keys, data integrity, and other security features.

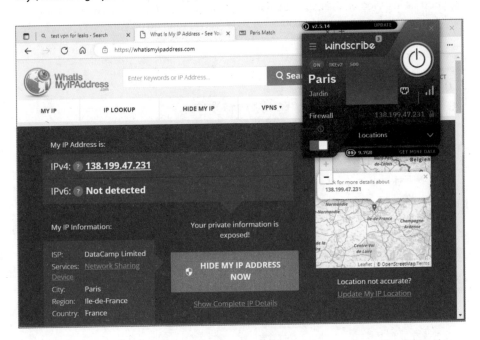

FIGURE 36.4 The Windscribe VPN is configured to report the author's location
as Paris, France.

Point-to-Point Protocol (*PPP*) is used as part of VPN tunneling as the data link protocol for
the connection. PPP is also used for dial-up network connections.

> **NOTE**
>
> See the ProPrivacy website's articles on VPN routers, firmware, and VPN apps at `https://proprivacy.com/router`.

Virtual Network Computing (VNC)

VNC (Virtual Network Computing) is a remote access system available for Windows, macOS, Linux, and the iOS and Android mobile platforms. VNC uses the Remote Frame Buffer (RFB) protocol (default TCP port 5900) to make a connection between the viewer (the remote user) and the VNC server.

VNC transmits user input (mouse movements, typing, clicks, and so on) to the server and sends screen output to the viewer. VNC is available in both free and commercial versions. Because VNC doesn't process input or output for speed, it's slower than RDP or other services. VNC is not encrypted by default but can be used with SSH tunneling.

The VNC server app must be installed on the computer to be accessed; the VNC viewer app must be installed on the computer that will connect remotely. Figure 36.5 shows the configuration dialog box for the popular TightVNC server running on Windows.

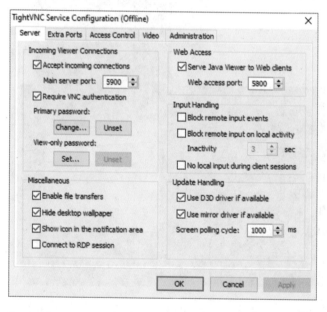

FIGURE 36.5 Configuring the TightVNC server to permit remote access on Windows

NOTE

To learn more about VNC and to access reviews of VNC software, go to www
.lifewire.com/vnc-virtual-network-computing-818104. To
learn how to set up a VNC server on Ubuntu Linux, visit www.tecmint.com/
install-and-configure-vnc-server-on-ubuntu.

Secure Shell (SSH)

Secure Shell (*SSH*) is a command-line protocol used for secure remote access using public key cryptography. SSH is built into Linux, macOS, and Windows.

NOTE

To learn more about using SSH from the Windows Terminal in Windows 10/11,
see https://docs.microsoft.com/en-us/windows/terminal/
tutorials/ssh.

SSH and OpenSSH are typically used by developers for creating public keys, for checking and creating security certificates, and for other security-related tasks as well as for remote access.

NOTE

To learn more about SSH, see https://phoenixnap.com/kb/
what-is-ssh.

In Linux and macOS, SSH is run from the command line with the syntax
ssh *sshservername*, where *sshservername* is the SSH server; see Figure 36.6. Windows can also use the PuTTY utility to log into an SSH server. For configuration details in Linux or macOS, open a Terminal session and enter **man ssh**.

The SSH server is not installed by default. In Ubuntu and similar Debian-based Linux distros, use **sudo apt install openssh-server**. For details on configuring an SSH server in Linux or macOS, open a Terminal session and enter **man sshd**.

EXAM TIP

SSH is often used by administrators to securely connect to remote systems. It provides secure logins and command execution using encryption. SSH runs over TCP port 22.

FIGURE 36.6 A typical first-time connection to an SSH server using the Linux SSH client

NOTE

To learn more about using SSH with Linux or macOS, see www.digital ocean.com/community/tutorials/ how-to-use-ssh-to-connect-to-a-remote-server. To download a copy of OpenSSL for 32-bit or 64-bit Windows, go to https://slproweb .com/products/Win32OpenSSL.html. For more information on OpenSSL, visit www.openssl.org. For more information on PuTTY, visit https:// putty.org.

Remote Monitoring and Management (RMM)

Remote monitoring and management (*RMM*), also called remote IT management, is used to remotely connect to computers and computing devices for management, configuration, updates, and repairs.

RMMs use clients installed on each computer or device to be monitored. An RMM dashboard is used to view, manage, and configure monitored devices. In Figure 36.7, a web-based RMM manager is being used to perform asset management.

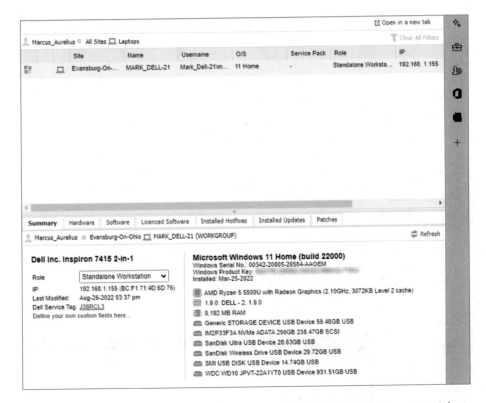

FIGURE 36.7 The remote access management of this RMM displays essential information about a Dell laptop, including its IP address, MAC address, and service tag (left pane), Windows license (obscured), processor, BIOS/UEFI version, and connected storage devices (right pane).

KVM (keyboard, video, mouse) originally referred to a hardware device that allows a single keyboard, display, and mouse to switch between connected PCs or servers. RMMs that feature virtual KVM support over IP can run a managed device as if the RMM user was directly in front of the keyboard.

RMM is available as software, web-based, or hardware-based products. An example of a hardware-based product is Intel vPro Enterprise for Windows. It can manage any supported system even if it's turned off as long as the system is connected to the Internet, a feature known as out-of-band management.

NOTE

For an introduction to RMM and a list of open source RMMs, see `https://heimdalsecurity.com/blog/rmm-software`. To learn more about vPro Enterprise for Windows, see `www.intel.com/content/www/us/en/business/enterprise-computers/resources/rmm.html`.

Microsoft Remote Assistance (MSRA)

Microsoft Remote Assistance (*MSRA*) is a remote screen-sharing program included in Windows. It enables users to request help from a specific user or to help the user who requested help from you. MSRA, unlike RDP, is designed for tech support.

Here's the process for setting up an MSRA connection via email:

1. The user who needs help searches for **MSRA** and starts it.
2. The user selects the option to request help.
3. MSRA creates an Invitation file and stores it in the `Documents` folder.
4. The user emails the file to the helper.
5. The helper opens the email and the invitation and this starts MSRA on their computer.
6. The person requesting help gives the session password to the helper. After the helper enters the password, the remote session starts (see Figure 36.8).
7. A chat window is available, and the helper must request permission from the user to control the screen.
8. Either party can end the connection at any time.

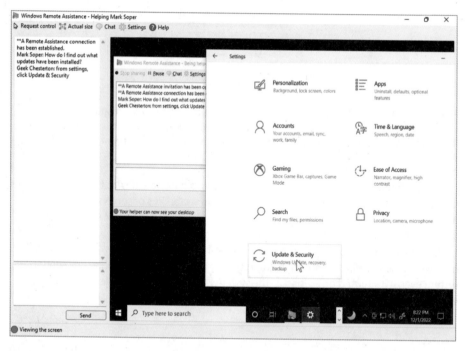

FIGURE 36.8   An MSRA remote session with the chat window in use

NOTE

To see an illustrated step-by-step tutorial on using MSRA, see www
.technotification.com/2014/02/remote-screen-sharing-
and-conroling-in.html. Windows 10 and Windows 11 can get a free
Microsoft alternative to MSRA called Quick Assist, which is easier to use. Quick
Assist is available from the Microsoft Store. Learn more at https://docs
.microsoft.com/en-us/windows/client-management/
quick-assist.

Third-Party Tools

In addition to tools built into or optionally provided for Windows, macOS, and Linux, several categories of third-party tools are available for remote access and support, including:

- ▶ Screen-sharing
- ▶ Videoconferencing
- ▶ File transfer
- ▶ Desktop management

Screen-Sharing Software

Screen-sharing software helps teachers provide instruction remotely and helps interactive remote meetings to get more done by allowing multiple users to share their screens. Figure 36.9 demonstrates using screen sharing during a training session using Microsoft Zoom.

FIGURE 36.9   Using screen-sharing in Zoom for training

Other examples of screen-sharing software are Webex, GoTo Meeting, Zoho Meeting, and TeamViewer.

Videoconferencing Software

Videoconferencing software such as Zoom, Microsoft Teams (Figure 36.10), ClickMeeting, Webex Events, and others are designed specifically for the give-and-take of interactive meetings with voice, video, and text chat. These products also typically support screen sharing and file transfer.

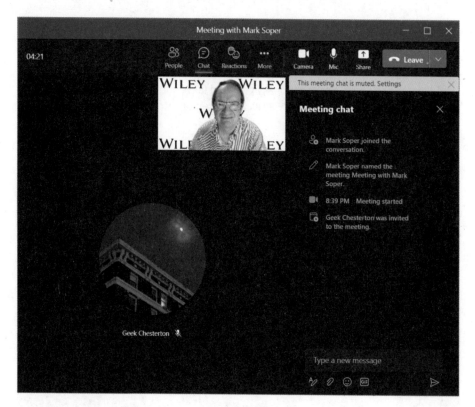

FIGURE 36.10 Using text chat in a Microsoft Teams meeting

File Transfer Software

Although many organizations now use cloud file sharing, there's still a place for products made for file transfer. It's especially important to look for products that support multiple operating systems and secure types of file transfers like SFTP (secure FTP), FTPS (FTP over SSL), WebDAV, and Amazon S3, among others.

Most FTP programs require you to download a client app, but some, such as FireFTP (a Firefox add-in), can work directly within a supported browser. FTP clients can also work in a command-line mode, such as `ftp.exe` included in Windows and the FTP clients included with many Linux distros. However, it's much easier to use a GUI with a split screen, as shown in Figure 36.11, which illustrates using the popular FileZilla FTP client to access the FTP server at GNU.org.

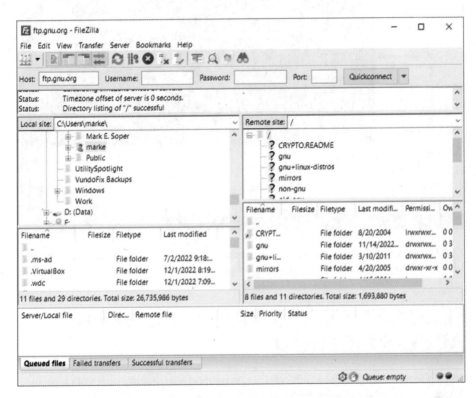

FIGURE 36.11 Accessing the GNU.org FTP server with FileZilla

Desktop Management Software

Desktop management software is a subset of remote monitoring and management (RMM). Desktop management concentrates on managing desktops, laptops, and mobile devices. Applications that also include server management are better classified as RMM software. In Figure 36.12, a desktop management application (Goverlan) is using its remote control capabilities to run `ipconfig` on a Windows 10 workstation.

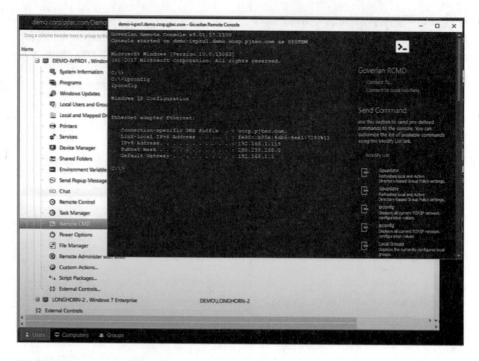

FIGURE 36.12 Using Goverlan to check IP settings remotely on a Windows 10 workstation (image from YouTube screen capture; YouTube courtesy of Goverlan)

SECURITY CONSIDERATIONS OF EACH ACCESS METHOD

One of the reasons to choose a particular access method is its security level. Let's look at the security considerations for the access methods discussed in this chapter.

RDP Security

RDP is more secure than VNC. RDP's security can also be strengthened by using strong passwords, implementing two-factor authentication, and enabling the Group Policy setting (Computer Configuration | Administrative Templates | Windows Components | Remote Desktop Services | Remote Desktop Session Host | Security) Require user authentication for remote connections by using Network Level Authentication, setting up user groups that are granted RDP access, and creating lockout policies.

> **NOTE**
>
> For additional security tips, see `https://security.berkeley.edu/education-awareness/securing-remote-desktop-rdp-system-administrators`.

VPN Security

VPN connections themselves are very secure, but if providers log your connections, use faulty encryption, don't support protocols stronger than IPsec or PPTP, and don't provide an Internet kill switch, the VPN isn't private enough. VPNs in a corporate environment can be risky if used for third-party access to the corporate network.

> **NOTE**
>
> For more information on best VPN features to consider, see `www.cactusvpn.com/vpn/vpn-security-risks`. For more information on hardening corporate VPNs, see `www.securelink.com/products/securelink-customer-connect`.

VNC Security

VNC is insecure out of the box, with nothing encrypted by default. To create a secure connection with VNC, you must set up a VPN tunnel and run your VNC session through it or create an SSH connection and run your VNC session through it.

> **NOTE**
>
> For details on using SSH, see `www.techrepublic.com/article/how-to-connect-to-vnc-using-ssh`. For details on creating a VPN connection with Windows for use with VNC, see `https://helpdeskgeek.com/how-to/tunnel-vnc-over-ssh`.

MSRA Security

MSRA is vulnerable to social engineering attacks, such as fake "Microsoft Support" calls that claim you have a virus and then ask you for permission to take over your computer. To protect corporate computers from social engineering attacks while enabling the use of MSRA, use Group Policy.

> **NOTE**
>
> For details setting up Group Policy to make MSRA safer, see `www.prajwaldesai.com/how-to-enable-remote-assistance-using-group-policy`.

FTP Security

The FTP protocol is not encrypted, so it is not secure. For security, use secure file transfer protocols such as SFPT and FTPS. To learn more about these protocols, visit www .cerberusftp.com/ftps-vs-sftp-understanding-the-difference.

EXAM TIP

Be sure you understand the differences between the various types of applica- tions and methods discussed in this chapter and the importance of security set- tings. Be ready to answer questions about how to make remote access methods more secure and the best choice for remote access given a scenario.

CertMike EXAM ESSENTIALS

▶ Some remote access technologies, such as Remote Desktop Protocol and Virtual Network Computing, are designed to allow users to run computers remotely, while others, like virtual private networks and Secure Shell, are designed to make connections more secure. Don't confuse them.

▶ There is a lot of overlap in the features of various types of remote access technol- ogies. Don't worry about what arbitrary category an application or web service has been placed into; instead, concentrate on the features you need and the devices and operating systems that an application or web service needs to support.

▶ Evaluate security issues carefully and know that some remote access products need additional configuration or VPN tunnels to make them more secure.

Practice Question 1

You are supporting remote users who have a lot of questions about using a new app on Windows and macOS. Which of the following remote access technologies will be the *best* choice to use to help them?

A. RDP
B. MSRA
C. FTP
D. VNC

Practice Question 2

Your client has decided to use VNC to support Windows and macOS computers both within the corporate network and remotely. Which of the following *best* identifies the security issues with this connection?

A. A VPN or SSH tunnel should be set up for the VNC connection.
B. VNC should be used along with RDP.
C. VNC should be configured to use SFTP.
D. No extra steps are needed. VNC is secure as provided.

Practice Question 1 Explanation

This question is designed to test your real-world understanding of the compatibility of remote access with different operating systems. Let's consider each of these answers.

1. The first answer (A, RDP) is incorrect. RDP is used to enable remote users to connect with their office computers, and it is a Microsoft product that works only on Windows.

2. The next answer (B, MSRA) is incorrect. While MSRA is made especially for remote assistance, it is a Microsoft product that works only on Windows.

3. The next answer (C, FTP) is incorrect. FTP is used to transfer files between computers. Although FTP clients are available for both Windows and macOS, FTP is not designed to provide desktop remote control or assistance.

4. The last answer (D, VNC) is correct. VNC is available for both macOS and Windows and can be used to help other users.

Correct Answer: D. VNC

Practice Question 2 Explanation

This question is designed to test your knowledge of remote access security. Let's evaluate these answers one at a time.

1. The first answer (A, A VPN or SSH tunnel should be set up for the VNC connection) is correct. An encrypted tunnel provides security for the VNC connection, which by itself isn't secure.

2. The second answer (B, VNC should be used along with RDP) is incorrect. VNC and RDP are different remote access technologies and cannot be used together.

3. The third answer (C, VNC should be configured to use SFTP) is incorrect. SFTP is the Secure File Transfer Protocol, which is not used for remote access.

4. The last answer (D, No extra steps are needed. VNC is secure as provided) is incorrect. VNC is insecure, and needs an encrypted tunnel to protect the connection.

Correct Answer: A. A VPN or SSH tunnel should be set up for the VNC connection

Index

W

ONLINE TEST BANK

To help you study for your CompTIA A+ Core 2 certification exam, register to gain one year of FREE access after activation to the online interactive test bank—included with your purchase of this book! All of the practice questions in this book are included in the online test bank so you can study in a timed and graded setting.

REGISTER AND ACCESS THE ONLINE TEST BANK

To register your book and get access to the online test bank, follow these steps:

1. Go to www.wiley.com/go/sybextestprep. You'll see the **"How to Register Your Book for Online Access"** instructions.
2. Click "here to register" and then select your book from the list.
3. Complete the required registration information, including answering the security verification to prove book ownership. You will be emailed a pin code.
4. Follow the directions in the email or go to www.wiley.com/go/ sybextestprep.
5. Find your book on that page and click the "Register or Login" link with it. Then enter the pin code you received and click the "Activate PIN" button.
6. On the Create an Account or Login page, enter your username and password, and click Login or, if you don't have an account already, create a new account.
7. At this point, you should be in the test bank site with your new test bank listed at the top of the page. If you do not see it there, please refresh the page or log out and log back in.